RICE

RICE

whitecap

This edition first published in Canada in 2003 by Whitecap Books,
351 Lynn Ave., North Vancouver, British Columbia, Canada, V7J 2C4.

First published in 2003 by Murdoch Books®, a division of Murdoch Magazines Pty Ltd.

Editor: Zoë Harpham Editorial Director: Diana Hill
Designer: Alex Frampton Design Concept: Marylouise Brammer
Food Consultant: Jane Lawson
Stylist (cover and special features): Mary Harris
Photographer (cover and special features): Ian Hofstetter
Food Preparation: Jo Glynn (special features), Ross Dobson (cover)
Picture Librarian: Anne Ferrier Indexer: Russell Brooks
Production: Janis Barbi

Chief Executive: Juliet Rogers
Publisher: Kay Scarlett

PRINTED IN CHINA by Toppan Printing Co. (HK) Ltd.

ISBN 1-55285-495-7

NOTE: We have used 20 ml tablespoon measures. If you are using a 15 ml tablespoon,
for most recipes the difference will not be noticeable. However, for recipes using small amounts
of flour and cornflour, add an extra teaspoon for each tablespoon specified.

IMPORTANT: Those who might be at risk from the effects of salmonella food poisoning
(the elderly, pregnant women, young children and those suffering from immune deficiency
diseases) should consult their GP with any concerns about eating raw eggs.

OUR STAR RATING: When we test recipes, we rate them for ease of preparation.
The following cookery ratings are used in this book:
☆ A single star indicates a recipe that is simple and generally quick to make—perfect for beginners.
☆☆ Two stars indicate the need for just a little more care, or perhaps a little more time.
☆☆☆ Three stars indicate special dishes that need more investment in time,
care and patience—but the results are worth it. Even beginners can make these
dishes as long as the recipe is followed carefully.

RICE

'The grain of life', rice is the staple food for almost half the world's population, and it is grown on every continent except Antarctica. Each culture has developed their own methods of using rice, and in this book we examine these cultures one by one. You may decide to move through the book country by country, or you may prefer to dip in at will and enjoy an Italian risotto one night and a Chinese rice noodle stir-fry the next. You will be amazed at the variety—there are risottos, paellas, pilaffs, pulaos, stir-fries, soups, puddings, cakes and much much more.

CONTENTS

SPECIAL FEATURES

THE GRAIN OF LIFE

One of the most versatile grains in the world, rice grows in all conditions on nearly every continent. What's more, it has proved to be incredibly adaptable. Many different cultures have embraced rice—thus we have dishes as diverse as the Italian risotto, American gumbos, Indian pulaos, Middle Eastern pilaffs and Southeast Asian rice noodle stir-fries, to name just a few. With just a few simple guidelines, it is easy to choose and buy the perfect rice for whatever meal you'd like to cook.

FOOD FOR THE WORLD

Rice is a member of the grass family—the fruit of a grass plant. It grows in 112 countries, and it can grow in all conditions—in paddy fields, in rivers, in hot and cool climates, in wet and dry areas. Rice is eaten daily by over 300 billion people. Nearly half of the world's population relies on it as a staple food, though its popularity across the globe is by no means evenly spread—Asia produces almost 90 per cent of the rice in the world, but consumes most of it as well.

The two main cultivated species are *Oryza sativa* (Asian rice) and *Oryza glaberrima* (African rice), and from these come thousands of varieties of rice, though many are only available in the area in which they are grown. It comes in many colours (black, white, brown, red), sizes (short-grain, long-grain, round), consistencies (sticky, glutinous) and forms (whole, milled, popped, flaked and ground). Most of the rice eaten is white rice, which means the husk has been removed and the grain milled. White rice not only keeps better, but it is also more highly esteemed than most other rice.

BUYING RICE

Only a few years ago the supermarket would have stocked two, maybe three, types of rice—long-grain, short-grain and perhaps brown. What a difference a few years make. Today, supermarkets stock enough varieties of rice to cover most of the basic uses. They will generally have arborio, which is a good rice for risottos and a fine stand-in for paella rice; fragrant jasmine rice, which is perfect for Southeast Asian dishes; basmati for pilaffs and to serve with Indian meals; as well as short-grain, long-grain and brown rice. Most will also include some wild rice, but you may have to venture to a healthfood store if your supermarket cannot help. If you want something a bit more specific, try ethnic grocery stores. They often have a wider selection, in larger quantities, at a cheaper price.

STORING RICE

If you eat a lot of rice, buy it in large quantities—it has a long shelf life and an unopened packet can be kept for several years without loss of quality. Once you have opened a fresh packet of rice, store it in a cool, dark, dry place in an airtight container. Rice bought in large sacks is best transferred to a dry, clean container with a lid.

Brown rice is an exception. Because it still contains the oil-rich germ or bran layer, it has a higher fat content than milled, or white, rice, and goes rancid if left in a warm place for too long. For this reason, it is best stored in an airtight container in the fridge.

You also need to take extra care with cooked rice. If it is not consumed immediately, cover it, then chill it quickly as harmful bacteria can grow rapidly. Cooked rice will store in the fridge for up to 2 days.

WHICH RICE DO I NEED?

As this book will show you, different rice is suitable for different uses because of its inherent characteristics. Sushi works because it is made with a slightly sticky rice which will ensure the grains of rice stick together and won't fall apart. Risottos need a short-grain rice that will release a lot of starch. And pilaffs are considered perfect when cooked with a rice that will remain separate and fluffy. This isn't to say that your recipe will be a failure if you use the wrong kind of rice. But the results won't be quite as good. Before you buy rice, have some idea of how you want to prepare it so you don't have to use a disappointing replacement.

WHAT RICE IS THAT?

Rice can be classified according to its culinary use (pudding rice), its method of processing (easy-cook), its grain shape (long-grain), its country or place of origin (Dhera Dun) or its degree of stickiness (glutinous).

Different types of rice have different cooking characteristics. The size of the grain is not the only distinction. Cultivated rice is further divided into two subspecies: the tropical *indica* rice which is long grained and non-sticky, like basmati; and *japonica* rice, a shorter grain grown in temperate climates with varying degrees of stickiness, which includes Japanese, Spanish and Italian rice. Added to these is a third subspecies, *javanica*, also known as bulu—a tropical to subtropical, medium- to long-grain rice that is somewhat sticky.

Sticky (glutinous/waxy) rice absorbs less water during cooking and, once cooked, the grains lose their shape and stick together. This makes sticky rice suitable for sushi, puddings or any dish eaten with chopsticks. Despite its name, sticky rice contains no gluten—its name is purely a description of its texture. It comes as white or black rice and generally includes japonicas, with the exception of Thai jasmine rice.

Aromatic rices have a distinctive taste and fragrance, and are delicious served plain with savoury dishes on the side. The most popular ones are jasmine—a soft, slightly clingy rice when cooked; basmati, which cooks into long, slender grains that are dry, separate and fluffy; and Della, a drier, fluffier rice when cooked.

For some extra colour, try some of the speciality coloured rices. The range includes black or purple rices, red rice and wild rice.

These are perfect for rice salads, stuffings, as an accompaniment to strong flavoured dishes or even for rice puddings.

To accommodate busy lifestyles, modern processing methods have been used to develop precooked (instant) rice—basically white rice that has been precooked and dehydrated so it cooks quickly. Its obvious advantage is convenience, but it is usually more expensive and lacks flavour.

A wonderful compromise between nutritious brown rice and tender, fast-cooking white rice is parboiled (converted) rice. The process was first discovered in ancient India where parboiling was used to preserve the rice and also had the benefit of retaining some of the nutrients which are usually destroyed in milling. Because it is milled, parboiled rice has better storage qualities as it has no bran or germ oil to go rancid. It can generally handle a wider range of cooking circumstances, too, and still emerge intact. Not all cooking methods are recommended for parboiled rice as it does not absorb water so easily. It is less suitable for dishes where flavour absorption is important, such as risotto or paella. The cooked grains of parboiled rice tend to have a slightly bouncy texture and are non-sticky; they also tend to look slightly yellow compared to normal rice.

THE HISTORY OF RICE

Rice was originally a wild grass that grew across Asia and Africa, and it still does grow wild in some parts of the world. But it is cultivated rice that we are interested in, for cultivation has given the world one of its major staple foods. Though it is impossible to give an exact date and location for when cultivation occurred, historians believe it was somewhere in Asia around 7,000 years ago. It is believed that rice was originally cultivated on dry land. As rice cultivation spread more and more methods of cultivation were developed and today it is grown all around the world, in very different conditions, from flooded rice paddies to dry fields.

COOKING RICE

One of the best things about rice is that it needs very little attention. Give it a quick rinse and then put it on to cook while you focus on the rest of the meal. There are several methods of cooking rice, all with good results. Experiment with each method and work out your favourite, then get cooking.

CLEANING

Traditionally, rice had to be picked over and any stones or rubble discarded. Most modern-day rice is clean enough that it does not require checking, though rice bought in sacks may still need picking over.

Once upon a time, all rice was washed prior to cooking. Today, personal preference dictates whether this is done or not—most rices sold commercially are clean enough that this step can be omitted. Many cooks in Asia often both wash their rice and soak it to shorten the cooking time.

Some rices cook better if they have been soaked first—basmati and sushi rice being two examples. Soaking makes the rice less brittle. But most rices can be cooked without being soaked.

One point to remember—if you do wash or soak your rice before cooking it, remember to drain it thoroughly, particularly when cooking by the absorption method, or you will have too much liquid to cook the rice properly.

COOKING

Rice can be cooked in a number of different ways. Some rices will lend themselves to being cooked using more than one method, but others suit just one method. Individual recipes will guide you.

If reheating cooked rice, make sure all the rice is piping hot to destroy any bacteria that may be present.

Absorption method

Probably the most familiar method of cooking rice, the absorption method is an efficient and nutritious way to cook rice, as nutrients are not discarded with the cooking water. Generally, long-grain rices suit this method. A measured amount of rice is cooked in a measured amount of water so that all the water is absorbed. To cook, put the rice in cold water, then bring to the boil, cover with a tight-fitting lid, then reduce the heat to a simmer so that the rice at the bottom of the pan doesn't burn. The rice is

COOKING RICE BY THE ABSORPTION METHOD

Put the rice in a saucepan, stick your finger into the rice, then add enough water so it comes up to the first finger joint.

Cover the pan with a tight-fitting lid and bring to the boil. Reduce the heat to low and cook until little steam holes appear on the surface of the rice.

Remove the lid and allow the steam to escape. Fluff up the grains of rice with a fork and transfer to a serving dish.

cooked by the hot water and by the remaining steam once the water has been absorbed. Once cooked, simply fluff up with a fork and serve immediately.

The electric rice cooker is designed to cook rice the absorption way. Sold in Asian stores, many kitchen stores and some department stores, they have markings on the inside to show the amount of water needed for the amount of rice. It automatically switches off when the grains are cooked, so the rice is then steam-dried. Usually, though, it is only the portion closer to the surface which is steamed—the rice at the bottom of the cooker is boiled. The rice cooker then keeps the rice warm until you're ready to eat it.

A general rule of thumb when cooking by the absorption method is to make sure that the depth of uncooked rice in the pan, pot or electric rice cooker is no more than 5 cm (2 inches) high, or the rice will cook unevenly.

Rapid boiling
Like pasta, many rices, from arborio to parboiled rices, cook well in plenty of water. Bring a large saucepan of water to the boil, uncovered.

Sprinkle in the rice and keep an eye on it, so it does not stick or overcook. Drain the rice in a sieve (if you are using jasmine or Japanese rice, rinse it with a little tepid water to prevent it cooking further).

Steaming rice
This method is preferred for sticky rice. Soak the rice overnight, then drain. Spread out the grains in a steamer, and put the steamer over a wok or pan of boiling water. The rice does not touch the water—it is cooked only by the steam.

LEFTOVERS
If you have any leftover rice, don't throw it away—most cultures have developed recipes specifically to use up leftover rice, from Italian arancini to use up leftover risotto, and fried rice in China and Southeast Asia, to sticky rice crackers in Thailand.

Once the cooked rice has cooled, store it in an airtight container in the refrigerator, and eat within 2 days—heat it thoroughly before eating it. We have included many recipes for leftover rice in the book.

RICE—A GLOSSARY

CAMARGUE RED RICE

Red rice is unusual because it has a red layer of bran once the husk of the grain has been removed. Camargue red rice is one of the most high-quality and expensive red rices. It has a distinctive nutty flavour and chewy texture. It is a medium- to short-grain japonica grown as a small crop in the Camargue region of southern France. It is not so readily available, but you may find it in speciality European food stores. A less expensive alternative is Bhutanese red rice. This is a coloured japonica from central Asia that is tender, absorbent, but slightly sticky, so it is easy to eat with chopsticks. Thai red rice (grown among jasmine rice) has similar qualities, as does Vietnamese red cargo.

BASMATI

This is a long-grained, needle-shaped rice used predominantly in Indian cooking. It has a light, dry texture and is lightly perfumed. The grains are very fluffy and stay separate when cooked, as well as elongating. Basmati grows in the Himalayan foothills in northern India and Pakistan, as well as in some parts of the United States of America, though the American-grown basmati does not expand as much as that grown in India. Other basmatis, from West Bengal, are labelled 'Patna'. These are ideal rices for Middle Eastern pilaffs, and north Indian pulaos and biryani. Basmati is sold as Punni, Dehra Dun, Jeera-Sali or Delhi.

JAPANESE SHORT-GRAIN RICE

This is the style of rice that the Japanese prefer. It is short-grain, relatively sticky rice. Japan does not produce enough Japanese-style rice to export, but other countries including Korea and the United States of America also grow Japanese-style rice. The raw grains are slightly glassy with a light powder on them to keep them separate—the powder used to be talc, but now the talc has been replaced by cornflour (cornstarch), and many packets will advertize 'no talc'. When properly cooked, the rice is slightly sticky, but with firm grains. The Japanese also have another type of rice, a sticky rice, called sweet rice.

BROWN RICE

The grains of brown rice have had their husk (hull) removed, but the outer bran layer left intact, not milled and polished like white rice. The result is a more nutritious rice, though that fact has not helped its popularity, which historically lags behind that of white rice. With a pronounced nutty flavour and chewy texture, brown rice requires a longer cooking time than other varieties of rice. It is available both as a short- and medium-grain rice. Brown rice has a higher fat content than white rice, so can be kept for much less time than white rice—only up to 2 years; it is best stored in the refrigerator or in a cool place. Also known as wholegrain rice.

JASMINE

This is a fragrant rice, usually long-grained. It is named after the sweet-smelling jasmine flower of Southeast Asia because, on cooking, it releases a similar floral aroma. Jasmine rice cooks to a soft, slightly sticky grain and its taste enhances the traditional spices of Thai dishes. It is also served plain as it needs no seasoning. However, it is not a good choice for puddings or risottos where the grains don't remain separate. Often sold as Thai fragrant rice, scented rice and aromatic rice. The best is reputed to be Thai Hom Mali rice, which is grown in Thailand from a traditional strain which originated in central Thailand.

LONG-GRAIN

Long-grain rice is not a strain of rice, but a descriptive term for the size of the rice grains—the grains are three to five times as long as they are wide. The long and slender grains usually stay separate and fluffy after cooking, so it is a good rice to choose when you want a dry, fluffy texture in your dish with every grain separate. There are several types of long-grain rice, some scented, like basmati and jasmine, and others that are quite plain, like Texmati. Long-grain is an absorbent, fine long-grained rice mainly used for savoury dishes; a good all-purpose rice. You can substitute medium-grain rice, though the result will be a little stickier and less fluffy.

PAELLA RICE

Varieties of short- to medium-grained Spanish paella rices include Bahia, Calasparra, sequia and the firm-grained bomba. They look very similar to Italian risotto rices with large white oval grains. Paella rices can absorb a lot of water and they soak up a lot of the delicious flavours from the paella; they are also suitable for puddings. Valencia is the most prized Spanish grain for paella as it cooks up tender, moist and clingy due to its high starch content. It is also the most widely available Spanish rice. Bomba, from the Spanish region of Calasparra, is another premium rice. Paella rice can be difficult to find; risotto rice makes a good substitute, if necessary.

RISOTTO RICE

Risotto rices are short-grain rices high in starch, which give risottos their classic creaminess. There are several types of risotto rice. Arborio is a large, plump grain. Vialone nano is a stubby small grain that gives a looser consistency but keeps more of a bite in the middle. Carnaroli is the best of all risotto rices. It is a relatively new variety, developed in 1945 by a Milanese rice grower as a cross between Vialone and a Japanese strain. Small production makes it more expensive than other grains. The outer skin has enough of the soft starch to dissolve and make the risotto creamy but it also keeps a firm consistency.

WILD RICE

Not technically a rice, wild rice is the name given to the rice-like seed of an aquatic grass that mainly grows in central and northern parts of America and southern Canada. Shiny black–brown to green in colour, it has a smoky, nutty flavour and chewy texture. Natural wild rice is still harvested from lakes and marshes by hand, though it is very expensive and hard to find (often labelled hand harvested). Today it is more widely available mechanically cultivated, though it is reputed to be less flavoursome than real wild rice. This grass seed is richer in protein and other nutrients that real rice, and it takes longer to cook. Also known as Indian rice.

SHORT-GRAIN

Though short-grain rices vary in total length, they are classified as such because the grains are less than twice as long as they are wide. The term is often used also to describe medium-grain rice, which has grains 2–3 times as long as they are wide. The grains looks almost round, with moist grains that stick together. When cooked, the grains swell without disintegrating and the high starch content makes it sticky and good for puddings, moulds and stuffings. These rices are generally higher in amylopectin, a starch which easily dissolves in water and creates a sticky, soft texture when cooked. Often sold as round or pudding rice.

WILD RICE BLEND

Natural wild rice can be very expensive, so it is often extended with brown or white rice—usually brown because the cooking times are similar. Sometimes the rices are precooked. By combining wild rice with 'real' rice, texture, colour and taste are added, and the wild rice has the effect of enhancing the nutritional value of plain rice. Now that mechanical harvesting methods have been perfected, there may be less call for wild rice blend. If you're making your own blend, cook the grains separately before combining them because the cooking times are so different.

THAI BLACK STICKY RICE

This attractive dark rice has had its husk removed, but not the black bran layer, hence, its colour. Under the bran lies a white sticky rice. Because the bran remains on the grains, when cooked the rice grains remain separate, unlike other sticky rices. Typically used in desserts, it is often mixed with white sticky rice to combine the best qualities of each—colour and stickiness. Grown in Indonesia and the Philippines it has a nutty flavour and turns a beautiful rich dark purple (almost black) colour when cooked. Also called black glutinous rice (though this is a misnomer because rice does not contain gluten), Thai black rice, Balinese black and purple rice.

RICE PRODUCTS

RICE NOODLES

Dried rice vermicelli

These thin rice noodles are dried. They are often used in stir-fries and soups or deep-fried. Often sold in nests.

Dried rice noodle sticks

These noodles are broader and thicker than rice vermicelli.

Fresh rice noodles

Made from a thin dough of rice flour, these are available uncut as fresh rice sheet noodles or pre-cut into different widths. Use the sheets within a few days as they shouldn't be stored in the fridge—they will go hard and be difficult to separate. Before use, cover them with boiling water and gently separate. Drain and rinse.

RICE PAPER WRAPPERS

From Vietnam, these paper-thin brittle wrappers are dipped in water to soften them and served soft or deep-fried wrapped around a filling. Available in varying shapes and sizes in sealed packets.

MOCHI CAKES

Blocks of pounded cooked glutinous rice, which are rehydrated and then grilled (broiled) or added to dishes.

RICE FLOUR

Used as a flour substitute or to dust foods before frying. Adds texture to biscuits and batters when used with flour.

RICE WINE

Chinese rice wine

A fermented rice wine with a rich, sweetish taste similar to dry sherry. It is amber coloured and made from glutinous rice in Shaoxing, China.

Mirin

A sweet spirit-based rice liquid used predominantly in Japanese cooking.

Sake

An alcoholic liquid made by fermenting cooked, ground rice mash. It has a dry, sherry-like taste and it is used as a cooking liquid and, in its more refined form, as a drink. Available both clear and amber in colour.

RICE VINEGAR

Made from vinegar and a natural rice extract. It is used in dressings and marinades. There are many different types of rice vinegar—Chinese black vinegar, Japanese rice vinegar and seasoned rice vinegar—but most of our recipes use plain rice vinegar.

CLOKWISE FROM TOP LEFT: Fresh rice noodle sheets, sake, Chinese rice wine (Shaoxing), rice noodle sticks, rice crackers and cakes sitting on rice paper wrappers, dried rice vermicelli

MEDITERRANEAN AND MIDDLE EAST

In this chapter we visit the Middle East and the sunny shores of the Mediterranean and surrounds—Italy, Greece, Turkey, Spain, Portugal and Morocco. Rice has been cultivated in the area for over a thousand years, first in Egypt, then spreading to Spain and Italy. The result has been the creation of some of the world's classic rice dishes—the creamy risottos of Italy, the vibrant paellas of Spain, the rice-stuffed vegetables of Greece and the spicy pilaffs of the Middle East.

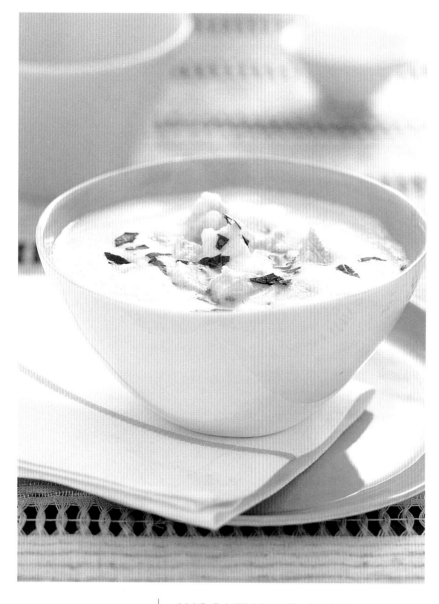

1 Put the chicken, carrot, leek, bay leaves and stock in a large saucepan. Bring to the boil over high heat, then reduce the heat and simmer for 10–15 minutes, or until the chicken is cooked. Strain into a clean saucepan and reserve the chicken fillets.

2 Add the rice to the liquid, bring to the boil, then reduce the heat and simmer for 15 minutes, or until tender. Meanwhile, cut the chicken into 1 cm (½ inch) cubes.

3 Whisk the egg whites in a clean dry bowl until firm peaks form. Beat in the yolks until light and creamy, then whisk in first the lemon juice, then 1 cup (250 ml/8 fl oz) of the hot liquid. Remove the pan of soup from the heat and gradually whisk in the egg mixture. Add the chicken pieces and stir over low heat for 2 minutes—do not boil or the egg will scramble. Ladle into bowls and serve with a sprinkling of parsley and dot of butter.

NOTE: This classic Greek soup will not stand well—make it just before serving.

CANJA
(Spicy Portuguese chicken soup)

Preparation time: 15 minutes
Total cooking time: 1 hour
Serves 6

3 tomatoes
2.5 litres (80 fl oz) chicken stock
1 onion, cut into thin wedges
1 celery stalk, finely chopped
1 teaspoon grated lemon zest
1 mint sprig
1 tablespoon olive oil
2 chicken breast fillets
1 cup (200 g/6½ oz) long-grain rice
2 tablespoons lemon juice
2 tablespoons shredded mint

1 Score a cross in the base of each tomato. Put the tomatoes in a bowl of boiling water for 30 seconds, then plunge into cold water and peel the skin away from the cross. Cut the tomatoes in half and scoop out the seeds with a teaspoon. Chop the flesh.

2 Combine the stock, onion, celery, lemon zest, chopped tomatoes, mint and olive oil in a large saucepan. Slowly bring to the boil, then reduce the heat, add the chicken and simmer gently

AVGOLEMONO SOUP WITH CHICKEN

Preparation time: 25 minutes
Total cooking time: 35 minutes
Serves 4

2 chicken breast fillets
1 carrot, chopped
1 large leek (white part only), chopped
2 bay leaves
2 litres (64 fl oz) chicken stock
⅓ cup (80 g/2¾ oz) short-grain rice
3 eggs, separated
⅓ cup (80 ml/2¾ fl oz) lemon juice
2 tablespoons chopped flat-leaf (Italian) parsley
40 g (1¼ oz) butter, diced

ABOVE: Avgolemono soup with chicken

for 20–25 minutes, or until the chicken is cooked through.

3 Remove the chicken from the saucepan and discard the mint sprig. Allow the chicken to cool, then thinly slice.

4 Meanwhile, add the rice to the pan and simmer for 25–30 minutes, or until the rice is tender. Return the sliced chicken to the pan, add the lemon juice and stir for 1–2 minutes, or until the chicken is warmed through. Season with salt and freshly ground black pepper, and stir in the shredded mint just before serving.

CALDO VERDE
(Portuguese green soup)

Preparation time: 15 minutes
Total cooking time: 1 hour
Serves 6

150 g (5 oz) chorizo sausage, thinly sliced
2 tablespoons olive oil
1 large onion, thinly sliced
4 garlic cloves, very finely chopped
2 teaspoons finely chopped oregano
1 large all-purpose potato (e.g. desiree), peeled and diced
1 cup (200 g/6½ oz) long-grain rice
1 litre (32 fl oz) chicken stock
1 small green chilli, split down the centre
6 cups (270 g/9 oz) very finely shredded kale, silverbeet (Swiss chard) or English spinach (see Notes)
1 cup (20 g/¾ oz) flat-leaf (Italian) parsley, chopped
extra virgin olive oil, for drizzling
lemon wedges, to serve

1 Fry the chorizo in a frying pan over medium heat for about 5 minutes, or until slightly crispy, then set aside. Heat the olive oil in a large saucepan, then add the onion, garlic and oregano and cook over medium heat for 8 minutes, or until the onion is softened but not browned. Add the potato and rice and cook for a few more minutes, stirring to make sure it doesn't catch on the bottom of the pan.

2 Pour in the stock, 1 litre (32 fl oz) water and the chilli, increase the heat and bring to the boil, stirring occasionally. Reduce the heat and simmer for about 20 minutes, or until the rice is tender and the potato is starting to fall apart, skimming as needed. Discard the chilli. Lightly crush the potato with a vegetable masher, then add the kale and chorizo. Cook for a further 15 minutes, or until kale is softened and loses its raw flavour.

3 Stir in the chopped parsley and season to taste. Ladle into bowls and drizzle with extra virgin olive oil, if desired. Serve with lemon wedges to squeeze over the top.

NOTES: Kale is a relative of the cabbage, with a similar but stronger flavour and, depending on the variety, dark green or purple, smooth or curly leaves. Also known as cole, colewart or curly kale.

Originating in the northern Portuguese province of Minho, this hearty soup is popular throughout the country. The authentic recipe calls for couve tronchuda, a dark green cabbage, and linguica, a spicy Portuguese sausage; however, as both are difficult to obtain outside the Iberian peninsula, we have used kale and chorizo instead.

BELOW: Caldo verde

SPANISH-STYLE RICE, MUSSEL, PRAWN AND CHORIZO SOUP

Preparation time: 45 minutes
Total cooking time: 45 minutes
Serves 4

☆

1 kg (2 lb) black mussels
1 cup (250 ml/8 fl oz) dry sherry
1 tablespoon olive oil
1 red onion, chopped
200 g (6^{1}/$_{2}$ oz) chorizo sausage,
    thinly sliced on the diagonal
4 garlic cloves, crushed
^{1}/$_{2}$ cup (100 g/3^{1}/$_{2}$ oz) long-grain rice
400 g (13 oz) tin chopped tomatoes
2 litres (64 fl oz) chicken stock
^{1}/$_{2}$ teaspoon saffron threads
2 bay leaves
1 tablespoon chopped oregano
500 g (1 lb) raw prawns (shrimp), peeled and
    deveined, tails intact
3 tablespoons chopped flat-leaf (Italian) parsley

CHORIZO SAUSAGE
The most famous of the Spanish and Portuguese sausages, chorizo (or *chouriço* in Portuguese) is a dried or cured sausage. It is based on minced (ground) pork, with flavourings from paprika and, sometimes, red capsicums (peppers), garlic and black pepper, depending on regional variations. Though chorizo is also available as a soft sausage, it is more commonly found dried. The process of drying the sausage causes its skin to wrinkle and enhances the spicy flavour.

1 Scrub the mussels with a stiff brush and pull out the hairy beards. Discard any broken mussels or open ones that don't close when tapped on the bench. Rinse well. Put the mussels in a saucepan with the sherry and cook, covered, over high heat for 3 minutes, or until the mussels have opened. Strain the liquid into a bowl. Discard any unopened mussels. Remove all but 8 mussels from their shells and discard the empty shells.

2 Heat the oil in a large saucepan over medium heat, add the onion and cook for 5 minutes, or until softened but not browned. Add the chorizo and cook for 3–5 minutes, or until browned, then add the garlic and cook for a further 1 minute.

3 Add the rice to the mixture and stir to coat with the chorizo mixture. Add the reserved mussel cooking liquid and cook for 1 minute before adding the chopped tomatoes, stock, saffron, bay leaves and oregano. Bring to the boil, then reduce the heat and simmer, covered, for 25 minutes.

4 Add the prawns and the mussels (except the ones in their shells) to the soup, cover with a lid, and cook for 3 minutes, then stir in the parsley. Ladle into four bowls, then top each bowl with 2 mussels still in their shells.

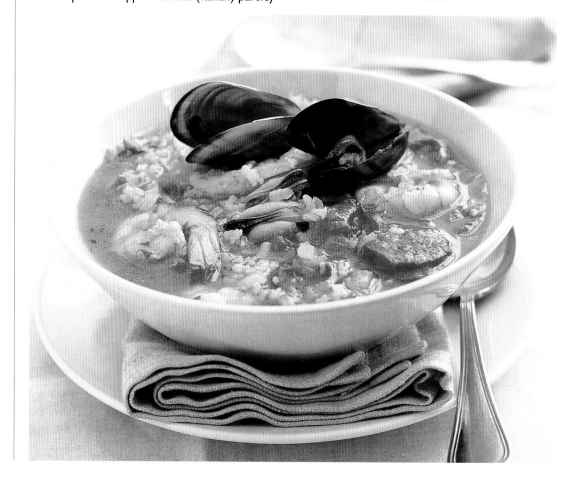

RIGHT: Spanish-style rice, mussel, prawn and chorizo soup

MINESTRONE SOUP WITH RICE

Preparation time: 20 minutes +
  overnight soaking
Total cooking time: 2 hours 30 minutes
Serves 6

☆ ☆

225 g (7 oz) dried borlotti beans
55 g (2 oz) butter
1 onion, finely chopped
1 garlic clove, finely chopped
3 tablespoons finely chopped parsley
2 sage leaves
100 g (3½ oz) pancetta, cubed
2 celery stalks, halved, then sliced
2 carrots, sliced
3 potatoes, peeled but left whole
1 teaspoon tomato paste (purée)
400 g (13 oz) tin chopped tomatoes
8 basil leaves
3 litres (96 fl oz) chicken or vegetable stock
2 zucchini (courgettes), sliced
225 g (7 oz) fresh peas
125 g (4 oz) green beans, cut into 4 cm
  (1½ inch) lengths
¼ cabbage, shredded
1 cup (220 g/7 oz) risotto rice
freshly grated Parmesan cheese, to serve

1 Put the dried beans in a large bowl, cover with cold water and soak overnight. Drain and rinse under cold water.
2 Melt the butter in a saucepan and add the onion, garlic, parsley, sage and pancetta. Cook over low heat, stirring once or twice, for 10 minutes, or until the onion is softened but not browned.
3 Add the celery, carrot and potatoes, and cook for 5 minutes. Stir in the tomato paste, chopped tomatoes, basil and borlotti beans. Season with freshly ground black pepper. Pour in the stock and bring slowly to the boil. Cover and leave to simmer for 2 hours, stirring once or twice.
4 If the potatoes have not broken up by the end of the 2 hours, roughly break them with a fork against the side of the pan. Season to taste with salt and pepper, then add the zucchini, peas, green beans, cabbage and rice. Simmer for a further 15–20 minutes, or until the rice is cooked. Divide among six soup bowls and sprinkle with a little Parmesan cheese.

CHICKEN STOCK

Put 2 kg (4 lb) chicken bones, 1 chopped onion, 1 chopped carrot, 1 chopped celery stalk, 1 chopped leek, 1 bay leaf, a few stalks of parsley, 1 sprig of thyme, 8 peppercorns and 6 litres (192 fl oz) cold water in a large saucepan or stockpot. Bring to the boil over high heat, skimming off any scum that rises to the surface. Reduce the heat and simmer for 2–3 hours, continuing to skim as needed. Strain the stock through a fine sieve into a heatproof bowl. Do not press on the solids or it may cloud the stock. Cover and refrigerate overnight. The next day, remove the layer of fat from the top of the stock. The stock will keep refrigerated for 3–4 days, or frozen for up to 4 months. Makes about 3.5 litres (112 fl oz).

ABOVE: Minestrone soup with rice

Spoon out the flesh into a strainer over a bowl. Strain the juice into the bowl. Finely dice the flesh and reserve in a separate bowl. Drain the tomato shells upside down on a rack.

2 Boil the rice in a saucepan of lightly salted water for 10–12 minutes, or until just tender. Drain and set aside to cool.

3 Heat the oil in a frying pan. Fry the onion, garlic and oregano for 8 minutes, or until the onion is soft. Add the pine nuts and currants and cook for 5 minutes, stirring frequently. Remove from the heat and stir in the herbs. Season.

4 Add the onion mixture and reserved tomato pulp to the rice and mix well. Fill the tomato shells with the rice mixture, piling it up over the top. Spoon 1 tablespoon of the reserved tomato juice on top of each tomato and replace the tops.

5 Lightly brush the tomatoes with the oil. Arrange them in the ovenproof dish. Bake for about 30 minutes, or until heated through.

STUFFED CABBAGE ROLLS

Preparation time: 40 minutes
Total cooking time: 2 hours
Serves 4

8 cabbage leaves from the outside of the cabbage
2 tablespoons olive oil
I onion, finely chopped
2–3 garlic cloves, chopped
250 g (8 oz) minced (ground) pork and veal
150 g (5 oz) ham, chopped
1/2 cup (110 g/3 1/2 oz) short-grain rice
1/2 cup (30 g/1 oz) chopped parsley
2 tablespoons chopped capers, rinsed and
   squeezed dry
I tablespoon malt vinegar
I tablespoon soft brown sugar
I teaspoon ground allspice
30 g (1 oz) butter, diced

TOMATO SAUCE
I tablespoon olive oil
I small onion, finely chopped
400 g (13 oz) tin chopped tomatoes
1/4 cup (60 g/2 oz) tomato paste (purée)
1/2 cup (125 ml/4 fl oz) red wine
2–3 teaspoons chopped thyme
I teaspoon caster (superfine) sugar

STUFFED TOMATOES

Preparation time: 40 minutes
Total cooking time: 55 minutes
Makes 8

8 tomatoes
1/2 cup (110 g/3 1/2 oz) short-grain rice
2 tablespoons olive oil
I red onion, chopped
I garlic clove, crushed
I teaspoon dried oregano
1/4 cup (40 g/1 1/4 oz) pine nuts
1/4 cup (35 g/1 1/4 oz) currants
1/2 cup (30 g/1 oz) chopped basil
2 tablespoons chopped parsley
I tablespoon chopped dill
olive oil, to brush

I Preheat the oven to warm 160°C (315°F/ Gas 2–3). Lightly grease a large ovenproof dish. Slice the top off each tomato and reserve them.

ABOVE: Stuffed tomatoes

22

1 Preheat the oven to warm 160°C (315°F/ Gas 2–3). Lightly grease a 30 x 20 x 8 cm (12 x 8 x 3 inch) ovenproof dish. Blanch the cabbage leaves, in batches, in boiling, salted water for 2 minutes, or until just wilted. Drain.
2 Heat the oil in a frying pan and cook the onion and garlic for 2–3 minutes, or until softened but not browned. Add the minced (ground) meat and cook for 2–3 minutes, breaking up any lumps. Add the ham and rice, stir for 2 minutes, then transfer to a bowl and add the parsley, capers, vinegar, sugar and allspice.
3 Divide the mixture into eight portions. Cut away the hard centre of each cabbage leaf. Then overlap pieces of leaf where the hard stem has been removed. Put a portion of filling on each leaf, fold in the sides and roll into a parcel, about 12 cm (5 inches) long. Pack the rolls together, seam-side down, in the ovenproof dish.
4 To make the tomato sauce, heat the oil in a frying pan and cook the onion for 2–3 minutes. Stir in the chopped tomatoes, tomato paste, wine, thyme and sugar and cook for another 10 minutes. Pour the sauce over the rolls.
5 Dot with butter, cover the dish tightly with a lid or a sheet of foil and bake for 1½ hours, or until tender.

STUFFED CAPSICUMS

Preparation time: 20 minutes
Total cooking time: 1 hour 10 minutes
Serves 6

☆ ☆

3/4 cup (150 g/5 oz) long- or medium-grain rice
1¼ cups (315 ml/10 fl oz) chicken stock
6 red, yellow or orange capsicums (peppers)
1/3 cup (80 ml/2¾ fl oz) olive oil
1 onion, chopped
1/2 cup (125 g/4 oz) tomato passata
60 g (2 oz) currants
2½ tablespoons chopped flat-leaf (Italian) parsley
2½ tablespoons chopped mint
1/2 teaspoon ground cinnamon
60 g (2¼ oz) pine nuts, toasted

1 Put the rice and stock in a saucepan and bring to the boil over medium heat. Reduce the heat a little, cover with a lid and cook for 15 minutes, or until the rice is tender. Remove from the heat and leave covered.

2 Bring a large saucepan of water to the boil. Cut the tops off the capsicums, reserving them for use later. Remove and discard the seeds and membrane from inside the capsicums. Blanch the capsicums (not the lids) in the boiling water for 2 minutes. Drain and upturn on paper towels to dry.
3 Preheat the oven to moderate 180°C (350°F/ Gas 4). Heat 2 tablespoons of the oil in a frying pan and cook the onion for 10 minutes, or until softened but not browned.
4 Add the tomato passata, currants, herbs, cinnamon, rice and pine nuts to the pan and stir for 2 minutes. Season.
5 Sit the capsicums in an ovenproof dish so they fit snugly. Divide the rice among the capsicum cavities. Replace the tops. Pour 100 ml (3½ fl oz) boiling water into the dish and drizzle the remaining oil over the tops of the capsicum. Bake for 40 minutes, or until cooked through and tender.

BELOW: Stuffed capsicums

STUFFED SQUID

Clean the squid by first pulling off the skin and wings. Pull out the transparent vertebrae and tentacles and scoop out the insides.

Cut the tentacles away from the rest of the innards at the front of the beak and eyes. Wash the inside of the squid and the tentacles.

Stuff the squid carefully and gently. If you force the filling in, the tubes may tear or burst.

Leave enough room that you can seal the squid tubes with cocktail sticks. If they are too full, they may burst out of the tube when cooking.

RIGHT: Stuffed squid

STUFFED SQUID

Preparation time: 30 minutes
Total cooking time: 1 hour
Serves 4

☆ ☆

8 squid (about 600 g/1 1/4 lb)

TOMATO SAUCE
1 garlic clove, thinly sliced
2 tablespoons extra virgin olive oil
2 x 400 g (13 oz) tins chopped tomatoes
100 ml (3 1/2 fl oz) red wine
2 tablespoons chopped flat-leaf (Italian) parsley

STUFFING
100 ml (3 1/2 fl oz) olive oil
1 small onion, finely chopped
1 small fennel bulb, finely chopped
2 garlic cloves, chopped
1/3 cup (75 g/2 1/2 oz) risotto rice
large pinch of saffron threads
1/2 large red chilli, chopped
155 ml (5 fl oz) white wine
3 tablespoons chopped flat-leaf (Italian) parsley

1 Prepare the squid by pulling off the skin and wings. Pull out the quill (the transparent cartilage), the head and tentacles and scoop out the innards. Cut the heads off below the eyes, leaving just the tentacles. Discard the heads. Rinse the tentacles and bodies, making sure any sand is removed, then leave to drain in a colander for a few minutes. Finely chop the tentacles and set aside with the bodies (put them in the fridge if the kitchen is hot).

2 To make the sauce, gently fry the garlic in the extra virgin olive oil for 1 minute. Add the chopped tomatoes and simmer until some of the liquid has evaporated and the sauce is quite thick. Add the wine and parsley and cook until it has reduced and thickened. Set aside.

3 To make the stuffing, heat the oil in a large saucepan and gently cook the onion, fennel and garlic for about 10 minutes, or until softened but not browned. Add the rice, saffron, chilli and chopped squid tentacles and cook for a few minutes, stirring frequently until the tentacles are opaque. Season, then add the wine and 6 tablespoons of the tomato sauce.

4 Cook, stirring frequently, until the tomato and wine has reduced into the rice. Cook for about 5 minutes, or until the liquid has reduced, then add 1/2 cup (125 ml/4 fl oz) water and continue cooking until the rice is tender and all the liquid has been absorbed. You may need to add a little

more water if the rice absorbs all the liquid and is not quite tender. Add 2 tablespoons of the parsley and set aside to cool for a few minutes.
5 Stuff the squid with the filling, using a teaspoon to push it down into the bottom of the tubes. Do not overfill the tubes—you need to be able to close them easily without any filling squeezing out. Seal the tops with cocktail sticks.
6 Put the remaining tomato sauce in a saucepan with 220 ml (7 fl oz) water. Cook for 2 minutes, then add the stuffed squid to the pan. Cover the saucepan and simmer gently for 30–45 minutes, or until the squid are soft and tender—the cooking time will depend on the size of the squid so test it and give it a little more time if you need to. Don't stir the squid too much when cooking or the filling will fall out. Shake the pan a little if you are worried about the squid sticking to the bottom. Remove the cocktail sticks and sprinkle with the remaining parsley just before serving. Serve with a salad.

BAKED EGGPLANT

Preparation time: 20 minutes
Total cooking time: 1 hour 5 minutes
Serves 4

3/4 cup (185 ml/6 fl oz) olive oil

2 large eggplants (aubergines), cut in half lengthways

3 onions, thinly sliced

3 garlic cloves, finely chopped

400 g (13 oz) Roma (plum) tomatoes, peeled and chopped, or a 400 g (13 oz) tin of good-quality chopped tomatoes

2 teaspoons dried oregano

4 tablespoons chopped flat-leaf (Italian) parsley

1/4 cup (35 g/1 1/4 oz) currants

1/4 teaspoon ground cinnamon

1 cup (185 g/6 oz) long-grain rice, cooked and drained

1/2 cup (125 ml/4 fl oz) tomato juice

2 tablespoons lemon juice

pinch of sugar

1 Preheat the oven to moderate 180°C (350°F/ Gas 4). Heat half the oil in a frying pan over medium heat and cook the eggplants all over for 8–10 minutes, or until the cut sides are golden. Remove from the pan and scoop out some of the flesh, leaving the skins intact and some of the flesh lining the skin. Finely chop the flesh and set aside.
2 Heat the remaining olive oil in the same pan and cook the onion over medium heat for about 10 minutes, or until softened but not browned. Add the garlic and cook for another minute. Now add the tomato, oregano, parsley, currants, cinnamon, rice and the eggplant flesh and mix it in well. Season with salt and freshly ground black pepper.
3 Put the eggplant shells in an ovenproof dish and fill each with the prepared tomato mixture. Mix the tomato juice, lemon juice, sugar and some salt in a bowl, and pour over the eggplant. Cover and bake for 30 minutes, then uncover and cook for another 10 minutes. Serve the eggplants on a platter with a light drizzle of oil and any of the remaining juice.

ABOVE: Baked eggplant

GREEK-STYLE STUFFED VEGETABLES

Preparation time: 15 minutes
Total cooking time: 1 hour 50 minutes
Serves 4

☆☆

4 large, firm, ripe tomatoes, of uniform size
4 green capsicums (peppers), of uniform
   size and shape
1 cup (250 g/8 oz) medium-grain rice
1/4 cup (60 ml/2 fl oz) olive oil, plus
   a little extra
1 onion, finely chopped
250 g (8 oz) lean minced (ground) beef
1/2 cup (125 g/4 oz) tomato passata
white pepper, to season
2 tablespoons finely chopped flat-leaf
   (Italian) parsley
1 tablespoon finely chopped dill
1 tablespoon finely chopped mint leaves
1/2 teaspoon ground allspice
15 g (1/2 oz) butter

1 Preheat the oven to moderate 180°C (350°F/
Gas 4). Slice the top off the tomatoes and reserve
them. Scoop out the seeds with a teaspoon
and discard. Scoop out the flesh and place in a
strainer to drain the juice. Finely dice 1/2 cup
(100 g/31/2 oz) of the flesh and set aside. Sit the
tomatoes upside down on a rack. Slice the tops
off the capsicums, reserving them. Remove the
seeds and membrane. Wash the rice and drain well.
2 Heat the oil over medium heat in a saucepan,
then add the onion and fry for 3–4 minutes, or
until softened but not browned. Add the beef
and cook over medium heat, stirring to break
up any lumps, for 4–5 minutes, or until evenly
browned. Add the chopped tomato flesh and
1/4 cup (60 g/2 oz) of the tomato passata, then
season. Reduce the heat a little and cook for
10 minutes. Add the rice, herbs and allspice and
mix well. Pour in 11/4 cups (310 ml/10 fl oz)
water, then cook, uncovered, over low heat for
10–15 minutes, or until all the liquid has been
absorbed and the rice is tender, but still slightly
under done. Stir occasionally to ensure that the
rice doesn't stick to the bottom of the pan.
3 Fill each vegetable with enough stuffing to fill
them two-thirds full. Dot the surface of the rice
in each vegetable with a little butter and replace
the lids. Lightly oil a large roasting tin and put
the tomatoes on one side of the pan and the
capsicums on the other. Drizzle with olive oil.
Combine the remaining tomato passata with
1 cup (250 ml/8 fl oz) water, then pour this
around the vegetables. Bake for 11/4 hours,
or until the vegetables are tender and lightly
browned, adding more water if the liquid dries
out. Cover the capsicums with foil if they brown
before the tomatoes. Serve warm or cold.

TIMBALLO OF LEEKS, ZUCCHINI AND BASIL

Preparation time: 15 minutes
Total cooking time: 1 hour
Serves 4–6

pinch of saffron threads

1/2 cup (125 ml/4 fl oz) dry white wine

3 cups (750 ml/24 fl oz) chicken stock

50 g (1³/₄ oz) butter

1 onion, finely chopped

2 garlic cloves, crushed

1²/₃ cups (360 g/12 oz) risotto rice

leaves from 2 thyme sprigs

1/2 cup (50 g/1³/₄ oz) freshly grated
    Parmesan cheese

2 tablespoons olive oil

2 leeks (white part only), thinly sliced

400 g (13 oz) thin zucchini (courgettes),
    thinly sliced on the diagonal

1/4 teaspoon freshly grated nutmeg

10 basil leaves, shredded

75 g (2¹/₂ oz) thinly sliced prosciutto,
    cut into strips

1/3 cup (80 g/2³/₄ oz) sour cream

1 Soak the saffron in the wine. Pour the stock and 1/2 cup (125 ml/4 fl oz) water into a saucepan and bring to the boil. Reduce the heat, cover with a lid and keep at a low simmer.
2 Melt half the butter in a large saucepan wider than it is high. Add the onion and garlic and cook over low heat for about 5 minutes, or until softened but not browned. Add the rice and stir until well coated. Stir in the thyme and season well. Stir in the saffron-infused wine, then increase the heat and cook, stirring constantly, until it is absorbed. Stir 1/2 cup (125 ml/4 fl oz) of the stock into the rice, then reduce the heat and cook until it is absorbed. Continue adding more liquid, 1/2 cup (125 ml/4 fl oz) at a time until all the liquid is absorbed and the rice is tender and creamy. This will take around 25–30 minutes. Remove from the heat and stir in the remaining butter and the Parmesan.
3 Heat the oil in a frying pan and cook the leeks without browning over low heat for 5 minutes. Add the zucchini slices and cook for about 5 minutes, or until softened. Add the nutmeg and season well with salt and freshly ground black pepper. Stir in the basil, prosciutto and sour cream. Cook, stirring, for 2–3 minutes, or until the sauce thickens.
4 Preheat the oven to moderate 180°C (350°F/Gas 4) and grease a 1.5 litre (48 fl oz) pudding basin or rounded ovenproof bowl. Cut out a piece of greaseproof paper the size of the basin's base and line the base. Cover with half the rice mixture, pressing it down firmly. Spoon in two-thirds of the zucchini mixture, keeping the remaining one-third warm in the pan. Press in the last of the rice mixture. Cover with foil and transfer to the oven.
5 Bake for 20 minutes. Remove from the oven and rest for 5 minutes. Carefully unmould onto a serving plate. Serve the reserved zucchini on the side and serve at once.
NOTE: The prosciutto can be eliminated and the stock changed to vegetable if you'd prefer a vegetarian version.

BELOW: Timballo of leeks, zucchini and basil

DOLMADES

Vigorously mix together the rice filling for the dolmades with a large spoon—the aim is to have an even mix of ingredients.

With the leaves vein-side down, put a small amount of filling in the middle of each leaf before rolling them up into little 'cigars'.

To prevent the dolmades from moving around too much during cooking, keep them tightly packed together.

ABOVE: Dolmades

DOLMADES

Preparation time: 40 minutes +
  25 minutes soaking
Total cooking time: 45 minutes
Makes 48

☆☆

200 g (6¹/2 oz) vine leaves in brine (see Note)
1 cup (250 g/8 oz) medium-grain rice
1 small onion, finely chopped
1 tablespoon olive oil
50 g (1³/4 oz) pine nuts, toasted
2 tablespoons currants
2 tablespoons chopped dill
2 tablespoons finely chopped mint
2 tablespoons finely chopped flat-leaf
  (Italian) parsley
¹/3 cup (80 ml/2³/4 fl oz) olive oil, extra
2 tablespoons lemon juice
2 cups (500 ml/16 fl oz) chicken or
  vegetable stock

1 Soak the vine leaves in cold water for 15 minutes. Remove, pat dry and cut off any stems. Reserve 5–6 leaves; discard any with holes. Meanwhile, pour boiling water over the rice and soak for 10 minutes, then drain.
2 Put the rice, onion, oil, pine nuts, currants, herbs and a little salt and freshly ground black pepper in a large bowl, and mix well.
3 Lay some leaves vein-side down on a flat surface. Put ¹/2 tablespoon of filling in the middle of each leaf, fold the stalk end over the filling, then the left and right sides into the middle, and finally roll firmly towards the tip. The dolmade should resemble a small, fat cigar. Repeat with the remaining filling and leaves to make 48 dolmades.
4 Line the base of a large saucepan or flameproof casserole dish with the reserved leaves. Drizzle with 1 tablespoon of the extra oil. Put the dolmades in the pan, tightly packing them in one layer. Pour the lemon juice and remaining oil over them.
5 Pour the stock over the dolmades and cover with an inverted plate to stop them moving while cooking. Bring to the boil, then reduce

the heat and simmer gently, covered, for
45 minutes. Remove with a slotted spoon.
Serve warm or cold.

NOTE: Fresh vine leaves can be used instead, but
they need to be blanched in boiling water first.

ARANCINI

Preparation time: 25 minutes +
   overnight refrigeration
Total cooking time: 50 minutes
Makes 20

large pinch of saffron threads

1 cup (250 ml/8 fl oz) white wine

100 g (3^1/2 oz) butter

1 onion, finely chopped

1 large garlic clove, crushed

2 tablespoons thyme

3 cups (750 ml/24 fl oz) chicken stock

1 cup (220 g/7 oz) risotto rice

^{1}/2 cup (50 g/1^3/4 oz) freshly grated
   Parmesan cheese

100 g (3^1/2 oz) fresh mozzarella or
   fontina cheese, cut into cubes

75 g (2^1/2 oz) dry breadcrumbs

oil, for deep-frying

1 Soak the saffron in the wine while you prepare
the risotto. Pour the stock into a saucepan and
bring to the boil. Reduce the heat, cover with
a lid and keep at a low simmer.

2 Melt the butter in a large saucepan. Cook the
onion and garlic over low heat for 3–4 minutes,
or until softened but not browned. Add the
thyme and rice to the onion and cook, stirring,
for 1 minute, or until the rice is well coated.
Add the wine and saffron and stir until the wine
is all absorbed. Add ^{1}/2 cup (125 ml) of the hot
stock and stir constantly over medium heat until
all the liquid is absorbed. Continue adding more
stock, ^{1}/2 cup (125 ml) at a time until all the
liquid is absorbed and the rice is tender and
creamy; this will take around 25–30 minutes.
When making arancini, it is not so essential
to keep the rice *al dente*—if it is a little more
glutinous, it will stick together better.

3 Remove the pan from the heat and stir in
the Parmesan, then spread the mixture out onto
a tray covered with plastic wrap. Leave to cool
and, for the best results, leave in the fridge to
firm up overnight.

4 To make the arancini, roll a small amount of
risotto into a walnut-sized ball. Press a hole in
the middle with your thumb, push a small piece
of cheese inside and press the risotto around
it to enclose in a ball. Repeat with the rest of
the risotto. Roll each ball in the breadcrumbs,
pressing down to coat well.

5 Heat enough oil in a deep-fat fryer or large
saucepan to fully cover the arancini. Heat the
oil to 180°C (350°F), or until a cube of bread
dropped into the oil browns in 15 seconds.
Cook the arancini in batches, without crowding,
for 3–4 minutes. Drain on crumpled paper towels
and leave for a couple of minutes before eating.
Serve either hot or at room temperature.

NOTE: Arancini means 'little oranges' and these
rice balls are a speciality of Sicily. Using saffron
risotto as a basis for arancini is traditional. If
you can find it, use vialone nano or another
riso semifino.

BELOW: Arancini

SUPPLI

Roll one portion of rice into a small ball, press a hole in the middle with your thumb, then put a piece of cheese in the middle.

Press the rice back around the filling to reform the ball.

SUPPLI

Preparation time: 25 minutes + cooling
Total cooking time: 45 minutes
Serves 6

☆ ☆

1.5 litres (48 fl oz) chicken stock
60 g (2 oz) butter
1 small onion, finely chopped
400 g (13 oz) risotto rice
3/4 cup (75 g/2 1/2 oz) freshly grated
    Parmesan cheese
2 eggs, beaten
9 basil leaves, torn in half
150 g (5 oz) fresh mozzarella cheese, cut into
    18 cubes (about 1.5 cm/5/8 inch square)
150 g (5 oz) dry breadcrumbs
oil, for deep-frying

1 Pour the stock into a saucepan and bring to the boil. Reduce the heat, cover with a lid and keep at a low simmer.

2 Melt the butter in a large saucepan. Cook the onion over low heat for 3–4 minutes, or until softened but not browned. Stir in the rice until well coated. Add 1/2 cup (125 ml) of the hot stock and stir constantly over medium heat until all the liquid is absorbed. Continue adding more liquid, 1/2 cup (125 ml) at a time until all the liquid is absorbed and the rice is tender and creamy, this will take around 25–30 minutes. When making suppli, it is not so essential to keep the rice *al dente*—if it is a little more glutinous, it will stick together better.

3 Remove the pan from the heat and stir in the Parmesan and eggs. Season with salt and freshly ground black pepper. Spread out on a large baking tray to cool completely.

4 Divide the rice into 18 portions. Take one portion in the palm of your hand and put a piece of basil and a cube of mozzarella in the centre. Fold the rice over to encase the cheese and at the same time mould the croquette into an egg shape. Roll the croquette in breadcrumbs and put on a baking tray while you make the rest.

5 Heat enough oil in a deep-fat fryer or large saucepan to fully cover the croquettes. Heat the oil to 180°C (350°F), or until a cube of bread dropped into the oil browns in 15 seconds. Deep-fry the suppli in batches, without crowding, for about 4 minutes, or until evenly golden brown. Drain on crumpled paper towels and serve at once, as they are or with a fresh tomato sauce.

RIGHT: Suppli

RISOTTO CAKES WITH PRESERVED LEMON MAYONNAISE

Preparation time: 30 minutes +
 2 hours 30 minutes standing
Total cooking time: 40 minutes
Makes 30

1 litre (32 fl oz) chicken stock
1 tablespoon olive oil
1 garlic clove, finely chopped
1 small onion, finely chopped
1 cup (220 g/7 oz) risotto rice
1/2 cup (125 ml/4 fl oz) dry white wine
4 marinated artichokes, drained and
 finely chopped
1/4 cup (25 g/3/4 oz) coarsely grated
 Parmesan cheese
1 teaspoon grated lemon zest
1/2 cup (60 g/2 oz) plain (all-purpose)
 flour, seasoned
2 eggs
1 cup (100 g/31/2 oz) dry breadcrumbs
3 slices (50 g/13/4 oz) pancetta
oil, for pan-frying
15 pitted Kalamata olives, halved
flat-leaf (Italian) parsley, to garnish

PRESERVED LEMON MAYONNAISE
1/3 cup (80 g/23/4 oz) whole-egg mayonnaise
2 teaspoons finely chopped preserved lemon

1 Pour the stock into a saucepan and bring to the boil. Reduce the heat, cover with a lid and keep at a low simmer.
2 Heat the oil in a large saucepan. Cook the garlic and onion over low heat for 4–5 minutes, or until the onion is softened but not browned. Stir in the rice until well coated. Add the wine and stir over medium heat until it has all been absorbed. Add 1/2 cup (125 ml/4 fl oz) of the hot stock, and stir constantly until nearly all the stock has been absorbed. Continue adding more liquid, 1/2 cup (125 ml/4 fl oz) at a time until all the liquid is absorbed and the rice is tender and creamy, this will take around 25–30 minutes.
3 Remove from the heat and stir in the artichokes, Parmesan and lemon zest. Spread the risotto out on a tray and allow it to cool for 2 hours.

4 Put the flour in one bowl, the eggs in another and the breadcrumbs in a third. Lightly beat the eggs. Using wet hands, roll the risotto into thirty 3 cm (11/4 inch) discs. First, coat them with flour, next dip them in egg and, finally, coat them in the breadcrumbs. Refrigerate for at least 30 minutes.
5 Cook the pancetta in a non-stick frying pan until crisp, then tear each slice into 10 pieces.
6 To make the preserved lemon mayonnaise, mix the preserved lemon into the mayonnaise.
7 Heat the oil in a frying pan and cook the risotto cakes in batches for 2–3 minutes on each side, or until golden and crisp. Drain on crumpled paper towels. Top each risotto cake with 1/2 teaspoon of the mayonnaise, a piece of pancetta, half an olive and a torn parsley leaf. Serve warm or hot.
NOTE: You can make the risotto 2 days ahead of time, then spread it out on a tray and keep covered in the fridge until needed.

ABOVE: Risotto cakes with preserved lemon mayonnaise

31

CHEESY RISOTTO FRITTERS WITH BACON AND TOMATOES

Preparation time: 20 minutes +
   refrigeration
Total cooking time: 50 minutes
Makes 12

 ☆☆

1.125 litres (36 fl oz) chicken stock

1 tablespoon olive oil

1 small onion, finely chopped

1¹/2 cups (330 g/11 oz) risotto rice

¹/2 cup (60 g/2 oz) freshly grated
   Cheddar cheese

¹/2 cup (50 g/1³/4 oz) freshly grated
   Parmesan cheese

2 tablespoons finely chopped parsley

3 spring onions (scallions), finely chopped

6 Roma (plum) tomatoes, halved

12 back bacon rashers

plain (all-purpose) flour, for dusting

¹/4 cup (60 ml/2 fl oz) olive oil, extra

ABOVE: Cheesy risotto fritters with bacon and tomatoes

1 Preheat the oven to 180°C (350°F/Gas 4). Pour the stock into a saucepan and bring to the boil. Reduce the heat, cover with a lid and keep at a low simmer.

2 Heat the oil in a large saucepan over medium heat. Cook the onion for 3 minutes, or until softened but not browned. Stir in the rice until well coated. Add ¹/2 cup (125 ml/4 fl oz) of the hot stock to the rice, and stir constantly over medium heat until all the liquid is absorbed. Continue adding more liquid, ¹/2 cup (125 ml/4 fl oz) at a time until all the liquid is absorbed and the rice is tender and creamy, this will take around 25–30 minutes.

3 Remove the pan from the heat and stir in the cheeses, parsley and spring onion. Refrigerate until completely cooled.

4 Preheat the grill (broiler), then cook the bacon until crisp.

5 Lay the tomatoes, skin-side down, on a baking tray and grill (broil) for 3–4 minutes.

6 Using wet hands, shape the cold risotto mixture into 12 patties, then toss in flour. Heat the extra oil in a frying pan. Cook the patties in batches over medium heat for 3 minutes on each side, or until golden. Drain well. Serve with the tomatoes and bacon.

FENNEL RISOTTO BALLS WITH CHEESY FILLING

Preparation time: 30 minutes +
  1 hour refrigeration
Total cooking time: 50 minutes
Serves 4–6

1.5 litres (48 fl oz) vegetable stock

1 tablespoon oil

30 g (1 oz) butter

2 garlic cloves, crushed

1 onion, finely chopped

2 fennel bulbs, thinly sliced

1 tablespoon balsamic vinegar

1/2 cup (125 ml/4 fl oz) white wine

3 cups (660 g/1 lb 5 oz) risotto rice

1/2 cup (50 g/1 3/4 oz) freshly grated
  Parmesan cheese

1/2 cup (25 g/3/4 oz) snipped chives

1 egg, lightly beaten

150 g (5 oz) sun-dried (sun-blushed)
  tomatoes, chopped

100 g (3 1/2 oz) fresh mozzarella cheese,
  diced

1/2 cup (80 g/2 3/4 oz) frozen peas,
  thawed

1/2 cup (60 g/2 oz) plain (all-purpose)
  flour, seasoned

3 eggs, extra

2 cups (200 g/6 1/2 oz) dry breadcrumbs

oil, for deep-frying

1 Pour the stock into a saucepan and bring to the boil. Reduce the heat, cover with a lid and keep at a low simmer.

2 Heat the oil and butter in a large saucepan and cook the garlic and onion over medium heat for 3 minutes, or until softened but not browned. Add the fennel and cook for 10 minutes, or until it starts to caramelize. Add the vinegar and wine, increase the heat and boil until the liquid evaporates. Stir in the rice until well coated.

3 Add 1/2 cup (125 ml/4 fl oz) hot stock, stirring constantly over medium heat until the liquid is absorbed. Continue adding more stock, 1/2 cup (125 ml/4 fl oz) at a time, stirring, for 20–25 minutes, or until all the stock is absorbed and the rice is tender and creamy.

4 Remove from the heat and stir in the Parmesan, chives, egg and tomato. Transfer to a bowl, cover and cool. Put the mozzarella and peas in a bowl and mash together. Season.

5 Put the flour in one bowl, the extra eggs in another and the breadcrumbs in a third. Lightly beat the eggs. With wet hands, shape the risotto into 14 even balls. Flatten each ball out, slightly indenting the centre. Put a heaped teaspoon of the pea mash into the indentation, then shape the rice around the filling to form a ball. Roll each ball in seasoned flour, then dip in the extra egg and roll in breadcrumbs. Place on a foil-covered tray and refrigerate for 30 minutes.

6 Fill a deep-fat fryer or large saucepan one-third full of oil and heat to 180°C (350°F), or until a cube of bread dropped into the oil browns in 15 seconds. Cook the risotto balls in batches for 5 minutes, or until golden and crisp and the cheese has melted inside. Drain on crumpled paper towels and season with salt. If the cheese has not melted by the end of the cooking time, cook the balls on a tray in a (180°C/350°F/Gas 4) oven for 5 minutes. Serve with a salad.

BELOW: Fennel risotto balls with cheesy filling

HOW TO MAKE THE PERFECT RISOTTO
Give a risotto a little love and patience and you will be well rewarded with tender pearls of rice.

The Italians invented risotto and now the rest of the world loves it as much as they do. And with a glass of wine in one hand and the wooden spoon in the other, making risotto can be very soothing.

FLAVOUR
The flavours of risotto are as interesting and varied as the regions they hail from and there are now risottos with flavours as diverse as red wine and Asian mushrooms.

One of the main elements of the flavour is the liquid used to cook the rice. Sometimes water, but more often a stock made from meat or vegetables, is used. The type of stock used should be appropriate to the main ingredient; for example, a seafood risotto will usually use a lighter fish stock or water whereas a hearty meaty risotto may use red wine and beef, lamb or veal stock. Most risottos can be made on a light chicken stock as its subtle flavour blends well with almost any flavour combination. Be

aware that some ready-made commercial brands of stock are quite salty and strongly flavoured and should be diluted with water to prevent the flavour intensifying over the long cooking time. Because stock is such an important element of a risotto, it's well worth using the home-made variety for its superior flavour.

Just before serving, a variety of ingredients may be added to enrich the risotto, such as butter, cream or cheese, which melt through the risotto. Other ingredients add a refreshing lift to a rich risotto: fresh herbs or lemon zest are two common examples. Most risottos are served with freshly grated, good-quality Parmesan cheese.

TEXTURE
Most people prefer their risotto *al dente*, which translates as tender but firm to the bite. However, many Italians from the north, particularly around the Veneto region, prefer their risotto served *al onda*, meaning wavy. When served in this

manner, the risotto is soft enough to pour and is soup-like.

The grains of rice should be reasonably separate and tender to the bite without being mushy and the sauce that binds the rice should have a smooth creaminess.

WHICH RICE?
Good risotto demands good rice—one that is short, fat, high in starch and that can absorb up to five times its weight in liquid without breaking up. The best rice for risotto comes from northern Italy. The rices are graded and rices from the top grade, *riso superfino* include arborio (the biggest grain) and carnaroli (the best grain). Rices a grade lower, *riso fino,* also make fine risottos; and the third grade, *riso semifino,* is very good for making suppli, arancini and in timballo.

TOOLS
All you need to make a first-class risotto are a couple of large heavy-based saucepans and a wooden spoon. A heavy base is

important so that the rice doesn't stick to the bottom.

Some people prefer to use frying pans to cook risotto; if you do, make sure it has a heavy base and high sides to minimize excess evaporation.

TECHNIQUE

Our recipes are based on the classic method of the Lombardy region, which involves careful stirring and gradual additions of hot liquid (usually stock).

Depending on the type of risotto you are making, you will need to add particular ingredients at different stages, taking into account varying cooking times of these ingredients. The recipe will guide you.

The liquid needs to be hot when it is added to the rice so that the temperature of the rice does not drop too much—which not only makes the process longer but can alter the texture.

Melt some butter or heat some oil until sizzling over medium heat then if the recipe calls for it, sauté some onion or garlic. Unless specified, don't let the onion brown. Add the rice to the pan and cook for a couple of minutes or until it turns translucent, not golden. This process coats the grains, allowing them to stay slightly separate but still allows the starch to be released.

Next, add any alcohol and stir until it is absorbed. Adding it before the rest of the liquid ensures the alcohol is cooked out and doesn't overpower the other flavours.

Add the hot stock, ½ cup (125 ml/ 4 fl oz) at a time, and stir until it is absorbed, then repeat this method until all the liquid is absorbed. In general, you will need about 1.5 litres (48 fl oz) of liquid to 2 cups (440 g/14 oz) of rice to serve 4 to 6 people. To use all the liquid and for the rice to be *al dente* should take you about 20–30 minutes.

Different types and batches of rice may absorb liquid at varying rates, the most common reason being humidity: rice can absorb moisture from the air, so you may not need to add all the liquid.

Often the final addition of stock is accompanied by raw seafood or other meats or vegetables that may have been browned off at an earlier stage and need to be returned to the pan. Vegetables, such as asparagus, that require little time to cook are also added at this stage.

Many risottos are finished by stirring in some cheese, usually a good-quality Parmesan, and perhaps a dob of butter or some chopped fresh herbs. Always stir the cheese in a couple of minutes before the risotto is completely cooked so that the melted cheese can completely envelop all the grains of rice.

Although most recipes say to serve risotto immediately, it actually benefits from a couple of minutes resting; this allows the flavours and the texture to settle. Italian diners often spread their risotto around their plate to allow the steam to escape and the risotto to cool slightly. That said, do not leave the

STEPS TO THE PERFECT RISOTTO

STEP ONE: Pour the stock into a saucepan and bring to the boil. Reduce the heat, cover with a lid and keep at a low simmer.

STEP TWO: Sauté the onion base in oil or butter until softened but not browned.

STEP THREE: Stir in the rice until well coated.

STEP FOUR: Add ½ cup (125 ml/4 fl oz) of the hot stock. Stir constantly over medium heat until nearly all the liquid is absorbed. Continue adding the stock, ½ cup (125 ml/4 fl oz) at a time, stirring constantly.

STEP FIVE: Add other ingredients, if necessary (follow the recipe). Continue adding stock until the rice is al dente.

STEP SIX: Remove from the heat and stir in any flavourings. Season to taste, then serve.

risotto to sit for too long or it will become a heavy and unappealing mass.

THE FINISHING TOUCH

Serve the risotto with freshly grated, good-quality Parmesan cheese. Invite your guests to sprinkle as little or as much as they like over the top. Even better, let them grate their own Parmesan for the best flavour.

There is some debate over whether the pungently flavoured Parmesan should be served with seafood risotto. There are those who believe it masks the delicate flavour of the seafood, but others who wouldn't serve a risotto without it—let your guests decide for themselves.

MASCARPONE
Mascarpone is a rich, fresh cream cheese originally from the Lombardy region in Italy. Made from cream coagulated by citric or tartaric acid, it has a relatively high fat content. Its creamy texture makes it particularly well suited to use in desserts and it makes an appearance in the traditional Italian dessert, tiramisu. Its use in savoury meals is usually limited to replacing cream in sauces and butter in risottos, providing a wonderful richness. Usually sold in tubs, mascarpone is available from the refrigerated section of some supermarkets or from delicatessens.

LEMON AND HERB RISOTTO WITH FRIED MUSHROOMS

Preparation time: 30 minutes
Total cooking time: 50 minutes
Serves 4

☆ ☆

1 litre (32 fl oz) chicken or vegetable stock
pinch of saffron threads
2 tablespoons olive oil
2 leeks (white part only), thinly sliced
2 garlic cloves, crushed
2 cups (440 g/14 oz) risotto rice
2–3 teaspoons finely grated lemon zest
2–3 tablespoons lemon juice
2 tablespoons chopped flat-leaf (Italian) parsley
2 tablespoons snipped chives
2 tablespoons chopped oregano
3/4 cup (75 g/2 1/2 oz) freshly grated
    Parmesan cheese
100 g (3 1/2 oz) mascarpone cheese
30 g (1 oz) butter
1 tablespoon virgin olive oil
200 g (6 1/2 oz) small flat mushrooms,
    cut into thick slices
1 tablespoon balsamic vinegar

1 Pour the stock into a saucepan and add the saffron threads. Bring to the boil, then reduce the heat, cover and keep at a low simmer.
2 Heat the olive oil in a large saucepan over medium heat. Add the leek, cook for 5 minutes, then add the garlic and cook for a further 5 minutes, or until golden. Add the rice and stir until well coated. Add half the lemon zest and half the juice, then add 1/2 cup (125 ml/4 fl oz) of the hot stock. Stir constantly over medium heat until all the liquid has been absorbed. Continue adding more liquid, 1/2 cup (125 ml/ 4 fl oz) at a time until all the liquid is absorbed and the rice is tender and creamy; this will take around 25–30 minutes. (You may not need to use all the stock, or you may need a little extra— every risotto will be slightly different.)
3 Remove the pan from the heat. Stir in the herbs, Parmesan, mascarpone and the remaining lemon zest and lemon juice, then cover and keep warm.
4 To cook the mushrooms, melt the butter and virgin olive oil in a large frying pan, add the mushroom slices and vinegar and cook, stirring, over high heat for 5–7 minutes, or until the mushrooms are tender and all the liquid has been absorbed.
5 Serve the risotto in large bowls topped with the mushrooms. Garnish with sprigs of fresh herbs, if desired.

RIGHT: Lemon and herb risotto with fried mushrooms

SEAFOOD RISOTTO

Preparation time: 20 minutes
Total cooking time: 35 minutes
Serves 4

185 g (6 oz) squid tubes

200 g (6¹/2 oz) prawns (shrimp)

16 scallops

¹/3 cup (80 ml/2³/4 fl oz) olive oil

2 garlic cloves, crushed

185 g (6 oz) firm white fish fillets
   (e.g. monkfish, sea bass or fresh haddock),
   skinned and cut into bite-size pieces

1 litre (32 fl oz) fish stock

1 leek (white part only), thinly sliced

1¹/2 cups (360 g/12 oz) risotto rice

¹/2 cup (125 ml/4 fl oz) dry white wine

3 Roma (plum) tomatoes, chopped

20 g (³/4 oz) butter

1¹/2 tablespoons finely chopped parsley

1¹/2 tablespoons finely chopped dill

1 Cut the squid tubes into thinner rings. Peel and devein the prawns. To clean the scallops, pull off any vein, membrane or hard white muscle from the meat.

2 Heat half the olive oil in a large wide saucepan. Add the garlic and cook gently without browning for 20–30 seconds. Add the squid and prawns and season lightly. Increase the heat and cook until they turn opaque. Remove the squid and prawns from the pan and set aside.

3 Add the fish and scallops to the pan and cook until they change colour. Remove from the pan and set aside.

4 Pour the stock into a saucepan and bring to the boil. Reduce the heat, cover with a lid and keep at a low simmer.

5 Heat the remaining olive oil in the large wide saucepan. Add the leek and cook for about 4 minutes, or until softened but not browned. Stir in the rice until well coated. Pour in the white wine, increase the heat and cook, stirring, until all the liquid has been absorbed. Add ¹/2 cup (125 ml/4 fl oz) of the hot stock and stir constantly over medium heat until all the liquid is absorbed. Continue adding more stock, ¹/2 cup (125 ml/4 fl oz) at a time until all the liquid is absorbed and the rice is tender and creamy, this will take around 25–30 minutes.

6 Add the tomato and cooked seafood and toss lightly. Remove the pan from the heat and gently stir in the butter and chopped herbs. Season to taste with salt and freshly ground black pepper.

FISH STOCK

Place 2 kg (4 lb) white fish bones and trimmings (remove any eyes with a teaspoon) in a bowl of salted water. Stand for 10 minutes, then drain. Transfer to a large saucepan or stockpot with 1 chopped onion, 1 chopped celery stick, 1 bay leaf, 6 peppercorns, the juice of 1 lemon and 2 litres (64 fl oz) cold water. Bring to the boil, skimming any scum that rises to the surface. Reduce the heat and simmer for 20 minutes, continuing to skim as needed. Strain through a fine sieve into a heatproof bowl. Do not press on the solids or it may cloud the stock. Will keep refrigerated for 2–3 days, or frozen for up to 3 months. Makes 1.5 litres (48 fl oz).

ABOVE: Seafood risotto

RISOTTO NERO

There may be an ink sac in the squid; if so, separate it from the rest of the innards without puncturing it and then rinse it gently.

Cut the tentacles off below the eyes, rinse them and remove the skin. Rinse the bodies well and remove the skin, then chop the flesh finely.

RISOTTO NERO
(Squid ink risotto)

Preparation time: 20 minutes
Total cooking time: 35 minutes
Serves 6

☆ ☆

3 squid
1 litre (32 fl oz) fish stock
100 g (3¹/₂ oz) butter
1 red onion, finely chopped
2 garlic cloves, crushed
1¹/₂ cups (360 g/12 oz) risotto rice
3 sachets of squid or cuttlefish ink or
    the ink sacs of the squid (see Note)
155 ml (5 fl oz) white wine
2 teaspoons olive oil

1 Prepare the squid by pulling the heads and tentacles out of the bodies along with any innards. If there is an ink sac, carefully remove it and rinse it. Cut the heads off below the eyes, leaving just the tentacles. Discard the heads and set the tentacles aside. Rinse the tentacles and bodies, pulling out the transparent quills. Pull the skin off the tentacles and bodies. Finely chop the bodies and cut the tentacles in half.

2 Pour the stock into a saucepan and bring to the boil. Reduce the heat, cover with a lid and keep at a low simmer.

3 Heat the butter in a deep heavy-based frying pan and cook the onion until softened but not browned. Increase the heat and add the squid bodies. Cook for 3 minutes, or until opaque. Add the garlic and stir briefly. Stir in the rice until well coated.

4 Squeeze the ink from the sachets (or use the ink sacs) and add with the wine. Increase the heat and stir until absorbed.

5 Add ¹/₂ cup (125 ml/4 fl oz) of the hot stock and stir constantly over medium heat until all the liquid is absorbed. Continue adding more stock, ¹/₂ cup (125 ml/4 fl oz) at a time until all the liquid is absorbed and the rice is tender and creamy, this will take around 25–30 minutes.

6 Heat the olive oil in a frying pan and fry the squid tentacles quickly. Use to garnish the risotto.
NOTE: Some squid have ink sacs in their bodies, others do not. You can buy sachets of ink from fishmongers and delicatessens—these have a long shelf life so you can keep them on standby just in case your squid doesn't contain any ink.

RIGHT: Risotto nero

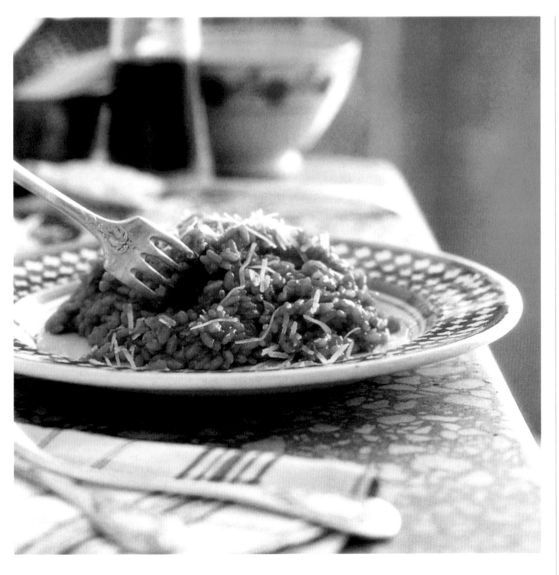

RISOTTO
Risotto originated in the rice-growing areas of northern Italy. The consistency of risotto is regional—some areas prefer it almost soup-like (Venice); others slightly thicker (Milan). Though risotto was originally an Italian peasant dish, it has now become much more sophisticated as the rest of the world has learnt to appreciate the dish. As its reputation has grown, there has been an explosion in the variety of flavourings as well; there are now many options that go beyond the original Italian flavours. Traditional risotto is somewhat of a labour of love for the cook, requiring almost constant stirring to achieve the soft, creamy texture so admired.

RED WINE RISOTTO

Preparation time: 20 minutes
Total cooking time: 25 minutes
Serves 4 as a starter

2 cups (500 ml/16 fl oz) chicken stock

100 g (3¹/₂ oz) butter

1 onion, finely chopped

1 large garlic clove, crushed

2 tablespoons chopped thyme

1 cup (220 g/7 oz) risotto rice

2 cups (500 ml/16 fl oz) dry red wine (see Note)

¹/₂ cup (50 g/1³/₄ oz) freshly grated
　Parmesan cheese

1 Pour the stock into a saucepan and bring to the boil. Reduce the heat, cover with a lid and keep at a low simmer.

2 Heat the butter in a large wide saucepan. Add the onion and garlic and cook until softened but not browned. Add the thyme and rice and stir until the rice is well coated. Season.

3 Add half the red wine and cook, stirring continuously, until it has all been absorbed. Add ¹/₂ cup (125 ml) of the hot stock and stir constantly over medium heat until all the liquid is absorbed. Continue adding more stock, ¹/₂ cup (125 ml) at a time until you have used half the stock. Add the remaining red wine to the risotto, stirring continuously until it has been absorbed. Keep adding ¹/₂ cup (125 ml/4 fl oz) of the stock until all the liquid is absorbed and the rice is tender and creamy, this will take around 25–30 minutes in total.

4 Remove the pan from the heat and stir in half the Parmesan. Serve with the remaining cheese sprinkled over the top.

NOTE: The traditional variety of wine used in Italy for this risotto is Amarone of Valpolicella, but you can use any dry but rich red.

ABOVE: Red wine risotto

until the rice is *al dente* and most of the stock has been absorbed. Stir in the remaining butter and the Parmesan, season and serve.

NOTE: The consistency of this classic Italian rice dish is thick, halfway between a risotto and a soup in texture and appearance. You can make it thin enough to eat with a spoon, or thick enough to use a fork. Some versions are very simple and do not even include pancetta.

RISOTTO PRIMAVERA

Preparation time: 15 minutes
Total cooking time: 35 minutes
Serves 6

 ☆ ☆

1.5 litres (48 fl oz) chicken or vegetable stock
2 tablespoons olive oil
75 g (2$^{1}/_{2}$ oz) butter
I large onion, finely chopped
I carrot, finely diced
2 garlic cloves, crushed
2 cups (440 g/14 oz) risotto rice
200 g (6$^{1}/_{2}$ oz) fresh, thin asparagus, cut into
  2 cm ($^{3}/_{4}$ inch) pieces
2 small zucchini (courgettes), thinly sliced
$^{3}/_{4}$ cup (115 g/4 oz) fresh peas
$^{1}/_{2}$ cup (15 g/$^{1}/_{2}$ oz) chopped flat-leaf
  (Italian) parsley
$^{1}/_{2}$ cup (50 g/1$^{3}/_{4}$ oz) freshly grated
  Parmesan cheese

I Pour the stock into a saucepan and bring to the boil. Reduce the heat, cover with a lid and keep at a low simmer.
2 Heat the oil and half the butter in a large heavy-based saucepan over medium heat. Add the onion and carrot and stir for 5 minutes. Add the garlic and cook, stirring, for 2 minutes, or until the onion is softened but not browned. Stir in the rice until well coated.
3 Add $^{1}/_{2}$ cup (125 ml/4 fl oz) of the hot stock. Stir constantly over medium heat until nearly all the liquid is absorbed. Continue adding the stock, $^{1}/_{2}$ cup (125 ml/4 fl oz) at a time, stirring constantly. After 10 minutes, add the asparagus, zucchini and peas. Continue adding the remaining stock. Cook for a further 10–15 minutes, or until the rice is tender and creamy.
4 Remove from the heat and stir in the parsley, Parmesan and remaining butter. Season to taste with salt and pepper.

RISI E BISI

Preparation time: 15 minutes
Total cooking time: 25 minutes
Serves 4

 ☆

1.5 litres (48 fl oz) chicken or vegetable stock
2 teaspoons olive oil
40 g (1$^{1}/_{4}$ oz) butter
I small onion, finely chopped
80 g (2$^{3}/_{4}$ oz) pancetta, cut into small cubes
2 tablespoons chopped parsley
370 g (12 oz) fresh young peas
I cup (220 g/7 oz) risotto rice
$^{1}/_{2}$ cup (50 g/1$^{3}/_{4}$ oz) freshly grated
  Parmesan cheese

I Pour the stock into a saucepan and bring to the boil. Reduce the heat, cover with a lid and keep at a low simmer.
2 Heat the oil and half the butter in a large wide heavy-based saucepan and cook the onion and pancetta over low heat for 5 minutes until softened. Stir in the parsley and peas and add 2 ladlefuls of the stock. Simmer for 6–8 minutes.
3 Add the rice and the remaining stock. Simmer

ABOVE: Risi e bisi

ASPARAGUS RISOTTO

Preparation time: 20 minutes
Total cooking time: 30 minutes
Serves 4

1 kg (2 lb) asparagus
2 cups (500 ml/16 fl oz) chicken stock
2 cups (500 ml/16 fl oz) vegetable stock
1/3 cup (80 ml/2 3/4 fl oz) olive oil
1 small onion, finely chopped
1 1/2 cups (360 g/12 oz) risotto rice
3/4 cup (75 g/2 1/2 oz) freshly grated
   Parmesan cheese
1/4 cup (60 g/2 oz) thick (double/heavy) cream

1 Wash the asparagus and remove the woody ends (hold each spear at both ends and bend it gently—it will snap at its natural breaking point). Separate the tender spear tips from the stems.

2 Cook the asparagus spears (but not the tips) in boiling water for 8 minutes, or until very tender. Drain and put in a blender with the chicken and vegetable stocks. Blend for 1 minute, then scoop the mixture into a saucepan. Bring to the boil, then reduce the heat, cover with a lid and keep at a low simmer.

3 Cook the asparagus tips in boiling water for 1 minute, then drain and refresh in iced water so they stop cooking.

4 Heat the olive oil in a large wide saucepan. Cook the onion until softened but not browned. Stir in the rice until well coated. Add 1/2 cup (125 ml/4 fl oz) of the hot stock and stir constantly over medium heat until all the liquid is absorbed. Continue adding more stock, 1/2 cup (125 ml/4 fl oz) at a time until all the liquid is absorbed and the rice is tender and creamy, this will take around 25–30 minutes.

5 Remove from the heat, then stir in the Parmesan and cream and gently stir in the asparagus tips. Season with salt and freshly ground black pepper and serve.

ASPARAGUS RISOTTO

Remove the woody end of the asparagus spears by holding the asparagus with both hands and bending gently—the tough end of the asparagus will snap away at its natural breaking point.

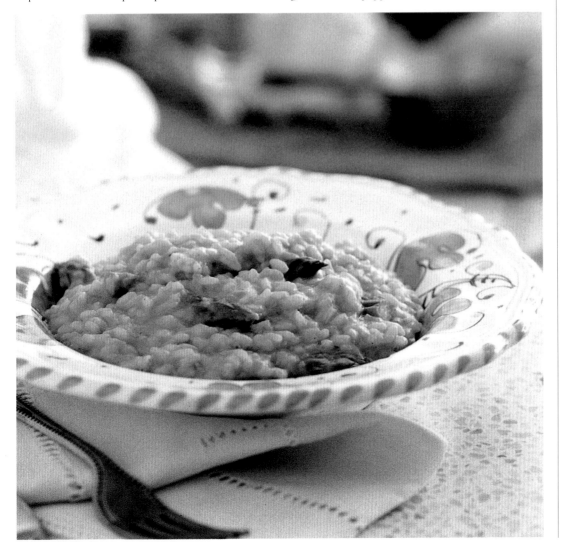

LEFT: Asparagus risotto

41

OSSO BUCCO ALLA MILANESE

Preparation time: 30 minutes
Total cooking time: 1 hour 40 minutes
Serves 4

12 pieces veal shank, about 4 cm
   (1 1/2 inch) thick
plain (all-purpose) flour, seasoned, for dusting
1/4 cup (60 ml/2 fl oz) olive oil
60 g (2 oz) butter
1 garlic clove, finely chopped
1 onion, finely chopped
1 celery stalk, finely chopped
1 cup (250 ml/8 fl oz) dry white wine
1 bay leaf or lemon leaf
pinch of ground allspice
pinch of ground cinnamon

GREMOLATA
2 teaspoons grated lemon zest
2 tablespoons finely chopped flat-leaf
   (Italian) parsley
1 garlic clove, finely chopped

1 Dust each piece of veal shank with seasoned flour. Heat the oil, butter, garlic, onion and celery in a heavy-based frying pan or saucepan that is big enough to hold the shanks in a single layer (but don't add the shanks yet). Cook for about 5 minutes over low heat until softened but not browned. Add the shanks to the pan and cook for 12–15 minutes, or until well browned all over. Arrange the shanks in the pan, standing them up in a single layer. Pour in the wine and add the bay leaf, allspice and cinnamon. Bring to the boil and cover the pan. Turn the heat down to low.
2 Cook at a low simmer for 15 minutes, then add 1/2 cup (125 ml/4 fl oz) warm water. Continue cooking, covered, for 45–60 minutes (the timing will depend on the age of the veal) or until the meat is tender and you can cut it with a fork. Check the volume of liquid once or twice during cooking time and add more warm water as needed.
3 To make the gremolata, mix together the lemon zest, parsley and garlic.
4 Transfer the veal shanks to a plate and keep warm. Discard the bay leaf. Increase the heat under the pan and stir for 1–2 minutes until the sauce has thickened, scraping up any bits off the bottom of the pan as you stir. Season to taste with salt and freshly ground black pepper and return the veal shanks to the sauce. Heat everything through, then stir in half the gremolata. Serve sprinkled with the remaining gremolata.

RISOTTO MILANESE

Preparation time: 20 minutes
Total cooking time: 25 minutes
Serves 6 as a side dish

200 ml (7 fl oz) dry white vermouth
   or white wine
large pinch of saffron threads
1.5 litres (48 fl oz) chicken stock
100 g (3 1/2 oz) butter
75 g (2 1/2 oz) beef marrow
1 large onion, finely chopped
1 garlic clove, crushed
1 1/2 cups (360 g/12 oz) risotto rice
1/2 cup (50 g/1 3/4 oz) freshly grated
   Parmesan cheese

1 Put the vermouth in a bowl, add the saffron and leave to soak. Pour the stock into a saucepan and bring to the boil. Reduce the heat, cover with a lid and keep at a low simmer.
2 Melt the butter and beef marrow in a large wide saucepan. Cook the onion and garlic until softened but not browned. Stir in the rice until well coated. Add the vermouth and saffron to the rice and stir continuously until the liquid has been absorbed. Add 1/2 cup (125 ml/4 fl oz) of the hot stock and stir constantly over medium heat until all the liquid is absorbed. Continue adding more stock, 1/2 cup (125 ml/4 fl oz) at a time until all the liquid is absorbed and the rice is tender and creamy, this will take around 25–30 minutes. (You may not need to use all the stock, or you may need a little extra—every risotto will be slightly different.)
3 Remove from the heat and stir in a handful of Parmesan, then serve the rest on the side for people to help themselves.

OSSO BUCCO ALLA MILANESE
There are versions of osso bucco that are made with tomatoes, but osso bucco is a Milanese dish and traditionally tomatoes are not used in the cooking of northern Italy. The absence of the tomato allows the more delicate flavours of the gremolata to come through. This version is usually accompanied by risotto Milanese. It takes its brilliant yellow colour from saffron and its rich flavour from beef marrow. If beef marrow is hard to find, you can use a fatty piece of lardo, prosciutto or pancetta, finely chopped.

OPPOSITE PAGE: Osso bucco alla Milanese with Risotto Milanese

PORCINI MUSHROOMS
The Italians consider porcini (the Italian name for a cep or boletus mushroom) to be the most flavoursome of all mushrooms. They are available fresh in autumn and spring. If fresh ones are out of season, or are simply too expensive, dried porcini can be used. Dried porcini give an earthiness to dishes and when used with fresh mushrooms they add an attractive depth of flavour. Dried porcini are sold in small packets and are widely available.

ABOVE: Mushroom risotto

MUSHROOM RISOTTO

Preparation time: 20 minutes +
  30 minutes soaking
Total cooking time: 35 minutes
Serves 4

20 g (³/4 oz) dried porcini mushrooms
1 litre (32 fl oz) vegetable or chicken stock
2 tablespoons olive oil
20 g (³/4 oz) butter
1 small onion, finely chopped
2 garlic cloves, crushed
1³/4 cups (385 g/13 oz) risotto rice
250 g (8 oz) flat mushrooms, sliced
pinch of freshly grated nutmeg
¹/2 cup (50 g/1³/4 oz) freshly grated
  Parmesan cheese
3 tablespoons finely chopped parsley

1 Soak the porcini mushrooms in 2 cups (500 ml/16 fl oz) boiling water for 30 minutes. Drain, reserving the liquid. Chop the porcini and pass the liquid through a fine sieve. Pour the stock into a saucepan and bring to the boil. Reduce the heat, cover with a lid and keep at a low simmer.

2 Heat the oil and butter in a wide heavy-based saucepan. Cook the onion and garlic until softened but not browned. Stir in the rice until well coated. Toss in the fresh mushrooms and nutmeg. Season and cook, stirring, for 1–2 minutes. Add the porcini and their liquid, increase the heat and cook until the liquid has been absorbed.
3 Add ¹/2 cup (125 ml/4 fl oz) of the stock and stir constantly over medium heat until all the liquid is absorbed. Continue adding more stock, ¹/2 cup (125 ml/4 fl oz) at a time until all the liquid is absorbed and the rice is tender and creamy; this will take 25–30 minutes. Remove from the heat and stir in the Parmesan and parsley. Serve.

SPANAKORIZO
(GREEK SPINACH RICE)

Preparation time: 15 minutes
Total cooking time: 30 minutes
Serves 6

400 g (13 oz) English spinach
6 spring onions (scallions)
2 tablespoons olive oil
1 large onion, chopped
2 garlic cloves, crushed

1¹/₂ cups (330 g/11 oz) short- or
   medium-grain rice

2 tablespoons lemon juice

1 tablespoon chopped dill

1 tablespoon chopped flat-leaf (Italian) parsley

1¹/₂ cups (375 ml/12 fl oz) vegetable stock

1 Wash the spinach in several changes of water, tear the leaves and chop the stalks. Finely chop the spring onions, including the green tops.
2 Heat the olive oil in a large, wide flameproof casserole dish. Add the onion and garlic and cook for 5–7 minutes over medium heat, or until the onion is softened but not browned. Add the spring onion and rice, stir to coat and cook for 2 minutes, stirring constantly. Add the spinach, 1 tablespoon of the lemon juice and the herbs. Season well. Stir in the stock and 1¹/₂ cups (375 ml/12 fl oz) water. Cover, bring to the boil, then reduce the heat to low and cook for 15 minutes.
3 Remove from the heat and set aside for 5 minutes. Stir in the remaining lemon juice and season to taste.

onion and garlic until softened but not browned. Stir in the rice until well coated. Season.
4 Add the vermouth to the rice and cook, stirring, until all the liquid has been absorbed. Add ¹/₂ cup (125 ml/4 fl oz) of the hot stock and stir constantly over medium heat until all the liquid is absorbed. Continue adding more stock, ¹/₂ cup (125 ml/4 fl oz) at a time until a quarter of the stock is left, then mix in the chopped spinach. Continue to add the last of the stock. When making risotto cake, it is not so essential to keep the rice *al dente*—if it is a little more glutinous, it will stick together better. Make sure all the liquid is absorbed or the cake may break up when you unmould it.
5 Remove the pan from the heat and stir in the nutmeg, Parmesan cheese and the rest of the butter.
6 Smear a little butter into a mould such as a 1.25 litre (40 fl oz) cake tin. Spoon the risotto into the mould, pressing it down firmly. Leave to rest for 5 minutes, then unmould and put on a warm serving plate with some Parmesan sprinkled over the top.
NOTE: Serve with a rich meat dish such as osso bucco.

SPINACH RISOTTO CAKE

Preparation time: 30 minutes
Total cooking time: 35 minutes
Serves 6

250 g (8 oz) baby English spinach leaves

3 cups (750 ml/24 fl oz) chicken stock

100 g (3¹/₂ oz) butter

1 onion, finely chopped

1 garlic clove, finely chopped

1 cup (220 g/7 oz) arborio rice

155 ml (5 fl oz) dry white vermouth or
   white wine

¹/₄ teaspoon freshly grated nutmeg

¹/₄ cup (25 g/³/₄ oz) freshly grated Parmesan
   cheese, plus extra to serve

1 Cook the spinach in a small amount of salted water until just wilted. Refresh in cold water and squeeze dry. Finely chop and set aside.
2 Pour the stock into a saucepan and bring to the boil. Reduce the heat, cover with a lid and keep at a low simmer.
3 Melt 75 g (2¹/₂ oz) of the butter in a deep heavy-based frying pan and gently cook the

BELOW: Spinach risotto cake

HOW TO MAKE THE PERFECT PAELLA

This impressive dish is surprisingly easy to prepare—after the initial stages you leave it to cook itself.

Paella is not only one of the best loved rice dishes within Spain itself—internationally it is perhaps the best known example of Spanish cuisine.

Traditionally, paellas were reserved for celebrations and they were cooked outdoors over the coals of a wood fire by men. The tradition of men being responsible for the cooking is still very much alive today.

An impressive, hearty one-pan meal of rice, meat, seafood and vegetables flavoured and coloured by saffron, tomato and paprika, a paella can be a simple affair or an elaborate centrepiece for groups of friends to enjoy. An average paella serves 6 to 8 people as a main course and, if accompanied by other smaller side dishes, can stretch to 10 or 12 servings.

FLAVOUR
Chicken, rabbit, pork, snails and beans were once the most common ingredients of paellas; however, as the dish became popular throughout other regions in Spain, ingredients were added or omitted according to their availability. In more recent times the most popular version is one in which a variety of seafood, in particular shellfish, is included.

There are several key ingredients that distinguish an excellent paella. Saffron threads are arguably the most important; these tiny strands possess a deep, earthy, musky flavour and merely a pinch will promote intense colour and flavour. Sweet paprika adds a little smokiness; tomatoes contribute sweetness and depth. Add to this base your choice of meats or seafood. A range of vegetables can be included not only for flavour but also for colour and texture—try capsicum (pepper), peas, beans, artichokes or olives.

WHICH RICE?
Bordering the Mediterranean sea, Valencia on the east coast of Spain enjoys the warm weather typical of the region—the kind climate combined with a well irrigated region to the south provide the perfect conditions for rice growing and consequently Valencia has become renowned for its high-quality short-grain crop prized for use in paellas. Calasparra or bomba rice will give the perfect paella texture—this firm, round, medium-grain rice cooks to a slightly sticky yet dry finish without being glutinous. Look for rice labelled 'Valencia rice' or 'rice for paella'. At a pinch, arborio or another risotto rice can be substituted but the result will be a little stickier.

TEXTURE
The trick to achieving the light, separate grains of a paella is to cook the rice in olive oil or butter or a mixture of the two for about 5 minutes until lightly golden. This method seals the grains of rice, which decreases and slows the release of starch, thus allowing the grains to stay quite separate and light.

The other key is stir the rice as little as possible to discourage the starches from being released. The rice should be well cooked and tender, not too firm to the bite but not mushy.

TOOLS

Paellas derive their name from the special pan (doubling as an attractive serving vessel) that they are cooked in. The *paella* or *paellera* is a wide, shallow pan most often made from cast iron, but also seen in earthenware. The pans have no lid, but often have a round handle on one or both sides.

Paella pans are now widely available at cookware stores or special Spanish food supply stores. When using a large paella pan on a stove top you may need to sit it across two burners to keep the heat evenly distributed. Paellas are just as easy to cook on a stove top in a large, wide heavy-based frying pan with shallow sides. If you are cooking large quantities, simply divide the ingredients between two pans. This is easier than it sounds—paellas demand very little attention.

TECHNIQUE

From town to town throughout Spain there are different ideas about the best technique to cook paella, each with merit. We have found the following method yields consistently good results, but have included other versions in the book.

The liquid (usually stock) should be hot when added to the rice so that it does not cool the mixture down. So, the first step is to bring the liquid to a simmer.

While the stock is simmering, brown any meats or seafood in a little olive oil in the paella pan—this allows the flavours to cling to the pan and permeate the paella from the start; however, these ingredients may need to be removed and returned to the dish later so they are not overcooked. The recipes will guide you.

Start the flavour base by sautéeing onions in a little olive oil over medium heat until lightly golden, then add any garlic and capsicum and cook until the capsicum is softened slightly.

Next, add the rice to the pan and cook until the rice is lightly golden; this seals the surface of the rice which helps to keep the grains separate.

Occasionally wine or sherry are used; if so add it to the pan now and stir until it is absorbed. Alcohol is added to the pan before other liquids so it will be cooked off and not override the other flavours or taste too sharp. Next add the tomatoes and stir well.

Add the saffron to the hot stock and crush with the back of a spoon to release the colour, then stir all the liquid into the rice. Bring to the boil, then reduce the heat to a simmer and leave for 25 minutes without stirring. You can occasionally shake the pan if you are worried about the rice sticking to the bottom and burning; however, in some parts of Spain the crust on the bottom of the paella is regarded as the highlight of the meal. The rice will cook evenly because it is in such a shallow layer.

STEPS TO MAKING THE PERFECT PAELLA
STEP ONE: Pour the stock into a large pan, bring to the boil, then reduce to a low simmer.
STEP TWO: Heat the oil in a paella pan or large, shallow frying pan. Add the onion, garlic, capsicum and chilli to the pan and cook over medium heat until the onion and capsicum are soft.
STEP THREE: Stir in the rice until it is well coated.
STEP FOUR: Pour the hot stock into the paella pan and simmer until almost absorbed, before reducing the heat and simmering for 20 minutes without stirring the rice.
STEP FIVE: Add the last ingredients to the pan— leave them on top of the rice; don't stir them in. Cover and cook for 2–3 minutes over low heat.
STEP SIX: Once all the ingredients have cooked, leave the paella to rest for 10 minutes, before garnishing and serving from the pan.

Once the time is up, meats such as chicken and pork should be placed on top of or very gently stirred through the rice, lightly covered, then cooked for an extra 10–15 minutes. If using seafood it should be added, along with any vegetables that need only brief cooking such as beans and peas, around the last 5 minutes of cooking.

Lastly, allow the paella to stand for about 10 minutes so that the rice can shrink slightly and any excess liquid can evaporate. Sprinkle on any herbs, and season with salt and pepper before serving with lemon wedges, if desired.

CLASSIC PAELLA

Preparation time: 20 minutes
Total cooking time: 45 minutes
Serves 4

☆ ☆

3 tomatoes
12 black mussels
1/2 cup (125 ml/4 fl oz) dry white wine
12 raw prawns (shrimp)
2 cups (500 ml/16 fl oz) chicken stock
1/4 cup (60 ml/2 fl oz) olive oil
600 g (1 1/4 lb) chicken thigh fillets, halved
1 large red onion, chopped
1 red capsicum (pepper), cut into 5 x 3 cm
  (2 x 1 1/4 inches) pieces
1 green capsicum (pepper), cut into 5 cm
  (2 inch) long thin strips

3 garlic cloves, crushed
2 teaspoons sweet Spanish paprika
1/4 teaspoon saffron threads, soaked in
  1/4 cup (60 ml/2 fl oz) hot water
1 1/3 cups (295 g/10 oz) paella rice
300 g (13 oz) white fish fillets
  (e.g. blue eye, snapper or ling),
  cut into 2–3 cm (3/4–1 1/4 inch) cubes
150 g (5 oz) fresh peas
lemon wedges, to serve

1 Score a cross in the base of the tomatoes. Place in a heatproof bowl and cover with boiling water. Leave for 30 seconds, then transfer to cold water and peel the skin away from the cross. Cut the tomatoes in half and scoop out the seeds with a teaspoon. Finely chop the flesh.
2 Scrub the mussels with a stiff brush and pull out the hairy beards. Discard any broken mussels, or open ones that don't close when tapped on the bench. Rinse well. Put them in a saucepan with the wine, cover with a lid and cook for 2–3 minutes, or until they have opened. Lift the mussels out of the liquid with tongs and set them aside on a plate, discarding any that have not opened.
3 Peel the prawns, leaving the tails attached. Gently pull out the dark vein from each prawn back, starting at the head end. Put the heads and shells in the pan with the mussel liquid, add 2 cups (500 ml/16 fl oz) water and simmer for 5 minutes. Strain the liquid into a bowl, then pour the liquid back into the pan and add the chicken stock. Bring to the boil, then reduce the heat and keep at a low simmer.
4 Heat 2 tablespoons of the oil in a paella pan or large, deep heavy-based frying pan. Add the chicken and cook over medium heat for 10 minutes, or until browned all over, then remove from the pan. Add the remaining oil to the pan, then add the onion and tomato and cook over low heat for 4–5 minutes, or until softened but not browned. Add the red and green capsicum and cook for 1 minute, then stir in the garlic, paprika and saffron with its soaking water, and cook for 30 seconds. Return the chicken to the pan, arranging it around the edge and stir to coat with the tomato mixture. Pour in the stock and bring it to simmering point, then add the rice, using a thin spatula. Do not stir the rice, instead use the spatula to gently move it down into the liquid. Using tongs, arrange the red and green capsicum on top of the rice. Bring back to the boil, then reduce the heat to medium and simmer briskly for

BELOW: Classic paella

8–10 minutes, or until the rice is starting to become tender. The paella should not be stirred after it has come to the boil.

5 Arrange the pieces of fish, mussels, prawns and peas evenly over the rice, taking care not to stir through to the bottom. Reduce the heat to very low and simmer without stirring for 15 minutes, or until the rice is tender and the prawns and fish are cooked through. Shake the pan from time to time to prevent the rice from burning, but do not stir to the bottom. This will allow a crust to form across the bottom. Pour in a little hot water if the mixture seems dry towards the end of cooking. Remove the pan from the heat, cover loosely with foil and leave to rest for 5–10 minutes. Season to taste with salt and freshly ground black pepper and serve, straight from the pan, with lemon wedges on the side.

PAELLA ANDALUCIA
(Chicken and chorizo paella)

Preparation time: 20 minutes +
    10 minutes standing
Total cooking time: 1 hour 15 minutes
Serves 6

☆ ☆

1/4 cup (60 ml/2 fl oz) olive oil

1 large red capsicum (pepper), seeded
    and cut into 5 mm (1/4 inch) strips

600 g (1 1/4 lb) chicken thigh fillets, cut
    into 3 cm (1 1/4 inch) cubes

200 g (6 1/2 oz) chorizo sausage, cut
    into 2 cm (3/4 inch) slices

200 g (6 1/2 oz) flat mushrooms, thinly
    sliced

3 garlic cloves, crushed

1 tablespoon grated lemon zest

700 g (1 lb 6 1/2 oz) ripe tomatoes,
    roughly chopped

200 g (6 1/2 oz) green beans, trimmed
    and cut into 3 cm (1 1/4 inch) lengths

1 tablespoon chopped rosemary

2 tablespoons chopped flat-leaf
    (Italian) parsley

1/4 teaspoon saffron threads soaked in
    1/4 cup (60 ml/2 fl oz) hot water

2 cups (440 g/14 oz) paella rice

3 cups (750 ml/24 fl oz) hot chicken stock

6 lemon wedges, to serve

1 Heat the olive oil in a paella pan, or in a large, deep heavy-based frying pan over medium heat. Add the capsicum and cook, stirring, for about 5 minutes. Remove from the pan. Toss in the chicken and cook for 10 minutes, or until browned all over. Remove from the pan. Add the chorizo to the pan and cook for 5 minutes. Remove from the pan. Add the mushrooms, garlic and lemon zest to the pan, and cook over medium heat for about 5 minutes.

2 Stir in the tomato and capsicum, and cook for another 5 minutes, or until the tomato is soft. Add the beans, rosemary, parsley, saffron mixture, rice, chicken and sausage. Stir briefly and add the stock. Do not stir at this point. Reduce the heat and simmer for 30 minutes. Remove from the heat, cover loosely with foil and leave to stand for 10 minutes. Season to taste with salt and freshly ground black pepper, then serve with lemon wedges.

ABOVE: Paella Andalucia

SEAFOOD PAELLA

Preparation time: 25 minutes
Total cooking time: 45 minutes
Serves 6

☆☆

2 tomatoes
500 g (1 lb) raw prawns (shrimp)
300 g (10 oz) skinless firm white fish fillets
250 g (8 oz) black mussels
200 g (6½ oz) squid rings
¼ cup (60 ml/2 fl oz) olive oil
1 large onion, diced
3 garlic cloves, finely chopped
1 small red capsicum (pepper), thinly sliced
1 small red chilli, deseeded and chopped (optional)
2 teaspoons paprika
1 teaspoon ground turmeric
1 tablespoon tomato paste (purée)
2 cups (440 g/14 oz) paella rice
½ cup (125 ml/4 fl oz) white wine
¼ teaspoon saffron threads, soaked in
   ¼ cup (60 ml/2 fl oz) hot water
1.25 litres (40 fl oz) fish stock
3 tablespoons chopped flat-leaf (Italian)
   parsley, to serve
lemon wedges, to serve

1 Score a cross in the base of the tomatoes. Place in a heatproof bowl and cover with boiling water. Leave for 30 seconds, then transfer to a bowl of cold water. Peel the skin away from the cross and finely chop the flesh.
2 Peel the prawns, leaving the tails intact. Gently pull out the dark vein from each prawn back, starting at the head end. Cut the fish fillets into 2.5 cm (1 inch) cubes. Scrub the mussels with a stiff brush and pull out the hairy beards. Discard any broken mussels, or open ones that don't close when tapped on the bench. Rinse well. Refrigerate the seafood (including the squid rings), covered, until ready to use.
3 Heat the oil in a paella pan or large, deep frying pan with a lid. Add the onion, garlic, capsicum and chilli to the pan and cook over medium heat for 2 minutes, or until the onion and capsicum are soft. Add the paprika, turmeric and 1 teaspoon salt and stir-fry for 1–2 minutes, or until fragrant.
4 Add the chopped tomatoes and cook for 5 minutes, or until softened. Add the tomato paste. Stir in the rice until it is well coated.
5 Pour in the wine and simmer until almost absorbed. Add the saffron and its soaking liquid and all the fish stock and bring to the boil. Reduce the heat and simmer for 20 minutes, or until almost all the liquid is absorbed into the rice. There is no need to stir the rice, but you may occasionally wish to fluff it up with a fork to separate the grains.
6 Add the mussels to the pan, poking the shells into the rice, cover and cook for 2–3 minutes over low heat. Add the prawns and cook for 2–3 minutes. Add the fish, cover and cook for 3 minutes. Finally, add the squid rings and cook for 1–2 minutes. By this time, the mussels should have opened—discard any unopened ones. The prawns should be pink and the fish should flake easily when tested with a fork. The squid should be white, moist and tender. Cook for another 2–3 minutes if the seafood is not quite cooked,

BELOW: Seafood paella

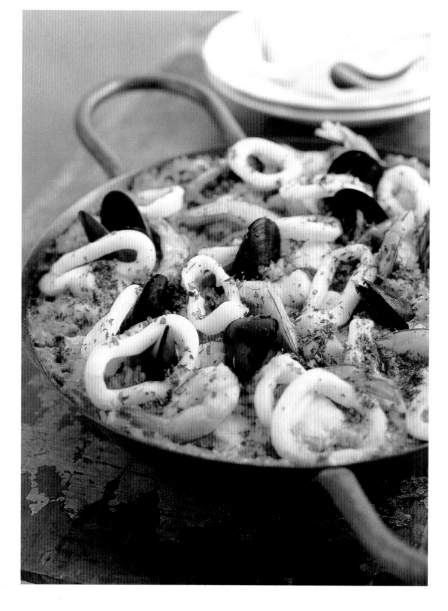

but avoid overcooking as the seafood will toughen and dry out. Remove the pan from the heat, cover loosely with foil and leave to rest for 5–10 minutes. Serve with parsley and lemon wedges. Delicious with a tossed salad.
NOTE: You can use just fish, or other seafood such as scampi, octopus or crabs. If using just fish, choose one with few bones and chunky flesh, such as ling, blue-eye or warehou. Other suggested fish include perch or ling.

SPICY MEAT PAELLA

Preparation time: 25 minutes +
  15 minutes standing
Total cooking time: 35 minutes
Serves 4

3 ripe tomatoes
8 lamb cutlets, trimmed of excess fat
1 tablespoon olive oil
200 g (6¹/₂ oz) pork fillet, cut into 3 cm
  (1¹/₄ inch) pieces
1 red capsicum (pepper), cut into strips
250 g (8 oz) green beans, trimmed
125 g (4 oz) chorizo sausage, thinly sliced
1 tablespoon paprika
1 teaspoon chilli flakes
1¹/₃ cups (295 g/10 oz) paella rice
¹/₄ teaspoon saffron threads, soaked in
  ¹/₄ cup (60 ml/2 fl oz) hot water
2 cups (500 ml/16 fl oz) hot chicken stock
1 tablespoon rosemary

1 Score a cross in the base of each tomato, put in a heatproof bowl and cover with boiling water. Leave for 30 seconds, then transfer to a bowl of cold water. Peel the skin away from the cross and finely chop the flesh.
2 Rub ¹/₂ teaspoon each of salt and freshly ground black pepper over the lamb cutlets.
3 Heat the oil in a paella pan or large, deep heavy-based frying with a lid. Add the lamb cutlets and cook over medium heat for 2–3 minutes, or until browned on both sides. Remove and set aside. Add the pork to the pan and cook, stirring, for 2–3 minutes, or until browned all over. Remove and set aside.
4 Add the capsicum and beans to the pan and cook, stirring, for 2–3 minutes, or until just soft. Increase the heat to high and add the chorizo, paprika and chilli flakes, and cook, stirring, for 30 seconds, or until fragrant.
5 Add the rice and stir to coat in the oil and spices. Add the chopped tomatoes and stir over high heat for 1 minute, or until bubbling. Return the pork to the frying pan with any accumulated juices and stir together.
6 Pour in the saffron and its liquid, the hot chicken stock and ¹/₂ teaspoon each of salt and pepper. Arrange the lamb cutlets on top of the rice mixture and sprinkle with the rosemary. Bring to the boil, then reduce the heat to medium and simmer gently. Check the heat frequently during cooking so the paella maintains a constant gentle simmer. Cook, covered, for 20 minutes without stirring. Shake the pan occasionally during cooking to keep the rice from sticking to the base. The rice should not be soft, it should still have a slight bite. Remove the pan from the heat, cover loosely with foil and leave to rest for 5–10 minutes, then serve.

ABOVE: Spicy meat paella

HOW TO MAKE THE PERFECT PILAFF
One of the most versatile methods of cooking rice, pilaffs can be as simple or as elaborate as you like.

A pilaff is essentially a rice dish with each grain of rice remaining separate and fluffy. Though the cooking method originated in the Middle East, you will find many versions of the technique around the world: pilaff in Turkey, polo in Iran, pilav in Russia, pulao in India and purloo in the deep south of America. And it is not only rice that is used as a base. Throughout the Middle East, pilaffs can be based on other grains, such as burghul (bulgar), or even lentils.

Pilaffs vary from the basic to the elaborate. They may be flavoured simply with a little onion, subtle spices and fresh herbs and served as an accompaniment, or they may be bulked out with meats, seafood and vegetables and served as a one-pot meal; for example the famous Spanish paella (pages 46–47) or Cajun jambalaya (pages 100–101).

In its more elaborate manifestation (mainly in the Middle East), the pilaff is offered at special occasions such as weddings or religious celebrations, moulded into shapes (often rings) and garnished decadently with rare or prized ingredients such as gold or silver leaf. And pilaffs are not only savoury; some versions are sweetened with dried fruits and nuts.

FLAVOURS
As the popularity of pilaff spread beyond the Middle East, new flavours were introduced and today the variations are infinite. In the Middle East and India, a combination of various aromatic spices such as cardamom, cumin, saffron, coriander, cinnamon and cloves are typical. Any meat will be influenced by dietary restrictions in accordance with religious beliefs and the local livestock; lamb is the most common.

In the Mediterranean, the base flavours reflect local ingredients and culinary heritage. For instance, Spanish cuisine is influenced by the Moors and many of their pilaffs use spices such as saffron and cinnamon, but they also use local ingredients such as tomatoes, lemons, olives or seafood, which are available in abundance. In Greece, there is less use of spices and more fresh and subtle flavours such as wild green leafy vegetables and herbs.

Pilaffs from the southern states of America display eclectic French, Spanish and African influences and are often strongly flavoured with garlic, bay leaves, celery, tomatoes, peppers, saffron, spicy sausage and a herb and spice mix containing at least several of the following: chilli, thyme, paprika, mustard, pepper, cumin and oregano.

WHICH RICE?
In general pilaffs are made with a long, thin rice grain with little starch, though this does depend on the particular region in which the pilaff originated. For instance, the pilaffs of Central Asia are unique in using short-grain rice. For most other pilaffs, basmati rice or long-grain rice gives a good result.

TEXTURE

A classic pilaff should have grains of rice that are light and separate in appearance and firm but tender to the bite, though some pilaffs are 'wetter' than others. The secret to achieving the texture is to use the appropriate rice as well as leaving the pilaff to cook on its own, without stirring. This inhibits the release of starch.

TOOLS

If cooking on a stove-top, you'll need a large, heavy-based saucepan or deep frying pan with a lid. Heavy-based pans allow even heat distribution, and prevent the rice from catching and burning on the bottom of the pan. Ideally, the pan should be made from copper, stainless steel or cast iron, which are all excellent heat conductors.

Oven-baked pilaffs should be cooked in a sturdy ceramic or cast iron casserole dish with a lid, though they may be started on the stove, then transferred to the oven.

THE DIFFERENCES

Every pilaff aficionado has their own secret technique for the best results. Some cooks soak the rice first (sometimes overnight) in order to wash out as much starch as possible. Some start by pouring boiling water over the top to soften the grains. Some pilaffs are stirred for a little and then left, some are covered while others are not (though most are), some are cooked on the stove and some are

baked (common in Indian cooking; for example, the traditional biryani). We have included several versions in our recipe pages. There are some general guidelines that work well for most pilaffs, which are outlined below.

BASIC TECHNIQUE

The liquid to be added should be hot, so bring your stock or water to a simmer prior to starting the cooking process.

Most traditional pilaffs begin with softening and sometimes browning some onions or garlic in butter or oil, which provides a great flavour base. Then the rice is added and cooked until lightly golden—this will take about 5 minutes—which seals the surface of the rice and helps to keep the grains separate.

Next, the liquid ingredients are added. If you are using any alcohol, it needs to be added first so the alcohol can cook off in order to avoid an overriding flavour. Now add the hot stock or water plus any other ingredients as instructed by the recipe, stir to combine and bring to the boil. Cover with a tight-fitting lid, then reduce the heat and cook without removing the lid for around 20 to 40 minutes in the oven or on the stove, by which time the liquid should have been absorbed and the grains of rice tender. (The time varies depending on the number of other ingredients that have to cook.) If the rice is still a little firm, continue cooking for a few more minutes. Some pilaffs have delicate

STEPS TO MAKING THE PERFECT PILAFF

Stove-top pilaff

STEP ONE: Create the flavour base by cooking the onion, capsicum (pepper) and paprika.
STEP TWO: Add the rice and stir it for a few minutes until it turns a light golden colour.
STEP THREE: Add the liquid and any ingredients that need a long cooking time and bring to the boil before covering with a lid and leaving to simmer.

Baked pilaff

STEP ONE: Stir the rice into the onion mixture—this will coat the grains and prevent them releasing too much starch.
STEP TWO: Pour in the stock, bring to a boil, then cover and put in the oven.
STEP THREE: After resting the rice, fluff it with a fork and in stir any herbs.

ingredients that need little cooking and which are stirred through towards the end.

Remove from the heat and stand the rice for about 10 minutes so that any excess moisture evaporates, then remove the lid and fluff with a fork. Some careful cooks line the lid with paper towels or a clean tea towel for the resting stage. As well as absorbing any condensation and minimizing drips onto the rice, the towel also steams the rice dry without cooling down too quickly. At this stage there may be the addition of fresh herbs or other seasonings, so add them while you are fluffing and try not to squash the grains.

and cook, stirring, for 2 minutes. Stir in the rice and bay leaf, mixing well to combine.
2 Pour in the stock and bring to the boil. Continue boiling until tunnels appear in the rice, stir quickly, then cover and reduce the heat to low. Cook for 20 minutes. Sprinkle the peas and capsicum strips over the top of the rice. Cover, remove from the heat and leave for a further 10 minutes. Sprinkle with the spring onion and fluff the mixture with a fork. Serve topped with the shaved Parmesan.

MOROCCAN CHICKEN PILAFF

Preparation time: 20 minutes +
  10 minutes soaking
Total cooking time: 1 hour 5 minutes
Serves 4

☆☆

1/2 teaspoon saffron threads, chopped
1 3/4 cups (440 ml/14 fl oz) hot chicken stock
2 tablespoons olive oil
1 kg (2 lb) chicken thigh cutlets, trimmed
1 large red onion, roughly chopped
1 green capsicum (pepper), roughly chopped
1 red capsicum (pepper), roughly chopped
3 garlic cloves, chopped
1/2 teaspoon chilli flakes
2 teaspoons ground cumin
3 teaspoons ground coriander
1 cup (200 g/6 1/2 oz) basmati rice
2 tablespoons finely chopped preserved
  lemon zest (see Note)
1/2 cup (95 g/3 oz) Kalamata olives

1 Preheat the oven to moderate 180°C (350°F/Gas 4). Put the saffron in a bowl with 1 tablespoon hot water. Soak for 10 minutes. Pour the stock into a saucepan, bring to the boil, then remove the pan from the heat.
2 Heat half the oil in a large frying pan over high heat. Cook the chicken for 2 minutes on each side, or until browned. Drain on paper towels.
3 Heat the remaining oil in a 2.75 litre (88 fl oz) flameproof casserole dish over medium heat. Add the onion and capsicum and cook, stirring, for 4 minutes, or until soft. Add the garlic, chilli flakes, cumin and coriander and cook for 30 seconds, or until fragrant. Stir in the rice and preserved lemon zest, mixing well.

SPICY SAUSAGE PILAFF

Preparation time: 20 minutes
Total cooking time: 40 minutes
Serves 4–6

☆

30 g (1 oz) butter
1 large onion, thinly sliced
2 garlic cloves, crushed
300 g (10 oz) chorizo sausage, thinly sliced
2 cups (400 g/13 oz) long-grain rice
1 bay leaf
1 litre (32 fl oz) chicken stock
1 cup (155 g/5 oz) frozen peas
1/2 cup (80 g/2 3/4 oz) sun-dried capsicums
  (peppers) in oil, drained and thinly sliced
4 spring onions (scallions), thinly sliced
shaved Parmesan cheese, to serve

1 Melt the butter in a large, deep frying pan over medium heat. Add the onion and garlic and cook, stirring, for 5 minutes, or until the onion is softened but not browned. Add the chorizo

ABOVE: Spicy sausage pilaff

4 Put the chicken on the rice. Combine the saffron liquid and hot stock, pour over the rice and season. Bring to the boil, then transfer to the oven, put the lid on and bake for 50 minutes, or until the liquid is absorbed and the rice is tender. Remove from the heat, cover with a lid and stand for several minutes. Stir in the olives just before serving.

SAFFRON CHICKEN AND RICE

Preparation time: 20 minutes
Total cooking time: 40 minutes
Serves 4

1/2 teaspoon saffron threads, chopped
1/4 cup (60 ml/2 fl oz) olive oil
4 chicken thighs and 4 drumsticks
1 large red onion, finely chopped
1 large green capsicum (pepper), two-thirds diced and one-third julienned
3 teaspoons sweet paprika
400 g (13 oz) tin chopped tomatoes
1 1/4 cups (250 g/8 oz) long-grain rice
3 1/4 cups (810 ml/26 fl oz) hot chicken stock

1 Soak the saffron threads in 1/4 cup (60 ml/ 2 fl oz) warm water. Heat 2 tablespoons of the oil in a large heavy-based saucepan or deep frying pan with a lid over high heat. Season the chicken pieces with salt and freshly ground black pepper and brown in batches. Remove the chicken from the pan and drain on crumpled paper towels.

2 Reduce the heat to medium and add the remaining oil. Add the onion and diced capsicum, and cook gently for 5 minutes, or until the onion is softened but not browned. Stir in the paprika and cook for about 30 seconds. Add the tomato and simmer for 1–3 minutes, or until the mixture thickens. Add the rice and cook until lightly golden.

3 Add the saffron water with the stock. Return the chicken to the pan and stir to combine. Season with salt and pepper. Bring to the boil, cover, reduce the heat to medium and simmer for 20 minutes, or until all the liquid has been absorbed and the chicken is tender. Stir in the julienned capsicum, then allow it to stand, covered, for several minutes before serving.

PAPRIKA
The origins of the Spanish version of paprika, *pimentón*, lie with Christopher Columbus and his discovery of the Americas. The seeds of the capsicums (peppers) he carried back to Spain were cultivated (supposedly in a monastery), and once the fruit was picked it was dried, then ground. The ground spice was so popular that cultivation of the fruit spread widely throughout Spain. Paprika is made from various species of *capsicum annum*, from the same family as the chilli. Today, Spain is still one of the most well known producers of paprika, along with Hungary. There are many grades of ground paprika, based on the quality of the fruit, the thoroughness of the grinding and the amount of seeds used. The three main types of the delicious smoked Spanish paprika are sweet, semi-sweet and hot.

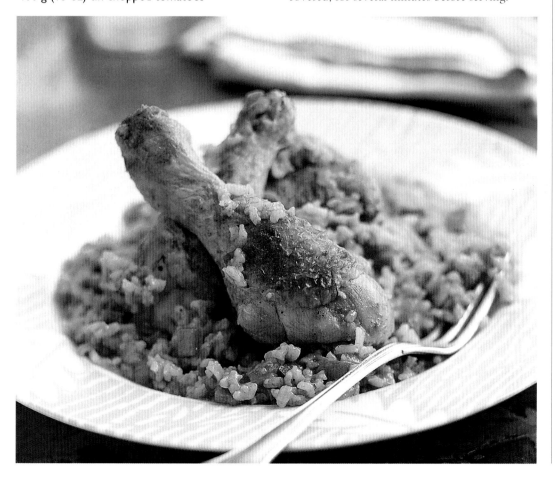

LEFT: Saffron chicken and rice

TURKISH LAMB PILAFF

Preparation time: 20 minutes + 1 hour standing
Total cooking time: 35 minutes
Serves 4

☆ ☆

1 large eggplant (aubergine), cut into small cubes
1/2 cup (125 ml/4 fl oz) olive oil
1 large onion, finely chopped
1 teaspoon ground cinnamon
2 teaspoons ground cumin
1 teaspoon ground coriander
1 1/2 cups (300 g/10 oz) long-grain rice
2 cups (500 ml/16 fl oz) stock
500 g (1 lb) minced (ground) lamb
1/2 teaspoon ground allspice
2 tablespoons olive oil, extra
2 tomatoes, cut into wedges
1/4 cup (35 g/1 1/4 oz) pistachios, toasted
2 tablespoons currants
chopped coriander (cilantro) leaves, to garnish

BELOW: Turkish lamb pilaff

1 Put the eggplant in a colander, sprinkle generously with salt and leave for 1 hour. Rinse well and squeeze dry in a clean tea towel. Heat 2 tablespoons of the oil in a large, deep frying pan with a lid, add the eggplant and cook over medium heat for 8–10 minutes, or until golden brown and cooked through. Drain on crumpled paper towels.

2 Heat the remaining oil in the same pan, add the onion and cook for 4–5 minutes, or until softened but not browned. Stir in half of each the cinnamon, cumin and coriander and cook for a minute, or until fragrant. Stir in the rice, mixing well to combine. Pour in the stock, season and bring to the boil. Reduce the heat to low, cover with a tight-fitting lid and simmer for 15 minutes, or until the stock has been absorbed and the rice is cooked. Add more water if the pilaff starts to dry out.

3 Meanwhile, put the lamb in a bowl with the allspice and the remaining cumin, cinnamon and coriander. Season with salt and freshly ground black pepper, and mix well. Roll into small balls, the size of macadamia nuts. Heat the extra oil in a clean frying pan and cook the meatballs in batches over medium heat for 5 minutes each batch, or until lightly browned and cooked through. Drain on crumpled paper towels.

4 Add the tomato wedges to the empty pan and cook, turning, for 3–5 minutes, or until lightly golden. Remove from the pan.

5 Stir the cooked eggplant, pistachios, currants and meatballs through the rice (this should be quite dry by now). Serve the pilaff surrounded by the cooked tomato and garnished with the coriander leaves.

GREEK-STYLE SPINACH RICE

Rinse 1 1/2 cups (330 g/11oz) medium-grain rice in a sieve under water runs clear. Stand for 30 minutes. Remove the stems from 400 g (13 oz) spinach (silverbeet), wash and roughly chop. Heat 1 1/2 tablespoons olive oil in a large saucepan, add 1 finely chopped onion and 1 crushed garlic clove and cook until the onion is soft but not brown. Add the rice, spinach, 2 tablespoons chopped fresh dill, 1 1/2 tablespoons lemon juice, 1/2 teaspoon sea salt and 2 cups (500 ml/ 16 fl oz) water. Bring to the boil, cover, reduce the heat to very low and simmer for 10 minutes. Remove from the heat, rest for 10 minutes then stir in 2 tablespoons toasted pine nuts. Serve with seafood or meat stews.

GREEN PILAFF WITH CASHEWS

Preparation time: 15 minutes
Total cooking time: 1 hour 10 minutes
Serves 6

200 g (6¹/₂ oz) baby English spinach leaves

²/₃ cup (100 g/3¹/₂ oz) cashew nuts, chopped

2 tablespoons olive oil

6 spring onions (scallions), chopped

2 garlic cloves, finely chopped

1 teaspoon fennel seeds

1¹/₂ cups (300 g/10 oz) long-grain brown rice

2 tablespoons lemon juice

2¹/₂ cups (600 ml/20 fl oz) vegetable stock

3 tablespoons chopped mint

3 tablespoons chopped flat-leaf (Italian) parsley

1 Preheat the oven to moderate 180°C (350°F/ Gas 4). Shred the English spinach into 1 cm (¹/₂ inch) pieces.

2 Put the cashew nuts on a baking tray and roast for 5–10 minutes, or until golden brown—watch them carefully so they don't burn.

3 Heat the oil in a large, deep frying pan and cook the spring onion over medium heat for 2 minutes, or until softened. Add the garlic and fennel seeds and cook for 1 minute, or until fragrant. Stir in the rice, mixing well to combine. Increase the heat to high, add the lemon juice, stock and 1 teaspoon salt and bring to the boil. Reduce the heat to low, cover with a tight-fitting lid and cook, without lifting the lid, for 45 minutes, or until the stock has been absorbed and the rice is cooked. Remove from the heat and sprinkle with the spinach and herbs. Stand, covered, for 8 minutes, then fork the spinach and herbs through the rice. Season. Serve sprinkled with cashews.

ABOVE: Green pilaff with cashews

57

CHICKEN WITH PILAFF

Preparation time: 20 minutes
Total cooking time: 1 hour 10 minutes
Serves 4

☆ ☆

2¹/₂ cups (600 ml/20 fl oz) chicken stock
1 tablespoon peanut oil
1 onion, finely chopped
2 garlic cloves, crushed
2 tablespoons finely chopped lemon grass
1 red capsicum (pepper), finely chopped
1¹/₂ cups (300 g/10 oz) basmati rice
1.4 kg (2 lb 13 oz) whole chicken
¹/₃ cup (80 ml/2³/₄ fl oz) coconut milk
2 tablespoons sweet chilli sauce
2 tablespoons lime juice
1 cup (50 g/1³/₄ oz) roughly chopped coriander
   (cilantro) leaves
2 teaspoons soft brown sugar

1 Pour the stock into a saucepan, bring to the boil, then remove from the heat. Preheat the oven to moderately hot 200°C (400°F/Gas 6).

2 Heat the oil in a large, 3 cm (1¹/₄ inch) deep flameproof casserole dish over medium heat. Add the onion, garlic, lemon grass and capsicum and cook, stirring, for 5 minutes, or until soft. Stir in the rice, mixing well to combine. Remove the dish from the heat. Add the hot stock and mix well.

3 Wash the chicken and pat dry inside and out with paper towels. Tie the legs together with string and tuck the wings under.

4 Combine the coconut milk, chilli sauce, lime juice, coriander and sugar in a bowl. Put the chicken on a rack over the rice. Brush half the coconut mixture over the chicken and bake for 15 minutes. Reduce the temperature to moderate 180°C (350°F/Gas 4) and stir 1 cup (250 ml/8 fl oz) water into the rice mixture. Cover the chicken tightly with lightly greased foil and bake for a further 30 minutes.

5 Remove the chicken and rack. Stir the rice, adding extra water if the rice is a little dry. Return the rack and chicken to the dish. Brush with the remaining coconut mixture. Bake, uncovered, for 15 minutes, or until the chicken is cooked and lightly browned and the juices run clear when a skewer is inserted into the thigh. Remove the chicken and stir the rice. Serve the pilaff with pieces of chicken.

ABOVE: Chicken with pilaff

FRUITY LAMB PILAFF

Preparation time: 20 minutes +
  30 minutes soaking
Total cooking time: 2 hours
Serves 4–6

2 cups (400 g/13 oz) basmati rice
600 g (1 1/4 lb) lamb fillets, cubed
1/2 teaspoon cayenne pepper
1 teaspoon ground coriander
1 teaspoon ground cumin
1 tablespoon olive oil
40 g (1 1/4 oz) butter
2 onions, sliced
1 bay leaf
1 cinnamon stick
1 teaspoon ground allspice
1/4 teaspoon ground cloves
2 tablespoons tomato paste (purée)
3 1/2 cups (875 ml/28 fl oz) beef stock
3 tablespoons finely chopped parsley
1/3 cup (50 g/1 3/4 oz) pine nuts, toasted
1/3 cup (40 g/1 1/4 oz) raisins

50 g (1 3/4 oz) dried apricots, halved
2 tablespoons mint
1/3 cup (80 g/2 3/4 oz) thick natural yoghurt,
  to serve

1 Soak the rice in boiling water for 30 minutes.
2 Toss the lamb in the cayenne, coriander and cumin. Heat the oil in a large saucepan over medium heat and cook the lamb in batches until browned all over. Remove from the pan.
3 Melt the butter in the same pan and cook the onion over medium heat for 5 minutes, or until soft. Add the bay leaf, cinnamon, allspice and cloves and cook for 30 seconds, then add the tomato paste. Cook for 1 minute, then return the lamb to the pan. Add 2 cups (500 ml/16 fl oz) of the stock, bring to the boil, then reduce the heat and cover with a lid. Simmer for 1 1/2 hours, or until the liquid has been absorbed and the lamb is tender.
4 Drain the rice and add it to the lamb mixture along with the remaining stock and the parsley, pine nuts, raisins and apricots. Bring to the boil, then reduce the heat and simmer, covered, for 20 minutes, or until the liquid has been absorbed and the rice is tender. Stir in the mint and serve with yoghurt.

PINE NUTS
These 'nuts' are actually the small edible seeds that grow at the base of the cone of certain varieties of pine tree. The nut is enclosed in a hard shell, which is always removed before the product goes to market. The most highly sought after pine nuts are grown in the northern hemisphere, and are harvested by hand. Though pine nuts may be eaten raw, the flavour is enhanced when they are roasted or fried. Because pine nuts have a high oil content, they burn quickly when heated. For the same reason, they also go rancid quickly, so buy them in small quantities, or freeze them.

LEFT: Fruity lamb pilaff

CHICKEN AND ALMOND PILAFF

Preparation time: 15 minutes +
    1 hour marinating + 30 minutes soaking
Total cooking time: 45 minutes
Serves 4–6

BAHARAT

1 1/2 tablespoons coriander seeds
3 tablespoons black peppercorns
1 1/2 tablespoons cassia bark
1 1/2 tablespoons cloves
2 tablespoons cumin seeds
1 teaspoon cardamom seeds
2 whole nutmeg
3 tablespoons paprika

700 g (1 lb 6 1/2 oz) chicken thigh fillets,
    trimmed, cut into 3 cm (1 1/4 inch) wide strips
2 cups (400 g/13 oz) basmati rice
3 cups (750 ml/24 fl oz) chicken stock
2 tablespoons ghee
1 large onion, chopped

1 garlic clove, finely chopped
1 teaspoon ground turmeric
400 g (13 oz) tin chopped tomatoes
1 cinnamon stick
4 cardamom pods, bruised
4 cloves
1/2 teaspoon finely grated lemon zest
3 tablespoons fresh coriander (cilantro)
    leaves, chopped
2 teaspoons lemon juice
1/3 cup (40 g/1 1/4 oz) slivered almonds, toasted

1 To make the baharat, grind the coriander seeds, peppercorns, cassia bark, cloves, cumin seeds and cardamom seeds to a powder in a mortar and pestle or spice grinder—you may need to do this in batches. Grate the nutmeg on the fine side of the grater and add to spice mixture with the paprika. Stir together.

2 Combine the chicken and 1 tablespoon of the baharat in a large bowl, cover with plastic wrap and refrigerate for 1 hour. Meanwhile, put the rice in a large bowl, cover with cold water and soak for at least 30 minutes. Rinse under cold running water until the water runs clear, then drain and set aside.

3 Bring the stock to the boil in a saucepan. Reduce the heat, cover and keep at a low simmer. Meanwhile, heat the ghee in a large, heavy-based saucepan over medium heat. Add the onion and garlic and cook for 5 minutes, or until soft and golden. Add the chicken and turmeric and cook for 5 minutes, or until browned. Add the rice and cook, stirring, for 2 minutes.

4 Add the tomato, simmering chicken stock, cinnamon stick, cardamom pods, cloves, lemon zest and 1 teaspoon salt. Stir well and bring to the boil, then reduce the heat to low and cover the saucepan with a tight-fitting lid. Simmer for 20 minutes, or until the stock is absorbed and the rice is cooked. Remove from the heat and allow to stand, covered, for 10 minutes.

5 Stir in the fresh coriander, lemon juice and almonds. Season to taste.

NOTE: Baharat is an aromatic spice blend used in Arabic cuisine to add depth of flavour to dishes such as soups, fish curries and tomato sauces. Leftover baharat can be stored in an airtight jar for up to 3 months in a cool, dry place. It can be used in Middle Eastern casseroles and stews, rubbed on fish that is to be grilled, pan-fried or barbecued, or used with salt to dry marinate lamb roasts, cutlets or chops.

BELOW: Chicken and almond pilaff

Spread half the rice over the base of the pan and smooth the surface with a wooden spoon.

Make a tunnel in the mound with the handle of a wooden spoon to the bottom of the pan and pour the remaining butter into the hole.

In a large, heavy-based casserole dish with a lid, arrange half the rice, top with the spinach and meat and then cover with another layer of rice.

Cover the spinach and meat with the final layer of rice before covering tightly with a lid.

PERSIAN LAYERED
LAMB POLO

Preparation time: 20 minutes
Total cooking time: 1 hour 35 minutes
Serves 4

☆ ☆

120 g (4 oz) butter

1 onion, finely chopped

800 g (1 lb 10 oz) lean lamb fillet,
   cut into 2 cm (3/4 inch) chunks

1/2 teaspoon ground turmeric

1/2 teaspoon ground cinnamon

1/4 cup (85 g/3 oz) prunes, pitted

1/2 cup (80 g) dried apricots, halved

2 cups (100 g/3 1/2 oz) English spinach leaves,
   washed and blanched

2 cups (400 g/13 oz) basmati rice

1 In a large heavy-based saucepan, melt half the butter over medium heat, add the onion and cook for 5 minutes, or until golden. Add the lamb and brown on all sides. Add the turmeric and cinnamon and a little salt and pepper. Add the prunes and apricots, then pour in enough water to cover the meat. Cover with a lid and simmer, stirring occasionally, over low heat for 1 1/4 hours, or until the mixture is thick and the meat is tender. Add a little more water if the mixture looks like it is drying out.

2 Meanwhile, pour 1 litre (32 fl oz) water into a large saucepan and add 1 teaspoon salt. Bring to the boil, then add the rice and stir until the water returns to the boil. Boil for 5 minutes, then drain the rice in a colander. Add half the remaining butter to the saucepan with 1/4 cup (60 ml/2 fl oz) water and bring to the boil. Swirl to coat the base and sides of pan, then spread half the rice over the base of the pan and smooth the surface with a wooden spoon. Spoon the remaining rice over the top and make a mound. Make a tunnel in the mound with the handle of a wooden spoon to the bottom of the pan and pour the remaining butter into the hole. Cover the pan with greaseproof paper, then secure the lid tightly. Cook over medium-low heat for 10 minutes, then reduce the heat to low and cook for another 10 minutes. The rice should be fluffy.

3 In large, heavy-based casserole dish with a lid, arrange half the rice, top with spinach and meat and cover with another layer of rice. You may need to drizzle with 2 tablespoons water if the rice is dry. Cover tightly and steam over low heat for 20 minutes, or until the rice is tender and has absorbed some of the sauce.

*ABOVE: Persian layered
lamb polo*

1 Preheat the oven to moderately hot 200°C (400°F/Gas 6). Lightly grease a 30 x 23 cm (12 x 9 inch) ovenproof dish.
2 Heat the oil in a large heavy-based frying pan, add the onion and cook over medium heat until softened but not browned. Add the garlic, cumin and 1 tablespoon of the oregano. Pour in the vinegar, cook for a further minute, then add the rice, stirring to coat. Add the tomatoes, tomato paste, currants and stock and season. Bring to the boil and pour into the ovenproof dish. Cover with foil and bake for 30 minutes, or until the rice is soft.
3 Add the prawns, poking them in under the rice, then sprinkle with fetta and the remaining oregano, and bake for a further 10 minutes. Serve with a salad.

STUFFED TROUT

Preparation time: 30 minutes
Total cooking time: 20 minutes
Serves 4

4 trout
³/4 cup (140 g/4¹/2 oz) chopped dates
¹/4 cup (45 g/1¹/2 oz) cooked long-grain rice
1 onion, finely chopped
4 tablespoons chopped coriander (cilantro) leaves
¹/4 teaspoon ground ginger
¹/4 teaspoon ground cinnamon
¹/3 cup (50 g/1³/4 oz) roughly chopped blanched almonds
40 g (1¹/4 oz) butter, softened
ground cinnamon, for dusting

1 Preheat the oven to moderate 180°C (350°F/Gas 4). Rinse the trout under cold running water and pat dry with paper towels. Season lightly.
2 Combine the dates, rice, half the onion, the coriander, ginger, cinnamon, almonds and half the butter in a bowl. Season well.
3 Spoon the stuffing into the fish cavities and put each fish on a well-greased double sheet of foil. Brush the fish with the remaining butter, season and divide the remaining onion among the four parcels. Wrap the fish neatly and seal the edges of the foil. Place the parcels on a large baking tray and bake for 15–20 minutes, or until cooked to your liking. Serve dusted with cinnamon.

GREEK PRAWN AND FETTA BAKE

Preparation time: 20 minutes
Total cooking time: 50 minutes
Serves 6–8

2 tablespoons extra virgin olive oil
1 red onion, chopped
3 garlic cloves, crushed
1 teaspoon ground cumin
3 tablespoons chopped oregano
2 tablespoons red wine vinegar
3 cups (660 g/1 lb 5¹/2 oz) risotto rice
2 x 400 g (13 oz) tins chopped tomatoes
1¹/2 tablespoons tomato paste (purée)
¹/4 cup (35 g/1¹/4 oz) currants
1 litre (32 fl oz) chicken stock
1 kg (2 lb) raw prawns (shrimp), peeled and deveined, tails intact
250 g (8 oz) fetta, crumbled

ABOVE: Greek prawn and fetta bake

STUFFED SARDINES

Preparation time: 25 minutes
Total cooking time: 15 minutes
Serves 4

☆☆

¹/₂ cup (100 g/3¹/₂ oz) long-grain rice

2 tablespoons olive oil

2 tablespoons chopped dried apricots

2 tablespoons raisins

1 tablespoon flaked almonds, toasted

1 tablespoon chopped parsley

1 tablespoon chopped mint

grated zest of 1 orange

2 tablespoons freshly squeezed orange juice

1 teaspoon finely chopped preserved
   lemon zest

1 teaspoon ground cinnamon

¹/₂ teaspoon harissa

16 whole large sardines, butterflied

16 large vine leaves (see Note)

1 cup (250 g/8 oz) thick natural yoghurt,
   to serve

1 Cook the rice in boiling water until it is tender. Drain and transfer to a bowl. Add 1 tablespoon of the olive oil, the dried apricots, raisins, almonds, parsley, mint, orange zest and juice, preserved lemon, cinnamon, harissa and the second tablespoon of oil. Season with salt and freshly ground black pepper, and mix together.

2 Divide the stuffing among the sardines, folding the two fillets of each fish together to enclose the rice mixture (save any extra stuffing to serve with the sardines). Wrap a vine leaf around each sardine and secure with a toothpick.

3 Preheat a chargrill pan or barbecue hotplate. Cook the sardines for 6 minutes, turning them over halfway through. Serve each one with a dollop of yoghurt and any extra rice.

NOTE: You can either use fresh vine leaves or vine leaves in brine. If you are using fresh ones, blanch them one by one for 30 seconds, then pat dry with paper towels. If you are using preserved vine leaves, rinse and dry them.

STUFFED SARDINES

Stir the rest of the stuffing ingredients into the cooked rice so that everything is evenly distributed.

Working one at a time, fold the sardine fillets over the rice stuffing to enclose it. Keep the sardine secure until it is wrapped tightly.

Wrap each stuffed sardine with a vine leaf, then secure the parcel with a toothpick.

LEFT: Stuffed sardines

ROAST CHICKEN STUFFED WITH PINE NUTS AND RICE

Preparation time: 30 minutes
Total cooking time: 2 hours 30 minutes
Serves 4–6

STUFFING

60 g (2 oz) clarified butter (see Note)
   or ghee, melted
1 onion, chopped
1 teaspoon ground allspice
$^{1}/_{3}$ cup (65 g/$2^{1}/_{4}$ oz) long-grain rice
$^{1}/_{4}$ cup (30 g/1 oz) walnuts, chopped
$^{1}/_{3}$ cup (50 g/$1^{3}/_{4}$ oz) pine nuts
$^{1}/_{3}$ cup (55 g/2 oz) sultanas
$^{1}/_{2}$ cup (125 ml/4 fl oz) chicken stock

1.6 kg ($3^{1}/_{2}$ lb) chicken
$^{2}/_{3}$ cup (170 ml/$5^{1}/_{2}$ fl oz) chicken stock

STUFFING
The process of filling cavities in meat, poultry, seafood, vegetables or fruit is called stuffing. Rice and bread are often the base for the stuffing, augmented by other ingredients to provide flavour.

1 Preheat the oven to moderate 180°C (350°F/ Gas 4). Pour half the butter into a large frying pan, then add the onion and cook for 5 minutes over medium heat until softened but not browned. Stir in the allspice.

2 Add the rice and nuts to the pan and cook for 3–4 minutes. Add the sultanas, stock and $^{1}/_{4}$ cup (60 ml/2 fl oz) water. Bring to the boil, then reduce the heat and simmer for 8–10 minutes, or until all the water is absorbed. Allow to cool.

3 Thoroughly rinse the cavity of the chicken with cold water, then pat dry inside and out with paper towels.

4 When the stuffing is cool, spoon the stuffing into the cavity. Tie the legs together and tuck the wing tips under. Put in a deep ovenproof dish, then rub $^{1}/_{2}$ teaspoon salt and $^{1}/_{4}$ teaspoon freshly ground black pepper into the skin using your fingertips.

5 Pour the rest of the butter over the chicken, then add the stock to the pan. Roast for 2 hours 10 minutes, basting every 20–25 minutes with juices from the pan, until the chicken is tender and the juices run clear when the thigh is pierced with a skewer. Rest the chicken for 15 minutes before carving. Serve with the stuffing.

NOTE: To clarify butter, melt it in a saucepan over low heat, then remove from the heat and let the milk solids drop to the base. Only use the yellow liquid part of the butter. Discard the white milk solids at the base of the saucepan.

RIGHT: Roast chicken stuffed with pine nuts and rice

MIDDLE EASTERN
RICE-STUFFED LAMB

Preparation time: 20 minutes
+ 20 minutes soaking + 25 minutes cooling
Total cooking time: 1 hour 40 minutes
Serves 6

$^1/_3$ cup (60 g/2 oz) dried figs

1 tablespoon olive oil

1 onion, finely chopped

2 garlic cloves, crushed

1 teaspoon ground cinnamon

$^1/_4$ teaspoon ground allspice

1 tablespoon red wine vinegar

$^1/_3$ cup (65 g/2$^1/_4$ oz) long-grain rice

2 tablespoons currants

2 tablespoons pistachios or pine nuts, toasted

3$^1/_2$ cups (875 ml/28 fl oz) chicken stock

2 tablespoons finely chopped flat-leaf
   (Italian) parsley

1 egg, lightly beaten

1.5 kg (3 lb) leg of lamb, deboned and
   butterflied

$^1/_4$ cup (60 ml/2 fl oz) olive oil, extra

2 tablespoons lemon juice

2–3 teaspoons finely chopped oregano

1 tablespoon sumac

1 cup (250 ml/8 fl oz) white wine

1 Preheat the oven to moderately hot 200°C (400°F/Gas 6). Soak the dried figs in warm water for 20 minutes. Drain and chop the figs coarsely.
2 To make the stuffing, heat the olive oil in a frying pan, then cook the onion for 3 minutes, or until softened but not browned. Add the garlic, cinnamon and allspice and cook for 30 seconds before adding the vinegar. Cook over high heat until all the vinegar has been absorbed. Reduce the heat to medium, then add rice, soaked figs, currants and pistachios and stir to coat. Pour in 1 cup (250 ml/8 fl oz) chicken stock, bring to the boil, then reduce the heat to low and cook, covered, for 20 minutes, or until the stock has been absorbed and the rice is tender. Season well and stir in the parsley. Set aside for 25 minutes to cool.
3 When the stuffing has cooled, mix the beaten egg into it with a metal spoon until it binds together. Open out the lamb leg on a work surface and spread the stuffing over the exposed surface, then roll up and tie with string. Combine the extra olive oil with the lemon juice, oregano and sumac, then pour onto the lamb, rubbing to cover evenly. Season with salt and freshly ground black pepper. Place in a roasting tin and roast for 10 minutes.
4 Remove the lamb from the oven and reduce the heat to moderate 180°C (350°F/Gas 4). Pour the remaining stock and white wine into the roasting tin and bake for a further 1 hour, or until cooked to desired level of doneness. Add extra stock or water if liquid is evaporating too quickly. Remove the lamb and set aside on a serving plate to rest.
5 Meanwhile, to make the sauce, put the roasting tin on top of stove and simmer over medium heat for 3 minutes, or until the liquid has reduced and thickened slightly. Serve the lamb with the stuffing, sauce and a green salad or steamed vegetables.

*ABOVE: Middle Eastern
rice-stuffed lamb*

then remove from the heat. Stir in the sugar, cinnamon, nutmeg and orange zest and set aside.
2 Soak the sultanas in the brandy. Meanwhile, add the rice to the infused milk and return to the heat. Bring to a simmer and stir slowly for about 35 minutes, or until the rice is creamy. Stir in the sultanas and remove the vanilla bean at the end. Serve warm or cold.

SWEET SICILIAN RICE FRITTERS

Preparation time: 20 minutes + 1 hour standing
Total cooking time: 25 minutes
Makes 8

☆ ☆

1/2 cup (110 g/3 1/2 oz) risotto rice
1 1/3 cups (330 ml/11 fl oz) milk
10 g (1/4 oz) unsalted butter
1 tablespoon caster (superfine) sugar
1 vanilla bean, split
1 teaspoon dried yeast
2 tablespoons candied citron, finely chopped
2 teaspoons grated lemon zest
oil, for deep-frying
flour, for dusting
2 tablespoons fragrant honey

1 Combine the rice, milk, butter, sugar, vanilla bean, and a pinch of salt in a heavy-based saucepan. Bring to the boil over medium heat, then reduce the heat to very low, cover and cook for 15–18 minutes, or until most of the liquid has been absorbed. Remove from the heat, cover and set aside.
2 Dissolve the yeast in 2 tablespoons tepid water and allow to stand for 5 minutes, or until frothy. If your yeast doesn't foam, it is dead and you will have to start again.
3 Discard the vanilla bean. Add the yeast, citron and lemon zest to the rice, mix well, cover and let stand for 1 hour.
4 Fill a deep-fat fryer or large saucepan one-third full of oil and heat to 180°C (350°F), or until a spoonful of the batter dropped into the oil browns in 15 seconds.
5 Shape the rice into eight croquettes about 2.5 x 8 cm (1 x 3 inches) and roll them in flour. Deep-fry for 5–6 minutes, or until golden brown on all sides. Remove with a slotted spoon and drain on crumpled paper towels. Drizzle with honey and serve immediately.

ITALIAN RICE PUDDING

Preparation time: 10 minutes
Total cooking time: 40 minutes
Serves 4

☆

2 1/2 cups (600 ml/20 fl oz) milk
1 cup (250 ml/8 fl oz) thick (double/heavy) cream
1 vanilla bean, split
50 g (1 3/4 oz) caster (superfine) sugar
1/4 teaspoon ground cinnamon
pinch of freshly grated nutmeg
1 tablespoon grated orange zest
1/2 cup (80 g/2 3/4 oz) sultanas
2 tablespoons brandy or sweet Marsala
1/2 cup (110 g/3 1/2 oz) risotto rice

1 Put the milk, cream and vanilla bean in a heavy-based saucepan and bring just to the boil,

ABOVE: Italian rice pudding

RICE PUDDING WITH LEMON THYME AND BALSAMIC STRAWBERRIES

Preparation time: 20 minutes + standing
Total cooking time: 1 hour 15 minutes
Serves 6–8

500 g (1 lb) strawberries
2 tablespoons good-quality balsamic vinegar
$1/3$ cup (90 g/3 oz) caster (superfine) sugar
$3/4$ cup (150 g/5 oz) long-grain rice
3 cups (750 ml/24 fl oz) milk
6 × 3 cm (1 $1/4$ inch) lemon thyme sprigs
$1/3$ cup (90 g/3 oz) sugar
3 egg yolks
1 egg

1 Trim the stalks from the strawberries and cut the strawberries in half. Put in a bowl with the vinegar. Sprinkle the caster sugar over the top and stir well. Set aside, turning occasionally.

2 Preheat the oven to warm 160°C (315°F/ Gas 2–3). Lightly grease a 1.5 litre (48 fl oz) ovenproof dish.

3 Thoroughly rinse the rice and put it in a medium saucepan with 1½ cups (375 ml/ 12 fl oz) water. Bring to the boil, cover and cook over low heat for 8–10 minutes. Remove from the heat and leave the pan with the lid on for 5 minutes, until the liquid is absorbed and the rice is soft.

4 Heat the milk with the lemon thyme and sugar in a small saucepan. When bubbles form at the edge, remove from the heat and set aside for 10 minutes so that it absorbs flavour from the lemon thyme. Strain. Beat the egg yolks and egg in a large bowl, add the rice and gradually stir in the warm milk. Pour into the prepared ovenproof dish. Place the dish in a baking dish and carefully pour in enough warm water to come halfway up the side of the pudding dish. Bake for 50–60 minutes, or until the pudding is just set (timing may vary according to the dish used). Remove from the oven and allow to stand for 10 minutes. Serve warm or cold with the balsamic strawberries.

LEFT: Rice pudding with lemon thyme and balsamic strawberries

67

ZERDE

(Turkish sweet saffron rice)

Preparation time: 10 minutes +
  30 minutes soaking
Total cooking time: 45 minutes
Serves 6

1 teaspoon saffron threads
1/2 cup (125 g/4 oz) medium-grain rice
1 cup (250 g/8 oz) caster (superfine) sugar
2 tablespoons rosewater
1/4 cup (40 g/1 3/4 oz) pine nuts, lightly
  toasted
1/4 cup (35 g/1 1/4 oz) pistachios, chopped
pomegranate seeds, to garnish
thick natural yoghurt, to serve

1 Crush the saffron threads with your fingers and soak in 2 tablespoons of boiling water for 30 minutes.
2 Bring 1.25 litres (40 fl oz) water to the boil in a large saucepan, then add the rice. Reduce to a simmer and cook, stirring occasionally, for 20 minutes. Stir in the sugar, rosewater and the saffron with the soaking liquid and simmer for another 10 minutes.
3 Add the pine nuts and chopped pistachios and simmer for another 10 minutes. The mixture should be thick and soupy. If it is too thick, add a little more water. Serve either hot or cold (it will thicken as it cools). Garnish with pomegranate seeds. Serve with thick natural yoghurt.
NOTE: This delectable rice pudding from Turkey is unusual in that is made without any milk, cream or butter. If serving it cold, top it with the pomegranate seeds just before serving.

ROSEWATER
Made from a distillation of rose petals, rosewater is used in the Middle East and India to flavour dishes such as Turkish delight, baklava and lassi. It is also used to impart a sweet fragrance to curries and rice dishes when sprinkled over the finished dish.

RIGHT: Zerde

CITRON
A citrus fruit that looks similar to a large knobbly lemon, citrons are grown for their thick peel rather than their flesh, which is quite sour and inedible. Citrons grow mainly in Corsica, as well as in Greece and Italy, and were believed to have been cultivated in Egypt as early as 300 BC. Citron peel is candied (pictured) and used in confectionery, in baking (particularly in fruit cakes or in Italian breads such as panettone and panforte) and in cassata, or it may be pressed to extract citron oil, which is used to flavour liqueurs. Citron peel is sold candied in chopped mixed peel, in slices or in pieces. Also known as cedro.

RICE ICE CREAM

Preparation time: 20 minutes + 2 hours cooling + 30 minutes standing + freezing
Total cooking time: 25 minutes
Serves 4

☆ ☆

1/2 cup (110 g/31/2 oz) risotto rice
3 cups (750 ml/24 fl oz) milk
1 vanilla bean
1/4 cup (60 g/2 oz) sugar
2 cups (500 ml/16 fl oz) thick (double/heavy) cream
3 teaspoons icing (confectioners') sugar
2 tablespoons finely chopped candied citron

Custard
1/2 cup (125 ml/4 fl oz) milk
3 egg yolks
1/2 cup (125 g/4 oz) sugar

1 Put the rice in a saucepan, add the milk, vanilla bean, sugar and a pinch of salt. Bring to a boil over medium heat, stirring constantly. Reduce the heat to low and simmer for about 12 minutes. Remove the rice from the heat and set aside for about 2 hours to cool completely.

2 Pour the contents of the pan through a colander and drain away the excess liquid. Let the rice stand for 30 minutes.
3 To make the custard, heat the milk in a saucepan over medium heat until it is almost boiling. In a bowl, whisk together the egg yolks and sugar, and add the milk. Mix well. Rinse the pan and return the milk mixture to the pan. Cook, stirring constantly, over a low heat until the custard thickens and will easily coat the back of a wooden spoon. Remove the custard from the heat and allow to cool.
4 Transfer the rice to a bowl, remove the vanilla bean, add the custard and mix well. Add the cream, icing sugar and candied citron, and stir well to combine.
5 Pour the mixture into a freezer box and freeze for 1 hour. Take the box out of the freezer and give the mixture a good stir, then refreeze. Repeat this process four times until the mixture is almost solid. The more you stir, the less icy the mixture. Alternatively, you can freeze the mixture in an ice-cream machine, following the manufacturer's instructions.
6 Remove the ice cream from the freezer 10 minutes before serving to soften. If it is too frozen the rice grains will be very hard.

ABOVE: Rice ice cream

RICE GROWING IN ITALY
It is not definitively known
how long rice has been
grown in Italy, but small
amounts have been
cultivated at least since the
14th century. The Spanish
are thought to have
introduced rice to the
area, and they are also
responsible for creating
a proper system for rice
growing. Cultivation
expanded until the Duke of
Milan restricted the export
of rice and the expansion
of its cultivation because
malaria was thought to be
caused by the flooded rice
fields. Today, Italy is a major
exporter of rice. For most
of the history of rice
growing in Italy, the rice has
been grown and harvested
by hand, back-breaking
work undertaken by poorly
paid labourers, a life that
was impressively illustrated
in the Italian 1948 classic
movie *Bitter Rice*. Most of
the rice grown in Italy
(particularly the Po Valley)
is medium- to short-grain
Italian-style rice, such as
the various types of risotto
rice: arborio, vialone nano
and carnaroli.

RIGHT: Torta di riso

TORTA DI RISO

(Italian rice tart)

Preparation time: 25 minutes +
    1 hour 30 minutes refrigeration
Total cooking time: 1 hour 35 minutes
Serves 8–10

PASTRY
1¼ cups (155 g/5 oz) plain (all-purpose) flour
¼ cup (60 g/2 oz) caster (superfine) sugar
125 g (4 oz) cold unsalted butter, cut into
    1 cm (½ inch) dice
2 egg yolks
1 teaspoon vanilla extract

FILLING
½ cup (110 g/3½ oz) arborio rice
½ cup (60 g/2 oz) raisins
2 tablespoons cognac or brandy
3 cups (750 ml/24 fl oz) cream
1 vanilla bean, split
2 cinnamon sticks

6 egg yolks
¾ cup (180 g/6 oz) caster (superfine) sugar
⅓ cup (50 g/1¾ oz) pine nuts, toasted
1½ teaspoons finely grated lemon zest

1 To make the pastry, sift the flour into a bowl
and add the sugar and a pinch of salt. Add the
butter and toss to coat in the flour mix. Rub
the butter into the flour with your fingertips
for about 5 minutes or until it resembles fine
breadcrumbs, then make a well in the centre.
2 Mix the egg yolks, vanilla and 3 tablespoons
of cold water together, then pour into the well.
Using a flat-bladed knife, cut into the mixture
while you turn the bowl until it is well combined
and comes together in small beads. Pinch a small
amount of dough together to see if it holds; if
it still crumbles add 1 more teaspoon of water.
3 Gather the dough together, press into a ball
then flatten into a 2 cm (¾ inch) thick disc.
Cover with plastic wrap and refrigerate for
30 minutes.
4 Roll the pastry out between two sheets of
baking paper or plastic wrap until it is 36 cm
(14 inches) in diameter. Remove the top layer
of baking paper and invert the pastry onto a

28 cm (11 inch) fluted tart dish or tin with 4 cm (1½ inch) sides. Remove the final layer of paper and carefully press the pastry into the dish, allowing any extra to hang over the sides, then trim the edges using a small sharp knife. Prick the base all over with a fork then put in the fridge for 1 hour or the freezer for 30 minutes.

5 Meanwhile, preheat the oven to moderate 180°C (350°F/Gas 4). Toss the raisins and cognac together and set aside to soak. Cook the rice in boiling water for 15 minutes, or until tender—there will still be some give. Drain, rinse with cold water and leave to drain and cool thoroughly. Place the cream, vanilla bean and cinnamon sticks in a saucepan and bring almost to the boil over medium heat. Remove from the heat and set aside to infuse and cool.

6 Remove the tart from the fridge, line with lightly crumpled baking paper and pour in some baking beads and spread evenly over the base. Bake for 15 minutes then remove the paper and beads and cook for a further 10–15 minutes, or until lightly golden all over. Remove from the oven and set aside. Reduce the temperature to slow 150°C (300°F/Gas 2).

7 Beat the egg yolks and sugar together until thick and creamy. Strain the cream mixture and stir into the eggs until well combined. Combine the cold rice with the raisins and pine nuts.

8 When the tart shell is at room temperature evenly spread the rice mixture over the base, then gently pour over the custard. Bake for 45 minutes, or until the centre has just set. Allow the tart to cool completely as it will break up if you try to cut it while it is still warm. Serve with lightly whipped cream.

SPANISH RICE PUDDING

Preparation time: 5 minutes
Total cooking time: 1 hour
Serves 6

1.25 litres (40 fl oz) milk
1 cup (220 g/7 oz) arborio rice
1 large strip of orange zest, pith removed
1 cinnamon stick
1 teaspoon natural vanilla extract
2/3 cup (145 g/5 oz) caster (superfine) sugar
orange zest, to garnish (optional)

1 Put the milk, rice, orange zest, cinnamon stick, vanilla, sugar and a pinch of salt in a large saucepan and stir over high heat until the sugar is dissolved. Allow to just come to the boil, then reduce the heat to a simmer.

2 Cook the rice mixture over low heat, stirring regularly, for 50 minutes, or until the rice is tender but not mushy. Stirring not only helps to ensure the rice mixture does not stick to the bottom of the pan but it also helps to produce a very creamy texture.

3 Lift out the zest and cinnamon stick from the pan with some tongs and serve the rice pudding warm or cold, garnished with some thin strips of orange zest.

NOTE: In Spanish, this dish is called *Arroz con leche* and it is found not only in Spain but also in Spanish influenced countries. The Spanish often dust the surface of the pudding with cinnamon just before serving—use only a little or you risk overpowering the subtle flavour.

ABOVE: Spanish rice pudding

EUROPE

Throughout Europe, recipes abound using rice as a delicious filling or stuffing for pies, poultry or meat. There are plump roasted chickens stuffed with rice, classic Russian dumplings, golden Dutch croquettes and many rice-based pies and tarts. Then, of course, there are all the sweet rice dishes. More than any other area in the world, Europe has a huge selection of delicious rice desserts. From the childhood favourite, Baked rice pudding, to the decadent Rice gateau and the celebratory Danish creamed rice with cherry sauce, there is a rice dessert as simple or as elaborate as you could possibly wish for.

100 ml (3^1/2 fl oz) chicken stock, extra
1 tablespoon tomato paste (purée)
1 tablespoon Worcestershire sauce
50 g (1^3/4 oz) gingernut biscuits, crushed
  (see Note)
2 tablespoons chopped flat-leaf (Italian) parsley
^{3}/4 cup (75 g/2^1/2 oz) dry breadcrumbs
oil, for deep-frying

1 To make the béchamel sauce, melt the butter in a small saucepan over medium heat. Stir in the flour and cook for 1 minute, or until foaming. Remove from the heat and gradually stir in the milk, beating well after each addition. After the last of the milk has been added, add the nutmeg and some salt and pepper. Return to the heat and stir constantly until the sauce boils and thickens. Set aside to cool.

2 Melt the butter in a saucepan. Add the rice and stir to coat. Gradually stir in the stock and continue stirring until it has come to the boil. Reduce the heat and simmer for about 20 minutes, or until the rice is very tender and all the stock has been absorbed.

3 Heat the oil in a large frying pan and cook the onion and garlic over low heat for about 5 minutes, or until softened but not browned. Add the beef and cook for 8 minutes, or until browned. Stir in the extra stock, tomato paste, Worcestershire sauce, crushed gingernut biscuits and parsley. Simmer, covered, for 20 minutes. If there is still some liquid left after this time, take the lid off and cook over high heat to reduce it.

4 Combine the béchamel, rice and beef and season well with salt and pepper. Cool slightly, then refrigerate for 1 hour.

5 Divide the mixture into twelve parts and roll each into a log approximately 7 cm (2^3/4 inches) long and 3 cm (1^1/4 inches) in diameter. The mixture will be soft, but manageable. Roll the logs in breadcrumbs to coat all over and place on a plate in a single layer. Cover with plastic wrap and refrigerate overnight.

6 Fill a deep-fat fryer or large saucepan one-third full of oil and heat to 180°C (350°F), or until a spoonful of the batter dropped into the oil browns in 15 seconds. Cook the croquettes, a few at a time, turning them with tongs to give an evenly golden brown surface. Drain on crumpled paper towels.

NOTE: If gingernut biscuits are unavailable, crush 50 g (1^3/4 oz) wheatmeal biscuits with ^{1}/2 teaspoon ground ginger.

DUTCH-STYLE BEEF AND RICE CROQUETTES

Preparation time: 30 minutes +
  1 hour refrigeration + overnight chilling
Total cooking time: 1 hour 30 minutes
Makes 12

☆☆

Béchamel sauce
20 g (^{3}/4 oz) butter
^{1}/4 cup (30 g/1 oz) plain (all-purpose) flour
^{2}/3 cup (170 ml/5^1/2 fl oz) milk
pinch of freshly grated nutmeg

10 g (^{1}/4 oz) butter
^{1}/3 cup (75 g/2^1/2 oz) arborio rice
1^2/3 cups (410 ml/13 fl oz) chicken stock
2 tablespoons olive oil
1 onion, finely chopped
2 garlic cloves, crushed
500 g (1 lb) lean minced (ground) beef

ABOVE: Dutch-style beef and rice croquettes

PIROZHKI

Preparation time: 50 minutes +
  1 hour refrigeration + cooling
Total cooking time: 25 minutes
Makes about 20

2¹/₂ cups (310 g/10 oz) plain (all-purpose) flour
180 g (6 oz) cold butter, cut into cubes
1 egg yolk
¹/₄ cup (60 g/2 oz) sour cream

FILLING
150 g (5 oz) mushrooms
50 g (1³/₄ oz) butter
1 small onion, finely chopped
¹/₂ cup (95 g/3 oz) cooked short-grain rice
1 hard-boiled egg, finely chopped
2 tablespoons finely chopped parsley
2 tablespoons finely chopped dill
1 egg, lightly beaten

1 Sift the flour and ¹/₂ teaspoon salt into a large bowl and add the butter. Rub the butter into the flour until the mixture resembles fine breadcrumbs. Add the combined egg yolk and sour cream. Cut the liquid in with a flat-bladed knife to form a dough, adding up to 1 tablespoon water, if necessary. Turn onto a lightly floured surface and gather together into a smooth ball. (Do not knead or you will have tough pastry.) Cover with plastic wrap and refrigerate for 30 minutes.

2 To make the filling, blitz the mushrooms in a food processor until finely chopped. Melt the butter in a frying pan, then cook the onion in it for 3 minutes, or until softened but not brown. Add the chopped mushrooms and cook, stirring, for a further 3 minutes. Stir in the rice. Transfer to a bowl and leave to cool. Stir in the chopped egg and herbs and season well.

3 Roll out the pastry thinly, half at a time, on a floured surface. Cut 20 rounds, with an 8 cm (3 inch) plain cutter. Put a tablespoon of filling in the centre of each round. Brush the pastry edges with the egg, then fold in half and pinch the edges to seal. Prick the tops with a fork. Put on a baking tray and refrigerate for 30 minutes. Preheat the oven to moderately hot 190°C (375°F/Gas 5). Brush the pastries with egg and bake for 15 minutes, or until golden. Serve hot as a starter or with soup.

PIROZHKI
Russian for 'little pie', these semicircular pastries are either baked or deep-fried and fillings include rice, fish, game, poultry, vegetables or cream. Pirozhki are served as an accompaniment to soup, especially borscht, with sour cream, or as a snack or hot starter. In Poland they are known as pierogi. Pirog are larger pies of varying shapes and can be served as a main meal.

LEFT: Pirozhki

STUFFED PUMPKINS

Preparation time: 35 minutes + cooling
Total cooking time: 1 hour
Serves 4

4 large golden nugget pumpkins
1 tablespoon olive oil
2/3 cup (140 g/4 1/2 oz) wild rice blend
30 g (1 oz) butter
1 onion, finely chopped
250 g (8 oz) orange sweet potato, peeled
   and cut into 1 cm (1/2 inch) cubes
1 cup (120 g/4 oz) chopped spring
   onions (scallions)
2 teaspoons ground cumin

BELOW: Stuffed pumpkins

1/2 teaspoon ground ginger
1 teaspoon ground coriander
1 teaspoon ground turmeric
1 teaspoon garam masala
2 tablespoons currants, soaked in hot
   water and drained
1/3 cup (40 g/1 1/4 oz) grated Cheddar cheese

1 Preheat the oven to moderate 180°C (350°F/
Gas 4). Slice the top third off each pumpkin.
Scoop out the seeds, leaving a deep cavity.
Brush the pumpkins lightly with oil. Stand the
pumpkins in an ovenproof dish. Pour in enough
water to come halfway up the sides of the
pumpkins. Put the lid on each, then bake for
20 minutes. Remove from the water bath and
allow to cool.
2 Meanwhile, cook the rice in a large saucepan
of boiling water for 25 minutes, or until tender.
Drain and allow to cool.
3 Melt the butter in a frying pan over medium
heat, then add the onion and sweet potato and
cook, covered, for 5 minutes. Add the spring
onion and cook, uncovered, for 1 minute. Stir
in the spices and cook for 2 minutes, or until
fragrant. Remove the pan from the heat. Fold
in the rice and currants.
4 Spoon the filling into the pumpkin cavities,
then sprinkle with cheese. Put the lids on at
an angle. Cover with foil, then put on a baking
tray and bake for 20 minutes. Serve hot with a
green salad.

CHICKEN AND RICE WITH GREEN CAPSICUM AND TOMATOES

Preparation time: 15 minutes
Total cooking time: 1 hour
Serves 4–6

1 1/2 tablespoons olive oil
1.2 kg (2 lb 6 1/2 oz) chicken pieces with
   skin on
1 onion, finely chopped
2 green capsicums (peppers), diced
3 garlic cloves, crushed
2 tablespoons paprika
1 1/2 cups (300 g/10 oz) long- or
   medium-grain rice
2 x 400 g (13 oz) tins chopped tomatoes

1 Heat the oil in a large saucepan over high heat, then add the chicken, (in batches, if necessary) skin-side down, and cook for 4 minutes on each side, or until well browned. Remove the chicken from the pan and drain on crumpled paper towels. Pour all but 1½ tablespoons of fat out of the pan.

2 Reduce the heat to medium, add the onion and capsicum and cook for 3–4 minutes, or until soft. Add the garlic, paprika and rice, and cook for a further 1 minute.

3 Add the tomato and 2¼ cups (560 ml/ 18 fl oz) water, scraping any browned bits off the bottom of the pan with a wooden spoon. Return the chicken to the pan and bring to the boil. Reduce the heat and simmer, covered, for 50 minutes, stirring occasionally to prevent sticking. Season to taste, then serve.

RED-RICE SALAD

Preparation time: 20 minutes + cooling
Total cooking time: 50 minutes
Serves 4

1 cup (220 g/7 oz) Camargue red rice (see Note)
1 red capsicum (pepper)
1 yellow capsicum (pepper)
⅓ cup (80 ml/2¾ fl oz) olive oil
1 red onion, cut into slivers
2 zucchini (courgettes), diced
1 tablespoon butter
1 garlic clove, crushed
1 chicken breast with skin on
2 tablespoons lemon juice
2 tablespoons chopped basil
2 tablespoons chopped parsley

1 Put the rice in a saucepan with plenty of boiling water and cook for 30 minutes, or until tender. Drain well, then cool.

2 Cut the red and yellow capsicums in half lengthways. Remove the seeds and membrane, then cut the flesh into large, flattish pieces. Grill or hold over a gas flame until the skin blackens and blisters. Place on a cutting board, cover with a tea towel and allow to cool. Peel the skin off and cut the flesh into smaller pieces. Add the capsicum strips to the rice.

3 Heat the oil in a frying pan, then cook the onion and zucchini until lightly charred around the edges. Add the onion and zucchini to the rice.

4 Mix the butter with the garlic. Push the mixture under the skin of the chicken breast so it is evenly distributed. Grill (broil) the chicken on both sides until the skin is crisp and the breast is cooked through. Leave the chicken to rest for 2 minutes, then slice it into strips (you can discard the skin, if you like).

5 Add the chicken slices to the rice with any juices. Add the lemon juice, any remaining olive oil and the herbs, and toss together. Season well and serve immediately.

NOTE: Camargue red rice from France is a superior grain, so it's more expensive than other varieties.

ABOVE: Red-rice salad

PUY LENTILS

Puy lentils are a small, slate green pulse from France. Reputed to have the best flavour and texture of all lentils, they are grown organically and contain more minerals than other varieties. They are also the most expensive of the lentils. *Lentilles vertes du Puy* are governed by the French *appellation d'origine contrôlée* (AOC) and must be from the Puy area. The same type of lentils are grown elsewhere—these are sold simply as Puy lentils.

ABOVE: Brown rice and Puy lentils with pine nuts and spinach

BROWN RICE AND PUY LENTILS WITH PINE NUTS AND SPINACH

Preparation time: 15 minutes
Total cooking time: 40 minutes
Serves 6–8

1 cup (200 g/6¹/₂ oz) brown rice
100 ml (3¹/₂ fl oz) extra virgin olive oil
1 red onion, diced
2 garlic cloves, crushed
1 carrot, diced
2 celery stalks, diced
1 cup (185 g/6 oz) Puy lentils
2 tomatoes, seeded and diced
3 tablespoons chopped coriander (cilantro)
3 tablespoons chopped mint
2 tablespoons balsamic vinegar

1 tablespoon lemon juice
2 tablespoons pine nuts, toasted
2 cups (90 g/3 oz) baby English spinach leaves, washed

1 Bring a large saucepan of water to the boil. Add 1 teaspoon salt and the rice, and cook for 20 minutes, or until tender. Drain and refresh under cold water.
2 Heat 2 tablespoons of the oil in a saucepan and add the onion, garlic, carrot and celery. Cook over low heat for 5 minutes, or until softened, then add the puy lentils and 1¹/₂ cups (375 ml/ 12 fl oz) water. Bring to the boil and simmer for 15 minutes, or until tender. Drain well, but do not rinse. Combine with the rice, tomato, coriander and mint in a large bowl.
3 Whisk the remaining oil with the balsamic vinegar and lemon juice, and season well with salt and freshly ground black pepper. Pour over the salad, add the pine nuts and the spinach, and toss well to combine.

KEDGEREE

Preparation time: 40 minutes + cooling
Total cooking time: 30 minutes
Serves 4

375 g (12 oz) smoked haddock

2 bay leaves

3 lemon slices

3 eggs

90 g (3 oz) butter

1 onion, finely chopped

1/2 teaspoon mild Indian curry paste

1/2 teaspoon ground cumin

3 cups (550 g/1 lb 1 3/4 oz) cooked cold
   long-grain rice

2 tablespoons chopped parsley

2 tablespoons lemon juice

1/2 cup (125 ml/4 fl oz) cream

chopped parsley and lemon wedges, to serve

1 Put the haddock in a frying pan with the bay leaves and lemon. Cover with cold water. Simmer for about 8 minutes, or until the fish flakes easily when tested with a fork. Remove the fish from the pan, then drain and cool. Flake into bite-size pieces.

2 Put the eggs in a pan of water. Bring to the boil and cook for 8–10 minutes, or until hard boiled. Remove. Run under cold water to cool, then peel and chop.

3 Melt the butter in a large, deep frying pan, and heat for 2 minutes, or until foaming. Add the onion, curry paste and cumin and cook, stirring, for 4 minutes. Add the rice, fish, parsley and lemon juice and cook over medium heat for 3 minutes, or until heated through, tossing regularly with two wooden spoons. Add the cream and half the egg. Toss gently to combine.

4 Garnish with the remaining egg and the extra parsley. Serve with lemon wedges.

NOTE: For a less spicy flavour, you can replace the curry paste and cumin with 1 teaspoon finely grated lemon zest and 1/4 teaspoon freshly grated nutmeg.

KEDGEREE
A popular English dish made of smoked fish, boiled eggs, curry powder and cream mixed into rice. The dish evolved from the Indian breakfast dish khichhari (see page 130), made with boiled rice, lentils and spices. Kedgeree is best made using smoked haddock though any white or smoked fish will do, and some recipes use salmon. Kedgeree is traditionally served for breakfast but it does make an enjoyable light lunch or supper.

LEFT: Kedgeree

BROWN RICE TART WITH FRESH TOMATO FILLING

Preparation time: 25 minutes + cooling
Total cooking time: 2 hours 25 minutes
Serves 6

☆ ☆

RICE CRUST

1 cup (200 g/6¹/₂ oz) brown rice
¹/₂ cup (60 g/2 oz) grated Cheddar cheese
1 egg, lightly beaten

FRESH TOMATO FILLING

6 Roma (plum) tomatoes, halved
6 garlic cloves, unpeeled
1 tablespoon olive oil
8 lemon thyme sprigs
50 g (1³/₄ oz) goat's cheese, crumbled
3 eggs, lightly beaten
¹/₄ cup (60 ml/2 fl oz) milk

1 To make the rice crust, cook the rice in plenty of boiling water for 35–40 minutes, or until tender, then drain and set aside to cool. Preheat the oven to moderately hot 200°C (400°F/Gas 6). Put the rice, cheese and egg into a bowl and mix together thoroughly. Spread the mixture over the base and sides of a lightly greased 25 cm (10 inch) flan tin or quiche dish and bake for 15 minutes.

2 To make the filling, put the tomatoes, cut-side up, and garlic on a non-stick baking tray, brush lightly with oil and sprinkle with a little freshly ground black pepper. Bake for 30 minutes. Remove from the oven and allow to cool slightly. When cool enough to handle, remove the skins from the garlic.

3 Reduce the oven temperature to moderate 180°C (350°F/Gas 4). Arrange the tomato halves, garlic, lemon thyme and goat's cheese over the rice crust.

4 Put the beaten eggs and milk in a bowl and whisk well. Pour over the tomatoes, then bake the tart for 1 hour, or until set. Cool slightly, then serve.

GOAT'S CHEESE
This cheese can have quite a pungent flavour depending on how long the cheese has been aged. It will soften when cooked but doesn't become really runny. When fresh, it is also known as chèvre, from the French for goat. The cheese is pure white in colour, with none of the yellow pigment associated with cheese from cow's and sheep's milk. Goat's cheese is available from the speciality cheese section of the supermarket, or from good delicatessens.

RIGHT: Brown rice tart with fresh tomato filling

FILO RICE PIE

Preparation time: 45 minutes
Total cooking time: 1 hour 45 minutes
Serves 8

☆ ☆ ☆

2 large red capsicums (peppers)
1 cup (250 ml/8 fl oz) dry white wine
1 litre (32 fl oz) vegetable stock
2 tablespoons oil
1 garlic clove, crushed
1 leek (white part only), sliced
1 fennel bulb, thinly sliced
2 cups (440 g/14 oz) arborio rice
2/3 cup (65 g/2 1/4 oz) freshly grated
   Parmesan cheese
10 sheets filo pastry
1/4 cup (60 ml/2 fl oz) olive oil
500 g (1 lb) English spinach leaves, blanched
250 g (8 oz) fetta cheese, sliced
1 tablespoon sesame seeds

1 Cut the capsicums in half lengthways. Remove the seeds and membrane and then cut into large, flattish pieces. Grill or hold over a gas flame until the skin blackens and blisters. Put on a cutting board, cover with a tea towel and allow to cool. Peel the skin off and cut the flesh into small pieces.
2 Pour the wine and stock into a large saucepan and bring to the boil. Reduce the heat, cover with a lid and keep at a low simmer.
3 Heat the oil and garlic in a large saucepan. Add the leek and fennel and cook over medium heat for 5 minutes, or until lightly browned. Add the rice and stir for 3 minutes, or until well coated.
4 Add 1 cup (250 ml/8 fl oz) of the stock to the rice and stir constantly until the liquid is absorbed. Continue adding stock, 1/2 cup (125 ml/4 fl oz) at a time, stirring constantly until all the stock has been used and the rice is tender. Remove from the heat, stir in the Parmesan and season. Cool slightly. Preheat the oven to moderate 180°C (350°F/Gas 4).
5 Brush each sheet of filo with olive oil and fold in half lengthways. Arrange like overlapping spokes on a wheel, in a 23 cm (9 inch) springform tin, with one side of each pastry sheet hanging over the side of tin.
6 Spoon half the rice mixture over the pastry and top with half the red capsicums, half the spinach and half the fetta cheese. Repeat with the remaining ingredients.
7 Fold the overhanging edge of the pastry over the filling, then brush lightly with oil and sprinkle with sesame seeds. Bake for 50 minutes, or until the pastry is crisp and golden and the pie is heated through.

VEGETABLE STOCK

Heat 1 tablespoon oil in a large saucepan or stockpot. Add 1 chopped onion, 2 chopped leeks, 4 chopped carrots, 2 chopped parsnips and 4 chopped celery stalks (with the leaves) and toss to coat in the oil. Cover and cook for 5 minutes without browning. Add 3 litres (96 fl oz) water and bring to the boil. Skim the surface if required and add 2 bay leaves, 4 unpeeled garlic cloves, 8 black peppercorns and a few parsley stalks. Reduce the heat to low and simmer for an hour. Strain the stock into a fine sieve sitting over a bowl. Gently press the solids to extract all the liquid. Cover and refrigerate. Makes about 2.5 litres (80 fl oz).

ABOVE: Filo rice pie

81

SALMON FILO PIE WITH DILL BUTTER

Preparation time: 25 minutes + cooling
Total cooking time: 50 minutes
Serves 6

☆ ☆

3/4 cup (150 g/5 oz) medium-grain white rice
80 g (2 3/4 oz) butter, melted
8 sheets filo pastry
500 g (1 lb) salmon fillet, skin and bones
    removed, cut into 1.5 cm (5/8 inch) chunks
2 French shallots, finely chopped
1 1/2 tablespoons baby capers, rinsed and
    squeezed dry
2/3 cup (160 g/5 1/2 oz) thick natural yoghurt
1 egg
1 tablespoon grated lemon zest
3 tablespoons chopped dill
1/4 cup (25 g/3/4 oz) dry breadcrumbs
1 tablespoon sesame seeds
2 teaspoons lemon juice

DILL

This herb with feathery leaves has a strong aniseed flavour. It goes well with fish, chicken, creamy sauces, in salads and as a garnish for vegetables. Chop it and add at the end of cooking. It is native to southern Russia and the Mediterranean and is a member of the same family as parsley and coriander (cilantro).

1 Put the rice in a large saucepan and add enough water to cover the rice by 2 cm (3/4 inches).

Bring to the boil over medium heat, then reduce the heat to low, cover and cook for 20 minutes, or until all the water has been absorbed and tunnels appear on the surface of the rice. Set aside to cool.

2 Preheat the oven to moderate 180°C (350°F/Gas 4). Grease a 20 x 30 cm (8 x 12 inch) tin with a little of the melted butter. Cover the sheets of pastry with a damp tea towel. Put the salmon in a large bowl with the shallots, capers, rice, yoghurt, egg, lemon zest and 1 tablespoon of the dill and season with salt and freshly ground black pepper. Mix together.

3 Layer four sheets of pastry in the base of the tin, brushing each one with melted butter and leaving the sides of the pastry overlapping the side of the tin. Spoon the salmon mixture onto the top and pat down well. Fold in the excess pastry. Top with four more sheets of filo, brushing each one with melted butter and sprinkling all but the top layer with a tablespoon of breadcrumbs. Sprinkle the top layer with sesame seeds.

4 Score the top of the pie into diamonds without cutting right through the pastry. Bake for 25–30 minutes on the lowest shelf of the oven until golden brown. Reheat the remaining butter, add the lemon juice and remaining dill and pour some over each portion of pie.

RIGHT: Salmon filo pie with dill butter

Cook the mushroom mixture until the mushrooms are buttery and slightly softened.

First, layer half the rice mixture, then follow with layers of the salmon mixture, mushrooms and a final layer of rice.

Crimp the edges of the pastry closed to ensure the filling doesn't escape during cooking.

COULIBIAC

Preparation time: 20 minutes +
 30 minutes refrigeration
Total cooking time: 45 minutes
Serves 6

☆ ☆

60 g (2 oz) butter

1 onion, finely chopped

200 g (6½ oz) button mushrooms, sliced

2 tablespoons lemon juice

225 g (7 oz) salmon fillet, skin and bones
 removed, cut into 1.5 cm (⅝ inch) chunks

2 hard-boiled eggs, chopped

2 tablespoons chopped dill

2 tablespoons chopped parsley

1 cup (185 g/6 oz) cooked, cold
 long-grain rice

¼ cup (60 ml/2 fl oz) thick
 (double/heavy) cream

370 g (12 oz) block puff pastry

1 egg, lightly beaten

1 Melt half the butter in a frying pan, add the onion and cook over medium heat until soft. Add the mushrooms and cook for 5 minutes. Stir in the lemon juice and transfer to a bowl.
2 Melt the remaining butter in a pan, then add the salmon and cook for 2 minutes. Transfer to a bowl, cool slightly and add the egg, dill and parsley. Season, combine gently and set aside. In a small bowl, combine the rice and cream, and season with salt and pepper.
3 Roll out half the pastry to an 18 x 30 cm (7 x 12 inch) rectangle and put it on the baking tray. Spread half the rice mixture onto the pastry, leaving a 3 cm (1 inch) border all around. Top with the salmon mixture, then the mushrooms and, finally, the remaining rice.
4 Roll out the remaining pastry to 20 x 32 cm (8 x 13 inch) and put it over the filling. Press the pastry edges together, then crimp to seal. Decorate with pastry cut-outs, if you like, then refrigerate for 30 minutes. Preheat the oven to hot 210°C (415°F/Gas 6–7).
5 Brush the pastry top with the beaten egg and bake for 15 minutes. Reduce the heat to moderate 180°C (350°F/Gas 4) and bake for another 15–20 minutes.

ABOVE: Coulibiac

MOZZARELLA
Traditionally made from
buffalo's milk, mozzarella
is now almost exclusively
made from the milk of
cows. Valued in cooking
for its stretchiness when
heated, mozzarella is a
favourite pizza topping, as
well as being used in all
manner of baked dishes.
True mozzarella from the
delicatessen is stored in
brine, smooth, fresh and
white with a mild, slightly
sweet flavour, and is
infinitely superior to the
hard, yellow variety sold
prepackaged in the
supermarket. Shapes vary
from egg to pear to block.

*ABOVE: Two-cheese
rice fritters*

TWO-CHEESE RICE FRITTERS

Preparation time: 30 minutes +
  1 hour 15 minutes refrigeration
Total cooking time: 30 minutes
Serves 6

☆ ☆

3^1/4 cups (810 ml/26 fl oz) chicken stock
1 tablespoon olive oil
20 g (^{3}/4 oz) butter
1 small onion, finely chopped
1^1/4 cups (275 g/9 oz) short-grain rice
^{1}/3 cup (35 g/1^1/4 oz) freshly grated
  Parmesan cheese
30 g (1 oz) fresh mozzarella cheese, cut
  into 1 cm (^{1}/2 inch) cubes
35 g (1^1/4 oz) sun-dried tomatoes, chopped
oil, for deep-frying
70 g (2^1/4 oz) mixed salad leaves, to serve

1 Pour the chicken stock into a small saucepan
and bring to the boil. Reduce the heat a little,
cover the pan with a lid and keep at a low
simmer until needed.

2 Heat the oil and butter in a large saucepan.
Cook the onion until softened but not brown.
Stir in the rice until well coated. Add a quarter
of the stock to the pan. Stir for 5 minutes, or
until all the liquid has been absorbed.
3 Repeat the process until all the stock has been
added and the rice is almost tender, stirring
constantly. Stir in the Parmesan. Remove from
heat. Transfer to a bowl to cool, then refrigerate
for 1 hour.
4 With wet hands, roll 2 tablespoonfuls of rice
mixture into a ball. Make an indentation into
the ball, and press in a cube of mozzarella and a
couple of pieces of sun-dried tomato. Reshape
the ball to completely encase the tomato, then
flatten slightly into a disc. Refrigerate for 15 minutes.
5 Fill a deep-fat fryer or large pot one-third
full of oil and heat to 180°C (350°F), or until
a cube of bread dropped into the oil browns in
15 seconds. Gently lower the rice fritters a few
at a time into the oil and cook for 1–2 minutes,
or until golden brown. Remove with a slotted
spoon, then drain on crumpled paper towels.
To serve, arrange salad leaves on each plate and
place three rice fritters on top.
NOTE: These fritters can be prepared up to
24 hours in advance. Store, uncooked, in the
refrigerator and fry just before serving.

ROAST CAPSICUM RICE TARTS

Preparation time: 45 minutes + cooling
Total cooking time: 1 hour 5 minutes
Serves 6

☆

1 litre (32 fl oz) vegetable stock
20 g (3/4 oz) butter
1/2 cup (95 g/3 oz) wild rice
2/3 cup (140 g/4 1/2 oz) short-grain brown rice
1 egg, lightly beaten with 1 egg yolk
1/2 cup (50 g/1 3/4 oz) freshly grated
    Parmesan cheese
2 green capsicums (peppers)
2 red capsicums (peppers)
2 yellow capsicums (peppers)
150 g (5 oz) Camembert cheese, thinly sliced
2 tablespoons oregano

1 Grease six 10 cm (4 inch) loose-based fluted flan tins. Pour the stock into a saucepan and bring to the boil. Reduce the heat, cover with a lid and keep at a low simmer.

2 Melt the butter in a large saucepan over low heat, then stir in the rice until well coated. Add 1/2 cup (125 ml/4 fl oz) of the hot stock to the rice, stirring well. Increase the heat to medium and add the remaining stock 1 cup (250 ml/8 fl oz) at a time, stirring, until it has been absorbed. This will take about 30 minutes. Remove from the heat and cool. Add the eggs and Parmesan and season to taste.

3 Divide the rice mixture among the prepared flan tins and press it around the base and sides. Allow to cool completely. Preheat the oven to moderately hot 200°C (400°F/Gas 6).

4 Cut the capsicums in half lengthways. Remove the seeds and membrane and then cut into large, flattish pieces. Grill or hold over a gas flame until the skin blackens and blisters. Put on a cutting board, cover with a tea towel and allow to cool. Peel the skin off and cut the flesh into smaller pieces.

5 Put the Camembert slices in the bottom of the lined tins and divide the capsicum evenly among the tarts. Bake for 30 minutes. Sprinkle the oregano leaves over the top and serve hot.

CAMEMBERT
A Frenchwoman named Marie Harel from Camembert is given credit for inventing this cheese. Legend has it that she was entrusted with cheesemaking secrets by a priest she was sheltering during the French Revolution. While this is a lovely story, the truth is that the region around Camembert had been making cheese for several centuries before that time. This famous French cheese is enjoyed both as a table cheese and in cooking. True Camembert, called Camembert de Normandie, is protected by the French *appellation d'origine contrôlée* (AOC), which recognizes and controls the production of foods (among them cheese) to strict standards. However, nowadays 'Camembert' is manufactured throughout the world.

LEFT: Roast capsicum rice tarts

ROAST TURKEY WITH RICE AND CHESTNUT STUFFING

Preparation time: 30 minutes +
   20 minutes soaking
Total cooking time: 3 hours 30 minutes
Serves 6–8

☆ ☆

STUFFING

12 prunes, pitted

180 g (6 oz) whole fresh chestnuts

40 g (1¼ oz) butter

1 red onion, finely chopped

2 garlic cloves, crushed

60 g (2 oz) pancetta (including any fat),
   finely chopped

100 g (3½ oz) wild rice blend

¼ cup (60 ml/2 fl oz) chicken stock

3 dried juniper berries, lightly crushed

2 teaspoons finely chopped rosemary

3 teaspoons finely chopped thyme

3 kg (6 lb) turkey

1 large red onion, cut into 4–5 slices

30 g (1 oz) butter, softened

1½ cups (375 ml/12 fl oz) dry white wine

1 carrot, quartered

1 celery stalk, quartered

1 large rosemary sprig

2 teaspoons finely chopped thyme

1 cup (250 ml/8 fl oz) chicken stock

2 tablespoons plain (all-purpose) flour

1 Preheat the oven to warm 170°C (325°F/ Gas 3). Soak the prunes in hot water for 20 minutes. Meanwhile, to prepare the chestnuts, make a small cut in the skin on the flat side, put under a hot grill (broiler) and cook on both sides until well browned. Put the hot chestnuts in a bowl lined with a damp tea towel and cover with the towel. Leave until cool enough to handle, then peel. Do not allow the chestnuts to cool completely before peeling, as they will become harder to peel as they cool. Coarsely chop the prunes and chestnuts and set aside.

2 To make the stuffing, melt the butter in a large saucepan and add the onion, garlic and pancetta. Cook over low heat for 5–6 minutes, or until the onion is softened but not brown. Add the rice, stock, juniper berries, prunes and chestnuts, stir well, then pour in 1½ cups (375 ml/12 fl oz) water. Bring to the boil and cook, covered, stirring once or twice, for 20–25 minutes, or until the rice is tender and all the liquid has been absorbed. Remove from the heat, stir in the rosemary and thyme, then season.

3 Fill the turkey cavity with the stuffing. Cross the turkey legs and tie them together, then tuck the wings underneath the body. Arrange the onion slices in the centre of a large roasting tin, then sit the turkey on top, breast-side up. Season well and dot with butter. Pour 1 cup (250 ml/ 8 fl oz) of the wine into the tin and scatter the carrot, celery, rosemary and 1 teaspoon of the thyme around the turkey.

4 Roast for 2–2½ hours, or until cooked through and the juices run clear, basting every 30 minutes. After 1 hour, pour half the chicken stock into the tin. Once the skin becomes golden brown, cover with buttered foil.

5 When cooked, transfer the turkey to a carving plate, cover with foil and leave to rest in a warm spot. Meanwhile, pour the juices into a small saucepan and reduce for 8–10 minutes. Stir in the flour, then add a little of the stock at a time, stirring to form a paste. Slowly add the rest of

BELOW: Roast turkey with rice and chestnut stuffing

Put the turkey breast-side down and cut the meat along the contours of the bone.

Scrape the flesh from the wing knuckle and carefully cut around the joint to remove the bone.

Spread the stuffing evenly along the centre of the turkey meat.

Fold the turkey breast inwards and sew the turkey together with a trussing needle and kitchen string.

the stock and wine, stirring so that no lumps form. Stir in the remaining thyme. Bring to the boil and continue to simmer for 6–8 minutes, or until reduced by one-third, then season to taste. Transfer to a gravy boat. Carve the turkey and serve with the stuffing and gravy.

TURKEY BUFFE WITH RICE AND FRUIT STUFFING

Preparation time: 1 hour
Total cooking time: 2 hours 10 minutes
Serves 6–8

 ☆☆☆

2.8 kg (5 lb 10 oz) turkey buffe

STUFFING

1¹/₂ cups (280 g/9 oz) cooked, cold long-grain rice
¹/₄ cup (40 g/1¹/₄ oz) pine nuts, toasted
180 g (6 oz) dried apricots, chopped
250 g (8 oz) chopped pitted prunes
4 spring onions (scallions), sliced
1 tablespoon finely grated orange zest
¹/₃ cup (80 ml/2³/₄ fl oz) orange juice
1 egg, lightly beaten

GLAZE

¹/₂ cup (125 ml/4 fl oz) orange juice
15 g (¹/₂ oz) butter
2 teaspoons soft brown sugar

1 Bone the turkey breast and remove the bone from the wings.
2 To make the stuffing, combine the rice, pine nuts, apricots, prunes, spring onion, orange zest, orange juice, ¹/₂ teaspoon salt and some white pepper. Mix well and stir in the egg.
3 Lay the turkey flat and spread the stuffing along the centre. Fold the breast inwards and sew the turkey together using a trussing needle and kitchen string. Tuck in the skin at the neck and press the wings in towards the breast. Sew or tie securely with string, or secure well with skewers. Preheat the oven to moderate 180°C (350°F/Gas 4).
4 To make the glaze, stir the orange juice, butter and sugar together in a small pan. Bring to the boil and stir until the sugar dissolves. Allow to cool.
5 Put the turkey on a rack in an ovenproof dish. Bake for 1³/₄–2 hours, basting with the glaze. (If the turkey is overbrowning, loosely cover it with foil.) When cooked, remove from the oven, cover and set aside for 20 minutes before removing the string or skewers. Slice and serve with the remaining glaze.

ABOVE: Turkey buffe with rice and fruit stuffing

HOW TO MAKE THE PERFECT RICE PUDDING

Rice pudding is proof that some of the best things in life are also the simplest.

Wherever there is rice, there is rice pudding: from the schoolrooms of England to the breakfast tables of Asia.

Europe, in particular has a diverse range of recipes based on rice pudding. These are often set in elaborate moulds or glazed with toffee; for example, the decadent French rice gateau (page 92). In countries with a strong Spanish influence, rice pudding goes by the name Arroz con leche (page 71) and is flavoured with cinnamon and citrus zest. In parts of the Middle East the local rice pudding, Zerde (page 68), is scented with rose water or orange blossom water, tinted yellow with saffron threads and garnished with jewel-like pomegranate seeds. In Thailand there is a sweet, sticky version using black or jasmine rice and coconut milk; usually accompanied by tropical fruits and eaten for breakfast or a filling snack (pages 209 and 211). And India has its own highly spiced rice pudding, Kheer, which on special occasions is decorated with gold or silver leaf (pages 156–157).

FLAVOURS

Rice pudding is an excellent example of what can be achieved by blending together a few staple and relatively inexpensive ingredients—rice, milk, cream, sugar and eggs and then adding a little flavour. The flavours can be as simple as a hint of vanilla, nutmeg or cinnamon or as decadent as rich, dark chocolate or exotic spices such as cardamom and saffron.

TEXTURE

Rice pudding should be creamy and tender, but not mushy. The texture is affected by several variables: the cooking method, the amount of eggs and the type of rice.

Cooking rice pudding on the stove results in a softer and creamier pudding than those baked in the oven. The constant stirring involved with the stove top method releases a lot of starch into the pudding, providing extra creaminess. For this reason it is sometimes referred to as creamed rice.

The baked version, however, develops a lovely golden crust on top and is generally firm enough to be able to cut through with a spoon.

The amount of eggs used can also affect the texture; though extra eggs add richness to the custard, they also make the pudding firmer.

WHICH RICE?

The texture and creaminess will also depend on the type of rice used—generally the rounder and fatter the grain the higher the starch content and the more liquid the grain will absorb; both these factors help to achieve a more creamy, tender result. Most rice puddings use short or medium-grain rice, though some will use arborio rice because it releases more starch than other varieties. And local areas will use their most common rice. For example, Indian rice puddings will use basmati rice and Thai rice puddings will use either jasmine rice or black rice.

WARM OR COLD?

Rice pudding can be eaten hot or cold but it will thicken on standing, even more on refrigeration; if this happens, simply add a little more milk or cream. In warmer climates, rice pudding is preferred chilled.

TOOLS

For a stove top pudding, it is essential to use a large heavy-based saucepan to promote even heat distribution and prevent the rice from sticking to the bottom of the pan. The only other essential piece of equipment is a wooden spoon for stirring.

A baked version requires a suitably sized ceramic or glass baking dish. Metal baking dishes get too hot and will end up overheating your ingredients and may cause any eggs in the mixture to toughen. Also, since this dish is often served on the table, try to pick an attractive dish.

Some rice puddings will also need a larger baking dish or roasting tin in which to sit the ceramic baking dish.

TECHNIQUE

Rice pudding is incredibly simple to prepare. It can be either cooked on the stove or baked in the oven; the aim of both methods is to cook the rice slowly to get a creamy pudding.

Stove top version

The most basic version is to combine all the ingredients in large heavy-based saucepan and stir regularly over low heat for about 40–50 minutes, or until the rice is tender but not mushy and the surrounding sauce is very creamy and thickened. The time will vary depending on what type of rice you use.

Next, stir in any egg yolks in the recipe (they add richness) and heat for a minute or so to gently cook through.

Generally, some cream is stirred into the pudding once it is cooked, to add a little richness. Other ingredients may also be added, depending on personal preference. If refrigerating, lay a piece of plastic wrap on the surface of the rice so that a skin does not form.

Baked pudding

Preheat your oven. Combine all the ingredients and pour into a suitably sized ceramic or glass baking dish (the recipe will guide you).

Either bake the dish as is, or cook in a water bath: this means, putting the ceramic dish inside a large tin, half filling the tin with water and then baking—this generally takes longer. Bake until the top is a deep golden colour and a knife inserted comes out clean.

QUICK TIP

As rice tends to take longer to cook in milk than in water, some recipes boil or soak the rice in boiling water before cooking it in the milk mixture. The result is often less creamy than the traditional method.

STEPS TO MAKING THE PERFECT RICE PUDDING

Stove-top rice pudding

STEP ONE: Rinse the rice in a colander until the water runs clear.
STEP TWO: Bring to the boil while stirring, reduce the heat to the lowest setting and cook for about 45 minutes, stirring frequently, until the rice is thick and creamy.
STEP THREE: Stir in the cream. Serve warm with stewed fruit.

Baked rice pudding

STEP ONE: In a bowl, mix together the rice, milk, sugar, cream and vanilla extract, and pour into the greased dish.
STEP TWO: Dust the surface with the grated nutmeg and float the bay leaf on top.
STEP THREE: Bake the rice pudding until the rice has absorbed most of the milk, the texture is creamy and a brown skin has formed on top. Serve hot.

LEFTOVERS

In the unlikely event that you have leftovers, try reheating gently for a breakfast treat instead of porridge—the texture will have altered slightly but will have developed a slightly more intense flavour. Chilled rice pudding also makes great fritters—just mould the mixture into small balls or croquettes, crumb and deep- or shallow-fry and sprinkle with icing sugar or serve with a fruit-based sauce or drizzle with honey.

DANISH CREAMED RICE
This is traditionally served in Denmark for dessert on Christmas Eve. The person who gets the whole almond receives a small gift or token from the host, often a marzipan pig. Superstition surrounds the almond: some believe whoever finds the almond will be the next person to be married or have a baby, others that the finder will have good luck for the following year.

ABOVE: Danish creamed rice with dark cherry sauce

DANISH CREAMED RICE WITH DARK CHERRY SAUCE

Preparation time: 15 minutes + cooling
Total cooking time: 50 minutes
Serves 6

☆

1 cup (220 g/7 oz) short-grain rice
1 litre (32 fl oz) milk
1 tablespoon vanilla sugar (see Note)
2 tablespoons caster (superfine) sugar
1¼ cups (310 ml/10 fl oz) cream
2 tablespoons whole blanched almonds

DARK CHERRY SAUCE
3 teaspoons cornflour (cornstarch)
425 g (14 oz) tin stoneless black cherries
   in syrup

1 Put the rice and milk in a saucepan, cover and cook over low heat for 40–45 minutes, or until the rice is cooked and the mixture is thick and creamy. Stir occasionally to prevent the rice forming lumps and sticking to the pan. Remove from the heat and stir in both the sugars. Spoon into a large bowl, cover the top of the rice with plastic wrap and allow to cool at room temperature, stirring occasionally.
2 When the rice is cool, stir to separate the grains. Beat the cream in a bowl with electric beaters until soft peaks form. Fold into the creamed rice. Reserve one whole almond and roughly chop the rest. Fold into the creamy rice and stir in the whole almond. Refrigerate the rice while preparing the sauce.
3 To make the sauce, blend the cornflour with 2 tablespoons water in a small bowl. Pour the cherries and their juice into a small saucepan, add the cornflour mixture and stir over medium heat until the mixture boils and thickens. Remove from the heat. Spoon the rice into serving bowls and top with the hot sauce.
NOTE: Vanilla sugar is simply normal sugar that has been infused with a vanilla bean or has had a vanilla bean chopped up into it. If you don't have any, add ¼ teaspoon natural vanilla extract.

INDIVIDUAL BAKED RICE PUDDINGS

Preparation time: 10 minutes
Total cooking time: 1 hour
Serves 4–6

¹/4 cup (55 g/2 oz) short- or
   medium-grain rice
1²/3 cups (410 ml/13 fl oz) milk
1¹/2 tablespoons caster (superfine) sugar
³/4 cup (185 ml/6 fl oz) cream, plus extra,
   to serve
¹/4 teaspoon natural vanilla extract
¹/4 teaspoon freshly grated nutmeg

1 Preheat the oven to slow 150°C (300°F/Gas 2) and grease four 1 cup (250 ml/8 fl oz) ramekins or six smaller ones. In a bowl, mix together the rice, milk, sugar, cream and vanilla extract, and pour into the greased dishes. Dust the surface of each one with grated nutmeg.
2 Bake the rice puddings for about 1 hour, or until the rice has absorbed most of the milk, the texture is creamy and a brown skin has formed on top. Serve hot with fresh cream.

SPICED CREAMED RICE WITH APRICOTS

Preparation time: 10 minutes +
   30 minutes soaking
Total cooking time: 30 minutes
Serves 4

24 dried apricots
700 ml (23 fl oz) skim milk
¹/2 cup (110 g/3¹/2 oz) arborio rice
1 vanilla bean, split lengthways
¹/4 teaspoon freshly grated nutmeg
pinch of ground cardamom
2 teaspoons caster (superfine) sugar
200 g (6¹/2 oz) sugar
2 cinnamon sticks
2 teaspoons orange zest
¹/4 cup (60 ml/2 fl oz) orange juice

1 Soak the apricots in boiling water for 30 minutes.

2 Pour the milk into a saucepan, add the rice, vanilla, nutmeg and cardamom, and bring to the boil. Reduce the heat and simmer gently, stirring frequently, for 25 minutes, or until the rice is soft and creamy, and has absorbed almost all of the milk. Remove the pan from the heat.
3 Remove the vanilla bean, scrape out the seeds and mix them back into the rice. Stir in the caster sugar.
4 Meanwhile, put the sugar, cinnamon sticks, orange zest and orange juice in a saucepan with 2¹/2 cups (625 ml /20 fl oz) water. Bring to the boil, then reduce the heat and simmer for 10 minutes. Drain the apricots and add to the pan. Return to the boil, then reduce the heat to low and simmer for 5 minutes, or until soft. Remove the apricots with a slotted spoon. Lift out the cinnamon stick. Return the sauce to the boil and boil until reduced by half. Remove from the heat, cool slightly and pour over the apricots. Serve the apricots with the rice.

ABOVE: *Individual baked rice puddings*

RICE GATEAU

As the sugar begins to dissolve, swirl the pan gently so the sugar melts evenly.

Before the caramel starts to harden, pour it into the ovenproof dish and tilt and swirl the dish so the base and side are covered.

Pour the rice mixture into the caramel-lined dish and smooth the top.

RICE GATEAU

Preparation time: 20 minutes + soaking +
  20 minutes resting + cooling
Total cooking time: 1 hour 25 minutes
Serves 10

1 cup (240 g/7$^{1}/_2$ oz) finely chopped
  glacé apricots
2 tablespoons very finely chopped glacé ginger
2 tablespoons cognac or amaretto
1 cup (250 g/8 oz) arborio rice
2$^{1}/_2$ cups (625 ml/20 fl oz) milk
300 ml (9$^{1}/_2$ fl oz) cream
1 teaspoon finely grated orange zest
1 vanilla bean, split
1$^{3}/_4$ cups (435 g/14 oz) caster (superfine) sugar
300 g (10 oz) crème fraîche
4 egg yolks
$^{1}/_4$ cup (25 g/$^{3}/_4$ oz) ground almonds,
  lightly toasted

1 Combine the glacé fruit with the cognac and set aside to soak.
2 Put the rice, milk, cream, orange zest and vanilla bean in a saucepan over medium heat and mix together. Stir occasionally until the mixture comes to the boil, then reduce the heat a little and cook, stirring frequently, for 30 minutes, or until the rice is tender and most of the liquid has been absorbed—it should look like a creamy rice pudding or risotto. Set aside to cool to room temperature, then discard the vanilla bean. Preheat the oven to warm 170°C (325°F/Gas 3).
3 While the rice is cooling, put 1 cup (250 g/ 8 oz) of the sugar in a small heavy-based saucepan over low heat. As the sugar begins to dissolve, swirl the pan gently to ensure the sugar melts evenly. Increase the heat to medium and boil, without stirring, until the caramel turns dark golden, being careful that the sugar doesn't burn. Working quickly, pour the caramel into the base of a 2 litre (64 fl oz) round ovenproof dish and tilt and swirl the dish until the entire base and side are covered; be very careful not to burn yourself on the hot caramel.
4 Add the crème fraîche, egg yolks, ground almonds, soaked glacé fruit and the remaining sugar to the cooled rice and mix well. Pour the rice mixture into the caramel-lined dish and smooth the top. Put the dish in a roasting tin and pour in enough warm water to come halfway up the side of the dish. Cook for 45 minutes, or until quite firm and lightly golden on top.
5 Cool for about 20 minutes before turning out onto a large serving plate. Cool completely before cutting. Serve with some lightly whipped cream and orange segments, if desired.

RIGHT: Rice gateau

NURSERY RICE PUDDING

Preparation time: 5 minutes +
   10 minutes standing
Total cooking time: 45 minutes
Serves 4–6

^{2}/$_3$ cup (140 g/4^1/$_2$ oz) arborio or
   short-grain rice
1 litre (32 fl oz) milk
^{1}/$_3$ cup (80 g/2^3/$_4$ oz) caster (superfine) sugar
1 teaspoon natural vanilla extract
^{1}/$_2$ cup (125 ml/4 fl oz) cream

1 Rinse the rice in a colander until the water runs clear. Drain well and place in a heavy-based pan with the milk, sugar and vanilla.
2 Bring to the boil while stirring, then reduce the heat to the lowest setting and cook for about 45 minutes, stirring frequently, until the rice is thick and creamy.
3 Remove the pan from the heat and leave to stand for 10 minutes. Stir in the cream. Serve warm with stewed fruit, if desired.
VARIATIONS: Add a cinnamon stick and a strip of lemon zest to the rice in place of vanilla extract. Or add a small sprig of washed lavender to the rice while cooking.

RICE PUDDING WITH STRAWBERRIES AND BLUEBERRIES

Preparation time: 10 minutes
Total cooking time: 25 minutes
Serves 4–6

1 cup (220 g/7 oz) short-grain white rice
^{1}/$_2$ cup (125 g/4 oz) thick natural yoghurt
300 ml (9^1/$_2$ fl oz) cream
^{1}/$_3$ cup (90 g/3 oz) caster (superfine) sugar
1 teaspoon natural vanilla extract
250 g (8 oz) strawberries, hulled and halved
300 g (10 oz) fresh or frozen blueberries
1 tablespoon caster (superfine) sugar, extra

1 Put the rice, ^{1}/$_2$ teaspoon salt and 2^1/$_2$ cups (625 ml/20 fl oz) water in a saucepan and bring to the boil over high heat, stirring once. Reduce the heat and simmer, covered, for 20 minutes, or until very soft and tender but still moist. Remove from the heat and leave for 5 minutes.
2 Meanwhile, put the yoghurt, cream, sugar and vanilla extract in a bowl and whisk together. Leave at room temperature, stirring occasionally to dissolve the sugar.
3 Toss the strawberries, blueberries and extra sugar together in a bowl. Cover and refrigerate until ready to serve.
4 Stir the hot rice into the cream mixture. Add more milk or cream if the mixture is too thick. Serve topped with the combined strawberries and blueberries.
NOTE: If you need to refrigerate the rice pudding it will thicken. Use cream or milk to thin it to the desired consistency.

ABOVE: Nursery rice pudding

93

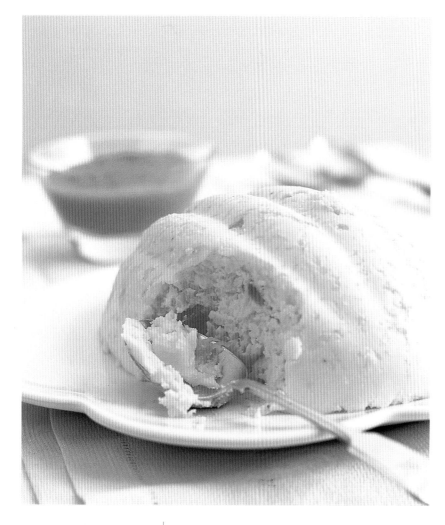

EMPRESS RICE

Preparation time: 45 minutes + refrigeration
Total cooking time: 1 hour
Serves 6–8

2/3 cup (140 g/4 1/2 oz) short-grain rice
2 cups (500 ml/16 fl oz) milk
1/2 teaspoon natural vanilla extract
1/4 cup (60 g/2 oz) caster (superfine) sugar
30 g (1 oz) unsalted butter
1/2 cup (125 g/4 oz) chopped mixed glacé fruit
2 tablespoons Kirsch (see Note)

CUSTARD
1 tablespoon gelatine
4 egg yolks
1/4 cup (60 g/2 oz) caster (superfine) sugar
1 teaspoon cornflour (cornstarch)
1 cup (250 ml/8 fl oz) milk
300 ml (9 1/2 fl oz) cream

ABOVE: Empress rice

APRICOT SAUCE
2/3 cup (125 g/4 oz) dried apricots
2 tablespoons Kirsch
1–2 tablespoons caster (superfine) sugar

1 Lightly grease a 2 litre (64 fl oz) decorative mould with oil. Put the rice in a saucepan with 2 cups (500 ml/16 fl oz) cold water. Bring slowly to the boil and cook for 2 minutes, then drain. Return the rice to the pan with the milk and vanilla extract. Cook, stirring frequently, over low heat for 25 minutes, or until the rice is tender and the milk has been absorbed. Stir in the sugar and butter while hot. Cover and cool completely. Put the glacé fruit in a bowl, add the Kirsch and soak.

2 To make the custard, put 2 tablespoons water in a small heatproof bowl, sprinkle with gelatine and leave over hot water until dissolved. Put the egg yolks, caster sugar and cornflour in a large bowl and whisk for 3 minutes, or until the mixture is pale and thickened. In a pan, heat the milk to scalding point. Pour the milk, whisking continuously, into the egg mixture, then return to the pan. Whisk over low heat until thickened to a thin custard that coats the back of a spoon (take care not to overheat and curdle). Stir in the dissolved gelatine. Cover and cool a little.

3 Combine the cooled rice and cooled custard. Beat the cream until firm peaks form. Gently fold the glacé fruit and cream into the rice custard. Spoon into the mould and flatten the surface. Cover and refrigerate for several hours until firm.

4 While the rice pudding is cooling, make the apricot sauce. Put the apricots in a small saucepan and cover with water. Leave to soak for 30 minutes, then cook gently for 10 minutes, or until softened. Drain, reserving the liquid. Cool, then purée the apricots in a food processor, adding enough cooking liquid to reach sauce consistency. Add Kirsch and sugar to taste.

5 Unmould the rice pudding—the easiest way to do this is to briefly dip the mould in hot water, wipe it dry and then invert onto a serving plate. Serve with some of the apricot sauce.

NOTE: Kirsch is a clear brandy distilled from fermented black cherries. The brandy has a bitter almond flavour and is often used in desserts.

CHOCOLATE RICE PUDDING

Preparation time: 10 minutes
Total cooking time: 30 minutes
Serves 6

1 cup (220 g/7 oz) medium-grain rice

3 cups (750 ml/24 fl oz) milk

125 g (4 oz) good-quality dark chocolate,
   chopped into small pieces

2–3 tablespoons Kahlúa

1–2 tablespoons caster (superfine) sugar

thick cream, to serve

1 Place the rice in a saucepan, add 2 cups (500 ml/16 fl oz) boiling water and stir until well combined. Boil, stirring occasionally, for 5 minutes, or until the water is nearly absorbed. Add the milk and bring to the boil. Reduce the heat and simmer, covered, over very low heat for 20 minutes, or until the rice is cooked and the pudding is thick and creamy. Do not let the pudding bubble over.
2 Add the chocolate and Kahlúa, and stir until the chocolate is melted and well combined. Add 1–2 tablespoons caster sugar, to taste. Spoon into six bowls and serve with thick cream.

LOW-FAT RICE POTS

Preparation time: 15 minutes
Total cooking time: 1 hour 10 minutes
Serves 4

1/2 cup (110 g/3 1/2 oz) short-grain rice

1 litre (32 fl oz) skim milk

1/4 cup (60 g/2 oz) caster (superfine) sugar

1 teaspoon grated orange zest

1 teaspoon grated lemon zest

1 teaspoon natural vanilla extract

20 g (3/4 oz) hazelnuts

1 tablespoon soft brown sugar

1 Wash the rice in a sieve under cold water until the water runs clear, then drain thoroughly. Put the milk and sugar in a saucepan and stir over low heat until the sugar has dissolved. Add the rice and citrus zest and stir briefly. Bring to the boil, then reduce the heat to as low as possible.

Cook for 1 hour, stirring occasionally, until thick and creamy and the rice is tender. Stir in the vanilla extract. Preheat the oven to moderate 180°C (350°F/Gas 4).
2 Spread the hazelnuts on a baking tray and toast in the oven for about 5 minutes. Rub the hot nuts in a tea towel to remove as much of the skin as possible. Cool and grind in a food processor to a coarse texture, not too fine. Preheat a grill (broiler) to very hot.
3 Spoon the rice into four heatproof 3/4 cup (185 ml/6 fl oz) ramekins. Combine the sugar and ground hazelnuts and sprinkle over the rice. Grill (broil) briefly until the sugar melts and the nuts are lightly browned. Serve immediately.

BELOW: Low-fat rice pots

BAKED RICE PUDDING

Preparation time: 10 minutes
Total cooking time: 2 hours
Serves 4

1/4 cup (55 g/2 oz) short- or medium-grain rice

1 2/3 cups (410 ml/13 fl oz) milk

1 1/2 tablespoons caster (superfine) sugar

1/4 cup (185 ml/6 fl oz) cream

1/4 teaspoon natural vanilla extract

1/4 teaspoon freshly grated nutmeg

1 bay leaf

BELOW: Baked rice pudding

1 Preheat the oven to slow 150°C (300°F/Gas 2) and grease a 1 litre (32 fl oz) ovenproof dish. In a bowl, mix together the rice, milk, caster sugar, cream and vanilla extract, and pour into the dish.
2 Dust the surface with the grated nutmeg and float the bay leaf on top.
3 Put the ovenproof dish into a larger baking dish or tin and pour in enough hot water to come halfway up the sides of the dish containing the pudding. Bake for about 2 hours or until the top is a deep golden colour and a knife inserted comes out clean. Serve hot.

CARAMEL RICE PUDDING

Preparation time: 15 minutes
Total cooking time: 1 hour 15 minutes
Serves 4

1/2 cup (110 g/3 1/2 oz) short- or
  medium-grain rice

2 eggs

2 tablespoons soft brown sugar

1 1/2 cups (375 ml/12 fl oz) milk

2 tablespoons caramel topping

1/2 cup (125 ml/4 fl oz) cream

1/2 teaspoon freshly grated nutmeg plus
  a little extra, to serve

1 Preheat the oven to warm 160°C (315°F/Gas 2–3). Grease a 1.5 litre (48 fl oz) ovenproof ceramic dish. Cook the rice in a saucepan of boiling water for 12 minutes, or until just tender. Drain and then allow the rice to cool slightly.
2 Put the eggs, sugar, milk, caramel topping and cream in a large bowl and whisk together well. Fold in the cooked rice. Pour the rice mixture into the prepared dish and sprinkle the surface with the nutmeg. Place the ceramic dish in a deep baking tin and pour in enough boiling water to come halfway up the sides.
3 Bake for 30 minutes, then stir with a fork to distribute the rice evenly. Cook for a further 30 minutes, or until the custard is just set. Serve hot or warm. Sprinkle with the extra ground nutmeg just before serving.

WHITE CHRISTMAS

Preparation time: 15 minutes +
  30 minutes refrigeration
Total cooking time: 5 minutes
Makes 24 pieces

1½ cups (45 g/1½ oz) puffed rice cereal

1 cup (100 g/3½ oz) milk powder

1 cup (125 g/4 oz) icing (confectioners') sugar

1 cup (90 g/3 oz) desiccated coconut

²/3 cup (160 g/5½ oz) chopped red and green
  glacé cherries

¹/3 cup (55 g/2 oz) sultanas

250 g (8 oz) copha (white vegetable shortening)

1 Line a shallow 18 x 28 cm (7 x 11 inch) tin with foil. Put the puffed rice, milk powder, icing sugar, coconut, glacé cherries and sultanas in a large bowl and stir. Make a well in the centre.
2 Melt the shortening over low heat, cool slightly, then add to the well in the puffed rice mixture. Stir with a wooden spoon until all the ingredients are moistened.
3 Spoon the mixture into the prepared tin and smooth down the surface. Refrigerate for 30 minutes, or until completely set. Remove from the tin, and peel away and discard the foil. Cut into 24 small triangles to serve.

SCOTTISH SHORTBREAD

Preparation time: 25 minutes
  + 20 minutes refrigeration
Total cooking time: 35 minutes
Makes two large rounds

250 g (8 oz) unsalted butter, softened

¹/2 cup (125 g/4 oz) caster (superfine) sugar

2 cups (250 g/8 oz) plain (all-purpose) flour

²/3 cup (115 g/4 oz) rice flour

1 teaspoon sugar, to decorate

1 Preheat the oven to warm 160°C (315°F/ Gas 2–3). Line two baking trays with baking paper. Mark a 20 cm (8 inch) circle on the paper on each tray and turn the paper over.
2 Cream the butter and sugar in a small bowl with electric beaters until light and fluffy. Add the sifted flours and a pinch of salt and mix with a knife, using a cutting action, to form a soft dough. Gather together and divide into two portions. Refrigerate in plastic wrap for 20 minutes.
3 Place one dough portion on each tray and press into a round, using the drawn circle as a guide. Pinch and flute the edges decoratively and prick the surface with a fork. Use a sharp knife to mark each circle into twelve segments. Sprinkle with sugar and bake for 30–35 minutes, until firm and pale golden. Cool on the trays. When cold, store in an airtight container.
NOTE: Usually, no liquid is used, but if the mixture is very crumbly, moisten with not more than 1 tablespoon of milk or cream.

ABOVE: White Christmas

97

THE AMERICAS

The Americas are home to some exciting rice recipes—colourful jambalayas and earthy gumbos from the deep south of America, dark, chocolaty moles and spicy fried rice from Mexico and many warming, soupy stews featuring seafood, rice and smoky spices from the Caribbean and South America. Then, of course, there is wild rice. Though technically not a rice, but an aquatic grain native to North America, it has a rich, nutty flavour that mixes well with other rices, and is particularly good in stuffings and salads.

1/4 teaspoon cayenne pepper

500 g (1 lb) chicken thigh fillets,
   cut into 4 pieces

2 tablespoons oil

250 g (8 oz) chorizo, cut into 1 cm
   (1/2 inch) slices

1 large onion, chopped

2 celery stalks, sliced

1 large green capsicum (pepper), cut
   into rough 2 cm (3/4 inch) pieces

4 garlic cloves, crushed

2 teaspoons thyme

400 g (13 oz) tin chopped tomatoes

2 bay leaves

1/4 teaspoon Tabasco sauce

1 cup (200 g/6 1/2 oz) long-grain white rice

3 1/2 cups (875 ml/28 fl oz) hot chicken stock

450 g (14 oz) raw prawns (shrimp), peeled
   and deveined, tails intact (optional)

5 spring onions (scallions), thinly sliced

3 tablespoons chopped parsley

1 Put the paprika, basil, thyme, garlic powder, onion powder, white pepper, oregano, cayenne, 3/4 teaspoon salt and 1/2 teaspoon freshly ground black pepper in a bowl. Add the chicken thigh pieces and mix to coat the chicken well.

2 Heat the oil in a wide, heavy-based frying pan over medium heat and cook the chorizo for 5–6 minutes, or until lightly browned. Remove with a slotted spoon, leaving as much oil in the pan as possible. Add the chicken to the pan in batches and cook over medium heat for 6–8 minutes, or until lightly browned, adding a little more oil if necessary. Remove from the pan with a slotted spoon, leaving as much fat in the pan as possible.

3 Add the onion, celery, capsicum, garlic and thyme to the pan and cook over medium heat for 6–8 minutes, stirring often with a wooden spoon to lift any sediment from the base of the pan. When the vegetables begin to brown, add the tomato, bay leaves and Tabasco and simmer for 2–3 minutes.

4 Return the chorizo and chicken to the pan. Add the rice, stir briefly, then pour in the stock. Don't stir at this point. Reduce the heat and simmer, uncovered, for 25–30 minutes, or until all the liquid has been absorbed and the rice is tender. Remove from the heat and add the prawns, if using them. Cover and leave for 10 minutes, then fluff the rice with a fork, season well and stir in the spring onion and parsley.

CHICKEN JAMBALAYA

Preparation time: 30 minutes
   + 10 minutes standing
Total cooking time: 1 hour 5 minutes
Serves 4–6

1 teaspoon paprika

3/4 teaspoon dried basil

3/4 teaspoon dried thyme

3/4 teaspoon garlic powder

3/4 teaspoon onion powder

1/2 teaspoon ground white pepper

1/2 teaspoon dried oregano

ABOVE: Chicken jambalaya

CLASSIC JAMBALAYA

Preparation time: 30 minutes
Total cooking time: 55 minutes
Serves 4–6

2 tablespoons olive oil

1 large red onion, finely chopped

1 garlic clove, crushed

2 back bacon rashers, finely chopped

1¹/₂ cups (300 g/10 oz) long-grain white rice

1 red capsicum (pepper), diced

150 g (5 oz) ham, chopped

400 g (13 oz) tin chopped tomatoes

400 g (13 oz) tomato passata

1 teaspoon Worcestershire sauce

dash of Tabasco sauce

¹/₂ teaspoon dried thyme

¹/₂ cup (30 g/1 oz) chopped parsley

150 g (5 oz) cooked, peeled, small prawns (shrimp)

4 spring onions (scallions), thinly sliced

1 Heat the oil in a large saucepan over medium heat. Add the onion, garlic and bacon and cook, stirring, for 5 minutes, or until the onion is softened but not browned. Stir in the rice and cook for a further 5 minutes, or until lightly golden.

2 Add the capsicum, ham, chopped tomatoes, tomato passata, Worcestershire and Tabasco sauces and thyme and stir until well combined. Bring the mixture to the boil, then reduce the heat to low. Cook, covered, for 30–40 minutes, or until the rice is tender.

3 Stir in the parsley and prawns and season with salt and freshly ground black pepper. Sprinkle with the spring onion, then serve.

CAJUN SPICE MIX

Combine 1 tablespoon garlic powder, 1 tablespoon onion powder, 2 teaspoons white pepper, 2 teaspoons freshly ground black pepper, 1¹/₂ teaspoons cayenne pepper, 2 teaspoons dried thyme and ¹/₂ teaspoon dried oregano in a small bowl. Store in a spice jar for several months.

JAMBALAYA
Pronounced jahm-buh-lie-uh, jambalaya is a New Orleans dish that has been adopted by the Cajuns (descendants of French settlers of 17th century Nova Scotia who were driven off their land; many of them found a home in Louisiana). Jambalaya probably originated during the time when the Spanish ruled Louisiana (1766–1800), and the name is thought to be an amalgamation of *jamón* (the Spanish word for ham, a prime ingredient in early jambalayas) and paella. Probably the most versatile dish of southern America, jambalaya may be made with beef, pork, chicken, duck, shrimp, oysters, crayfish, sausage or any combination of the above. Most jambalayas start with sautéeing capsicum (pepper), celery and onions, then cooking any meat. A broth, or water, tomatoes and seasonings with uncooked rice is then added and the jambalaya is left to simmer until the rice is done. Prawns (shrimp) or other foods which need little cooking are added towards the end of the cooking time.

LEFT: Classic jambalaya

MEXICAN RICE

Preparation time: 10 minutes
Total cooking time: 30 minutes
Serves 4

1¹/₂ tablespoons oil
1¹/₂ cups (300 g/10 oz) long-grain rice
1 small onion, chopped
2 garlic cloves, crushed
¹/₂ teaspoon ground cumin
¹/₂ teaspoon paprika
2 large ripe tomatoes, peeled, seeded
    and chopped
100 g (3¹/₂ oz) sliced mild salami, cut
    into strips
1 small carrot, diced
2 cups (500 ml/16 fl oz) hot chicken stock
¹/₂ cup (80 g/2³/₄ oz) frozen peas
2 tablespoons chopped coriander
    (cilantro) leaves

1 Heat the oil in a large saucepan and gently cook the rice, onion and garlic over medium heat for 10 minutes, or until the onion is softened but not browned. Add the spices and cook, stirring frequently, for 30 seconds, or until fragrant.
2 Add the tomato, salami, carrot and stock. Bring to the boil, then reduce the heat and simmer, covered, for 15 minutes. Stir in the peas and coriander and cook, covered, for a further 4 minutes, or until the rice is tender and all the liquid has been absorbed.

MEXICAN CORN AND RICE BAKE

Preparation time: 15 minutes
Total cooking time: 45 minutes
Serves 6–8

1¹/₂ cups (375 g/12 oz) medium-grain rice
1 tablespoon olive oil
20 g (³/₄ oz) butter
1 large onion, finely chopped
1 red capsicum (pepper), finely chopped
3 garlic cloves, crushed
2 small red chillies, seeded and very
    finely chopped
2 teaspoons ground cumin
1 teaspoon paprika
1¹/₂ cups (300 g/10 oz) corn kernels
2 tablespoons tomato paste (purée)
5 spring onions (scallions), chopped
¹/₂ cup (25 g/³/₄ oz) finely chopped coriander
    (cilantro) leaves
300 g (10 oz) sour cream
2¹/₂ cups (310 g/10 oz) grated Cheddar cheese

1 Preheat the oven to moderately hot 200°C (400°F/Gas 6). Bring a large saucepan of water to the boil, add the rice and cook for about 12 minutes, stirring occasionally. Drain, rinse, drain well again and set aside.
2 Meanwhile, heat the oil and butter in a saucepan over medium heat, add the onion and capsicum and cook for 10 minutes, or until the vegetables are softened but not browned. Add the garlic, chilli, cumin and paprika and stir for 1 minute, or until fragrant. Remove from the heat and stir in the corn, tomato paste and spring onion.
3 Combine the rice, corn mixture, coriander, sour cream and 1¹/₂ cups (185 g/6 oz) of the

BELOW: Mexican rice

MEXICAN MEALS
The main meal in Mexico is often eaten in the middle of the day (this is less common in the bigger cities where travel home at midday can be difficult). The first course is usually a traditional 'wet' soup, followed by a so called 'dry soup', usually a rice, noodle or pasta dish. For a complete Mexican meal, these would be followed by a meat or fish dish accompanied by tortillas and beans; then fruit or dessert, such as custard flan, with coffee.

cheese in a large bowl and season with salt and pepper. Transfer to a greased 20 x 25 cm (8 x 10 inch) ovenproof dish and smooth the top. Sprinkle the remaining cheese over the top and bake for 30 minutes.

MEXICAN CHICKEN BAKE

Preparation time: 15 minutes
Total cooking time: 1 hour
Serves 4

3/4 cup (165 g/5 1/2 oz) short-grain rice
1 tablespoon oil
600 g (1 1/4 lb) boneless, skinless chicken
    thigh fillets, unrolled
400 g (13 oz) spicy taco sauce
300 g (10 oz) tin red kidney beans,
    drained and rinsed
3 1/2 tablespoons chopped coriander
    (cilantro) leaves
2 cups (250 g/8 oz) grated Cheddar cheese
1/2 cup (125 g/4 oz) sour cream

1 Preheat the oven to moderate 180°C (350°F/ Gas 4). Lightly grease a 7 cm (2 3/4 inch) deep, 21 cm (8 1/2 inch) round ceramic casserole dish. Bring a large saucepan of water to the boil, add the rice and cook for 10–12 minutes, stirring occasionally. Drain.
2 Heat the oil in a large frying pan over medium heat. Add the chicken thighs and sauté for 3 minutes, then turn over. Pour in the spicy taco sauce, stir well and then cook for a further 3 minutes.
3 To assemble the Mexican chicken bake, combine the beans, rice and 1 1/2 tablespoons of the coriander in a large bowl and toss together. Lightly press the mixture into the bottom of the prepared casserole dish. Spread half the cheese over the rice mixture. Arrange the chicken thighs and sauce on top in a star shape, sprinkle with 1 1/2 tablespoons of the coriander, then sprinkle with the rest of the Cheddar cheese. Cover with foil.
4 Bake for 35–40 minutes, or until the mixture is bubbling and the cheese is melted and slightly browned—remove the foil for the last 5 minutes of cooking. Cut into four servings with a knife and scoop out each serving carefully, trying to keep the layers intact. Serve sprinkled with the remaining coriander and a dollop of sour cream.

ABOVE: Mexican chicken bake

Rice was introduced to Mexico by the Spanish after the Spanish Conquest in 1519. Interestingly, the predominant type of rice used is medium-grain Asian style rice rather than Spanish style paella rice; probably because the Spanish originally imported rice from their colony in the Philippines. Mexicans like their rice light, fluffy and perfectly dry. Their secret to achieving this is to first fry the rice, then to cook it in broth. The three main rice dishes in Mexico are red, green and white rice, distinguishable mainly by the colour of the chillies used.

ABOVE: Mexican green rice

MEXICAN GREEN RICE

Preparation time: 15 minutes
Total cooking time: 35 minutes
Serves 8 as a side dish

3 large mild green chillies, such as
    poblano or banana
1 small green chilli, chopped
4 garlic cloves, chopped
1 small onion, chopped
1¹/₂ cups (45 g/1¹/₂ oz) coriander (cilantro)
    leaves
40 g (1¹/₄ oz) butter
2 cups (400 g/13 oz) long-grain white rice
3 cups (750 ml/24 fl oz) hot chicken or
    vegetable stock
2 tablespoons finely chopped coriander
    (cilantro) leaves, extra

1 Grill (broil) the large chillies or hold over a gas flame until the skin blackens and blisters. Place on a cutting board, cover with a tea towel and allow to cool. Peel the skin off, then deseed and roughly chop the chillies. Put the flesh in a food processor with the small chilli, garlic, onion and coriander leaves and process until smooth.
2 Melt the butter in a saucepan and, when sizzling, add the rice and cook, stirring, over medium heat for about 5 minutes, or until lightly golden. Add the chilli purée and mix well.
3 Gradually stir in the stock and bring to the boil. Cover and reduce the heat to low. Cook, without lifting the lid, for 20 minutes, or until all the liquid has been absorbed and the rice is tender. Fluff with a fork, stir in the extra coriander and season to taste.

PLAIN MEXICAN RICE

Preparation time: 10 minutes
Total cooking time: 35 minutes
Serves 8 as a side dish

1 tablespoon olive oil
1 small onion, chopped
1 garlic clove, chopped
1 cup (200 g/6¹/₂ oz) long-grain white rice
¹/₂ cup (125 g/4 oz) tomato passata
1 cup (250 ml/8 fl oz) chicken stock

1 Heat the oil in a large saucepan, add the onion and cook for 5 minutes, or until softened but not browned. Add the garlic and cook for 1 minute. Add the rice and stir for 1–2 minutes, or until well coated in the oil.

2 Add the tomato passata and stock to the pan and bring to the boil. Reduce the heat to very low, cover tightly with a lid and simmer for 25 minutes, or until the liquid is absorbed and the rice is tender. Fluff up the grains with a fork, and serve as a side dish.

MEXICAN BEEF CHILLI WITH BEANS AND RICE

Preparation time: 20 minutes
  + soaking
Total cooking time: 2 hours
Serves 4–6

2 cups (400 g/13 oz) long-grain rice

2 tablespoons olive oil

600 g (1 1/4 lb) chuck steak, cut into
  2 cm (3/4 inch) cubes

1 red onion, chopped

3 garlic cloves, crushed

1 long green chilli, finely chopped

2 1/2 teaspoons ground cumin

2 teaspoons ground coriander

1 teaspoon chilli powder

3 teaspoons dried oregano

400 g (13 oz) tin chopped tomatoes

2 tablespoons tomato paste (purée)

3 cups (750 ml/24 fl oz) beef stock

400 g (13 oz) tin kidney beans, drained
  and rinsed

2 tablespoons fresh oregano, chopped

sour cream, to serve

burritos, to serve

1 Put the rice in a heatproof bowl, add enough boiling water to cover it and leave it to soak until cool.

2 Meanwhile, heat 1 tablespoon of the oil in a large, heavy-based saucepan. Cook the beef in two batches until browned, then remove from the pan.

3 Heat the remaining oil in the pan and cook the onion for 2 minutes, or until softened but not browned. Add the garlic and chilli and cook for a further minute, then add the cumin, ground coriander, chilli powder and dried oregano, and cook for a further 30 seconds. Return the beef to the pan and add the chopped tomatoes, tomato paste and 1 cup (250 ml/ 8 fl oz) of the stock. Bring to the boil, then reduce the heat and simmer, covered, for 1 1/2 hours, or until the beef is tender.

4 Drain the rice and stir it into the beef mixture along with the kidney beans and remaining stock. Bring the mixture to the boil, then reduce the heat and simmer, covered, for 20 minutes, or until the rice is tender and all the liquid has been absorbed. Stir in the fresh oregano and serve with warmed burritos and a dollop of sour cream. Let your guests assemble their own burritos at the table.

BELOW: Mexican beef chilli with beans and rice

CHICKEN GUMBO

Preparation time: 15 minutes
Total cooking time: 2 hours 30 minutes
Serves 4–6

1/3 cup (80 ml/2³/4 fl oz) vegetable oil
1/4 cup (30 g/1 oz) plain (all-purpose) flour
600 g (1 1/4 lb) chicken thigh fillets
60 g (2 oz) unsalted butter
100 g (3 1/2 oz) smoked ham, diced
150 g (5 oz) chorizo, thinly sliced
2 onions, chopped
2 garlic cloves, finely chopped
2 celery stalks, thinly sliced
1 red capsicum (pepper), finely chopped

450 g (14 oz) tomatoes, peeled, seeded and chopped
2 cups (500 ml/16 fl oz) chicken stock
1 bay leaf
2 teaspoons thyme
Tabasco sauce, to taste
350 g (11 oz) okra, cut into 1 cm (1/2 inch) slices
2 spring onions (scallions), sliced
2 tablespoons chopped fresh parsley, to garnish

1 Heat 3 tablespoons of the oil in a small, heavy-based saucepan, add the flour and stir to make a smooth paste. Stir over very low heat for 1 hour, or until the roux turns very dark brown, but is not burnt. This requires a great deal of patience and stirring but provides the gumbo with its dark look and rich flavour—when it is done, the roux should be the colour of dark chocolate. Remove from the heat.

2 Pat dry the chicken thigh fillets with paper towels, cut into quarters and lightly season with salt and pepper. Heat the remaining oil and half the butter in a heavy-based frying pan over medium heat. Cook the chicken for about 5 minutes, or until golden brown. Remove the chicken with a slotted spoon. Add the ham and chorizo and cook for another 4–5 minutes, or until lightly golden. Remove, leaving as much rendered fat in the pan as possible.

3 Add the remaining butter to the same pan and cook the onion, garlic, celery and capsicum over medium heat for 5–6 minutes, or until the vegetables have softened but not browned. Transfer the vegetables to a heavy-based, flameproof casserole dish. Add the tomato and the roux to the vegetables and stir well. Gradually stir the stock into the pan. Add the herbs and season with the Tabasco. Bring to the boil, stirring constantly.

4 Reduce the heat, add the chicken, ham and chorizo to the casserole dish and simmer, uncovered, for 1 hour. Add the okra and cook for another hour. Skim the surface as the gumbo cooks because a lot of oil will come out of the chorizo. The gumbo should thicken considerably in the last 20 minutes as the okra softens. Remove the bay leaf and serve. Garnish with spring onion and parsley, if desired. Serve with rice.

NOTE: Gumbo is a speciality of Cajun cuisine and is a cross between a soup and a stew. Traditionally, gumbo is often served in deep bowls, each containing a few tablespoons of cooked rice in the bottom.

BELOW: Chicken gumbo

CRAWFISH ÉTOUFFÉE

Preparation time: 10 minutes
Total cooking time: 30 minutes
Serves 6

☆ ☆

¹/₄ cup (60 ml/2 fl oz) oil

¹/₄ cup (30 g/1 oz) plain (all-purpose) flour

45 g (1¹/₂ oz) unsalted butter

¹/₂ onion, finely chopped

1 short celery stalk, finely chopped

1 red capsicum (pepper), cut into
    thin strips

¹/₂ green capsicum (pepper), cut into
    thin strips

1 teaspoon Cajun spices

1 teaspoon celery salt

¹/₂ teaspoon dried basil

1 red chilli, seeded and finely chopped

2 cups (500 ml/16 fl oz) fish stock

500 g (1 lb) lobster tail, cut into bite-sized
    pieces

3 spring onions (scallions), finely chopped

1 Start by making the roux. Heat the oil in a small, heavy-based saucepan, add the flour and stir to make a smooth paste. Cook over very low heat, stirring constantly, until it turns into a rich, dark, mahogany brown roux. Remove the pan from the heat.

2 Heat the butter in a large frying pan. Cook the onion, celery and capsicums for 5 minutes, then add the Cajun spices, celery salt, basil and chopped chilli.

3 Bring the stock to the boil in a separate saucepan, whisk in the roux and simmer over medium heat for 5 minutes. Add the cooked vegetables and simmer over medium heat for 15 minutes.

4 Add the lobster and spring onions and cook for 3–4 minutes, or until just tender. Season to taste with salt and freshly ground black pepper. Serve on a bed of steamed white rice.

NOTES: Étouffée means 'smothered' or 'covered' and refers to a dish with plenty of sauce.

Louisiana crawfish are small crayfish. Lobster, marron, scampi or crayfish tails cut into medallions can also be used.

CAJUN FOOD
The Cajuns are descended from the French Acadians, driven from Canada when the territory was ceded to the English in the 1700s. Some Acadians went back to France, some moved to the Caribbean and others arrived in Louisiana just as it transferred to Spanish rule. Thus Cajun food is a melange of French and southern American cuisine, largely influenced by the African ingredients used by the local, French-descended Creoles of Louisiana. Cajun cuisine relies heavily on food from the bayous (swampy rivers), such as alligator, rabbit and, most importantly, crayfish, and is heavily spiced. An important element in Cajun cooking is the roux, a thick paste made of lard and flour cooked until almost burnt, essential in gumbo and other dishes.

ABOVE: Crawfish étouffée

1 Heat the oven to 200°C (400°F/Gas 6). Put the wild rice and chicken stock in a saucepan and bring to the boil. Simmer for 30 minutes, or until tender, then drain.

2 Sauté the onion in the butter for 5 minutes, or until softened but not browned. Then add the apricots, prunes, parsley and chervil. Add the rice and season well.

3 Loosely fill the quails with the prepared rice stuffing and fasten them closed with cocktail sticks or toothpicks.

4 Heat the oil in a frying pan and brown the quails all over—you may need to do this in batches. Transfer to a roasting tin and cook for 15–20 minutes, or until a skewer inserted into the cavity comes out very hot. Serve the quails with a green salad and potatoes.

DIRTY RICE

Preparation time: 35 minutes
Total cooking time: 50 minutes
Serves 6

☆ ☆

¹/₄ cup (60 ml/2 fl oz) oil
¹/₄ cup (30 g/1 oz) plain (all-purpose) flour
60 g (2 oz) butter
1 onion, finely chopped
2 garlic cloves, crushed
1 green capsicum (pepper), diced
1 celery stalk, diced
180 g (6 oz) chicken livers, chopped
250 g (8 oz) minced (ground) pork
2 teaspoons chicken stock powder
1 teaspoon Tabasco sauce
1 teaspoon garlic powder
1 teaspoon onion powder
¹/₂ teaspoon dried thyme
¹/₂ teaspoon white pepper
¹/₂ teaspoon freshly ground black pepper
¹/₄ teaspoon cayenne pepper
¹/₄ teaspoon dried oregano
2 cups (400 g/13 oz) long-grain rice
3 cups (750 ml/24 fl oz) chicken stock

1 Heat the oil in a heavy-based frying pan. When hot, sprinkle over the flour; mix together then whisk continuously for 3–4 minutes, or until the mixture is nut brown in colour but not burnt. Remove the roux from the pan to stop further cooking.

QUAIL STUFFED WITH WILD RICE

Preparation time: 15 minutes
Total cooking time: 1 hour
Serves 4

☆ ☆

¹/₄ cup (50 g/1³/₄ oz) wild rice
1 cup (250 ml/8 fl oz) chicken stock
1 onion, finely chopped
20 g (³/₄ oz) butter
1 tablespoon finely chopped dried apricots
1 tablespoon finely chopped prunes
1 tablespoon chopped mixed parsley
  and chervil
4 quails
¹/₃ cup (80 ml/2³/₄ fl oz) olive oil

ABOVE: Quail stuffed with wild rice

2 Heat the butter in a large saucepan. Add the onion, garlic, capsicum and celery. Cook, stirring often, for 5 minutes, or until the vegetables are softened but not browned. Transfer to a plate.

3 Add the livers and pork to the pan. Cook for 2–3 minutes, breaking up any lumps with a fork. Return the vegetables to the pan and cook, stirring, for a further 2–3 minutes. Stir in the prepared roux, stock powder, Tabasco, garlic and onion powders, herbs and spices. Stir well for 1–2 minutes.

4 Stir in the rice and chicken stock. Bring slowly to the boil, then reduce the heat to very low and simmer, stirring often, for 30 minutes, or until the rice is tender. Serve at once.

4 Bring a large saucepan of water to the boil. Add the white rice and cook, stirring occasionally, for 12 minutes, or until tender. Drain and mix with the wild rice and pecans in a large, shallow bowl. Add the parsley and spring onion. Add half the dressing and toss well.

5 Put the duck, skin-side down, in a cold frying pan, then heat the pan over high heat. Cook for 5 minutes, or until crisp, then turn over and cook for another 5 minutes. Tip out any excess fat and add the remaining dressing and the orange zest, and cook until bubbling. Transfer the duck to a serving dish and slice on the diagonal. Serve with the rice, drizzled with any juices.

DUCK WITH WILD RICE

Preparation time: 15 minutes
Total cooking time: 1 hour
Serves 4

DRESSING
1/3 cup (80 ml/2³/4 fl oz) olive oil
2 tablespoons orange juice
2 teaspoons walnut oil
1 teaspoon grated orange zest
1 tablespoon chopped preserved ginger

1/2 cup (95 g/3 oz) wild rice
2 teaspoons oil
50 g (1³/4 oz) pecans, roughly chopped
1/2 teaspoon ground cinnamon
1/3 cup (65 g/2¹/4 oz) long-grain white rice
2 tablespoons finely chopped parsley
4 spring onions (scallions), thinly sliced
2 duck breasts
zest of 1 orange

1 To make the dressing, thoroughly mix the ingredients together. Season with salt and freshly ground black pepper. Set aside.

2 Put the wild rice in a saucepan with 300 ml (9¹/2 fl oz) water. Bring to the boil, then cook, covered, for 30 minutes, or until tender. Drain away any excess water.

3 Meanwhile, heat the oil in a large frying pan. Add the pecans and cook, stirring, until golden. Add the cinnamon and a pinch of salt, and cook for 1 minute.

RED BEANS AND RICE

Preparation time: 20 minutes + overnight soaking
Total cooking time: 3 hours 10 minutes
Serves 4

☆ ☆

1 cup (210 g/7 oz) dried red kidney beans

2 tablespoons oil

1 onion, finely chopped

1 green capsicum (pepper), chopped

3 celery stalks, finely chopped

2 garlic cloves, crushed

225 g (7 oz) andouille or other spicy sausage,
   cut into pieces (see Notes)

2 ham hocks

2 bay leaves

1 cup (200 g/6¹/₂ oz) long-grain rice

spring onions (scallions), thinly sliced,
   to garnish

BELOW: Red beans and rice

1 Soak the red kidney beans overnight in cold water. Drain and put into a saucepan with enough cold water to cover the beans. Bring to the boil, then reduce the heat to a simmer.
2 Heat the oil in a frying pan and sauté the onion, capsicum, celery and garlic until the onion is softened but not browned. Add the sausage and cook until it begins to brown around the edges.
3 Add the sautéed vegetables and sausage to the saucepan with the beans, then add the ham and bay leaves. Bring to the boil, then reduce to a simmer and cook for 2¹/₂–3 hours, adding more water if necessary—the beans should be saucy but not too wet. When the beans are almost cooked, boil the rice in a separate saucepan until it is tender.
4 Top the cooked rice with the red kidney beans. Tear some meat off the ham hocks and add to each serving plate. Garnish with the sliced spring onions.
NOTES: Andouille is the name of the smoked pork sausage used in Louisiana cooking.

Commonly called 'red and white', this southern American dish is traditionally served on Mondays. The reasons why are left to folklore—either it was easy to prepare on wash day; it made good use of Sunday's leftover ham; or it soaked up the alcohol consumed on the weekend.

BAKED SEA BASS WITH WILD RICE STUFFING

Preparation time: 20 minutes
Total cooking time: 1 hour 10 minutes
Serves 4

☆ ☆

2 small fennel bulbs

¹/₃ cup (65 g/2¹/₄ oz) wild rice

1 cup (250 ml/8 fl oz) fish stock

40 g (1¹/₄ oz) butter

2 tablespoons olive oil

1 onion, chopped

1 garlic clove, crushed

grated zest of 1 lemon

2 kg (4 lb) sea bass, bass or any large
   white fish, gutted and scaled

extra virgin olive oil

1 lemon, quartered

2 teaspoons chopped oregano

lemon wedges, to serve

Once the fennel, onion
and garlic are softened, add
the cooked wild rice and
stir thoroughly.

Using a heaped tablespoon
of the fennel and rice
mixture, carefully stuff
the fish.

Sprinkle the fish with the
rest of the oregano and
chopped fennel fronds.

1 Preheat the oven to moderately hot 190°C (375°F/Gas 5) and lightly grease a large, shallow ovenproof dish. Thinly slice the fennel, reserving and chopping the green fronds.
2 Put the wild rice and stock in a saucepan with ¼ cup (60 ml/2 fl oz) water and bring to the boil. Simmer for 30 minutes, or until tender, then drain.
3 Heat the butter and olive oil in a large frying pan and gently cook the fennel, onion and garlic for 12–15 minutes, or until softened but not browned. Add the lemon zest, then stir in the rice and season with salt and freshly ground black pepper.

4 Stuff the fish with a heaped tablespoon of the fennel mixture and a quarter of the reserved fronds. Brush with extra virgin olive oil, squeeze over some lemon juice and season well with salt and pepper.
5 Spoon the remainder of the cooked fennel and rice mixture into the ovenproof dish and sprinkle with half the oregano. Put the fish on top of the fennel. Sprinkle the remaining oregano and fennel fronds over the fish and loosely cover the dish with foil. Bake for 25 minutes, or until the fish is just cooked through. Serve with lemon wedges.

*ABOVE: Baked sea bass
with wild rice stuffing*

111

OKRA

Also known as bhindi, gumbo and ladies' fingers this is a slender, five-sided pod that contains numerous white seeds. When young, okra is eaten as a vegetable; the older pods are usually dried, then powdered and used as a flavouring. When cooked, okra releases a sticky, gelatinous substance, which serves to thicken stews and soups such as the Cajun and Creole dish, gumbo. Okra is used extensively in India, the Caribbean, Southeast Asia and the Middle East. It can also be eaten raw in salads or blanched, then dressed in a vinaigrette. Buy pods that are tender and healthy green in colour. They should snap rather than bend and should be no more than 10 cm (4 inches) long. If too ripe, the pod will feel very sticky. To prepare, gently scrub with a paper towel or vegetable brush. Rinse and drain, then slice off the top and tail.

ABOVE: Prawn and okra gumbo

PRAWN AND OKRA GUMBO

Preparation time: 35 minutes
Total cooking time: 3 hours
Serves 8

☆☆☆

PRAWN STOCK
1 kg (2 lb) raw prawns (shrimp)
1 tablespoon olive oil
1 onion, chopped
1 carrot, chopped
1 celery stalk, chopped
1 bay leaf
2 cloves
3 garlic cloves, bruised
a few parsley stalks
thyme sprig
1/2 teaspoon black peppercorns

2 tablespoons olive oil
500 g (1 lb) okra, thickly sliced
200 g (6 1/2 oz) chorizo sausage, thickly sliced
250 g (8 oz) smoked ham, diced
1/4 cup (60 ml/2 fl oz) olive oil, extra
1/4 cup (30 g/1 oz) plain (all-purpose) flour

2 onions, chopped
2 celery stalks, diced
1 red capsicum (pepper), diced
6 garlic cloves, finely chopped
1/2 teaspoon cayenne pepper
2 teaspoons sweet paprika
2 teaspoons mustard powder
large pinch of ground allspice
400 g (13 oz) tomato passata
1 tablespoon tomato paste (purée)
2 teaspoons finely chopped thyme
2 teaspoons finely chopped oregano
2 bay leaves
2 1/2 tablespoons Worcestershire sauce
500 g (1 lb) scallops without roe
12 oysters
3 tablespoons chopped flat-leaf (Italian) parsley
cooked long-grain rice, to serve

1 To make the stock, peel the prawns, reserving the shells. Gently pull out the dark vein from each prawn back, starting at the head end. Cover the prawn meat and refrigerate until ready to use. Heat the oil in a large saucepan, add the prawn shells and cook over high heat for about 8 minutes, or until bright orange. Add 2 1/2 litres (80 fl oz) cold water and the remaining stock

ingredients and bring to the boil. Reduce the heat to low and simmer for 30 minutes, skimming occasionally, then strain well and set aside—you should have about 2 litres (64 fl oz).

2 Meanwhile, heat the olive oil in a frying pan and sauté the okra over medium heat for 10 minutes, or until slightly softened, then remove the okra from the pan and set aside. Add the chorizo to the pan and cook for about 5 minutes, or until well browned, then set aside. Add the ham to the pan and cook for a few minutes, or until lightly browned.

3 Heat the extra olive oil in a large saucepan, add the flour and stir to combine. Cook, stirring regularly, over medium heat for 30 seconds, or until the roux turns a colour somewhere between milk and dark chocolate, but do not allow to burn.

4 Add the onion, celery, capsicum and garlic to the roux and cook for about 10 minutes, or until softened. Add the cayenne, paprika, mustard and allspice and stir for 1 minute. Add the tomato passata, tomato paste, prawn stock, thyme, oregano, bay leaves, Worcestershire sauce, chorizo and ham and bring to the boil. Reduce the heat to low and simmer for 1 hour, then add the okra and continue cooking for a further hour or until the gumbo is thick and glossy.

5 Add the prawns, scallops and oysters and cook for about 5–8 minutes, or until all the seafood is cooked through. Stir in the parsley and season to taste. Ladle over hot rice in individual bowls and accompany with lemon wedges if desired.

HOPPIN' JOHN

Preparation time: 10 minutes +
   overnight soaking
Total cooking time: 30 minutes
Serves 4

☆☆

1 1/2 cups (300 g/10 oz) black-eyed beans
1 tablespoon oil
1 onion, finely chopped
1 red capsicum (pepper), finely chopped
4 back bacon rashers, diced
1/2 cup (100 g/3 1/2 oz) long-grain rice
Louisiana hot sauce or chilli sauce (see Notes)

1 Soak the black-eyed beans in cold water overnight, then drain.
2 Heat the oil in a frying pan over medium heat. Add the onion, capsicum and bacon and cook for 10 minutes, or until the bacon is crisp and the vegetables are soft.

3 Add the beans, rice and 2 cups (500 ml/16 fl oz) water. Cover, bring to the boil and simmer for about 20 minutes, or until the rice is cooked. Season with salt, freshly ground black pepper and some Louisiana hot sauce.

NOTES: Hoppin' John is said to have originated with the African slaves who worked on southern American plantations. The most well known rice dish from the southern American region, it it is traditionally served there on New Year's day with collards (a green leafy vegetable related to kale). The rice is said to bring good luck, and the collards to bring 'greenbacks', or wealth.

There are hundreds of varieties of Louisiana hot sauce, which come in varying degrees of heat. Made from red peppers or chillies, and sometimes with the addition of garlic, onion and other spices, hot sauce is ubiquitous in southern America and is used to spice up anything from hot dogs to rice dishes.

BELOW: Hoppin' John

ARROZ CON POLLO
(Rice with chicken)

Preparation time: 25 minutes
Total cooking time: 1 hour 15 minutes
Serves 6

☆ ☆

2 kg (4 lb) whole chicken or chicken pieces

2 tablespoons olive oil

100 g (3 1/2 oz) chorizo sausage, finely diced

1 large onion, finely chopped

1 green capsicum (pepper), diced

3 teaspoons sweet paprika

1 long red chilli, seeded and finely chopped

3 garlic cloves, crushed

2 cups (440 g/14 oz) paella rice

pinch of saffron threads

1 litre (32 fl oz) hot chicken stock

4 very ripe tomatoes, peeled, seeded
  and chopped

2 1/2 tablespoons tomato paste (purée)

1/3 cup (80 ml/2 3/4 fl oz) sherry

2/3 cup (100 g/3 1/2 oz) frozen peas

3 tablespoons finely chopped flat-leaf
  (Italian) parsley

1/3 cup (55 g/2 oz) stuffed green olives
  (optional)

1 Cut the chicken into eight pieces, pat dry with paper towels, then season with salt and pepper. Heat a little oil in the base of a large heavy-based saucepan or flameproof casserole dish, then cook the chicken in batches over medium heat for about 10 minutes, or until well browned all over. Remove from the pan and set aside

2 Add the chorizo to the pan and cook, stirring, for 1 minute, then remove with a slotted spoon and add to the chicken. Drain off any excess fat, if necessary, leaving 2 tablespoons in the pan. Add the onion and capsicum and cook for 5 minutes, or until softened and starting to brown. Add the paprika, chilli and garlic and stir for a further minute, or until fragrant. Add the rice and saffron and stir to coat well. Stir in the hot chicken stock until well combined, then add the tomatoes, tomato paste and sherry.

3 Return the chicken and chorizo to the pan, stirring well to combine. Allow the liquid to come to the boil, then reduce the heat to low and cover. Simmer, stirring occasionally, for about 25 minutes, or until most of the liquid has been absorbed, then stir in the peas, re-cover and cook for a further 10 minutes, or until the rice is tender and the chicken is cooked through—the liquid should be almost completely absorbed. Stir in the parsley and olives, if desired, and season to taste with salt and freshly ground black pepper. Serve immediately.

ARROZ CON POLLO
There are many versions of Arroz con pollo (rice with chicken) throughout the Americas. Its Spanish origins are evident—many of the main ingredients were introduced to the area by the Spaniards after the Spanish Conquest, including rice, olives and sherry. But the tomato, chilli and capsicum (pepper) are all native to South America. So this meal is an amalgamation of two cultures.

RIGHT: Arroz con pollo

CREOLE SHRIMP WITH RICE

Preparation time: 20 minutes
Total cooking time: 1 hour 10 minutes
Serves 4

40 g (1 1/4 oz) butter
1 tablespoon oil
1 large onion, finely chopped
200 g (6 1/2 oz) smoked ham, diced
2 celery stalks, diced
1 large red capsicum (pepper) finely diced
3 garlic cloves, crushed
3 teaspoons sweet paprika
large pinch of cayenne pepper
1 teaspoon ground cumin
2 teaspoons finely chopped thyme
2 teaspoons finely chopped oregano
400 g (13 oz) tin chopped tomatoes
1 tablespoon tomato paste (purée)
1 bay leaf
1/2 teaspoon finely grated lemon zest
2 tablespoons Worcestershire sauce
24 large raw prawns (shrimp), peeled
   and deveined

3 tablespoons finely chopped flat-leaf
   (Italian) parsley
cooked long-grain rice, to serve
lemon wedges, to serve

1 Melt half the butter with the oil in a large saucepan over medium heat. Add the onion and ham and sauté for about 5 minutes, or until the onion is softened but not browned. Add the celery and capsicum and cook for 10 minutes longer. Add the garlic, paprika, cayenne, cumin, thyme and oregano, stir to combine and cook for a further minute, or until fragrant. Add the chopped tomatoes, tomato paste, bay leaf, lemon zest, Worcestershire sauce and 3 cups (750 ml/ 24 fl oz) water to the pan and bring to the boil. Reduce to a simmer and cook for 45 minutes, or until you have a thick and chunky sauce.
2 Melt the remaining butter in a frying pan over medium heat. When the butter is sizzling, sauté the lightly seasoned prawns in batches until just pink and slightly curled, then add them to the sauce in the saucepan and cook for a further 2 minutes.
3 Remove the saucepan from the heat, stir in the parsley and season to taste with salt and freshly ground black pepper. Serve on a bed of the hot rice with lemon wedges, if desired.

CAPSICUM (PEPPER)
All capsicums are native to the Americas. The capsicum family includes sweet peppers as well as the hot ones, chillies. The capsicum was deliberately misnamed pepper by Christopher Columbus in order to sell its close relation the chilli as an alternative to the spice pepper that was, at the time, much in demand. Although capsicums are a fruit, they are treated more as a vegetable. Most sweet (bell) capsicums are green at first, then turn red, yellow or orange, or even purple–black as they ripen, depending on the variety. When used in the Americas, they are most often grilled (broiled) and gain a smoky flavour.

*ABOVE: Creole shrimp
with rice*

JAMAICAN RICE WITH PEAS

Preparation time: 5 minutes
Total cooking time: 35 minutes
Serves 6–8 as a side dish

☆

2 cups (400 g/13 oz) long-grain rice
3 cups (750 ml/24 fl oz) coconut milk
400 g (13 oz) tin kidney beans, drained
   and rinsed
2 teaspoons finely chopped thyme
4 garlic cloves, crushed
large pinch of ground allspice
4 whole spring onions (scallions), bruised
1 small red chilli

1 Combine all the ingredients in a large saucepan and add enough water to come about 2.5 cm (1 inch) above the rice. Slowly bring to the boil over medium heat, cover, reduce the heat to low and simmer for about 25 minutes, or until the rice is tender and the liquid has been absorbed.
2 Remove the spring onion and chilli, season well and serve.

BELOW: Jamaican rice with peas

NOTES: As a variation, add 1 cup (155 g/5 oz) chopped smoked ham to the other ingredients before you start to cook.

This Jamaican staple is actually rice with beans; however beans are often referred to as peas in Jamaica. Kidney beans are commonly used, though some authentic versions contain hard-to-find gungo or pigeon peas.

VEAL WRAPPED IN PROSCIUTTO

Preparation time: 25 minutes
Total cooking time: 35 minutes
Serves 4–6

☆ ☆ ☆

1 bunch (500 g/1 lb) English spinach, stalks
   removed and leaves washed
4 veal steaks, each about 200 g (6¹/2 oz),
   slightly flattened
2 tablespoons wholegrain mustard
16 prosciutto slices
2 tablespoons olive oil
2 garlic cloves, crushed
¹/2 cup (125 ml/4 fl oz) dry white wine
1 cup (250 ml/8 fl oz) chicken stock
1 tablespoon Dijon mustard
1 teaspoon cornflour (cornstarch) blended
   with 2 tablespoons cold water
1 tablespoon chervil sprigs

HONEYED WILD RICE
1 cup (210 g/7 oz) wild rice blend
30 g (1 oz) butter
1 onion, finely chopped
1 garlic clove, crushed
1 tablespoon honey
1 tablespoon light soy sauce

1 Preheat the oven to moderate 180°C (350°F/ Gas 4). Steam the spinach until just wilted, then rinse in cold water, drain and pat dry. Put a few spinach leaves on a board to form a square, a little larger than the veal steak. Also on the board, lay out 4 prosciutto slices, slightly overlapping, with the short ends towards you. Put the steak on the spinach square, spread it with wholegrain mustard and roll up both the veal and spinach to form a log. Lay the veal and spinach log across the bottom edge of the pieces

of prosciutto and roll up, folding in the sides as you go to form a parcel. Repeat with the remaining spinach, veal and prosciutto until you end up with four parcels.

2 To make the Honeyed wild rice, bring a large saucepan of water to the boil. Add the rice and cook, stirring occasionally, for 25 minutes, or until tender. Drain. Heat the butter in a small frying pan, add the onion and garlic and cook until the onion is softened but not browned. Add the rice, honey and soy sauce, toss thoroughly, then remove from the heat.

3 Meanwhile, heat the oil in a frying pan over medium heat and cook the steak parcels until lightly browned, turning frequently. Remove from the pan and transfer to a roasting tin. Bake for 10–15 minutes. Remove from the oven, cover and keep warm.

4 Put the roasting tin on the stove-top over medium heat, add the garlic and wine and cook for 2 minutes. Add the stock, Dijon mustard and cornflour paste. Stir until the sauce boils and thickens. Strain. Slice the veal thickly, pour over the sauce and sprinkle with chervil leaves.

CHICKEN BOG
(Southern chicken and rice stew)

Preparation time: 25 minutes + cooling
Total cooking time: 1 hour 45 minutes
Serves 8

☆ ☆

40 g (1¼ oz) butter

1 large onion, chopped

2 carrots, cut into large chunks

2 celery stalks, cut into 4 cm (1½ inch)
   lengths, a few leaves reserved and chopped

4 garlic cloves, crushed

large pinch of cayenne pepper

1 teaspoon finely chopped oregano

2 kg (4 lb) whole chicken

1 small smoked ham hock

400 g (13 oz) tomato passata

¼ cup (60 ml/2 fl oz) lemon juice

1 litre (32 fl oz) chicken stock

2 cups (400 g/13 oz) long-grain rice

3 hard-boiled eggs, finely chopped

2 tablespoons Worcestershire sauce

3 tablespoons finely chopped flat-leaf
   (Italian) parsley

20 g (¾ oz) butter

1 Melt the butter in a very large, deep pot, add the onion and cook over medium heat for about 8 minutes, or until softened and lightly golden. Add the carrot, celery, garlic, cayenne and oregano and stir for 1 minute, or until fragrant.

2 Add the chicken, ham hock, celery leaves, tomato passata, lemon juice and the stock—the liquid should only just cover the chicken. Bring to the boil, then reduce the heat to low and simmer, skimming the surface regularly, for an hour, or until chicken is cooked through.

3 Carefully remove the chicken and ham hock from the broth and allow them to sit until cool enough to handle, then pull all the meat off the bones, discarding the skin and bones and cutting the flesh into bite-size chunks.

4 Bring the broth back to the boil, add the rice and chunks of ham and cook for about 20 minutes, or until the rice is tender. Add the pieces of chicken, the egg and Worcestershire sauce and cook for a few more minutes to heat through. Stir in the parsley and butter and season to taste with salt and pepper. Serve with cornbread to mop up the 'bog'.

ABOVE: Chicken bog

SCALLOPS
Named for their fan-shaped shells, scallops are found throughout the Atlantic, Mediterranean and Pacific oceans. Because they deteriorate rapidly once out of the water, they are usually sold shucked and should be refrigerated quickly and used within 1 day. When used in stews, as here, they are added at the last minute to prevent the flesh becoming tough.

CREOLE SEAFOOD STEW

Preparation time: 25 minutes
Total cooking time: 1 hour 10 minutes
Serves 4

☆ ☆

400 g (13 oz) raw prawns (shrimp)
250 g (8 oz) squid tubes
1/4 cup (60 ml/2 fl oz) olive oil
1 large onion, chopped
4 back bacon rashers, chopped
1 small green capsicum (pepper), diced
1 green serrano chilli, chopped
3 garlic cloves, chopped
1 teaspoon paprika
1 1/2 teaspoons dried thyme
2 teaspoons dried oregano
1/4 teaspoon cayenne pepper
1/4 cup (60 ml/2 fl oz) sherry
1/4 cup (30 g/1 oz) plain (all-purpose) flour
3 1/2 cups (875 ml/28 fl oz) chicken stock
400 g (13 oz) tin chopped tomatoes
1 1/2 cups (300 g/10 oz) long-grain rice
1 bay leaf
250 g (8 oz) scallops

1 Peel and devein the prawns, keeping the tails intact. Cut the squid tubes into 5 mm (1/4 inch) rings. Refrigerate on a plate covered with plastic wrap until needed.
2 Heat the oil in large heavy-based saucepan, add the onion, bacon and capsicum and cook over high heat for 5 minutes, or until the bacon is cooked.
3 Add the chilli and garlic to the bacon mixture and cook for 1 minute. Add the herbs and spices and cook for 30 seconds, then pour in the sherry. Continue cooking until the sherry has evaporated, then reduce the heat to medium and stir in the flour. Cook for 3 minutes, or until the flour is cooked, then gradually pour in the stock. Slowly bring the mixture to the boil, then simmer for 3 minutes, or until the mixture has thickened.
4 Stir in the chopped tomatoes rice and bay leaf and simmer, covered, for 30–40 minutes, stirring reasonably often to prevent the mixture from catching on the base of the pan.
5 Add the prawns, squid rings and scallops, and cook for a further 8 minutes, stirring after 4 minutes, or until the seafood is cooked through and tender. Add a little water or extra stock with the seafood if the mixture seems too thick and gluggy. Remove the bay leaf. Ladle into deep bowls and serve immediately.

ABOVE: Creole seafood stew

PRAWN PURLOO

Preparation time: 20 minutes
Total cooking time: 55 minutes
Serves 4–6

1 tablespoon olive oil

3 streaky bacon rashers, chopped

1 onion, finely chopped

1 celery stalk, finely chopped

1 red capsicum (pepper), finely diced

1 bay leaf

1½ teaspoons finely chopped thyme

40 g (1¼ oz) butter

2 cups (400 g/13 oz) long-grain rice

3 cups (750 ml/24 fl oz) chicken stock

1½ tablespoons Worcestershire sauce

1 kg (2 lb) raw prawns (shrimp), peeled
   and deveined

2 tablespoons chopped flat-leaf (Italian) parsley

2 spring onions (scallions), finely chopped

Tabasco sauce, to serve

lemon wedges, to serve

1 Heat 1 teaspoon of the oil in a large, deep frying pan, add the bacon and cook for 5 minutes over medium heat, or until slightly crispy, then remove from the pan. Heat the remaining oil in the pan, then sauté the onion, celery, capsicum, bay leaf and thyme for about 5 minutes, or until softened and just starting to brown. Remove from the pan.

2 Add the butter to the pan and allow to melt. Add the rice and cook, stirring, for 4 minutes, or until the rice is lightly golden. Return the vegetables and bacon to the pan, stir to combine, then stir in 1 cup (250 ml/8 fl oz) of the stock and keep stirring for 3 minutes, or until the liquid has absorbed. Repeat with another cup of stock. Add the final cup of stock with the Worcestershire sauce, then cover. Reduce the heat to low and cook for about 15 minutes, then quickly stir in the prawns, re-cover and cook for a further 3 minutes, or until prawns are pink and curled.

3 Remove the pan from the heat, allow to sit for a couple of minutes, then stir in the parsley and spring onion and season to taste. Serve with Tabasco and lemon wedges.

NOTE: Purloo is a southern American term for pilaff. It is also known as perlieu, perlo, perlu and perloo.

LEFT: Prawn purloo

119

FISH STEW WITH RICE

Preparation time: 20 minutes +
  overnight soaking + 30 minutes refrigeration
Total cooking time: 40 minutes
Serves 4

☆ ☆

115 g (4 oz) dried white fish, such as salted cod
1/2 cup (125 ml/4 fl oz) oil
3 tablespoons chopped parsley
1 1/2 teaspoons chilli flakes
5 large garlic cloves, crushed
6 x 150 g (5 oz) mixed white fish steaks

2 onions, chopped
1/4 cup (60 g/2 oz) tomato passata
1.5 litres (48 fl oz) well-flavoured fish stock
2 cups (400 g/13 oz) long-grain rice
400 g (13 oz) orange sweet potato, peeled and
  cut into chunks
150 g (5 oz) carrot, peeled and cut into chunks
1 red capsicum (pepper), seeded and cut into
  chunks
300 g (10 oz) white cabbage, cut into chunks

BELOW: Fish stew with rice

1 Soak the dried fish in water overnight, changing the water three to four times. Drain, then put it in a saucepan with clean water and simmer for 15–20 minutes, or until soft. Drain and remove any skin and bones.

2 Mix together 1/4 cup (60 ml/2 fl oz) of the oil, 2 tablespoons of the parsley, 1/2 teaspoon of the chilli flakes and 3 of the crushed garlic cloves. Rub into the fresh fish, transfer to a non-metallic dish, cover and refrigerate for 30 minutes.

3 Heat a tablespoon of the remaining oil in a large saucepan and add the onion. Cook for about 6 minutes, or until the onion has softened but not browned. Stir in the remaining garlic and cook for a further minute. Add the tomato passata and the remaining chilli flakes to the cooked onions, then pour in the stock. Season with salt, bring to the boil, then gently simmer for 10 minutes.

4 Meanwhile, heat a frying pan with the remaining 2 tablespoons of oil and cook the fresh fish for 1 minute on each side. Transfer to a plate and set aside. Tip the rice into a saucepan. Add 3 1/2 cups (875 ml/28 fl oz) water and a generous pinch of salt. Bring the liquid back to the boil, then reduce the heat to low. Cover and cook for 15 minutes, or until tender.

5 Stir the sweet potato and carrot into the stew, and simmer for 10 minutes. Add the capsicum, cabbage and dried fish. Simmer for 5 minutes, season and add more chilli flakes, if desired. Put the fish steaks on top and cook, covered, for 6 minutes, or until the fish is cooked through. Scatter with the remaining parsley. Drain the cooked rice and serve with the fish.

NOTE: Rice culture in much of the Americas has its roots in Africa. Plantation slaves from West Africa brought with them a knowledge of how to grow and cook rice. This meal can be traced back to Senegal, West Africa. Fish stew with rice (diebou dien) is the national dish there. As it is common for local fishermen to dry part of their catch, the stew combines both fresh and dried fish. If dried fish is unavailable, or you don't have time to soak it, just leave it out.

ARROZ CON MARISCOS
(Rice with shellfish)

Preparation time: 30 minutes
Total cooking time: 1 hour 10 minutes
Serves 4

1 large garlic clove, peeled

1 onion, quartered

2 firm tomatoes

1 red capsicum (pepper), seeded
  and quartered

1/4 cup (60 ml/2 fl oz) olive oil

55 g (2 oz) bacon, chopped

1 1/3 cups (265 g/8 oz) long-grain rice

2 1/2 cups (625 ml/20 fl oz) hot fish stock
  or water

2 tinned and drained, or fresh, poblanos
  chillies, finely shredded

16 raw prawns (shrimp), peeled and deveined,
  tails intact

250 g (8 oz) firm fish, such as snapper, skinned
  and cut into chunks

2 tablespoons chopped coriander (cilantro)
  leaves

1 lime, cut into 4 wedges

1 Dry-roast the garlic, onion, tomatoes and capsicum in a heavy-based frying pan over low heat, turning now and then, for about 45 minutes, or until the ingredients are browned all over.
2 When cool enough to handle, peel the tomato and capsicum, and roughly chop the flesh. Put the flesh in a food processor with the garlic and onion, and blend to a purée. Alternatively, finely chop the ingredients by hand.
3 Heat the olive oil in a deep frying pan. Add the bacon and cook until crisp. Add the rice and cook for 1 minute, stirring the grains to make sure they are completely coated in oil.
4 Add the puréed tomato mixture and cook for 3 minutes. Add the stock and 1 teaspoon salt. Bring to the boil and stir once. Reduce the heat to low and cover with a lid. Cook gently for 15 minutes.
5 Add the chillies, prawns and fish to the frying pan, and cook for another 5 minutes. Add a little hot water to the rice if it is becoming too dry. When ready, taste to check the seasoning, adding more salt if necessary.
6 Sprinkle the coriander over the top of the dish and serve with the lime wedges.

NOTE: This is the Mexican version of paella. It includes firm-fleshed fish and a unique, delicious flavour derived from roasting the base ingredients before adding them to the sauce.

SUCCOTASH

Soak 100 g (3 1/2 oz) lima beans overnight. Drain, then cover the beans in water and cook for 1 hour, or until tender. Boil 1 cup (250 ml/8 fl oz) cream until reduced by half. Combine the beans, cream, 250 g (8 oz) fresh corn kernels and simmer for 10 minutes. Add 20 g (3/4 oz) butter, 1 teaspoon chopped thyme, some salt and pepper. Serve as a side dish for poultry, pork or American rice dishes. Serves 4.

ABOVE: Arroz con mariscos

8 minutes, or until the onion has softened and the bacon browned. Add the mushroom and cook for 1–2 minutes. Pour in the chicken stock and bring to the boil, then add the rice, stir and cook the mixture for 2 minutes. Remove the pan from the heat.

3 Stir in the cream and parsley, then reheat until the soup is almost boiling. Serve in deep bowls with bread.

CHICKEN MOLE

Preparation time: 25 minutes
Total cooking time: 1 hour 40 minutes
Serves 6

2 onions
10 garlic cloves
1 chicken cut into 8 pieces
6 sprigs of thyme
6 sprigs of oregano
6 sprigs of parsley
6 whole black peppercorns
6 whole dried mulato chillies
4 whole dried pasilla chillies
1/2 small chipotle chilli
1/4 cup (40 g/1 1/4 oz) raisins
400 g (13 oz) tin chopped tomatoes
1 tablespoon dried oregano
1/2 teaspoon ground allspice
1 slice of day-old white toast bread, crust
    removed
1/4 cup (40 g/1 1/4 oz) sesame seeds, toasted
2 cloves
1 teaspoon cumin seeds
1 teaspoon coriander seeds
2 tablespoons canola oil
1 tablespoon tomato paste (purée)
1 cinnamon stick
1/4 teaspoon sugar
20 g (3/4 oz) Mexican chocolate, chopped
1/2 cup (25 g/3/4 oz) finely chopped fresh
    coriander leaves

1 Cut 1 onion into quarters, and 4 cloves of garlic into slices, and place in a large saucepan with the chicken pieces, thyme, oregano, parsley and peppercorns. Cover with cold water, add 1 teaspoon of salt and bring to the boil. Reduce the heat and simmer for 20–25 minutes, or until

WILD RICE SOUP

Preparation time: 15 minutes
Total cooking time: 1 hour
Serves 6

1/2 cup (95 g/3 oz) wild rice
1 tablespoon oil
1 onion, finely chopped
2 celery stalks, finely chopped
1 green capsicum (pepper), finely chopped
4 back bacon rashers, finely chopped
4 open cap mushrooms, thinly sliced
1 litre (32 fl oz) chicken stock
1/2 cup (125 ml/4 fl oz) cream
1 tablespoon finely chopped parsley

1 Put the wild rice in a saucepan with plenty of water and bring to the boil. Cook for 40 minutes, or until the rice is tender. Drain.
2 Heat the oil in a large saucepan and add the onion, celery, capsicum and bacon. Fry for

ABOVE: Wild rice soup

the chicken is cooked through and tender. Reserve 1 cup (250 ml/9 fl oz) cooking liquid.

2 Meanwhile, cut open the chillies, discarding the stems, seeds and membranes. Toast for 20 seconds in a hot frying pan, then transfer to a bowl. Cover with 3 cups (750 ml/24 fl oz) boiling water and soak for 15 minutes. Soak the raisins in hot water for 20 minutes, then drain.

3 Blend the tomatoes in a food processor until smooth. Add the oregano, allspice, bread, raisins, sesame seeds, and chillies with their soaking water, and blend until smooth. Strain, pressing the liquid through the sieve. Reserve the liquid and discard the pulp. In a small frying pan over low heat, dry-fry the cloves and cumin and coriander seeds for 1–2 minutes, or until fragrant. Grind to a fine powder in a mortar and pestle.

4 Finely dice the remaining onion and crush the remaining garlic. In a heavy-based frying pan, large enough to fit all the chicken pieces in one layer, heat the oil over medium heat. Cook the onion and garlic for 5 minutes. Add the ground spices and stir for 1–2 minutes, or until fragrant. Add the tomato paste, stir for 2 minutes, then add the tomato mixture, cinnamon stick and sugar. Cook over low heat for 20 minutes. Add the chocolate and the reserved cooking liquid from the chicken. Bring to a simmer, and add the chicken. Cook, covered, over low heat for 30 minutes, or until the chicken is tender. Stir in the coriander. Season and serve with white rice and tortillas.

1 Put the wild rice and stock in a saucepan, add the butter, bring to the boil, then cook, covered, over low heat for 1 hour. Drain.

2 Meanwhile, put the basmati rice in a separate saucepan with cold water and bring to the boil. Cook at a simmer for 12 minutes, then drain.

3 Mix the rices together in a bowl and leave to cool to room temperature.

4 Lightly toast the slivered almonds in a dry frying pan for a few minutes, or until lightly golden, watching carefully to make sure they don't burn. Heat the oil in the same pan and cook the bacon for 5 minutes, or until cooked. Remove from the pan and cool.

5 Combine the rice with the bacon, currants, almonds, parsley, spring onion and lemon zest and juice. Season with salt and freshly ground black pepper, drizzle with olive oil and serve with lemon wedges.

BELOW: Wild rice salad

WILD RICE SALAD

Preparation time: 20 minutes + cooling
Total cooking time: 1 hour
Serves 4

☆

1/2 cup (95 g/3 oz) wild rice

1 cup (250 ml/8 fl oz) chicken stock

20 g (3/4 oz) butter

1/2 cup (100 g/3 1/2 oz) basmati rice

1/2 cup (60 g/2 oz) slivered almonds

1 tablespoon olive oil

2 back bacon rashers, chopped

125 g (4 oz) currants

1 cup (30 g/1 oz) chopped parsley

6 thinly sliced spring onions (scallions)

grated zest and juice of 1 lemon

olive oil, to drizzle

lemon wedges, to serve

CHILLIES
Chillies belong to the Capsicum family and are native to South and Central America. Chillies were taken by the Spanish and Portuguese to southern Italy, India and Southeast Asia, where they became integrated into local diets. Each type of chilli has its own flavour and varies in its degree of 'hotness'. In countries that use a lot of chilli in their cooking, it is important to have the right chilli for each dish.

MEXICAN RED RICE

Preparation time: 12 minutes
Total cooking time: 50 minutes
Serves 8 as a side dish

4 streaky bacon rashers, chopped
40 g (1 1/4 oz) butter
1 onion, finely chopped
3 garlic cloves, crushed
2 cups (400 g/13 oz) long-grain rice
1 large red capsicum (pepper), finely diced
1 celery stalk, finely chopped
1 long red chilli, finely chopped
2 teaspoons sweet paprika
2 teaspoons ground cumin
400 g (13 oz) tin chopped tomatoes
1 tablespoon tomato paste (purée)
2 teaspoons finely chopped oregano
3 cups (750 ml/24 fl oz) chicken stock
3 spring onions (scallions), finely chopped
20 g (3/4 oz) butter (optional)

1 Cook the bacon, with a little oil if necessary, in a large saucepan over medium heat for about 8 minutes, or until crispy and brown. Remove from the pan. Add the butter and, when sizzling, add the onion and garlic and cook, stirring frequently, for about 10 minutes, or until softened and golden.
2 Add the rice and stir to coat, then add the capsicum, celery and chilli and cook for a few minutes or until softened. Add the paprika and cumin and cook for 1 minute, or until fragrant. Return the bacon to the pan, then add the chopped tomatoes, tomato paste, oregano and chicken stock and stir to combine. Bring to the boil, then reduce the heat to low and cover with a lid. Cook for 20 minutes, or until all the liquid has been absorbed. Allow to sit, still covered, for about 5 minutes before fluffing with a fork and stirring in the spring onions and extra butter if desired. Season to taste and serve immediately.
NOTE: To turn this side dish into a main course sauté 500 g (1 lb) peeled and deveined prawns (shrimp) in a little butter and stir through the rice before serving.

RIGHT: Mexican red rice

ROAST CHICKEN STUFFED WITH WILD RICE

Preparation time: 30 minutes + cooling
Total cooking time: 1 hour 45 minutes
Serves 6

50 g (1³/4 oz) wild rice

200 g (6¹/2 oz) basmati rice

¹/4 cup (60 ml/2 fl oz) orange juice

100 g (3¹/2 oz) dried cranberries

¹/2 teaspoon ground cinnamon

100 g (3¹/2 oz) roasted, roughly chopped
   macadamias

50 g (1³/4 oz) shelled pistachios

2 teaspoons chopped fresh rosemary

1 large orange, zested

20 g (³/4 oz) butter, melted

40 g (1¹/4 oz) butter, extra, softened

1 cup (250 ml/8 fl oz) chicken stock

1.6–2 kg (3¹/4 lb–4 lb) chicken

1 large onion, cut into large chunks

1 carrot, cut into large chunks

2 celery stalks, cut into large chunks

1 tablespoon plain (all-purpose) flour

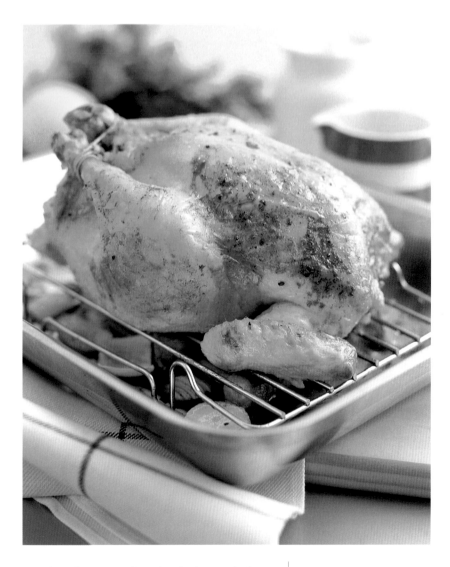

1 Add the wild rice to a saucepan of cold, salted water. Bring to the boil and simmer for 10 minutes, then add the basmati rice and cook for 15 minutes. At the same time, bring the orange juice to the boil in a small saucepan and add the cranberries. Turn off the heat and soak for 15 minutes. Drain the rice under cold water, then cool. Transfer to a bowl and add the cranberries, cinnamon, macadamias, pistachios, rosemary and orange zest. Season, then stir in the melted butter. Cool completely.

2 Pat the inside of the chicken dry with paper towels. Using clean hands, fill the cavity of the chicken with the cold stuffing.

3 Truss the chicken. To do this, use a 90 cm (36 inch) piece of kitchen string, tie both chicken legs together, twisting the string around a couple of times. Run the string around the thighs and under the wings on both sides of the bird, then pull it tightly and tie a firm knot at the neck. Trim off any excess string. Any excess skin at the neck of the bird can be tucked under the wings.

4 Preheat the oven to moderately hot 200°C (400°F/Gas 6). Spread the remaining butter over the skin of the chicken, then season well with sea salt and pepper. Place the chicken with the breast-side up on a roasting rack.

5 Spread the vegetables in the base of a sturdy roasting tin. Place the chicken, on its rack, over the vegetables and roast for 45 minutes. Baste the chicken, then return to the oven and roast for another 30 minutes, or until the chicken is cooked. Test by piercing through the lower part of the thigh with a skewer. If the juices run clear, it is cooked, but if not, return it to the oven for another 10–15 minutes. Cover loosely with foil if browning too quickly. Leave the chicken to rest while you prepare the gravy.

6 Remove the vegetables from the roasting tin with a slotted spoon and discard. Spoon all but 3 tablespoons of the fat from the roasting tin, then place the tin on the stove-top. Stir in the flour and cook for 1 minute, until it starts to brown. Scrape the crusty bits from the base. Add the remaining chicken stock and cook for 3–4 minutes. Add any juices from the chicken. Strain the gravy through a sieve. Serve the chicken with the gravy.

ABOVE: Roast chicken stuffed with wild rice

NUTMEG
The hard kernel or nut of an evergreen plant native to Indonesia, nutmeg has a warm spicy flavour. Nutmegs lose their aroma and flavour quite soon after grating, so the best flavour is achieved with freshly grated nutmeg—there are mini graters for just this purpose, but a normal one will do the job just as well. Nutmeg is used to flavour both sweet and savoury food.

ABOVE: Creole rice fritters

CREOLE RICE FRITTERS

(Calas)

Preparation time: 20 minutes +
  40 minutes resting
Total cooking time: 15 minutes
Makes about 24

☆ ☆

3/4 cup (90 g/3 oz) plain
  (all-purpose) flour
1/2 cup (115 g/4 oz) caster
  (superfine) sugar
1/2 teaspoon freshly grated nutmeg
1 teaspoon ground cinnamon
1 x 8 g (1/4 oz) sachet instant dry yeast
2 eggs, lightly beaten
2 cups (370 g/12 oz) well cooked short-grain
  rice, lightly mashed
1 teaspoon pure vanilla extract
vegetable oil, for deep-frying
icing (confectioners') sugar, to sprinkle

1 Sift the flour into a bowl and add the sugar, nutmeg, cinnamon, yeast and a large pinch of salt and combine well. Gradually stir in 1/3 cup (80 ml/2^3/4 fl oz) very hot but not boiling water until you have a thick paste. Gradually beat in the eggs and continue beating until you have a smooth batter, then mix in the rice and vanilla until well combined. Cover and allow to rise in a warm, draft-free place for about 20 minutes, or until doubled in size. Stir well, then rest again for a further 20 minutes.

2 Heat enough oil in a deep-fat fryer or large saucepan to fully cover the fritters. Heat the oil to 180°C (350°F), or until a piece of batter dropped into the oil browns in 15 seconds. Stir the batter again, then drop tablespoons of the mixture (in batches) into the hot oil and cook, turning occasionally for 2–3 minutes, or until deeply golden. Drain on paper towels, sprinkle with icing sugar and serve immediately.

NOTE: Cooked and sold on the streets of New Orleans this popular treat is enjoyed most often as a breakfast food or a snack but makes a great dessert served with ice cream.

OAXACAN RICE PUDDING

Preparation time: 15 minutes + soaking
Total cooking time: 1 hour 20 minutes
Serves 6

☆

1/3 cup (40 g/1 1/4 oz) raisins

2 tablespoons white rum

1 1/2 cups (330 g/11 oz) paella or arborio rice

1 cinnamon stick

1 strip lime zest

1 vanilla bean, split

1 cup (250 ml/8 fl oz) milk

300 ml (9 1/2 fl oz) cream

395 g (13 oz) tin condensed milk

3 egg yolks, beaten

20 g (3/4 oz) butter

ground cinnamon, to serve

1 Soak the raisins in the rum in a small bowl until needed.

2 Combine the rice with 2 1/2 cups (625 ml/ 20 fl oz) water, the cinnamon stick, lime zest and the split vanilla bean and seeds in a large saucepan and bring to the boil over medium heat. Cook, stirring frequently so it doesn't catch on the bottom of the pan, for about 10 minutes, or until the water has almost absorbed, then reduce the heat to very low.

3 Combine the milk, cream, condensed milk and gradually stir into the pan until well combined with the rice. Cook over a gentle heat for 1 hour, stirring frequently until the rice is very tender and most of the liquid has been absorbed—it should be a creamy consistency. Again, be careful not to let the mixture catch.

4 Carefully remove the vanilla, lime and cinnamon stick, then add the beaten yolks, butter and the raisins and stir for 2 minutes before pouring into a serving platter or individual dishes. Sprinkle with a little ground cinnamon before serving. This dish is delicious served warm or chilled.

NOTE: Very similar to the Spanish rice pudding, this originates in the Mexican town of Oaxaca. Some versions include a little fresh ginger to add some punch.

CINNAMON
A member of the laurel family native to Sri Lanka. The inner bark is dried and sold as quills or sticks, which are used whole to flavour milk puddings, curries, pickles and mulled wine. Ground or powdered cinnamon is used in baking and desserts, and is sometimes added to savoury dishes such as curries and stews.

LEFT: Oaxacan rice pudding

INDIA

Indian meals are a vibrant mixture of texture, colour and flavour. In northern and central India, rice is an essential part of the meal and it is accompanied by a wide variety of vegetarian or meat dishes as well as chutneys, relishes and dairy foods, such as yoghurt or curd. In India it is customary for people to scoop up a pile of rice with their right hand, then add a few pieces of each accompanying dish until the perfect blend of flavours has been achieved. The little pile is then formed into a tasty ball and popped into the mouth. Whichever way you choose to eat, there is a wonderful world of Indian food to explore.

KHICHHARI
Khichhari or kitcheri is the precursor to kedgeree, a dish taken up with much enthusiasm by the British in India. In the south of India khichhari is a breakfast dish and is eaten with minced (ground) meat, poppadoms and chutney.

ABOVE: Khichhari

KHICHHARI

Preparation time: 10 minutes +
   2 hours soaking + 10 minutes standing
Total cooking time: 25 minutes
Serves 6

1/4 cup (60 g/2 oz) yellow lentils

1 1/2 cups (300 g/10 oz) basmati rice

60 g (2 oz) ghee

1 teaspoon cumin seeds

6 cloves

1/2 cinnamon stick

2 onions, finely chopped

2 garlic cloves, finely chopped

2 cm (3/4 inch) piece of ginger, finely chopped

1 teaspoon garam masala

1/4 cup (60 ml/2 fl oz) lemon juice

1 teaspoon salt

1 Soak the lentils in 2 cups (500 ml/16 fl oz) water in a large saucepan for 2 hours. Wash the rice in a sieve under cold water until the water from the rice runs clear. Drain.
2 Heat the ghee in a heavy-based saucepan over low heat and fry the cumin seeds, cloves and cinnamon for a few seconds. Increase the heat to medium, add the onion, garlic and ginger and cook for a few minutes until they soften and begin to brown.
3 Add the rice and lentils and toss to thoroughly coat in ghee. Add the garam masala, lemon juice, salt and 3 cups (750 ml/24 fl oz) boiling water. Bring to the boil, then reduce the heat to very low, cover tightly and cook for 15 minutes. Remove from the heat and gently fluff up with a fork. Cover the pan with a clean cloth and leave for 10 minutes. Fluff up again and season with salt, to taste.

CHICKEN MULLIGATAWNY

Preparation time: 25 minutes +
 overnight refrigeration
Total cooking time: 4 hours
Serves 6

STOCK

1.5 kg (3 lb) chicken

1 carrot, chopped

2 celery stalks, chopped

4 spring onions (scallions), cut into
 3 cm (1¼ inch) lengths

2 cm (³/4 inch) piece of ginger, sliced

2 tomatoes, peeled

20 g (³/4 oz) ghee

1 large onion, finely chopped

3 garlic cloves, crushed

8 curry leaves

¼ cup (60 g/2 oz) Madras curry paste

1 cup (250 g/8 oz) red lentils, washed
 and drained

⅓ cup (75 g/2½ oz) short-grain rice

1 cup (250 ml/8 fl oz) coconut cream

2 tablespoons coriander (cilantro)
 leaves, chopped

mango chutney, to serve

1 To make the stock, put all the ingredients and 4 litres (128 fl oz) cold water in a large stockpot or saucepan. Bring to the boil, removing any scum that rises to the surface. Reduce the heat to low and simmer, partly covered, for 3 hours. Continue to remove any scum from the surface.
2 Carefully remove the chicken and cool. Strain the stock into a bowl and cool. Cover and refrigerate overnight. Discard the skin and bones from the chicken and shred the flesh into small pieces. Cover and refrigerate overnight.
3 Score a cross in the base of the tomatoes. Put in a heatproof bowl and cover with boiling water. Leave for 30 seconds then transfer to a bowl of cold water and peel the skin away from the cross. Chop the flesh.
4 Remove the fat from the surface of the stock. Melt the ghee in a large saucepan over medium heat. Cook the onion for 5 minutes, or until softened but not browned. Add the garlic and curry leaves and cook for 1 minute. Add the curry paste, cook for 1 minute, then stir in the lentils until coated. Pour in the stock and bring

to the boil over high heat, removing any scum on the surface. Reduce the heat, add the tomato and simmer for 30 minutes, or until the lentils are completely soft.
5 Bring a large saucepan of water to the boil. Add the rice and cook for 12 minutes, stirring once or twice. Drain. Stir the rice into the soup with the chicken and coconut cream until warmed through—don't allow it to boil or it will curdle. Season. Sprinkle with the coriander and serve with the mango chutney.

GARAM MASALA

Remove the seeds from 8 cardamom pods. Break 2 Indian bay leaves (cassia leaves) into small pieces. Put them in a spice grinder or mortar and pestle with 1 teaspoon black peppercorns, 2 teaspoons cumin seeds, 2 teaspoons coriander seeds, a 5 cm (2 inch) piece of cinnamon stick and 1 teaspoon cloves and grind to a fine powder. Store in a small airtight container until needed. Makes 3 tablespoons.

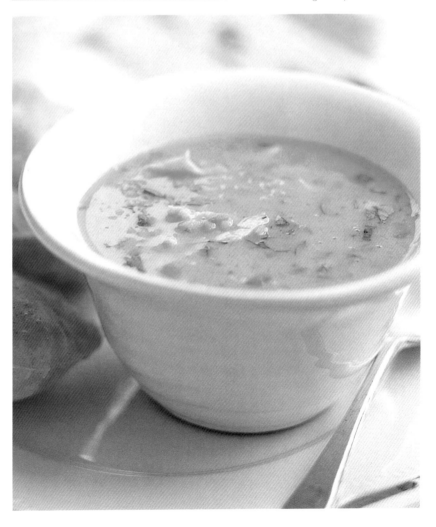

BELOW: Chicken mulligatawny

LAMB BIRYANI

Run the dough sausage around the edge of the casserole dish.

Once you have put the rope of dough around the edge of the dish, put the lid on; don't lift it off until the biryani is cooked.

LAMB BIRYANI

Preparation time: 30 minutes + overnight marinating + 10 minutes standing
Total cooking time: 1 hour 40 minutes
Serves 6

☆ ☆ ☆

1 kg (2 lb) boneless lamb leg or shoulder, cut into 3 cm (1 1/4 inch) cubes
7 cm (2 3/4 inch) piece of ginger, grated
2 garlic cloves, crushed
2 tablespoons garam masala
1/2 teaspoon chilli powder
1/2 teaspoon ground turmeric
4 green chillies, finely chopped
3 tablespoons chopped mint
4 tablespoons chopped coriander (cilantro) leaves
2 1/2 cups (500 g/1 lb) basmati rice
4 onions, thinly sliced
1/4 teaspoon salt
1/2 cup (125 ml/4 fl oz) oil
125 g (4 oz) unsalted butter, melted

250 g (8 oz) thick natural yoghurt
1/2 teaspoon saffron threads, soaked in 2 tablespoons hot milk
1/4 cup (60 ml/2 fl oz) lemon juice

SEALING DOUGH
1 1/3 cups (200 g/6 1/2 oz) wholemeal flour
1 teaspoon salt

1 Mix the lamb in a bowl with the ginger, garlic, garam masala, chilli powder, turmeric, chilli, mint and coriander. Cover and refrigerate overnight.
2 Wash the rice in a sieve under cold, running water until the water from the rice runs clear. Put the sliced onion in a sieve, sprinkle with the salt and leave for 10 minutes to drain off any liquid that oozes out. Rinse and pat dry.
3 Heat the oil and butter in a large, heavy-based saucepan, add the onion and fry for about 10 minutes, or until golden brown. Drain through a sieve, reserving the oil and butter.
4 Remove the lamb from the marinade, reserving the marinade, and fry in batches in a little of the oil and butter until the lamb is well browned all over. Transfer to a heavy casserole

dish and add the onion, any remaining marinade and the yoghurt and cook over low heat for 30–40 minutes, or until the lamb is tender.

5 In a separate saucepan, boil enough water to cover the rice. Add the rice to the pan. Return the water to the boil, cook the rice for 5 minutes, then drain and spread the rice over the meat. Pour 2 tablespoons of the leftover oil and ghee over the rice and drizzle with the lemon juice and saffron and milk mixture.

6 Preheat the oven to hot 220°C (425°F/Gas 7). Make a dough by mixing the flour and salt with a little water. Roll the dough into a sausage shape and use to seal the lid onto the rim of the pot or casserole, pressing it along the rim where the lid meets the pot. Put the pot over high heat for 5 minutes to bring the contents to the boil, then transfer it to the oven for 40 minutes. Remove the pot and break the seal of dough.

CHICKEN BIRYANI

Preparation time: 20 minutes +
 10 minutes standing
Total cooking time: 1 hour
Serves 8

4 cups (800 g/1 lb 10 oz) basmati rice

3 onions, sliced

1/2 cup (125 ml/4 fl oz) oil

180 g (6 oz) ghee or unsalted butter

4 cm (1 1/2 inch) piece of cinnamon stick

2 cardamom pods

3 cloves

2 star anise

2 stalks of curry leaves

2 cm (3/4 inch) piece of fresh ginger, grated

6 garlic cloves, crushed

1.3 kg (2 lb 10 oz) chicken pieces

4–6 green chillies, slit lengthways

2 cups (500 ml/16 fl oz) buttermilk

4 ripe tomatoes, diced

3/4 cup (185 ml/6 fl oz) coconut milk

1 litre (32 fl oz) chicken stock

1 lemon, cut into wedges

1 Wash the rice in a sieve under cold, running water until the water runs clear. Drain well. Put the onion in a sieve, sprinkle with 1/2 teaspoon of salt and leave for 10 minutes to drain off any liquid that oozes out. Rinse and pat dry.

2 Heat the oil and ghee over medium heat in a large, heavy-based ovenproof casserole. Add the cinnamon, cardamom and cloves, and heat until they begin to crackle. Reduce the heat to low and add the star anise and the curry leaves from one stalk. Stir in the sliced onion and cook for a few minutes until golden brown. Toss in the ginger and garlic, and cook until golden.

3 Mix in the chicken, increase the heat a little and fry until the pieces are browned on all sides. Add the chillies, the remaining curry leaves, buttermilk and some salt. Cook for 12 minutes, or until the chicken is cooked through and the liquid is reduced by half. Stir in the tomato and coconut milk. Cook until the tomato is tender, then pour in the stock and bring to the boil.

4 Preheat the oven to hot 220°C (425°F/Gas 7). Add the drained rice to the chicken and stir well. Season, then cook for 10 minutes, or until most of the liquid is absorbed.

5 Remove the pot from the heat, cover with a clean wet cloth, then a tight-fitting lid, and put the pot in the oven for 15 minutes, or until the rice is cooked. Serve hot with lemon wedges.

ABOVE: Chicken biryani

PULAO

Pulao, or pilaff as it is known in the Middle East, can be plain or a festive, elaborate dish with fruit, nuts and spices. Originally a Middle Eastern dish of cooked rice, the important feature of a pulao is that each grain of rice remains separate and fluffy. There are many variations of pulao, found as far afield as Southern Russia, Persia and Morocco, a legacy of dishes travelling with conquerors and traders. Indian pulaos are very closely related to those of Central Asia.

ABOVE: Pulao

PULAO

Preparation time: 20 minutes
Total cooking time: 15 minutes
Serves 6

☆ ☆

500 g (1 lb) basmati rice
1 teaspoon cumin seeds
4 tablespoons ghee or oil
2 tablespoons chopped almonds
2 tablespoons raisins or sultanas
2 onions, thinly sliced
2 cinnamon sticks
5 cardamom pods
1 teaspoon sugar
1 tablespoon ginger juice
15 saffron threads, soaked in
   1 tablespoon warm milk
2 Indian bay leaves (cassia leaves)
1 cup (250 ml/8 fl oz) coconut milk
2 tablespoons fresh or frozen peas
rosewater (optional)

1 Wash the rice in a sieve under cold, running water until the water from the rice runs clear. Drain the rice and put in a saucepan, cover with water and soak for 30 minutes. Drain.
2 Place a small frying pan over low heat and dry-fry the cumin seeds until aromatic.
3 Heat the ghee or oil in a karhai (Indian wok) or heavy-based frying pan and fry the almonds and raisins until browned. Remove from the pan, fry the onion in the same ghee until dark golden brown, then remove from the pan.
4 Add the rice, roasted cumin seeds, cinnamon, cardamom, sugar, ginger juice, saffron and salt to the pan and fry for 2 minutes, or until aromatic.
5 Add the bay leaves and coconut milk to the pan, then add enough water to come about 5 cm (2 inches) above the rice. Bring to the boil, cover and cook over medium heat for 8 minutes, or until most of the water has evaporated.
6 Add the peas to the pan and stir well. Reduce the heat to very low and cook until the rice is cooked through. Stir in the fried almonds, raisins and onion, reserving some for garnishing. Drizzle with a few drops of rosewater if you would like a more perfumed dish. Garnish with the reserved almonds, raisins and onion, then serve.

YAKHNI PULAO

Preparation time: 20 minutes +
  10 minutes standing
Total cooking time: 20 minutes
Serves 4

225 g (7 oz) basmati rice

2 cups (500 ml/16 fl oz) chicken stock

6 tablespoons ghee or oil

5 cardamom pods

5 cm (2 inch) piece of cinnamon stick

6 cloves

8 black peppercorns

4 Indian bay leaves (cassia leaves)

1 onion, finely sliced

1 Wash the rice in a sieve under cold running water until the water runs clear. Drain.
2 Pour the stock into a saucepan and heat to near boiling point.
3 Meanwhile, heat 2 tablespoons of the ghee or oil over medium heat in a large, heavy-based saucepan. Add the cardamom, cinnamon, cloves, peppercorns and bay leaves and fry for 1 minute. Reduce the heat to low, add the rice and stir constantly for 1 minute. Add the heated stock and some salt to the rice and bring rapidly to the boil. Cover and simmer over low heat for 15 minutes. Leave the rice to stand for 10 minutes before uncovering. Lightly fluff up the rice before serving.
4 Meanwhile, heat the remaining ghee or oil in a frying pan over low heat and fry the onion until soft. Increase the heat and fry until the onion is brown. Drain on paper towels, then use as garnish.

BOILED ROSEMATTER OR PATNI RICE

Rinse 400 g (13 oz) rosematter or patni rice under cold running water until the water running away is clear, then drain well. Bring a large, heavy-based saucepan of water to the boil and add 1 teaspoon of salt. When the water is at a rolling boil, add the rice and bring back to the boil. Keep at a steady boil for 20 minutes, then test a grain to see if it is cooked. Drain the rice and then serve. Serves 6.
NOTE: Rosematter and patni rice look red and speckled because the rice has been precooked in its husk, leaving some bran and husk stuck to the grain.

RICE IN INDIA
Rice is a staple across most of India. Hundreds of varieties exist, most with their own flavour, aroma and texture. Probably the most widely known Indian rice outside of India is basmati rice. Basmati is ideal for many of the Indian rice-based dishes because the grains remain separate and firm when cooked. In India, rice is typically an accompaniment to meat, vegetables or pulses.

LEFT: Yakhni pulao

PRAWN PULAO

Preparation time: 30 minutes
Total cooking time: 25 minutes
Serves 4

☆ ☆

200 g (6 1/2 oz) basmati rice
300 g (10 oz) small prawns (shrimp)
1/4 cup (60 ml/2 fl oz) oil
1 onion, finely chopped
3 cm (1 1/4 inch) piece of cinnamon
6 cardamom pods
5 cloves
4 Indian bay leaves (see Note)
1 stem lemon grass, finely chopped
4 garlic cloves, crushed
5 cm (2 inch) piece of ginger, grated
1/4 teaspoon ground turmeric

1 Wash the rice in a sieve under cold running water until the water from the rice runs clear. Drain. Peel and devein the prawns, then wash thoroughly and pat dry with paper towels.
2 Heat the oil in a karhai (Indian wok) or heavy-based frying pan over low heat and fry the onion, cinnamon, cardamom, cloves, bay leaves and lemon grass until the onion is lightly browned. Stir in the garlic, ginger and turmeric. Add the prawns and stir until the prawns turn pinkish. Add the rice and fry over medium heat for 2 minutes. Add 2 cups (500 ml/16 fl oz) boiling water and some salt and bring to the boil. Reduce the heat and simmer for about 15 minutes. Remove from the heat, cover tightly with a lid and leave for 10 minutes. Lightly fluff up the rice before serving.
NOTE: Indian bay leaves are the dried leaves of the cassia tree. They look somewhat like European bay leaves but they have a cinnamon flavour. They are available from Indian grocery shops.

GRATING GINGER
There are two types of graters specifically designed to cope with ginger. The first is a porcelain Japanese version with rows of pyramid-like teeth angled in two directions (as above). The teeth capture the fibres while releasing the flesh and juice. The second is a much more rustic version made out of bamboo that is commonly used in Southeast Asia, and it essentially does the same thing. If you are using a box grater, use the side with small, one-directional holes.

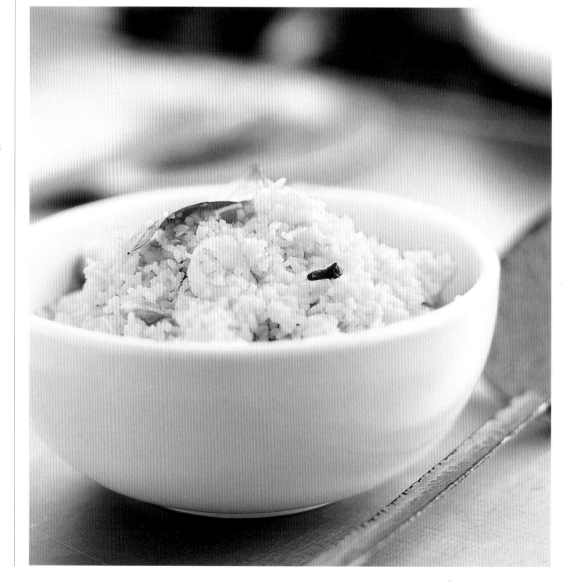

RIGHT: Prawn pulao

ANDHRA-STYLE CHICKEN PULAO

Preparation time: 30 minutes +
10 minutes standing
Total cooking time: I hour
Serves 8

1.5 kg (3 lb) chicken or chicken pieces

1 kg (2 lb) basmati rice

3 onions, sliced

1/2 teaspoon salt

100 ml (3 1/2 fl oz) oil

175 g (6 oz) ghee

4 cm (1 1/2 inch) piece of cinnamon stick

2 cardamom pods

3 cloves

2 star anise

2 stalks of curry leaves

2 cm (3/4 inch) piece of ginger, grated

6 garlic cloves, crushed

4–6 green chillies, slit lengthways

400 ml (13 fl oz) buttermilk

4 ripe tomatoes, diced

200 ml (6 1/2 fl oz) coconut milk

1 litre (32 fl oz) chicken stock

1 lemon, cut into wedges

1 If using a whole chicken, cut it into 16 pieces by removing both legs and cutting between the joint of the drumstick and thigh. Cut each of these in half through the bone with a cleaver or poultry shears (make sure there are no bone shards). Cut down either side of the backbone and remove the backbone. Turn the chicken over and cut through the cartilage down the centre of the breastbone. Cut each breast into three pieces and cut off the wings. Trim off the wing tips. Trim off any excess fat or skin from the pieces of chicken.

2 Wash the rice in a sieve under cold, running water until the water from the rice runs clear. Drain well. Put the sliced onion in a sieve, sprinkle with the salt and leave for 10 minutes to drain off any liquid that oozes out. Rinse and then pat dry.

3 Heat the oil and ghee over medium heat in a large, ovenproof 'degchi' (thick-based pot), or heavy casserole dish. Add the cinnamon, cardamom and cloves and heat until they begin to crackle. Reduce the heat to low and add the star anise and the curry leaves from one stem. Add the sliced onion and cook until golden brown. Add the ginger and garlic and cook until golden. Add the chicken, increase the heat to medium and fry until the pieces are browned on all sides. Add the slit chillies, the remaining curry leaves, the buttermilk and some salt. Cook for 12 minutes, or until the chicken is cooked through and the liquid is reduced by half. Add the diced tomato and the coconut milk. Cook until the tomato is tender, then pour in the stock and bring up to the boil.

4 Preheat the oven to 220°C (425°F/Gas 7). Add the drained rice to the chicken and stir it in well. Check the seasoning, adjust if necessary, and cook for 10 minutes, or until nearly all the liquid is absorbed.

5 Remove the pot from the heat, cover it with a clean wet cloth, then a tight-fitting lid, and put it in the oven for 15 minutes, or until the rice is cooked through. Serve hot with lemon wedges.

ABOVE: Andhra-style chicken pulao

1 Soak eight wooden skewers in water for 30 minutes to prevent them burning during cooking. Meanwhile, combine the yoghurt, tandoori paste and lemon juice in a non-metallic dish. Add the chicken and coat well, then cover with plastic wrap and marinate for at least 10 minutes.

2 Heat the oil in a saucepan. Add the onion and cook for 3 minutes, then add the rice and cardamom pods. Cook, stirring often, for 3–5 minutes, or until the rice is slightly opaque. Add the hot chicken stock and bring to the boil. Reduce the heat to low, cover with a lid, and cook the rice, without removing the lid, for 15 minutes.

3 Preheat a barbecue plate or grill (broiler) to very hot. Thread the chicken cubes onto the soaked bamboo skewers, leaving the bottom quarter of the skewers empty. Cook the skewers on each side for 4–5 minutes, or until the chicken is cooked through.

4 Wash the spinach and put it in a large saucepan with just the water clinging to the leaves. Cook, covered, over medium heat for 1–2 minutes, or until the spinach has wilted. Uncover the rice, fluff up with a fork and serve with the spinach, chicken and a dollop of yoghurt.

NOTE: Tandoori paste is usually made up of a mixture of cumin, coriander, cinnamon, cloves, chilli, ginger, garlic, turmeric, mace, salt, colouring and yoghurt, though recipes do vary. There are many commercial varieties of paste available in jars from Indian grocery stores and large supermarkets.

TANDOORI CHICKEN WITH CARDAMOM RICE

Preparation time: 15 minutes +
  30 minutes soaking
Total cooking time: 45 minutes
Serves 4

☆☆

1 cup (250 g/8 oz) thick natural yoghurt, plus extra, to serve
1/4 cup (60 g/2 oz) tandoori paste (see Note)
2 tablespoons lemon juice
1 kg (2 lb) chicken breast fillets, cut into 4 cm (1 1/2 inch) cubes
1 tablespoon oil
1 onion, finely diced
1 1/2 cups (300 g/10 oz) long-grain rice
2 cardamom pods, bruised
3 cups (750 ml/24 fl oz) hot chicken stock
400 g (13 oz) English spinach leaves

ABOVE: Tandoori chicken with cardamom rice

HOME-MADE YOGHURT

Bring 2 1/2 cups (625 ml/20 fl oz) milk to the boil in a heavy-based saucepan, then allow to cool to lukewarm. Stir in 2 tablespoons thick natural yoghurt, cover and leave in a warm place for about 8 hours, or overnight. The yoghurt should be thick. If it is too runny, the milk was probably too hot for the starter yoghurt; if it is too milky, the yoghurt was probably not left in a warm enough place to ferment. From each batch, use 2 tablespoons to make the next batch. When the yoghurt is set, put it in a sieve lined with a piece of muslin and leave to drain overnight. This will give a thick yoghurt which does not contain too much moisture. Makes 2 1/2 cups (600 g/1 1/4 lb).

MADRAS LAMB PULAO

Preparation time: 15 minutes
Total cooking time: 35 minutes
Serves 4

¹/₄ cup (60 ml/2 fl oz) oil

2 onions, thinly sliced

I cup (250 g/8 oz) thick natural yoghurt

¹/₄ cup (60 g/2 oz) good-quality Madras
  curry paste

2 cups (400 g/13 oz) basmati rice, rinsed well

8 large French-trimmed lamb cutlets

4 tablespoons chopped mint

¹/₂ cup (60 g/2 oz) slivered almonds,
  lightly toasted

1 Heat 2 tablespoons of the oil in a large saucepan, add the onion and cook over medium heat for 4–5 minutes, or until soft. Remove half with a slotted spoon, set aside and keep warm. Add 200 g (6¹/₂ oz) of the yoghurt and 2 tablespoons of the curry paste to the pan. Cook, stirring, for 2 minutes. Stir in the rice until well coated. Pour in 2 cups (500 ml/16 fl oz) water, bring to the boil, then reduce the heat a little and cook for 15–20 minutes, or until all the water has been absorbed and the rice is tender.

2 Meanwhile, smear the cutlets with the remaining curry paste and marinate for at least 5 minutes. Heat the remaining oil in a frying pan over high heat, then cook the cutlets for 3–4 minutes on each side, or until cooked to your liking. Remove from the heat, cover with foil and allow to rest. Combine the remaining yoghurt with 1 tablespoon of the mint.

3 To serve, stir the remaining mint through the rice, season, then divide among four serving plates. Top with the remaining onions, the lamb and the almonds. Serve with a dollop of the minted yoghurt on the side.

MINT
There are hundreds of varieties of mint, including applemint, peppermint and spearmint. Many Indian recipes are accompanied by cooling dishes that combine mint and yoghurt; they might be as simple as mint and yoghurt blended together in a basic raita, more complex mint-based chutneys or the traditional accompaniment to biryani, Churri (page 142), which also includes buttermilk and spices.

LEFT: Madras lamb pulao

SPICED LAMB RICE

Preparation time: 30 minutes
Total cooking time: 2 hours
Serves 6 as a side dish

☆ ☆

3 lamb shanks (about 1 kg/2 lb)
1 large onion, sliced
10 whole cloves
1 cinnamon stick
5 cardamom pods
3 tablespoons ghee or oil
1 teaspoon crushed garlic
2 onions, thinly sliced, extra
1/4 teaspoon ground cinnamon
1/4 teaspoon ground cloves
1/4 teaspoon freshly grated nutmeg
3 cups (600 g/1 1/4 lb) long-grain rice
1/4 teaspoon saffron threads
currants and shelled pistachios, to garnish

1 Put the lamb in a large pan with the onion, cloves, cinnamon stick, cardamom pods, 2 litres (64 fl oz) water and 1 1/2 teaspoons salt. Bring to the boil. Simmer for 1–1 1/2 hours, or until the meat is tender, occasionally skimming any scum off the surface. Remove the shanks from the cooking liquid, then cool slightly. Strain the remaining liquid into a large measuring jug—you need 1.25 litres (40 fl oz); if necessary, add some water.

2 Heat the ghee in a small pan, cook the garlic and extra onion gently until well reduced and just golden. Add the ground spices and 1/4 teaspoon freshly ground black pepper.

3 Remove the meat from the shanks and cut into cubes. Put in a bowl with the onion and spice mixture.

4 Wash and drain the rice. Put half of it in a large saucepan with a well-fitting lid and cover with the onion and lamb mixture. Put the remaining rice on top. Cook the saffron threads in a dry frying pan over a low heat until dry and crisp, stirring constantly. Cool. Put the strands in a bowl and crush with the back of a spoon. Add 1/4 cup (60 ml/2 fl oz) water and dissolve. Gently pour the reserved cooking liquid and dissolved saffron into the saucepan with the rice and lamb mixture and bring to the boil. Cover, reduce the heat to very low and cook for 20 minutes. Remove the lid, then lightly fluff up the rice. Serve garnished with currants and pistachios.

BELOW: Spiced lamb rice

SAFFRON CHICKEN PULAO

Preparation time: 25 minutes
Total cooking time: 30 minutes
Serves 6

☆

1/2 teaspoon saffron threads
2 cups (400 g/13 oz) long-grain rice
80 g (2 3/4 oz) ghee
1 cinnamon stick, broken
3 cloves
2 cardamom pods, lightly crushed
2 tablespoons sultanas
2 tablespoons blanched almonds
300 g (10 oz) skinless chicken breast fillet, diced

1 Soak the saffron in 1/4 cup (60 ml/2 fl oz) water. Put the rice and half the ghee in a large, heavy-based pan and stir until the rice grains are well coated with ghee. Add the saffron, cinnamon, cloves, cardamom pods and 2 1/2 cups (625 ml/20 fl oz) water. Cover and bring to the boil, then reduce the heat to as low as possible

and cook without removing the lid for 20 minutes.

2 Heat the remaining ghee in a frying pan, add the sultanas, almonds and chicken and cook over medium heat for about 5 minutes, or until the chicken is cooked through. Season to taste with salt.

3 Stir the chicken mixture into the rice and leave to stand for 5 minutes before serving.

TANDOORI LAMB WITH MINT PULAO

Preparation time: 30 minutes +
　overnight marinating
Total cooking time: 1 hour 30 minutes
Serves 4–6

2 kg (4 lb) leg of lamb, butterflied

1 teaspoon chilli powder

2¹/₂ tablespoons lime juice

200 g (6¹/₂ oz) thick natural yoghurt

1 onion, finely chopped

4 garlic cloves, crushed

1 tablespoon grated fresh ginger

1 teaspoon cayenne pepper

1 tablespoon ground cumin

1 tablespoon ground coriander

1 teaspoon turmeric

1 teaspoon ground cinnamon

1 teaspoon sea salt

MINT PULAO

1 tablespoon olive oil

1 onion, finely chopped

2 cups (400 g/13 oz) basmati rice

3¹/₂ cups (875 ml/28 fl oz) hot chicken stock

¹/₂ cup (25 g/³/₄ oz) chopped mint

1 Sprinkle the lamb with the chilli powder and half the lime juice.

2 To make the marinade, combine the yoghurt, onion, garlic, ginger, cayenne pepper, cumin, coriander, turmeric, cinnamon, sea salt and the remaining lime juice. Put the lamb in a large non-metallic dish and cover it with the marinade. Turn to coat well. Cover and refrigerate overnight.

3 Preheat the oven to moderately hot 200°C (400°F/Gas 6). Bring the meat to room temperature, then roll up and tie at intervals with string. Roast for about 1¹/₂ hours for medium–well done, or until cooked to your liking, basting regularly with the marinade. Rest for 15 minutes. Remove the string and carve into slices.

4 Meanwhile, to make the pulao, heat the oil in a large saucepan and add the onion. Cook for 5–6 minutes over medium heat, or until soft. Add the rice and cook for 2 minutes, then add the stock and bring to the boil. Reduce the heat, cover with a lid and simmer for 15 minutes, or until all the liquid has been absorbed and the rice is tender. Stir in the mint and season to taste with salt and pepper. Serve with the lamb.

ABOVE: Tandoori lamb with mint pulao

ACCOMPANIMENTS

CARROT PACHADI

Heat 1 tablespoon oil in a small saucepan or frying pan over medium heat, add 1 teaspoon black mustard seeds and 2–3 dried chillies, then cover the pan with a lid and shake it until the seeds start to pop. Remove the pan from the heat and immediately stir in ¼ teaspoon asafoetida and 1 stalk's worth of curry leaves. Scoop 600 g (1¼ lb) thick natural yoghurt into a bowl and lightly whisk it to remove any lumps. Add 4 finely grated carrots and stir together until combined. Add the spices from the pan, stir well, then season with a little salt. Traditionally this is served with biryani or pulao. Serves 4.

CHURRI

Put 1 teaspoon cumin seeds in a dry frying pan and cook until fragrant. Grind the seeds to a fine powder in a spice grinder or mortar and pestle. Chop ½ cup (10 g/¼ oz) mint, ½ cup (15 g/½ oz) coriander (cilantro) leaves, a 2 cm (¾ inch) piece of ginger and 2 green chillies into a fine paste in a blender, or chop together finely with a knife. Add 300 g (10 oz) thick natural yoghurt and 300 ml (9½ fl oz) buttermilk and a pinch of salt to the mixture and blend until all the ingredients are well mixed. Season to taste, then mix in 1 thinly sliced onion and the ground cumin, reserving a little cumin to sprinkle on top. Traditionally this is served with biryani, but it is cooling when eaten with hot or spicy dishes. Serves 4.

MINT AND CORIANDER CHUTNEY

Discard the tough stalks from 30 g (1 oz) each of mint and coriander (cilantro), but keep the soft ones. Blend 1 green chilli, 1 tablespoon tamarind purée, 1½ teaspoons sugar and ½ teaspoon salt with the herbs in a food processor. Serves 4.

MANGO SALAD

Put 300 g (10 oz) grated coconut, 2 seeded and chopped dried chillies and 1 tablespoon grated jaggery or soft brown sugar in a blender and add enough water to make a thick, coarse paste. Transfer to a bowl and toss in 300 g (10 oz) cubed ripe mango. Season with salt. Heat a tablespoon of oil in a small frying pan over low heat and add ½ teaspoon each of coriander seeds and mustard seeds and 6 curry leaves. Cover and shake the pan until the seeds start to pop. Pour the oil and seeds over the mango mixture and stir. Serve with any Indian meal. Serves 4.

EGGPLANT SAMBAL
Preheat the oven to moderately hot 200°C (400°F/Gas 6). Slice 2 medium eggplants (aubergines) in half and brush the cut halves with 2 teaspoons oil and ½ teaspoon ground turmeric. Put the eggplants in a roasting tin and roast for 30 minutes, or until they are browned all over and very soft. Scoop the eggplant pulp into a bowl, then mash with ¼ cup

(60 ml/2 fl oz) lime juice, 2 seeded and finely diced red chillies and 1 finely diced red onion, reserving some chilli and onion for garnish. Season with salt, then fold in ⅓ cup (80 g/2¾ oz) thick natural yoghurt. Garnish with the remaining onion and chilli. Use as an accompaniment or a dip with bread. Serves 4.

POTATO MASALA
Heat 2 tablespoons oil in a heavy-based frying pan, add 1 teaspoon black mustard seeds, cover and when they start to pop add 10 curry leaves, ¼ teaspoon ground turmeric, 2 teaspoons grated ginger, 2 finely chopped green chillies and 2 chopped onions and cook, uncovered, until the onion is soft. Add 500 g (1 lb) of cubed waxy potato and 1 cup (250 ml/ 8 fl oz) water, bring to the boil, cover and cook until the potato is tender and

almost breaking up. If there is any liquid left in the pan, simmer, uncovered, until it evaporates. Add 1 tablespoon tamarind purée and season with salt. Roll in dosas (page 145) or serve on the side. Serves 4.

FROM LEFT: Carrot pachadi, Churri, Mint and coriander chutney, Mango salad, Eggplant sambal, Potato masala

143

IDIYAPPAM
In this dish from Kerala, the rice noodles are often made at home. However, this is quite labour intensive so we have used rice sticks or vermicelli as a convenient substitute.

IDIYAPPAM

Preparation time: 10 minutes +
    30 minutes soaking
Total cooking time: 20 minutes
Serves 4

☆

225 g (7 oz) rice sticks or
    dried rice vermicelli
1/3 cup (80 ml/2 3/4 fl oz) oil
50 g (1 3/4 oz) cashew nuts
1/2 onion, chopped
3 eggs
150 g (5 oz) fresh or frozen peas
10 curry leaves
2 carrots, grated
2 leeks (white part only), finely shredded
1 red capsicum (pepper), diced
2 tablespoons tomato ketchup
1 tablespoon soy sauce

1 Soak the rice sticks in cold water for about 30 minutes, then drain and put them in a saucepan of boiling water. Remove from the heat and leave in the pan for 3 minutes. Drain and refresh in cold water.

2 Heat 1 tablespoon of the oil in a frying pan and fry the cashews until golden. Remove, add the onion to the pan, fry until dark golden, then drain on paper towels. Cook the eggs in boiling water for 10 minutes to hard-boil, then cool them immediately in cold water. When cold, peel them and cut into wedges. Cook the peas in boiling water until tender.

3 Heat the remaining oil in a frying pan and briefly fry the curry leaves. Add the carrot, leek and red capsicum and stir for 1 minute. Add the ketchup, soy sauce, 1 teaspoon salt and rice sticks and mix, stirring constantly to prevent the rice sticks from sticking to the pan. Serve on a platter and garnish with the peas, cashews, fried onion and egg wedges.

ABOVE: Idiyappam

DOSAS

Preparation time: 5 minutes +
  overnight soaking + 8 hours standing
Total cooking time: 25 minutes
Makes 20

☆ ☆ ☆

110 g (3½ oz) urad dal (see Notes)
300 g (10 oz) rice flour (see Notes)
oil, for cooking

1 Put the dal in a bowl and cover with water. Soak for at least 4 hours or overnight.

2 Drain, then grind the dal with 1 teaspoon salt and a little water in a food processor, blender or mortar and pestle to form a fine paste. Mix the paste with the rice flour, add 1 litre (32 fl oz) water and mix well. Cover with a cloth and leave in a warm place for 8 hours, or until the batter ferments and bubbles. The batter will double in volume.

3 Heat a tava (traditional Indian hot-plate) or non-stick frying pan over medium heat and leave to heat up. Don't overheat it—the heat should always be medium. Lightly brush the surface with oil. Stir the batter and pour a ladleful into the middle of the griddle and quickly spread it out with the back of the ladle or a palette knife, to form a thin pancake. Don't worry if the dosa is not perfect, they are very hard to get exactly right. Drizzle a little oil or ghee around the edge to help it crisp up. Cook until small holes appear on the surface and the edges start to curl. Turn over with a spatula and cook the other side. (The first dosa is often a failure but it will season the pan.)

4 Repeat with the remaining mixture, oiling the pan between each dosa. Roll the dosas into big tubes and keep warm. Dosas are often filled with potato masala (page 143) and served with chutneys, or with curries.

NOTES: Urad dal is a kind of bean similar to mung beans; black or green when whole and white when split and skinned. It is special to southern India.

For the best result, rice flour that is specially made for making dosas should be sought out as it is ground to the right consistency. The specific type used for dosas is called *chaaval ka atta*, and is available at Indian grocery stores.

DOSAS

Pour a ladleful of the batter into the middle of the pan.

Working quickly, spread out the batter so that it covers most of the surface of the pan.

Keep cooking until holes start to appear on the surface and the edges start to curl, then turn over and cook the other side.

LEFT: Dosas

IDLIS

Idlis are cooked in their own mould, called an idli steamer. The moulds should be filled almost full, then covered and steamed until the idlis are puffed.

IDLIS

Preparation time: 10 minutes +
    overnight soaking + 8 hours standing
Total cooking time: 30 minutes
Makes 20

☆☆☆

220 g (7 oz) urad dal
100 g (3½ oz) rice flour (see Notes)
1 teaspoon fenugreek seeds

1 Put the the dal in a bowl, cover with water and soak for at least 4 hours, or overnight.
2 Drain the dal, then grind in a food processor or blender with a little water, to form a fine paste.
3 Combine the rice flour, fenugreek seeds and 1 teaspoon salt in a large bowl and mix in enough water to make a thick, pourable batter. Mix the batters together. Cover with a cloth and leave in a warm place for 8 hours, until the batter ferments and bubbles. The batter will double in volume.
4 Pour the mixture into a greased idli mould, filling the cups almost full. Cover and steam the idlis over simmering water for 10–15 minutes, until they are firm and puffed.
NOTES: Traditionally, these are eaten with podi (see boxed recipe below), or as an accompaniment for dishes that have plenty of sauce.

For the best results, use rava-idli rice flour; it is a coarse flour specially for making idlis.

PODI

Dry-fry 110 g (3½ oz) urad dal, stirring constantly until brown. Remove from the pan and repeat with 100 g (3½ oz) chana dal, 10 g (¼ oz) dried chillies and ½ cup (80 g/2¾ oz) sesame seeds. Grind the mixture to a powder with ½ teaspoon each of sugar and salt, using a spice grinder or mortar and pestle. Cool completely and store in a jar or an airtight container. When ready to serve, heat 1 tablespoon ghee in a frying pan and add 2 teaspoons of podi per person. Toss together until well mixed. Makes 220 g (7 oz). Use as a dip or as a seasoning or eat it with idlis.

ABOVE: Idlis

YOGHURT RICE

Preparation time: 10 minutes +
 3 hours soaking + 15 standing
Total cooking time: 15 minutes
Serves 4

☆

2 tablespoons urad dal (see Notes)

2 tablespoons chana dal (see Notes)

225 g (7 oz) basmati rice

2 tablespoons oil

1/2 teaspoon mustard seeds

12 curry leaves

3 dried chillies

1/4 teaspoon ground turmeric

pinch of asafoetida

2 cups (500 g/1 lb) thick natural yoghurt

1 Soak the dals in 1 cup (250 ml/8 fl oz) boiling water for 3 hours. Wash the rice under cold running water until the water runs clear. Drain.
2 Put the rice and 2 cups (500 ml/16 fl oz) water in a saucepan and bring rapidly to the boil.

Stir, cover, reduce the heat to a slow simmer and cook for 10 minutes. Leave for 15 minutes before fluffing up with a fork.
3 Drain the dals and pat dry with paper towels. For the final seasoning (tarka), heat the oil in a small saucepan over low heat, add the mustard seeds, cover and shake the pan until the seeds start to pop. Add the curry leaves, dried chillies and dals and fry for 2 minutes, stirring occasionally. Lastly, stir in the turmeric and asafoetida.
4 Put the yoghurt in a large bowl, pour the fried dal mixture into the yoghurt and mix thoroughly. Mix the rice into the spicy yoghurt. Season with salt, to taste. Cover and refrigerate. Serve cold, but before serving, stand the rice at room temperature for about 10 minutes. Serve as part of a meal. It goes very well with meat dishes.
NOTES: In India dal relates to any type of dried split pea, bean or lentil.

This is a popular dish to prepare for taking on journeys as the dish is served cold and the acid in the yoghurt acts as a preservative. Indians have developed special boxes of stackable enamel, tin or aluminium, called tiffin boxes, specially for carrying food.

ASAFOETIDA
Available as a yellowish powder or a lump of resin, asafoetida is made from the dried resin of a type of fennel. In its powdered form it is used as a flavour enhancer in Indian and Middle Eastern cooking, in curries, fish and vegetable stews and pickles. Use it in very small quantities as it has a strong sulphurous odour and taste, which has earned it the name 'devil's dung'. An effective anti-flatulent, asafoetida is used to make pulses and legumes more digestible.

LEFT: Yoghurt rice

SAFFRON

Saffron threads are the stigmas of a particular type of crocus and have to be harvested by hand. They can be bought in small packets or as a ground powder (the whole stigmas are preferable). It is often pointed out that saffron is one of the most expensive commodities in the world, and is literally worth more than its own weight in gold. However as the flavour is quite strong very little is needed, which means it is not an expensive item to buy.

SAFFRON RICE

Preparation time: 10 minutes +
    30 minutes soaking
Total cooking time: 25 minutes
Serves 6

2 cups (400 g/13 oz) basmati rice
25 g (3/4 oz) butter
3 bay leaves
1/4 teaspoon saffron threads
2 cups (500 ml/16 fl oz) boiling vegetable stock

1 Wash the basmati rice thoroughly, cover with cold water and soak for 30 minutes. Drain.
2 Heat the butter gently in a frying pan until it melts. Add the bay leaves and washed rice, and cook, stirring, for 6 minutes, or until all the moisture has evaporated.
3 Meanwhile, soak the saffron in 2 tablespoons hot water for a few minutes. Add the saffron, and its soaking liquid, to the rice with the vegetable stock, 1½ cups (375 ml/12 fl oz)

boiling water and salt to taste. Bring to the boil, then reduce the heat and cook, covered, for 12–15 minutes, or until all the water is absorbed and the rice is cooked. Serve with curries.

TAMARIND PUREE

Break a 150 g (5 oz) tamarind block into small pieces, then put the pieces in a bowl. Pour in 1 cup (250 ml/8 fl oz) very hot water and soak for 3 hours, or until the tamarind is soft. (If you are in a hurry, simmer the tamarind in the water for 15 minutes. Although this is efficient, it doesn't give as good a result.) Mash the tamarind thoroughly with a fork. Push the mixture through a sieve and extract as much of the pulp as possible by pushing it against the sieve with the back of a spoon. Put the tamarind in the sieve back in the bowl with another 100 ml (3½ fl oz) water and mash again. Strain again. Discard the fibres left in the sieve. The purée can be frozen in 1 tablespoon portions and thawed as needed. Makes 300 ml (9½ fl oz).

RIGHT: Saffron rice

BHEL PURI

Preparation time: 40 minutes
Total cooking time: 25 minutes
Serves 6

MINT CHUTNEY

1²/₃ cups (50 g/1³/₄ oz) coriander (cilantro)

2¹/₂ cups (50 g/1³/₄ oz) mint

6 garlic cloves, chopped

3 red chillies, chopped

¹/₂ red onion, chopped

¹/₄ cup (60 ml/2 fl oz) lemon juice

TAMARIND CHUTNEY

60 g (2 oz) fennel seeds

1³/₄ cups (440 ml/14 fl oz) tamarind purée

100 g (3¹/₂ oz) fresh ginger, sliced

300 g (10 oz) jaggery or soft brown sugar

1 teaspoon chilli powder

1 tablespoon ground cumin

1 tablespoon chaat masala (see Notes)

1 teaspoon black salt (see Notes)

3 potatoes, peeled

1 tomato

120 g (4 oz) puffed rice (see Notes)

60 g (2 oz) sev noodles (see Notes)

1 green unripe mango, sliced into thin slivers

1 onion, finely chopped

4 tablespoons finely chopped coriander
   (cilantro) or mint leaves

1 teaspoon chaat masala (see Notes)

12 crushed puri crisps (see Notes)

coriander (cilantro) leaves

1 To make the mint chutney, blend the ingredients together in a food processor or mortar and pestle. Transfer to a saucepan and bring to the boil. Remove from the heat, leave to cool, then season with salt.

2 To make the tamarind chutney, place a small frying pan over low heat and dry-fry the fennel seeds until fragrant. Mix together the tamarind, ginger and sugar with 1 cup (250 ml/8 fl oz) water in a saucepan. Cook over low heat until the tamarind blends into the mixture and the sugar completely dissolves.

3 Strain out the ginger and cook the remaining mixture to a thick pulp. Add the fennel seeds, chilli powder, cumin, chaat masala and black salt. Season with salt and reduce, stirring occasionally, over medium heat until thickened to a dropping consistency (it will fall in sheets off the spoon). Leave to cool.

4 To make the bhel puri, cook the potatoes in boiling water for 10 minutes, or until tender, then cut into small cubes. Score a cross in the top of the tomato. Plunge into boiling water for 20 seconds, then drain and peel. Roughly chop the tomato, discarding the core and seeds and reserving any juices.

5 Put the puffed rice, noodles, mango, onion, chopped coriander, chaat masala and puri crisps in a large bowl and toss them together. When well mixed, stir in a little of each chutney. Vary the chutney amounts depending on the flavour you want to achieve. The tamarind chutney has a tart flavour and the mint chutney is hot. Serve in small bowls and garnish with coriander leaves.

NOTES: Black salt, puffed rice, sev noodles, chaat masala and puri crisps are all available at Indian grocery stores.

Bhel puri is India's most famous chaat (snack), and is sold by street vendors who make up a mixture to suit your tastes.

ABOVE: Bhel puri

RASAM
This soup-like dish was originally known as 'mulliga thanni', literally translated as 'pepper water'. The Anglo-Indian version is called Mulligatawny (page 131). Rasam is a southern Indian dish where it normally forms the second course in a traditional menu. It is usually mixed with plain cooked rice and eaten with curries. It can also be enjoyed on its own as a soup.

ABOVE: Rasam

RASAM

Preparation time: 15 minutes
Total cooking time: 45 minutes
Serves 4

^{1}/4 cup (80 g/2^3/4 oz) tamarind purée

1^1/2 tablespoons coriander seeds

2 tablespoons cumin seeds

1 tablespoon black peppercorns

1 tablespoon oil

5 garlic cloves, skins on, roughly pounded

1 red onion, thinly sliced

2–3 dried chillies, torn into pieces

2 stalks of curry leaves

200 g (6^1/2 oz) skinless, boneless chicken thighs, cut into small pieces

^{1}/3 cup (65 g/2^1/4 oz) basmati rice

1 Mix the tamarind purée with 3 cups (750 ml/ 24 fl oz) water. Put a small frying pan over low heat and dry-fry the coriander seeds until fragrant. Remove, then dry-fry the cumin seeds, followed by the black peppercorns. Grind them together using a spice grinder or a mortar and pestle.

2 Heat the oil in a large, heavy-based saucepan over low heat, add the garlic and onion and fry until golden. Add the chilli and the curry leaves and fry for 2 minutes, or until they are fragrant. Add the tamarind water, the ground spices and season with salt. Bring to the boil, reduce the heat and simmer for 10 minutes.

3 Add the chicken pieces and rice to the saucepan with 1 cup (250 ml/8 fl oz) water and simmer for 20 minutes, gradually adding another 1 cup (250 ml/8 fl oz) water as the soup reduces and thickens. Remove any garlic skin which has floated to the top. Season with salt, to taste, then serve.

QUAIL MASALA

Preparation time: 30 minutes +
  overnight marinating + cooling
Total cooking time: 50 minutes
Serves 6

6 x 150 g (5 oz) quails

MARINADE

$^2/_3$ cup (100 g/3$^1/_2$ oz) blanched almonds

3 garlic cloves, crushed

3 cm (1$^1/_4$ inch) piece of ginger, grated

$^1/_2$ onion, finely chopped

$^1/_2$ teaspoon chilli powder

$^1/_2$ teaspoon ground cloves

$^1/_2$ teaspoon ground cinnamon

1 teaspoon ground cumin

1 teaspoon garam masala

2 tablespoons mint, finely chopped

200 g (6$^1/_2$ oz) thick natural yoghurt

1 teaspoon jaggery or soft brown sugar

RICE STUFFING

60 g (2 oz) basmati rice

1 teaspoon amchoor powder (see Notes)

$^1/_3$ cup (50 g/1$^3/_4$ oz) chopped pine nuts

1$^1/_2$ tablespoons lemon juice

2 young banana leaves

$^1/_4$ cup (60 ml/2 fl oz) lemon juice

cucumber slices

mango or green mango slices

mint leaves

1 Clean the quails by rinsing them well and wiping them dry. Prick the flesh all over so the marinade will penetrate the meat.

2 To make the marinade, grind the almonds in a food processor or finely chop them with a knife, then mix them with the remaining marinade ingredients. Coat the quails evenly with the marinade, then cover and marinate for 4 hours, or overnight, in the fridge.

3 To make the rice stuffing, preheat the oven to moderately hot 200°C (400°F/Gas 6). Cook the rice in boiling water for 15 minutes, or until just tender. Drain well and allow to cool. Combine the rice, amchoor powder, pine nuts and lemon juice and season with salt. Just before cooking, fill the quails with the rice stuffing and brush some marinade on the quails. If you are making the stuffing in advance, make sure you refrigerate it until you are ready to use it.

4 Cut the banana leaves into neat pieces big enough to wrap a quail. Soften the leaves by dipping them into a pan of very hot water. Wipe them dry as they become pliant. If you can't get banana leaves, use foil. Brush with oil.

5 Wrap each quail individually in a piece of banana leaf, drizzling with any excess marinade. Tie firmly with a piece of kitchen string. Place the parcels, with the seam-side up, on a rack above a baking tray and bake for 25–30 minutes. Check to see if the quails are cooked by opening one—the flesh should be slightly pink but the juices should run clear when the flesh is pierced. If necessary, cook the quails for another 5 minutes. Open the packets completely for 3 minutes at the end of cooking, to brown the quail slightly. Sprinkle a dash of lemon juice over each quail. Serve in the packets with some sliced cucumber, sliced mango and mint leaves.

NOTES: Amchoor powder is a fine beige powder made by drying green mangoes.

Quail is an exotic dish, even in India. Many of the royal households traditionally used quail in many different ways. Tender young chicken or poussin can be successfully used instead.

BELOW: Quail masala

CURRIES

LAMB KORMA

Put 1 chopped onion, 2 teaspoons grated fresh ginger, 3 garlic cloves, 2 teaspoons each of ground coriander and ground cumin, 1 teaspoon cardamom seeds, a large pinch of cayenne pepper and 1/2 teaspoon salt in a food processor, and process to a smooth paste. Scoop into a large bowl with 1 kg (2 lb) cubed lamb leg. Marinate for 1 hour. Heat 2 tablespoons ghee in a large saucepan, add a sliced onion and cook, stirring, over low heat for 7 minutes, or until the onion is soft. Add the lamb and cook, stirring constantly, for 10 minutes, or until the lamb changes colour. Stir in 2½ tablespoons tomato paste (purée), 1/2 cup (125 g/4 oz) thick

natural yoghurt, 1/2 cup (125 ml/4 fl oz) coconut cream and 1/2 cup (55 g/2 oz) ground almonds. Reduce the heat and simmer, covered, stirring occasionally, for 50 minutes, or until the meat is tender. Garnish with pistachios. Serves 4–6.

BOMBAY-STYLE FISH

Mix together 2 crushed garlic cloves, 3 small seeded and finely chopped green chillies, 1 tablespoon tamarind purée, 1/2 cup (125 ml/4 fl oz) oil and 1/2 teaspoon each of ground turmeric, ground cloves, ground cinnamon and cayenne pepper. Put 800 g (1 lb 10 oz) skinned sole or leatherjacket fish fillets in a shallow dish and cover with the

marinade. Cover and refrigerate for 30 minutes. Heat 2 tablespoons oil in a large frying pan and add the fish in batches. Cook for 1 minute on each side. Return all the fish to the pan, then reduce the heat to low and add any remaining marinade and 300 ml (9½ fl oz) coconut cream. Season with salt and gently cook for 3–5 minutes, or until the fish is cooked through and flakes easily. Garnish with coriander. Serves 4.

SPICED CHICKEN WITH ALMONDS

Heat 1 tablespoon oil in a large saucepan. Add 1/4 cup (30 g/1 oz) slivered almonds and cook over low heat for 15 seconds, or until lightly golden. Remove and drain on paper towels. Heat 2 tablespoons oil in the same pan, add 2 finely chopped red onions, and cook, stirring, for 8 minutes, or until golden. Add 5 chopped garlic cloves and 1 tablespoon grated fresh ginger and cook, stirring, for 2 minutes, then stir in 4 bruised cardamom pods, 4 whole cloves, 1 teaspoon each of ground cumin, ground coriander and ground turmeric and 1/4–1/2 teaspoon chilli powder. Reduce the heat to low and cook for 2 minutes, or until fragrant. Add 1 kg (2 lb) trimmed chicken thigh fillets and cook, stirring constantly, for 5 minutes, or until well coated with the spices and starting to colour. Stir in 2 large, peeled and chopped tomatoes, 1 cinnamon stick, 1/2 cup (55 g/2 oz) ground almonds and 1 cup (250 ml/ 8 fl oz) hot water. Simmer, covered, over low heat for 1 hour, or until the chicken

is cooked through and tender. Stir often and add a little more water, if needed. Leave the pan to stand, covered, for 30 minutes for the flavours to develop, then remove the cinnamon. Scatter with slivered almonds. Serves 6.

GOAN BEEF CURRY
Remove the seeds from 8 cardamom pods and grind them with 1 teaspoon fennel seeds, 8 cloves, a 10 cm (4 inch) cinnamon stick, 1/2 teaspoon each of fenugreek seeds and freshly ground black pepper and 3 teaspoons each of coriander and cumin seeds, until they form a fine powder. Heat 1/2 cup (125 ml/4 fl oz) oil in a heavy-based frying pan over medium heat and fry 2 finely chopped onions, 6 finely chopped garlic cloves and 3 tablespoons grated ginger until lightly browned. Add 1 kg (2 lb) cubed stewing steak and fry until brown all over. Add

1/2 teaspoon ground turmeric and 2 teaspoons chilli powder and the ground powder. Fry for 1 minute. Add 300 ml (9 1/2 fl oz) coconut milk and bring slowly to the boil. Cover, reduce the heat and simmer for about 1 hour, or until the meat is tender, adding more boiling water if needed. Season with salt. Serves 6.

FROM LEFT: Lamb korma, Bombay-style fish, Spiced chicken with almonds, Goan beef curry

PULSES AND VEGETABLES

CAULIFLOWER BHAJI
Heat ¹/4 cup (60 ml/2 fl oz) oil over low heat in a saucepan. Add ¹/4 teaspoon black mustard seeds and ³/4 teaspoon cumin seeds, cover and pop for a few seconds. Uncover, add 250 g (8 oz) diced potato and fry for 1 minute, stirring occasionally. Add 750 g (1¹/2 lb) cauliflower florets, ¹/2 teaspoon ground cumin, ¹/2 teaspoon ground coriander, ¹/4 teaspoon ground turmeric, ¹/2 teaspoon garam masala, 2 finely chopped garlic cloves, 2 seeded and finely chopped green chillies and 5 curry leaves

and stir well. Add ¹/4 cup (60 ml/2 fl oz) water and bring to the boil. Cover and simmer for 6 minutes, or until the cauliflower is cooked and tender. Serves 4.

MIXED VEGETABLE CURRY
Bring 2 cups (500 ml/16 fl oz) water to the boil in a saucepan, add ¹/2 teaspoon ground turmeric and 200 g (6¹/2 oz) thickly sliced carrots, reduce the heat and simmer for 5 minutes. Add 200 g (6¹/2 oz) thickly sliced sweet potato and 200 g (6¹/2 oz) halved green beans, return to the

boil, then reduce the heat and simmer for 5 minutes, or until the vegetables are almost cooked. Put 50 g (1³/4 oz) grated coconut, 2 tablespoons grated ginger and 3 finely chopped green chillies in a blender with a little water, and blend to a paste. Add to the vegetables with 1¹/2 teaspoons ground cumin and some salt and simmer for 2 minutes. Stir in 400 g (13 oz) thick natural yoghurt and heat through. Heat 1 tablespoon oil over low heat in a small saucepan. Add 10 curry leaves and allow to crisp. Pour over the vegetables. Serves 4.

BALTI OKRA

Remove the stems from 750 g (1½ lb) okra, then cut into 2.5 cm (1 inch) lengths. Heat ⅓ cup (80 ml/2¾ fl oz) oil in a frying pan, add 1 finely chopped onion and cook for 10 minutes, or until golden. Add the okra, 1 teaspoon chilli powder, ½ teaspoon ground turmeric, 2 quartered tomatoes, and salt and cook, covered, stirring often, for 30 minutes, or until the okra is tender. Add 1 tablespoon garam masala, ¼ teaspoon ground cardamom and a pinch of freshly grated nutmeg, and cook, stirring, for 1–2 minutes. Serves 6.

CHICKPEA CURRY

Soak 1 cup (220 g/7 oz) dried chickpeas in a bowl of water overnight. Drain, rinse and put in a large saucepan. Cover with plenty of water and bring to the boil, then reduce the heat and simmer for 40 minutes, or until soft. Drain. Heat 2 tablespoons oil in a large saucepan, add 2 finely chopped onions and cook over medium heat for 15 minutes, or until golden. Add 2 chopped tomatoes, 1 tablespoon channa (chole) masala, 1 teaspoon each of cumin and chilli powder, ½ teaspoon ground coriander, ¼ teaspoon turmeric and 2 cups (500 ml/ 16 fl oz) water, and cook for 10 minutes, or until the tomato is soft. Add the chickpeas, season with salt and cook for 7–10 minutes, or until the sauce thickens. Transfer to a serving dish. Put 20 g (¾ oz) ghee or butter on top and allow to melt before serving. Garnish with sliced onion, mint and coriander (cilantro). Serves 6.

EGG CURRY

Put 8 eggs at room temperature in a saucepan of cold water and bring to the boil. Reduce the heat and simmer for 8 minutes. Remove from the pan and allow to cool in cold water. Peel the eggs. Heat 2 tablespoons oil in a saucepan, add 2 finely chopped onions, 1 teaspoon grated fresh ginger, 2 crushed garlic cloves and 3 bay leaves, and cook for 4 minutes, or until the onion is soft. Add a 400 g (13 oz) tin chopped tomatoes, ¼ teaspoon ground turmeric, ½ teaspoon chilli powder, 1 teaspoon ground cumin, 1 teaspoon ground coriander, 1 teaspoon salt and 1 cup (250 ml/8 fl oz) water. Bring to the boil, then reduce the heat and simmer for 3 minutes. Add 1 tablespoon garam masala and the whole hard-boiled eggs, and simmer for another 1–2 minutes. Garnish with coriander leaves. Serves 4–6.

FROM LEFT: Cauliflower bhaji, Mixed vegetable curry, Balti okra, Chickpea curry, Egg curry.

CLASSIC KHEER

Preparation time: 10 minutes +
   30 minutes soaking
Total cooking time: 2 hours 5 minutes
Serves 6

155 g (5 oz) basmati rice
20 cardamom pods
2.5 litres (80 fl oz) milk
1/3 cup (30 g/1 oz) flaked almonds
175 g (6 oz) sugar
30 g (1 oz) sultanas

1 Wash the rice, then soak for 30 minutes in cold water. Drain well. Remove the seeds from the cardamom pods and lightly crush them in a spice grinder or mortar and pestle.

2 Bring the milk to the boil in a large heavy-based saucepan and add the rice and cardamom. Reduce the heat and simmer for 1 1/2–2 hours, or until the rice has a creamy consistency. Stir occasionally to stop the rice sticking to the pan.

3 Dry-fry the almonds in a frying pan for a few minutes over medium heat. Add the sugar, almonds and sultanas to the rice, reserving some for a garnish. Mix, then divide among bowls. Serve warm, garnished with almonds and sultanas.

INDIAN SWEETS
Most Indians have a really sweet tooth. Unlike in the West there is no distinction between sweets and desserts; both are sold at sweet shops. They are not commonly eaten at the end of a meal. Instead, they represent a form a greeting, are used as religious offerings and are symbolic of hospitality. Many of the sweets are dairy-based, such as Kheer, a milky rice-based dessert.

RIGHT: Classic kheer

KHEER RICE PUDDING

Preparation time: 15 minutes +
  30 minutes soaking
Total cooking time: 1 hour 50 minutes
Serves 4

1/3 cup (65 g/21/4 oz) basmati rice

1.5 litres (48 fl oz) full-cream milk

6 cardamom pods, lightly crushed

1/2 cup (125 g/4 oz) caster (superfine) sugar

1/4 cup (30 g/1 oz) chopped raisins

1/4 cup (30 g/1 oz) slivered almonds

pinch of saffron threads

1 tablespoon rose water (optional)

ground cinnamon (optional)

1 Soak the rice in water for 30 minutes, then drain.
2 Pour the milk into a saucepan with the cardamom pods and bring to the boil. Add the rice, reduce the heat and simmer for 1 hour, stirring often (the rice will be soft). Add the caster sugar, raisins and slivered almonds and bring to a low boil and cook for 50 minutes, or until it is the consistency of porridge. Stir frequently to avoid sticking to the base of the pan. Remove the cardamom pods.
3 Mix the saffron threads with a little water and add to the mixture—just enough to give a pale yellow colour to the pudding. Stir in the rose water, if you're using, when cooled. Serve warm or cold, with a sprinkling of cinnamon on top, if desired.
NOTE: Served at banquets, weddings and religious ceremonies, kheer is the 'Queen of desserts' or 'Queen of creams' in India, and is particularly popular in northern India. The Indian version of rice pudding, it is cooked on the stove-top. It is exotically delicious, rich and creamy, with the cardamom and almonds giving it a distinctive texture and flavour.

CARDAMOM
There are several varieties of cardamom, with green being the best. Green cardamom is native to southern India, where it is referred to as the 'Queen of spices'. Use the whole pod or the seeds whole or ground to flavour both sweet and savoury Indian food from curries and rice dishes to sweet milk desserts. When a recipe asks for ground cardamom, you will get the best flavour by crushing the cardamom seeds into a powder yourself; either use a mortar and pestle, or a rolling pin. Choose black seeds, not brown, dry ones.

ABOVE: Kheer rice pudding

SOUTHEAST ASIA

Such is the importance of rice in Southeast Asia that it comprises 60 per cent of all food intake, and a bowl of perfectly steamed rice is rarely absent from the Asian table. But try it in other ways as well. Form a small ball of Thai sticky rice, dip it in a little sauce, then pop it in your mouth. Snack on perfectly formed fresh spring rolls with their delicate wrapping of rice paper. Feast on one of the many fried rice dishes that abound. Slurp up the rice noodles in a spicy laksa or other fragrant soup. Or enjoy a salad enlivened by the crunch of crispy deep-fried noodles.

1 Preheat the grill (broiler) to its highest setting. To make the dipping sauce, combine all the ingredients in a small bowl and stir until the sugar is dissolved.

2 Beat the eggs with the fish sauce, sugar and a pinch of black pepper.

3 Divide the cooked rice into six portions and form each one into three small balls. Press each ball to flatten. Thread three flat rounds onto each skewer.

4 Line a grill tray with foil and brush it lightly with oil. Dip each rice skewer into the egg mixture, shake off any excess and put it on the grill tray. Grill (broil) the rice until it is browned on one side, then turn it over and cook the other side. Serve with the dipping sauce.

LAOTIAN CHICKEN

Preparation time: 30 minutes
Total cooking time: 20 minutes
Serves 4–6

1/4 cup (55 g/2 oz) short-grain rice

2 tablespoons peanut oil

4 garlic cloves, crushed

2 tablespoons grated fresh galangal (see Note)

2 small red chillies

4 spring onions (scallions), finely chopped

1 kg (2 lb) chicken thigh fillets, minced (ground)

1/4 cup (60 ml/2 fl oz) fish sauce

1 tablespoon shrimp paste

3 tablespoons chopped Vietnamese mint

2 tablespoons chopped basil

1/3 cup (80 ml/2 3/4 fl oz) lime juice

1 Preheat the oven to moderate 180°C (350°F/ Gas 4). Spread the rice on an oven tray and roast it for 15 minutes, or until golden. Cool slightly, then transfer to a food processor and process until finely ground. Set aside.

2 Heat the oil in a wok, add the garlic, galangal, chilli and spring onion and cook over medium heat for 3 minutes. Add the chicken and stir for 5 minutes, or until browned, breaking up any large lumps. Stir in the fish sauce and shrimp paste and bring to the boil, then reduce the heat and simmer for 5 minutes.

3 Remove the wok from the heat, stir in the rice, mint, basil and lime juice, and mix well.

NOTE: Galangal is a rhizome related to ginger. It is available from greengrocers.

GRILLED RICE WITH DIPPING SAUCE

Preparation time: 30 minutes
Total cooking time: 15 minutes
Makes 6

DIPPING SAUCE

1/2 cup (125 ml/4 fl oz) rice vinegar

1/2 cup (110 g/3 1/2 oz) sugar

2 garlic cloves, crushed

2 bird's eye chillies, finely chopped

2 eggs

1 tablespoon fish sauce

1/2 teaspoon sugar

3 cups (650 g/1 lb 5 oz) cooked glutinous short-grain rice, well drained

ABOVE: Grilled rice with dipping sauce

MALAYSIAN SPICED FISH AND RICE

Preparation time: 20 minutes
Total cooking time: 30 minutes
Serves 4–6

6 garlic cloves

4 cm (1¹/2 inch) piece of ginger, chopped

1¹/2 tablespoons coriander seeds

1 teaspoon cumin seeds

1 cinnamon stick

3 cloves

1¹/2 teaspoons ground turmeric

¹/4 teaspoon cayenne pepper

750 g (1¹/2 lb) thick fish fillet (e.g. blue eye cod
    or snapper), cut into 5 cm (2 inch) pieces

2¹/2 tablespoons peanut oil

2 small red chillies, thinly sliced

1 large onion, sliced

2 cups (400 g/13 oz) long-grain rice,
    washed and drained

1 cup (250 ml/8 fl oz) coconut milk

¹/2 cup (125 ml/4 fl oz) good-quality fish stock

3 large ripe tomatoes, peeled, seeded
    and finely diced

1 teaspoon grated lime zest

¹/4 cup (60 ml/2 fl oz) lime juice

3 tablespoons coriander (cilantro)
    leaves, chopped

3 tablespoons crisp fried shallots

1 In the small bowl of a food processor, blend the garlic and ginger with 1 tablespoon water to form a smooth paste.

2 Dry-fry the coriander seeds, cumin seeds, cinnamon and cloves for 2 minutes until the seeds start to brown and pop. Transfer to a spice grinder or mortar and pestle and grind to a fine powder. Mix them together with the turmeric and cayenne pepper and spread out on a plate.

3 Lightly coat the pieces of fish with the spices, then shake any excess spices back onto the plate and reserve for later.

4 Heat 2 teaspoons of the oil in a deep, non-stick frying pan with a lid, over high heat, add the pieces of fish in batches and brown on either side for 1 minute. Add more oil if required. Remove the fish with a slotted spoon and set aside.

5 Reduce the heat to medium and add the remaining oil. Add the chilli and onion and stir for 3 minutes, or until the onion is soft. Stir in the garlic and ginger purée and cook for 1 minute, or until the mixture starts to brown slightly and begins to catch on the base of the pan. Sprinkle in the reserved spices and stir for 30 seconds. Add the rice and coat with the mixture.

6 Increase the heat to high and quickly pour in the coconut milk and bring to the boil. Add the fish stock and 1 cup (250 ml/8 fl oz) water and bring to the boil again.

7 When nearly all the water has evaporated, reduce the heat to a low simmer, add 2 of the diced tomatoes, the lime zest and juice, half the coriander leaves and the fish, including any juices. Season with salt, stirring through gently to avoid breaking up the fish. Cover the pan with the lid and cook for 20 minutes, or until the rice is cooked. Gently stir the rice halfway through cooking.

8 Let the rice stand for 5 minutes before fluffing with a fork. To serve, spoon out the rice and arrange pieces of fish on top, then scatter the crisp fried shallots, remaining diced tomato and coriander on top.

BELOW: Malaysian spiced fish and rice

SHRIMP PASTE
Many Southeast Asian countries use shrimp paste to add a salty flavour to food, in particular Thailand, Malaysia and Indonesia, where it is known as *blachan*. Shrimp paste is made out of dried, salted and fermented prawns (shrimp). Sold in blocks or in jars, it has a strongly pungent taste and odour. Keep it tightly wrapped in the fridge to reduce the smell. Always roast or fry shrimp paste before adding it to a dish.

NASI GORENG

Preparation time: 35 minutes
Total cooking time: 30 minutes
Serves 4

☆ ☆

2 eggs
1/3 cup (80 ml/2³/4 fl oz) oil
3 garlic cloves, finely chopped
1 onion, finely chopped
2 red chillies, seeded and very finely chopped
1 teaspoon shrimp paste
1 teaspoon coriander seeds
1/2 teaspoon sugar
400 g (13 oz) raw prawns (shrimp), peeled and deveined
200 g (6¹/2 oz) rump steak, thinly sliced
1 cup (200 g/6¹/2 oz) long-grain rice, cooked and cooled
2 teaspoons kecap manis
1 tablespoon soy sauce
4 spring onions (scallions), finely chopped
half a lettuce, finely shredded
1 cucumber, thinly sliced
3 tablespoons crisp fried onion

1 Beat the eggs and 1/4 teaspoon salt until foamy. Heat a frying pan and lightly brush with a little of the oil. Pour about one-quarter of the egg into the pan and cook for 1–2 minutes over medium heat, or until the omelette sets. Turn the omelette over and cook the other side for about 30 seconds. Remove from the pan and repeat with the remaining egg mixture. Allow to cool, then roll them up, cut into strips and set aside.
2 Combine the garlic, onion, chilli, shrimp paste, coriander and sugar in a food processor or mortar and pestle, and process or pound until a paste is formed.
3 Heat 1–2 tablespoons of the oil in a wok or large, deep frying pan; add the paste and cook over high heat for 1 minute, or until fragrant. Add the prawns and steak, and stir-fry for 2–3 minutes, or until they change colour.
4 Add the remaining oil and the cold rice to the wok. Stir-fry, breaking up any lumps, until the rice is heated through. Add the kecap manis, soy sauce and spring onion, and stir-fry for another minute.
5 Arrange the lettuce around the outside of a large platter. Put the rice in the centre, and garnish with the omelette, cucumber slices and fried onion. Serve immediately.
NOTE: This is one of the best known Indonesian dishes. The influences are Dutch (the omelette) and Chinese (the rice).

RIGHT: Nasi goreng

FRAGRANT LEMON GRASS RICE AND PRAWNS

Preparation time: 20 minutes
Total cooking time: 30 minutes
Serves 4

5 garlic cloves, peeled

4 cm (1 1/2 inch) piece of ginger, chopped

3 coriander (cilantro) roots, washed thoroughly

2 long green chillies, seeded and chopped

1 onion, chopped

2 tablespoons lime juice

1 teaspoon grated palm sugar

1/4 cup (60 ml/2 fl oz) oil

2 stems lemon grass (white part only), bruised

4 makrut (kaffir) lime leaves

750 g (1 1/2 lb) raw prawns (shrimp), peeled
    and deveined

2 cups (400 g/13 oz) long-grain rice, washed
    and drained

1 cup (250 ml/8 fl oz) fish stock

100 g (3 1/2 oz) snake beans, cut into
    3 cm (1 1/4 inch) lengths

1 Lebanese (short) cucumber

2 tablespoons coriander (cilantro) leaves

2 tablespoons crisp fried shallots

1 In the small bowl of a food processor, put the garlic, ginger, coriander roots, green chillies and onion. Add 2–3 tablespoons of water, and blend to a smooth paste.

2 In a small bowl, combine the lime juice and palm sugar, stirring until the sugar is dissolved. Set aside.

3 In a heavy-based, deep frying pan with a tight-fitting lid, heat half the oil on medium heat. Add the prepared paste, lemon grass and lime leaves, and cook for 5 minutes, or until the mixture is soft and fragrant, taking care not to brown it. Add the prawns and cook for 2 minutes, or until pink. Remove with a slotted spoon and set aside.

4 Add the rice to the pan, stir for 1 minute to coat well, then pour in the fish stock and 2 cups (500 ml/16 fl oz) water, and stir again. Increase the heat to high and bring the mixture to the boil. Stir in the beans and lime juice mixture, then season well with salt. Cover with a lid and simmer over low heat for 15–20 minutes, or until most of the water has been absorbed. Meanwhile, cut the cucumber in half,

lengthways, remove the seeds with a teaspoon and dice the flesh.

5 When most of the water has been absorbed by the rice, reduce the heat to very low, stir in the prawns, then replace the lid and cook for an additional 5 minutes, or until the rice is tender and the prawns are cooked through. Let the rice stand, covered, for 5 minutes before fluffing with a fork. Discard the lemon grass and lime leaves. Serve sprinkled with the diced cucumber, coriander leaves and crisp fried shallots.

ABOVE: Fragrant lemon grass rice and prawns

1 Heat a wok over high heat, add the oil and swirl. Stir-fry the shallots, garlic and chilli for 3 minutes, or until the shallots start to brown. Add the beans, capsicum and mushrooms, stir-fry for 3 minutes, or until cooked, then stir in the cooked jasmine rice and heat through.
2 Dissolve the palm sugar in the soy sauce, then pour over the rice. Stir in the herbs. Garnish with the crisp fried shallots and basil.

VIETNAMESE FRIED RICE

Preparation time: 30 minutes
Total cooking time: 35 minutes
Serves 4

1/4 cup (60 ml/2 fl oz) fish sauce
2 tablespoons soy sauce
2 teaspoons sugar
3 eggs
1/2 cup (125 ml/4 fl oz) oil
1 large onion, finely chopped
6 spring onions (scallions), chopped
4 garlic cloves, finely chopped
5 cm (2 inch) piece of ginger, finely grated
2 small red chillies, seeded and finely chopped
250 g (8 oz) pork loin, finely chopped
125 g (4 oz) Chinese sausage (lap cheong), thinly sliced
100 g (3 1/3 oz) green beans, chopped
100 g (3 1/3 oz) carrots, cut into small cubes
1/2 large red capsicum (pepper), chopped
2 1/2 cups (470 g/15 oz) cold cooked jasmine rice

1 Combine the fish sauce, soy sauce and sugar and stir until the sugar dissolves.
2 Whisk the eggs and 1/4 teaspoon salt together. Heat 1 tablespoon of the oil in a wok and swirl it around. Pour in the egg and cook over medium heat, stirring regularly for 2–3 minutes, or until just cooked. Remove from the wok.
3 Heat another tablespoon of oil in the wok and stir-fry the onion, spring onion, garlic, ginger and chilli for 7 minutes, or until the onion is soft, then remove from the wok. Add a little more oil and stir-fry the pork and sausage for 3–4 minutes, then remove. Add the rest of the oil and stir-fry the beans, carrot and capsicum for 1 minute before adding the rice and cooking for 2 minutes. Return everything except the egg to the wok, add the fish sauce mixture and toss. Add the egg and serve.

THAI BASIL FRIED RICE

Preparation time: 20 minutes
Total cooking time: 15 minutes
Serves 4

2 tablespoons oil
3 red Asian shallots, sliced
1 garlic clove, finely chopped
1 small red chilli, finely chopped
100 g (3 1/2 oz) snake beans, cut into short pieces
1 small red capsicum (pepper), cut into batons
90 g (3 oz) button mushrooms, halved
2 1/2 cups (470 g/15 oz) cold cooked jasmine rice
1 teaspoon grated palm sugar
1/4 cup (60 ml/2 fl oz) light soy sauce
3 tablespoons shredded Thai basil
1 tablespoon coriander (cilantro) leaves, chopped
crisp fried shallots, to garnish
Thai basil, to garnish

ABOVE: Thai basil fried rice

NASI LEMAK

Preparation time: 40 minutes +
  15 minutes standing
Total cooking time: 2 hours 40 minutes
Serves 4

RENDANG

2 onions, roughly chopped

2 garlic cloves, crushed

400 ml (13 fl oz) tin coconut milk

2 teaspoons ground coriander

1/2 teaspoon ground fennel

2 teaspoons ground cumin

1/4 teaspoon ground cloves

1.5 kg (3 lb) chuck steak, cut into cubes

4–6 small red chillies, chopped

1 tablespoon lemon juice

1 stem lemon grass (white part only),
  bruised and cut lengthways

2 teaspoons grated palm sugar

COCONUT RICE

1 1/2 cups (300 g/10 oz) long-grain rice

2 red Asian shallots

2 slices ginger

pinch of fenugreek seeds

2 pandanus leaves, knotted

400 ml (13 fl oz) tin coconut milk

SAMBAL IKAN BILIS

1/4 cup (60 ml/2 fl oz) oil

5 red Asian shallots, sliced

2 garlic cloves, crushed

1 stem lemon grass (white part only), thinly sliced

1/2 teaspoon shrimp paste

2 tablespoons chilli paste

100 g (3 1/2 oz) ikan bilis, soaked and
  washed (see Notes)

1 teaspoon sugar

2 tablespoons lime juice

1 To make the rendang, process the onion, garlic and 1 tablespoon of water to form a smooth paste. Pour the coconut milk into a wok and bring to the boil, then reduce the heat to medium and cook, stirring occasionally, for 15 minutes, or until the milk is reduced by half and the oil has separated. Do not allow the milk to brown. Add the coriander, fennel, cumin and cloves to the pan and stir for 1 minute. Add the meat and cook for 2 minutes, or until it browns. Add the chilli, lemon juice, lemon grass, sugar and prepared onion mixture. Cook, covered, over medium heat for about 2 hours, or until the liquid is reduced and thickened. Stir often.

2 Uncover and continue cooking until the oil separates again. Take care not to burn the sauce. The curry is cooked when it is brown and dry.

3 Meanwhile, to make the coconut rice, put the rice, shallots, ginger, fenugreek, pandanus leaves and 1 teaspoon salt in a saucepan. Pour enough coconut milk over the rice so there is 2 cm (3/4 inch) of liquid above the surface of the rice. Cover and cook until dry, then remove the pandanus leaf, sprinkle the rest of the coconut milk over the rice, then fluff up the grains. Stand for 15 minutes, until the coconut milk is absorbed.

4 To make the sambal, heat the oil in a wok, add the shallots, garlic, lemon grass, shrimp paste and chilli paste, and stir-fry until fragrant. Add the ikan bilis and stir-fry for a few more minutes. Mix in the sugar and lime juice. Serve with the rendang and rice.

NOTES: Ikan bilis are dried anchovies. In Malaysia, Nasi lemak is traditionally served for breakfast.

BELOW: Nasi lemak

STIR-FRIES

VIETNAMESE-STYLE BEEF AND BAMBOO SHOOTS

Freeze 400 g (13 oz) lean beef fillet for 20 minutes, then thinly slice it—freezing makes it easier to slice the meat. Heat a wok over high heat, add 2 tablespoons oil and swirl to coat the side of the wok. Add the beef in two batches and stir-fry each batch for 1 minute, or until it starts to turn pink. Remove from the wok. Add an extra tablespoon of oil to the wok, if necessary, then stir-fry 230 g (7½ oz) bamboo shoots for 3–4 minutes, or until starting to brown. Add 3 crushed garlic cloves, 2 tablespoons fish sauce and ¼ teaspoon salt and stir-fry for 2–3 minutes. Add 8 chopped spring onions (scallions) and stir-fry for a further 1 minute, or until the spring onions are starting to wilt. Return the beef to the wok, stir briefly and cook for 1 minute, or until heated through. Remove the wok from the heat, then toss in ¼ cup (40 g/1¼ oz) lightly toasted sesame seeds. Serves 4.

THAI PORK AND GINGER STIR-FRY

To make the stir-fry sauce, combine 2 tablespoons each of soy sauce, fish sauce, grated palm sugar and lime juice in a bowl and set aside until needed. Heat a wok over high heat. Add 1 tablespoon oil and swirl to coat the side of the wok. Add 1 crushed garlic clove and cook for 30 seconds. Stir-fry 400 g (13 oz) thinly sliced pork loin fillet in batches for 1–2 minutes each batch, or until lightly browned. Remove from the wok. Heat another 2 tablespoons oil in the wok, add 2 tablespoons julienned ginger and 3 thinly sliced red Asian shallots and stir-fry for 1 minute, or until the shallots are tender. Add 1 thinly sliced small red capsicum (pepper), 4 chopped spring onions (scallions) and 100 g (3½ oz) snow peas (mangetout). Stir-fry for a further 1 minute, then return the pork to the wok. Stir in the stir-fry sauce and 2 tablespoons chopped coriander (cilantro) leaves and toss everything together for 1 minute, or until combined, coated with the sauce and the pork is heated through. Serves 4.

STIR-FRIED VEGETABLES

To make the stir-fry sauce, combine 1/4 cup (60 ml/2 fl oz) chicken or vegetable stock, 2 tablespoons soy sauce, 1 tablespoon oyster sauce, 1 teaspoon fish sauce and 1/2 teaspoon grated palm sugar in a small bowl and set aside until needed. Heat a wok over high heat, add 2 tablespoons peanut oil and swirl to coat the side of the wok. Add 4 chopped spring onions (scallions), 3 crushed garlic cloves and 1 seeded and sliced red chilli. Stir-fry for 20 seconds. Add 75 g (2 1/2 oz) button mushrooms and 100 g (3 1/2 oz) roughly chopped Chinese cabbage (wom bok) and stir-fry for 1 minute. Stir in the stir-fry sauce and 150 g (5 oz) each of snow peas (mangetout), cauliflower

florets, broccoli florets and cook for 2 minutes, or until all the vegetables are tender and coated with the sauce. Garnish with coriander (cilantro) leaves, if desired. Serves 4.

CHICKEN WITH THAI BASIL

To make the stir-fry sauce, combine 1 tablespoon each of fish sauce, oyster sauce and grated palm sugar and 2 teaspoons lime juice in a small bowl and set aside until needed. Heat a wok over high heat, add 1 tablespoon peanut oil and swirl to coat the side of the wok. Cook 500 g (1 lb) thin strips of chicken breast fillet in batches for 3–5 minutes each batch, or until lightly browned and almost cooked—add more oil if needed. Remove from the wok. Heat another 2 tablespoons oil in the wok. Add 1 crushed garlic clove, 4 thinly sliced spring onions (scallions), 150 g (5 oz)

chopped snake beans and 2 thinly sliced red chillies, and stir-fry for 1 minute, or until the onion is tender. Return the chicken to the wok. Toss in 3/4 cup (35 g/1 1/4 oz) tightly packed Thai basil and 2 tablespoons chopped mint, then add the stir-fry sauce and 2 tablespoons water and cook for 1 minute. Garnish with extra basil. Serves 4.

FROM LEFT: Vietnamese-style beef with bamboo shoots, Thai pork and ginger stir-fry, Stir-fried vegetables, Chicken with Thai basil

THAI STUFFED MUSSELS

Firmly grip the cleaned mussels, then pull off and discard the beard.

Break open the mussels and remove the upper shell.

THAI STUFFED MUSSELS

Preparation time: 45 minutes
Total cooking time: 45 minutes
Serves 6

☆ ☆

2 kg (4 lb) black mussels
1/2 cup (125 ml/4 fl oz) white wine
3 garlic cloves, chopped
4 coriander (cilantro) roots
1 stem lemon grass
1 lime, sliced
2 small red onions, chopped
1 tablespoon peanut oil
1 cup (200 g/6 1/2 oz) jasmine rice
1/2 cup (80 g/2 3/4 oz) roasted unsalted
    peanuts, chopped
2 teaspoons finely chopped ginger
1 tablespoon fish sauce
1 tablespoon tamarind purée
4 tablespoons coriander (cilantro)
    leaves, chopped
4 makrut (kaffir) lime leaves, shredded
shredded Vietnamese mint, to garnish

1 Scrub the mussels with a stiff brush and remove the beards. Discard any mussels that are broken or don't close when tapped on the bench. Rinse well. Put the mussels in a large bamboo steamer and cover.

2 Put the wine, 1 1/2 cups (375 ml/12 fl oz) water, 2 of the garlic cloves, the coriander roots, the green part of the lemon grass stem, the lime slices and one of the chopped onions in a wok. Bring to a simmer.

3 Sit the steamer over the wok and steam for about 5 minutes, or until the mussels open. Discard any that have not opened. Remove and discard the upper shell. Strain and reserve the cooking liquid.

4 Heat the oil in a wok over medium heat. Add the remaining onion and garlic, the finely chopped white part of the lemon grass stem and the rice, and stir-fry for 2–3 minutes, or until the onion is soft. Add 2 cups (500 ml/16 fl oz) of the reserved liquid and simmer for 20 minutes. Preheat the oven to 200°C (400°F/Gas 6).

5 Toss in the peanuts, ginger, fish sauce, tamarind, coriander and lime leaves. Spoon a little of the mixture onto each shell half, transfer to an ovenproof baking dish and bake for 10 minutes. Garnish with the shredded mint and serve immediately.

RIGHT: Thai stuffed mussels

LEMPER
(Coconut rice in banana leaves)

Preparation time: 40 minutes + cooling
Total cooking time: 1 hour 30 minutes
Makes about 12

2–3 young banana leaves, or foil (see Notes)
2 cups (400 g/13 oz) glutinous rice
3/4 cup (185 ml/6 fl oz) coconut milk

CHICKEN FILLING
2 tablespoons oil
2–3 garlic cloves, crushed
6 curry leaves
1 teaspoon shrimp paste
2 teaspoons ground coriander
2 teaspoons ground cumin
1/2 teaspoon ground turmeric
250 g (8 oz) minced (ground) chicken
1/4 cup (60 ml/2 fl oz) coconut milk, extra
1 teaspoon lemon juice

1 With a sharp knife, cut away the central ribs of the banana leaves. The leaves will split into large pieces—cut into pieces about 15 cm (6 inches) square. Blanch in boiling water briefly to soften them, then spread out on a tea towel and cover.
2 Wash the rice, drain and put in a large heavy-based saucepan with 1 3/4 cups (440 ml/14 fl oz) water. Bring slowly to the boil, then reduce the heat to very low, cover tightly and cook for 15 minutes.
3 Pour the coconut milk and 1/2 cup (125 ml/4 fl oz) water into a small saucepan and heat without boiling. Stir through the rice with a fork. Transfer to a bowl and set aside to cool.
4 To make the chicken filling, heat the oil in a large heavy-based frying pan, add the garlic and curry leaves and stir over medium heat for 1 minute. Add the shrimp paste, coriander, cumin and turmeric and cook for another minute. Add the chicken and cook, breaking up with a fork, for 3–4 minutes, or until the chicken changes colour. Add the extra coconut milk and continue to cook over low heat for 5 minutes, or until absorbed. Remove the curry leaves. Add the lemon juice and season to taste with salt and freshly ground black pepper. Cool.
5 Place 1 heaped tablespoon of rice in the centre of each piece of banana leaf and flatten to a 4 cm (1 1/2 inch) square. Top with a heaped teaspoon of the chicken filling. Roll the leaf into a parcel and place, seam-side down, in a steamer lined with leftover banana leaf scraps or baking paper. Steam, in batches, for 15 minutes, or if you have a double-layered steamer, cook with one basket on top of the other, swapping halfway through—you'll need to cook them for a little longer.
NOTES: Banana leaves are used throughout Asia to wrap foods for steaming or baking. They keep the food moist and impart a mild flavour. They can be bought at Asian food stores if you don't have access to fresh leaves from a plant.

Lemper is a popular Indonesian snack and can be eaten hot or at room temperature.

ABOVE: Lemper

SAUCE

2 small red chillies, seeded and chopped

4 garlic cloves, roughly chopped

1 1/2 tablespoons finely chopped ginger

3 coriander (cilantro) roots, chopped

2 tablespoons dark soy sauce

2 tablespoons lime juice

2 tablespoons sugar

pinch of ground white pepper

1 Remove any excess fat from around the cavity of the chicken and reserve it. Rinse and salt the inside of the chicken and rinse again. Insert the spring onions, ginger slices and garlic into the chicken cavity then place, breast-side down in a large saucepan and cover with cold water. Add 1 teaspoon of salt and bring to the boil over high heat, skimming the surface as required. Reduce the heat to low and simmer gently for 15 minutes, then carefully turn over without piercing the skin and cook for another 15 minutes, or until the thigh juices run clear when pierced.

2 Carefully lift the chicken out of the saucepan, draining any liquid from the cavity into the rest of the stock. Reserve 1 litre (32 fl oz) of the stock. Plunge the chicken into iced water for 5 minutes to stop the cooking process and to firm the skin. Rub the entire surface with the combined vegetable and sesame oils and allow to cool while you make the rice.

3 To make the rice, cook the reserved chicken fat over medium heat for about 8 minutes, or until you have about 2 tablespoons of liquid fat, then discard the solids. (If you prefer, use vegetable oil instead.) Add the shallots and cook for a few minutes, or until lightly golden, then add the garlic and ginger and stir until fragrant. Add both the rices and cook for 5 minutes, or until lightly golden, then pour in the reserved chicken stock and 1 teaspoon salt and bring to the boil. Cover and reduce the heat to low and cook for about 20 minutes, or until tender and the liquid has evaporated. Cool, covered, for 10 minutes, then fluff with a fork.

4 Meanwhile, to make the sauce, pound the chillies, garlic, ginger and coriander roots into a paste using a mortar and pestle. Stir in the rest of the ingredients and season to taste.

5 Cut the chicken up. Divide the rice into six slightly wetted Chinese soup bowls and press down firmly, then turn out onto serving plates. Serve the pieces of chicken on a platter with the tomato, cucumber and coriander and pour the dipping sauce into a small bowl or individual sauce dishes and let your guests help themselves.

HAINANESE CHICKEN RICE

Preparation time: 50 minutes +
 10 minutes resting
Total cooking time: 1 hour 30 minutes
Serves 6

☆ ☆

2 kg (4 lb) whole chicken

6 spring onions (scallions)

a few thick slices of ginger

4 garlic cloves, bruised

1 teaspoon vegetable oil

1 teaspoon sesame oil

RICE

5 red Asian shallots, finely chopped

2 garlic cloves, crushed

1 tablespoon very finely chopped ginger

1 1/2 cups (300 g/10 oz) jasmine rice

1/2 cup (100 g/3 1/2 oz) long-grain glutinous rice

3 Roma (plum) tomatoes, cut into thin wedges

3 Lebanese (short) cucumbers, sliced diagonally

sprigs of coriander (cilantro), to garnish

ABOVE: Hainanese chicken rice

BALINESE FRIED RICE

Preparation time: 20 minutes
Total cooking time: 20 minutes
Serves 6

500 g (1 lb) raw prawns (shrimp)

2 teaspoons oil

2 eggs

2 onions, chopped

2 garlic cloves

1/4 cup (60 ml/2 fl oz) oil, extra

1/4 teaspoon shrimp paste

125 g (4 oz) rump steak, thinly sliced

1 cooked chicken breast, thinly sliced

1 1/2 cups (300 g/10 oz) long-grain rice,
    cooked and cooled

1 tablespoon soy sauce

1 tablespoon fish sauce

1 tablespoon sambal oelek

1 tablespoon tomato paste (purée)

6 spring onions (scallions), finely chopped

sliced cucumber, to garnish (optional)

1 Peel and devein the prawns, then chop the meat.

2 Heat the oil in a wok or large, heavy-based frying pan. Lightly beat the eggs and season with salt and freshly ground black pepper. Add the eggs to the pan and cook over medium heat for 1–2 minutes, or until cooked. When set, transfer the omelette to a plate, cool, and cut into thin strips—this is easy if you first roll the omelette.

3 Put the onion and garlic in a food processor and process until finely chopped.

4 Heat the extra oil in the wok, add the onion mixture and cook over medium heat, stirring frequently until it has reduced in volume and is translucent. Add the shrimp paste and cook for a further minute. Add the prawns and steak and cook over high heat for 3 minutes. Add the cooked chicken and rice and toss until heated.

5 Combine the soy sauce, fish sauce, sambal oelek, tomato paste and spring onion and add to the rice mixture. Mix well. Remove the rice from the heat and transfer to a serving platter. Top with the omelette strips and garnish with sliced cucumber, if desired.

FEASTS IN BALI
Feasts are an important feature of Balinese family and community life. For temple festivals an entire community prepares foods and offerings. Pork (a largely forbidden food in the rest of Indonesia, where the population is mostly Moslem) is festive food in Bali, with babi guling, roast suckling pig, the usual centrepiece. And, of course, rice is an important part of any feast.

LEFT: Balinese fried rice

171

THAI STICKY RICE WITH BARBECUED CHICKEN

Preparation time: 30 minutes +
  6 hours marinating
Total cooking time: 1 hour
Serves 4–6

2 kg (4 lb) whole chicken, cut into 8–10 pieces
8 garlic cloves, chopped
6 coriander (cilantro) roots, chopped
1/2 cup (15 g/1/2 oz) coriander (cilantro)
  leaves, chopped
1 tablespoon finely chopped ginger
1 teaspoon ground white pepper
1/4 cup (60 ml/2 fl oz) fish sauce
1/4 cup (60 ml/2 fl oz) lime juice
1/4 cup (60 ml/2 fl oz) whisky (optional)
3 cups (600 g/1 1/4 lb) long-grain glutinous rice
cucumber slices, to serve

Sauce
6 coriander (cilantro) roots, chopped
4 garlic cloves, chopped
2 bird's eye chillies, deseeded and chopped
3/4 cup (185 ml/6 fl oz) vinegar
4 tablespoons grated palm sugar or soft
  brown sugar

1 Put the chicken in a non-metallic bowl. Combine the garlic, coriander roots and leaves, ginger, white pepper and a pinch of salt and pound to a paste using a mortar and pestle. Mix in the fish sauce, lime juice and whisky, then pour over the chicken and mix well. Marinate for at least 6 hours in the refrigerator. At the same time, soak the rice for at least 3 hours in cold water.
2 To make the sauce, pound the coriander root, garlic, chillies and a pinch of salt to a paste using a mortar and pestle. Combine the vinegar, sugar and 3/4 cup (185 ml/6 fl oz) water and stir until the sugar has dissolved. Bring to the boil, then add the paste and cook for 8–10 minutes, or until reduced by half. Set aside until ready to serve.
3 Drain the rice well, then line a bamboo steamer with muslin or banana leaves, spread the rice over and cover with a tight-fitting lid. Steam over a wok or large saucepan of boiling water for 40 minutes, or until the rice is translucent, sticky and tender. If steam is escaping, wrap some foil over the top of the steamer. Keep covered until ready to serve.
4 Meanwhile, heat a barbecue to medium heat, then cook the chicken, turning regularly for about 25 minutes, or until tender and cooked through. The breast pieces may only take about 15 minutes so take them off first and keep warm.
5 Serve the chicken, rice, dipping sauce and cucumber on separate plates in the centre of the table and allow your guests to help themselves. Serve with the Green papaya salad.

GREEN PAPAYA SALAD

Preparation time: 25 minutes +
  30 minutes standing
Total cooking time: 5 minutes
Serves 6

370 g (12 oz) green papaya, peeled and seeded
90 g (3 oz) snake beans, cut into 2 cm
  (3/4 inch) lengths
2 garlic cloves
2 small red chillies, chopped
5 teaspoons dried shrimp
8 cherry tomatoes, halved
50 g (1 3/4 oz) coriander (cilantro) sprigs
1/4 cup (40 g/1 1/4 oz) chopped roasted peanuts

Dressing
1/4 cup (60 ml/2 fl oz) fish sauce
2 tablespoons tamarind purée
1 tablespoon lime juice
3 tablespoons grated palm sugar

1 Grate the papaya, sprinkle with salt and stand for 30 minutes. Rinse well.
2 Cook the beans in boiling water for 3 minutes, or until tender. Drain, plunge into cold water, then drain again.
3 To make the dressing, combine the fish sauce, tamarind purée, lime juice and palm sugar in a small bowl. Set aside.
4 Pound the garlic and chilli in a mortar and pestle until crushed. Add the dried shrimp and pound until puréed. Add the papaya and snake beans and lightly pound for 1 minute. Add the tomato and pound briefly to bruise.
5 Combine the coriander with the papaya mixture and spoon onto serving plates. Pour the dressing over the top. Sprinkle with the peanuts and, if desired, sliced red chilli.

GREEN PAPAYA

Papayas are a large tropical melon with a slightly pear-like shape. The flesh is juicy and creamy orange, red or yellow in colour. Unripe or green papayas are used as a vegetable; sometimes cooked, sometimes raw in salads, particularly in Thailand, and sometimes made into pickles. Confusingly, papaya is often called pawpaw, which is a different fruit altogether and a member of the custard apple family.

OPPOSITE PAGE: Thai sticky rice with barbecued chicken

2 Pour the coconut milk into a saucepan and heat until nearly boiling. Pour the milk over the rice, stirring constantly until the mixture comes to the boil. Add the curry leaves and 1 teaspoon salt. Cover with a tight-fitting lid, reduce the heat to very low and cook for 25 minutes.
3 Remove the lid, stir well and leave to cool for 10 minutes. Remove the curry leaves and pile the rice onto a platter. Arrange the egg and chilli over the rice and scatter with crisp fried onion.

INDONESIAN PEANUT FRITTERS

Preparation time: 10 minutes
Total cooking time: 15 minutes
Makes 25

DIPPING SAUCE
2 tablespoons kecap manis
1 tablespoon rice vinegar
1 tablespoon mirin
1/4 teaspoon finely grated ginger

1 cup (175 g/6 oz) rice flour
1 garlic clove, crushed
1 teaspoon ground turmeric
1/2 teaspoon ground cumin
3 teaspoons sambal oelek
1 1/2 teaspoons ground coriander
1 tablespoon finely chopped coriander
   (cilantro) leaves
220 ml (7 fl oz) coconut milk
1 1/4 cups (200 g/6 1/2 oz) roasted unsalted
   peanuts
oil, for deep-frying

1 To make the dipping sauce, combine all the ingredients in a small bowl.
2 To make the fritters, combine the flour, garlic, turmeric, cumin, sambal oelek, ground coriander, coriander leaves, and 1/2 teaspoon salt in a bowl. Gradually stir in the coconut milk until the mixture is smooth. Mix in the peanuts and 2 1/2 tablespoons hot water.
3 Fill a wok or deep-fat fryer one-third full of oil and heat to 180°C (350°F), or until a cube of bread dropped into the oil browns in 15 seconds. Cook level tablespoons of batter in batches for 1–2 minutes, or until golden. Drain on paper towels and season. Serve with the dipping sauce.

FESTIVE COCONUT RICE

Preparation time: 25 minutes
Total cooking time: 40 minutes
Serves 4

1/4 cup (60 ml/2 fl oz) oil
1 red onion, cut into thin wedges
4 cm (1 1/2 inch) piece of ginger, grated
2 garlic cloves, finely chopped
2 1/2 cups (500 g/1 lb) long-grain rice
1 teaspoon ground turmeric
1 litre (32 fl oz) coconut milk
6 curry leaves
3 hard-boiled eggs, cut into quarters
2 red chillies, thinly sliced
1/2 cup (35 g/1 1/4 oz) crisp fried onion

1 Heat the oil in a large saucepan, add the onion, ginger and garlic and cook over low heat for 5 minutes. Add the rice and turmeric, and cook for 2 minutes, stirring well.

ABOVE: Festive coconut rice

INDONESIAN COCONUT AND SPICE RICE

Preparation time: 5 minutes
Total cooking time: 20 minutes
Serves 4

1 tablespoon oil
1/2 cup (85 g/3 oz) unsalted peanuts,
    roughly chopped
1 tablespoon shredded coconut
1 cup (250 ml/8 fl oz) coconut milk
10 cm (4 inch) stem of lemon grass,
    lightly crushed with the side of
    a knife
8 curry leaves
2 spring onions (scallions), cut into
    2.5 mm (1/8 inch) slices
1 teaspoon ground cumin
1/2 teaspoon ground cardamom
1/2 teaspoon ground turmeric
2 1/2 cups (465 g/15 oz) long-grain rice

1 Heat the oil in a wok. Add the peanuts and cook, stirring often, until they turn golden brown. Add the coconut and stir until it darkens slightly and becomes fragrant.

2 Pour the coconut milk and 2 cups (500 ml/16 fl oz) water into the wok. Add the lemon grass stem, curry leaves and spring onions, then bring to the boil. Reduce the heat and simmer for 2 minutes. Add the cumin, cardamom and turmeric, and bring to the boil again. Lift out the stem of lemon grass, then add the rice and cook until steam holes appear at the surface of the rice.

3 Cover the wok with a tight-fitting lid, reduce the heat to very low and cook for a further 10 minutes. Lift the lid, check if rice is cooked, and continue cooking (with the lid on) if required.

NOTES: Basmati or jasmine rice can be used instead of long-grain rice, if you prefer.

Avoid lifting the lid of the wok while the rice is cooking, as all the steam will escape, resulting in thick, starchy rice.

CURRY LEAVES
Curry leaves are dark and shiny and have a distinctive curry flavour though, despite the name, they are not an ingredient in curry powder. They are widely used in Malay and southern Indian cooking, where the trees grow wild. Curry leaves are available fresh and dried and may either be added whole to a dish or broken up to intensify their flavour. Whole leaves are generally removed before food is served. They may also be fried and used as a garnish.

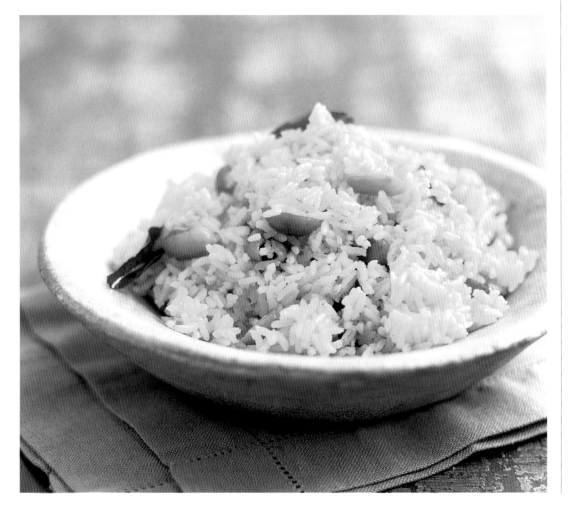

LEFT: Indonesian coconut and spice rice

VEGETARIAN STICKY
RICE POCKETS

Fold one end of the
bamboo leaf over on
the diagonal to form a
cone shape.

Spoon 2 tablespoons of
the rice mixture into
each cone.

Fold over the excess
bamboo leaf to totally
enclose the filling.

VEGETARIAN STICKY RICE POCKETS

Preparation time: 1 hour +
    10 minutes soaking
Total cooking time: 2 hours
Makes 20

 ☆ ☆

20 dried bamboo leaves (see Note)
1/2 cup (125 ml/4 fl oz) oil
6 spring onions (scallions), chopped
400 g (13 oz) eggplant (aubergine), cut
    into 1 cm (1/2 inch) cubes
1/2 cup (90 g/3 oz) drained water chestnuts,
    chopped
1 tablespoon mushroom soy sauce
3 small red chillies, seeded and finely chopped
2 teaspoons sugar
3 tablespoons chopped coriander (cilantro)
4 cups (800 g/1 lb 10 oz) white glutinous rice,
    washed and well drained
2 tablespoons soy sauce
1 teaspoon ground white pepper

1 Soak the bamboo leaves in boiling water for
10 minutes, or until soft. Drain.

2 Heat half the oil in a wok and swirl to coat the
side. Cook the spring onion and eggplant over
high heat for 4–5 minutes, or until golden. Stir
in the water chestnuts, soy sauce, chilli, sugar
and coriander. Allow to cool.

3 Bring 3 cups (750 ml/24 fl oz) water to a
simmer. Heat the remaining oil in a saucepan,
add the rice and stir for 2 minutes, or until
coated. Stir in 1/2 cup (125 ml/4 fl oz) of the
hot water over low heat until it is all absorbed.
Repeat until all the water has been added; this
should take about 20 minutes. Add the soy sauce
and season with white pepper.

4 Fold one end of a bamboo leaf on the diagonal
to form a cone. Hold securely in one hand and
spoon in 2 tablespoons of rice. Make an indent
in the rice, add 1 tablespoon of the eggplant
filling, then top with another tablespoon of rice.
Fold the other end of the bamboo leaf over to
enclose the filling, then secure with a toothpick.
Tie tightly with kitchen string. Repeat with the
remaining bamboo leaves, rice and filling.

5 Put the rice parcels in a single layer inside a
double bamboo steamer. Cover with a lid and
sit over a wok half filled with simmering water.
Steam for 1 1/2 hours, or until the rice is tender,
adding more boiling water to the wok as
needed. Serve hot.

NOTE: Bamboo leaves are used to wrap food
prior to cooking, but they are not eaten.

*RIGHT: Vegetarian
sticky rice pockets*

FISH SAUCE
This thin, clear, brown, salty sauce with its characteristic 'fishy' smell and pungent flavour is an important ingredient in Vietnamese, Laotian, Cambodian and Thai cooking. It is made from prawns (shrimp) or small fish that have been fermented in the sun. Its strong flavour diminishes when it is cooked with other ingredients.

BEEF FONDUE WITH RICE PAPER WRAPPERS AND SALAD

Preparation time: 20 minutes
Total cooking time: 30 minutes
Serves 4

 ☆☆

1 red onion, thinly sliced

3/4 cup (185 ml/6 fl oz) rice vinegar

3 red chillies, finely chopped

2 tablespoons fish sauce

2 tablespoons lime juice

6 garlic cloves, finely chopped

2 tablespoons sugar

500 g (1 lb) beef fillet

75 g (2¹/₂ oz) lettuce leaves, shredded

¹/₂ cup (10 g/¹/₄ oz) mint

1 small Lebanese (short) cucumber, sliced

400 g (13 oz) tin chopped tomatoes

12 rice paper wrappers (plus a few extras to allow for breakages)

1 Combine the onion and ¹/₄ cup (60 ml/2 fl oz) of the vinegar in a small bowl, then set aside. To make the dipping sauce, combine the chilli, fish sauce, lime juice, half the garlic and half the sugar in a small bowl, then set aside for the flavours to meld. Cut the beef into thin slices, season well with pepper and set aside.

2 Put the lettuce, mint and cucumber in separate piles on a platter, then cover with plastic wrap.

3 Bring 1 litre (32 fl oz) water to the boil in a large saucepan. Add the tomato and the remaining garlic, sugar and vinegar and simmer for 20 minutes.

4 Using a pastry brush, brush both sides of each rice paper wrapper liberally with water. Leave for 2 minutes to become soft and pliable. Stack the wrappers on a plate. Sprinkle a little extra water over them, then cover the plate with plastic wrap to keep the wrappers moist until they are needed.

5 Put the tomato mixture in a food processor and process until smooth. Return to the pan and reheat to simmering point. Add the beef in batches to the liquid, and cook it briefly, just until it changes colour, then transfer it to a serving bowl.

6 To serve, put all the food on the table. Each diner makes their own parcel, then dips it in the dipping sauce to eat.

ABOVE: Beef fondue with rice paper wrappers and salad

THAI RICE CRACKERS WITH DIPS

Preparation time: 40 minutes + cooling
Total cooking time: 2 hours
Serves 8–10 as a starter

☆ ☆ ☆

370 g (12 oz) long-grain or jasmine rice
2 cups (500 ml/16 fl oz) oil

CHILLI JAM
3 tablespoons dried shrimp
2 cups (500 ml/16 fl oz) oil
2 cups (220 g/7 oz) sliced red Asian shallots
35 garlic cloves, thinly sliced
4–5 long red chillies, seeded and finely chopped
1/2 cup (90 g/3 oz) grated light palm sugar
3 tablespoons tamarind syrup
2 tablespoons fish sauce

TAMARIND AND PORK DIP
2 teaspoons shrimp paste
3 garlic cloves, roughly chopped
1 small red chilli, roughly chopped
2 teaspoons grated ginger
1 tablespoon finely chopped spring
    onion (scallion)
1–2 tablespoons tamarind concentrate
100 g (3 1/2 oz) lean minced (ground) pork
100 g (3 1/2 oz) raw prawn (shrimp) meat
4 tablespoons finely chopped coriander
    (cilantro)
1 tablespoon peanut oil
1/2 cup (125 ml/4 fl oz) coconut milk
1 tablespoon fish sauce
1 tablespoon grated light palm sugar
1 tablespoon lime juice
2 tablespoons chopped coriander
    (cilantro) leaves

1 Wash the rice several times in cold water until the water runs clear. Put the rice and 3 cups (750 ml/24 fl oz) water in a saucepan over high heat. When the water boils, reduce the heat to low, cover with a tight-fitting lid and cook for 15 minutes, or until the rice is cooked. Allow the rice to cool.
2 Preheat the oven to very slow 140°C (275°F/ Gas 1) and lightly grease a flat baking tray with oil. Spread the cooked rice over the bottom of the tray in a thin layer. Use wet hands to prevent the rice from sticking and spread the rice to a thickness of about two or three grains. Use a knife to score a grid in the rice forming 4 cm (1 1/2 inch) squares.
3 Put the tray of rice in the oven and bake for 1 hour, or until the rice is completely dry. When cool enough to handle, break the rice along the scored lines and store in an airtight container.
4 To cook the rice squares, heat the vegetable oil in a wok or deep-fat fryer over high heat to 180°C (350°F), or until a cube of bread dropped in the oil browns in 15 seconds. When hot, add several of the rice squares at a time and cook for 1–2 minutes, or until golden. Remove and drain on paper towels. Serve immediately with the Chilli jam and Tamarind and pork dip.
5 To make the chilli jam, soak the dried shrimp in hot water for 5 minutes, drain well, then dry and roughly chop. Heat the oil in a saucepan over medium–high heat, add the shallots and garlic and cook for 10 minutes, stirring constantly, until the shallots and garlic turn golden. Add the shrimp and chillies and cook for 5 minutes, stirring constantly. Remove from the heat. Drain and reserve the oil. Put the fried mixture in a food processor and blend, gradually adding 1/4 cup (60 ml/2 fl oz) of the reserved cooking oil to form a paste. Put the mixture in a saucepan over medium heat and when it begins to simmer add the palm sugar, tamarind syrup and fish sauce. Cook for 5 minutes, stirring frequently, until it thickens. Cool before serving.
6 To make the tamarind and pork dip, wrap the shrimp paste in foil and put under a hot grill (broiler) for 2–3 minutes. Put the garlic, chilli, ginger, spring onion, shrimp paste and tamarind concentrate with 1 teaspoon salt in a small food processor and combine to form a smooth paste.
7 Combine the pork, prawn meat and coriander in a bowl. Heat the peanut oil in a frying pan over medium heat and add the tamarind paste mixture. Cook for 2–3 minutes, or until fragrant. Add the pork and prawn mixture, stir well and cook for an additional 2–3 minutes, or until browned, stirring constantly.
8 Pour in the coconut milk and cook over medium heat for 5 minutes, or until the liquid is absorbed and the meat is cooked through, stirring constantly to prevent the mixture from sticking to the bottom of the pan. Remove the pan from the heat, then stir in the fish sauce, sugar, lime juice and coriander leaves. Best served warm.

TAMARIND
The tropical tamarind tree is prized for its pods, each containing a sticky, fleshy, sweet–sour pulp wrapped around small hard seeds. Tamarind is sold in ready-made concentrated paste in jars, or in blocks or cakes that still contain the seeds. Cut off a little, mix with hot water and press through a sieve to extract the pulp. The pulp can also be turned into syrup with the addition of sugar.

OPPOSITE PAGE: Thai rice crackers with dips

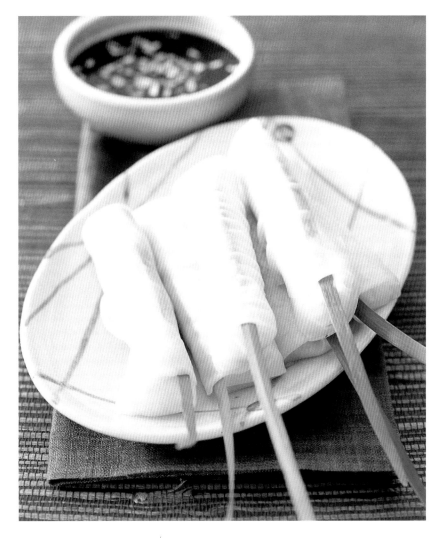

1 Soak the vermicelli in boiling water for 15 minutes, or until tender. Drain, pat dry and cut into shorter lengths with scissors.

2 Dip one rice paper wrapper at a time into a bowl of lukewarm water and allow it to soak for 30 seconds, or until soft.

3 Place the wrappers onto a dry surface, spoon one heaped tablespoon of the noodles along the bottom third of each one, top with two mint leaves and two prawn halves.

4 Fold in the sides and roll up firmly, enclosing a garlic chive halfway through each one. Lay the rolls seam-side down on a plate and cover with a damp tea towel to prevent them from drying out. Serve with the dipping sauce.

5 To make the dipping sauce, mix the hoisin, soy and sweet chilli sauces in a bowl with the chilli. Top with the chopped peanuts.

STEAMED RICE DUMPLINGS

Preparation time: 5 minutes + cooling
Total cooking time: 2 hours 15 minutes
Serves 4

☆ ☆

2 cups (400 g/13 oz) long-grain rice
4 pieces of banana leaf, each 25 x 14 cm
    (10 x 5¹/₂ inches) (see Note)
oil, for greasing

1 Rinse the rice under cold running water, then drain. Put in a saucepan with 2 cups (500 ml/ 16 fl oz) water and bring to the boil. Reduce the heat to low and simmer for 5 minutes, or until all the water has been absorbed. Allow the rice to cool.

2 Lightly oil the pieces of banana leaf and divide the cooled rice among them. Form the rice into a log along the long side of the leaf, then roll up to enclose the rice. Secure the ends with string or toothpicks.

3 Bring a large saucepan of water to the boil, add the rice packages, cover and simmer over medium heat for 2 hours. Top up with boiling water occasionally to keep the packages afloat. Remove the packages, then refrigerate until cold and firm. Unwrap before serving.

NOTE: If you can't find banana leaves, use pieces of clean, unbleached calico.

VIETNAMESE RICE PAPER ROLLS

Preparation time: 25 minutes +
    15 minutes soaking
Total cooking time: Nil
Makes 20

☆

100 g (3¹/₂ oz) dried rice vermicelli
20 x 16 cm (6¹/₂ inch) round rice paper wrappers
40 mint leaves
20 cooked prawns (shrimp), peeled, deveined and cut in half through the back
10 garlic chives, halved

Dipping sauce
¹/₄ cup (60 ml/2 fl oz) hoisin sauce
2 tablespoons soy sauce
1 tablespoon sweet chilli sauce
1 small red chilli, finely chopped
1 tablespoon chopped roasted peanuts

ABOVE: Vietnamese rice paper rolls

CHICKEN NOODLE LARB IN BANANA LEAF CONES

Preparation time: 25 minutes
Total cooking time: 15 minutes
Makes 12

50 g (1³/4 oz) dried rice vermicelli

vegetable oil, for deep-frying

1 tablespoon peanut oil

500 g (1 lb) minced (ground) chicken

¹/3 cup (80 ml/2³/4 fl oz) fish sauce

¹/2 cup (125 ml/4 fl oz) lime juice

1 tablespoon grated light palm sugar

6 red Asian shallots, thinly sliced

4 spring onions (scallions), chopped

2 small red chillies, finely chopped

¹/2 cup (10 g/¹/4 oz) mint, finely shredded

¹/2 cup (15 g/¹/2 oz) Thai basil, finely shredded

12 banana leaves, cut into 15 cm (6 inch) squares

1 Separate the vermicelli and break it into shorter lengths. Fill a wok or deep-fat fryer one-third full of oil and heat to 180°C (350°F), or until a cube of bread dropped into the oil browns in 15 seconds. Cook the vermicelli in batches until puffed and crisp. Drain on crumpled paper towels.

2 Heat the peanut oil in a wok, add the chicken and cook over medium heat until the meat is tender and cooked. Add the fish sauce, lime juice and palm sugar and stir until the sugar dissolves. Remove the wok from the heat and set aside. When cool, stir in the shallots, spring onions, chillies, mint and basil. Drain off any excess liquid.

3 Shape the banana leaves into cones and secure them with toothpicks. Fold the noodles through the salad and then spoon the mixture into the cones. Don't eat the banana leaves—they are merely a container for the filling. Serve with small forks.

NOTE: You can use pork or beef instead of the chicken, though in Thailand, where larb originates, chicken is almost always used. For the best results, finely chop the meat yourself.

BANANA LEAVES
The large flexible leaves of the banana plant are used throughout Asia to wrap foods for steaming or baking. They keep the food moist and impart a mild flavour. Remove the thick central stalk, rinse the leaves well and blanch in boiling water to soften. Packaged banana leaves are available at Asian food stores.

LEFT: Chicken noodle larb in banana leaf cones

181

BABY SQUID STUFFED WITH PORK AND VERMICELLI NOODLES

Preparation time: 30 minutes +
   10 minutes soaking + cooling
Total cooking time: 35 minutes
Serves 6

☆ ☆ ☆

12 baby squid tubes (about 100 g/3^{1}/$_{2}$ oz each)

75 g (2^{1}/$_{2}$ oz) dried rice vermicelli

2 tablespoons peanut oil

2 small red chillies, halved lengthways
   with the stem attached

2 garlic cloves, finely chopped

1^{1}/$_{2}$ tablespoons grated palm sugar

^{1}/$_{2}$ cup (80 g/2^{3}/$_{4}$ oz) roughly chopped
   unsalted peanuts

750 g (1^{1}/$_{2}$ lb) minced (ground) pork

2 teaspoons yellow bean sauce (see Note)

^{1}/$_{2}$ cup (30 g/1 oz) finely chopped Thai basil

^{1}/$_{2}$ cup (25 g/^{3}/$_{4}$ oz) finely chopped coriander
   (cilantro) leaves

cornflour (cornstarch), to dust

^{1}/$_{4}$ cup (60 ml/2 fl oz) oil

lime wedges, to serve

1 To clean the squid, pull out the tentacles and remove the quill—the transparent cartilage. Pull the skin away from the tubes and discard. Rinse well under cold running water. Pat dry.
2 Put the vermicelli in a large heatproof bowl, cover with boiling water and soak for 7 minutes, or until softened. Drain and rinse under cold water. Cut into short lengths.
3 Heat the peanut oil and chilli in a wok over low heat for 2 minutes to infuse. Remove the chilli and increase the heat to high. Add the garlic, palm sugar and peanuts and stir-fry for 5 seconds. Add the pork and stir for 7 minutes, or until cooked through, stirring to break up any lumps. Stir in the vermicelli until well combined. Remove from the heat and stir in the yellow bean sauce. Allow to cool slightly, then stir in the herbs. Divide the filling into 12 even portions.
4 Fill each squid tube with a portion of filling, then lightly dust with cornflour.
5 Heat a clean wok over high heat, add the oil and swirl to coat. Cook the squid in batches, two at a time, and sear for 2 minutes on each side, or until golden and tender. Drain on paper towels and repeat with the remaining squid. Season with salt and serve with lime wedges.
NOTE: Yellow bean sauce here refers to the Southeast Asian version, which is made from salted and fermented yellow soy beans. It has a runnier consistency and is paler in colour than the Chinese variety.

RIGHT: Baby squid stuffed with pork and vermicelli noodles

Holding the wing securely,
push the flesh down the
bone towards the joint,
using a small, sharp knife.

Twist and pull the cleaned,
exposed bone from the
socket while trying not to
pierce the skin.

Using your fingers, stuff
each chicken wing with a
ball of the pork mixture.

STUFFED CHICKEN WINGS

Preparation time: 30 minutes + cooling time
Total cooking time: 20 minutes
Makes 12

☆ ☆ ☆

12 large chicken wings

20 g (³/4 oz) dried rice vermicelli

1 tablespoon grated palm sugar

2 tablespoons fish sauce

200 g (6¹/2 oz) minced (ground) pork

2 spring onions (scallions), chopped

3 garlic cloves, chopped

1 small red chilli, chopped

3 tablespoons chopped coriander
   (cilantro) leaves

peanut oil, for deep-frying

rice flour, well seasoned, to coat

sweet chilli sauce, to serve

1 Using a small sharp knife and starting at the fatter end of the wing, scrape down the bone, pushing the flesh and skin as you go until you reach the connecting joint. Twist and pull the exposed bone from its socket and discard the bone. Take care not to pierce the skin. Repeat with the remaining wings.

2 Meanwhile, soak the vermicelli in boiling water for 7 minutes. Drain and cut into 2 cm (³/4 inch) pieces with scissors. Stir the palm sugar and fish sauce together in a small bowl until the sugar has dissolved.

3 Combine the pork, spring onion, garlic, chilli and the fish sauce mixture in a food processor until well mixed. Transfer to a bowl, then stir in the coriander and vermicelli. Divide the mixture into 12 even-sized balls. Stuff each boned-out section of chicken wing with a ball of mixture and secure firmly with a toothpick.

4 Put the wings in a bamboo or metal steamer over a wok of simmering water—ensure the base of the steamer doesn't touch the water. Cover and steam for 8 minutes. Remove the wings from the steamer, then set aside to firm and cool.

5 Fill a wok or deep-fat fryer one-third full of oil and heat to 200°C (400°F), or until a cube of bread dropped into the oil browns in 5 seconds. Coat the wings in the seasoned flour. Cook in batches for 3 minutes each batch, or until the wings are golden brown and cooked through. Drain on paper towels. Remove the toothpicks and serve with the sweet chilli sauce.

ABOVE: Stuffed chicken wings

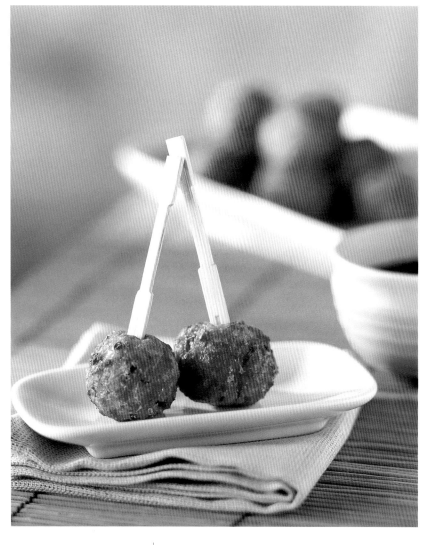

DIPPING SAUCE

¹/₂ cup (125 ml/4 fl oz) sweet chilli sauce

¹/₂ cup (125 ml/4 fl oz) soy sauce

1 tablespoon Chinese rice wine

1 Cover the dried rice vermicelli with boiling water and soak for 6–7 minutes. Drain, then cut into short lengths.

2 Combine the chicken, garlic, ginger, chilli, egg, spring onion, coriander, flour and water chestnuts in a large bowl. Mix in the vermicelli and season with salt. Refrigerate for 30 minutes. Roll heaped tablespoons of the mixture into balls.

3 Fill a wok or deep-fat fryer one-third full of oil and heat to 180°C (350°F), or until a cube of bread dropped into the oil browns in 15 seconds. Deep-fry the balls in batches for 2 minutes, or until golden brown and cooked through. Drain on paper towels.

4 To make the dipping sauce, combine the sweet chilli sauce, soy sauce and rice wine. Serve with the hot chicken balls.

CURRIED RICE NOODLES WITH CHICKEN

Preparation time: 25 minutes
Total cooking time: 10–15 minutes
Serves 4–6

200 g (6¹/₂ oz) dried rice vermicelli

1¹/₂ tablespoons oil

1 tablespoon red curry paste

450 g (14¹/₃ oz) chicken thigh fillets, cut into fine strips

1–2 teaspoons chopped red chilli

2 tablespoons fish sauce

2 tablespoons lime juice

100 g (3¹/₃ oz) bean sprouts

¹/₂ cup (80 g/2²/₃ oz) chopped unsalted roasted peanuts

¹/₄ cup (20 g/²/₃ oz) crisp fried shallots

¹/₄ cup (25 g/³/₄ oz) crisp fried garlic

1 cup (25 g/³/₄ oz) coriander (cilantro) leaves

1 Cover the vermicelli with boiling water and soak for 6–7 minutes. Drain, then toss with 2 teaspoons of the oil.

2 Heat the remaining oil in a wok. Add the curry paste and stir for 1 minute or until

DEEP-FRIED CHICKEN BALLS

Preparation time: 20 minutes +
30 minutes refrigeration
Total cooking time: 15 minutes
Makes about 30

50 g (1³/₄ oz) dried rice vermicelli

500 g (1 lb) minced (ground) chicken

3 garlic cloves, finely chopped

1 tablespoon chopped ginger

1 red chilli, seeded and finely chopped

1 egg, lightly beaten

2 spring onions (scallions), thinly sliced

4 tablespoons chopped coriander (cilantro) leaves

¹/₃ cup (40 g/1¹/₄ oz) plain (all-purpose) flour

¹/₃ cup (60 g/2 oz) finely chopped water chestnuts

oil, for deep-frying

ABOVE: Deep-fried chicken balls

fragrant. Add the chicken in batches and stir-fry for 2 minutes or until golden brown. Return all the chicken to the pan.

3 Add the chilli, fish sauce and lime juice, then bring to the boil and simmer for 1 minute. Add the bean sprouts and rice vermicelli and toss together well. Arrange the mixture on a serving plate and sprinkle with peanuts, crisp fried shallots, crisp fried garlic and coriander leaves. Serve immediately.

THAI BEEF SALAD RICE PAPER ROLLS

Preparation time: 35 minutes +
  2 hours marinating
Total cooking time: 5 minutes
Makes 16

DIPPING SAUCE
1/4 cup (60 ml/2 fl oz) soy sauce
1 tablespoon rice vinegar
1 teaspoon sesame oil
1 tablespoon mirin
2 teaspoons finely julienned ginger

1/3 cup (80 ml/2 3/4 fl oz) kecap manis
  (see Notes)
1/3 cup (80 ml/2 3/4 fl oz) lime juice
1 tablespoon sesame oil
2 small red chillies, finely chopped
300 g (10 oz) piece of beef eye fillet
1 stem lemon grass, white part only,
  finely chopped
3 tablespoons finely chopped mint
3 tablespoons finely chopped coriander
  (cilantro) leaves
1 1/2 tablespoons fish sauce
1/4 cup (60 ml/2 fl oz) lime juice, extra
16 square (16 cm/6 1/2 inch) rice paper wrappers
  (see Notes)

1 To make the dipping sauce, combine all the ingredients in a small bowl. Set aside until ready to serve.

2 Mix the kecap manis, lime juice, sesame oil and half the chilli in a large bowl. Add the beef and toss well to ensure all the beef is coated. Cover with plastic wrap and refrigerate for 2 hours.

3 Heat a barbecue or chargrill plate over high heat and cook the beef for 2–3 minutes on each side, or until cooked to your liking. It should be cooked just until it is quite pink in the middle so that it remains tender. Cool, then slice into thin strips, against the grain.

4 Combine the beef with the lemon grass, mint, coriander, fish sauce, extra lime juice and remaining chilli, then toss well.

5 Dip one rice paper wrapper at a time in warm water for a few seconds until softened. Drain, then place on a flat surface. Put a tablespoon of the mixture in the centre of the rice paper wrapper and roll up, tucking in the edges. Repeat with the remaining ingredients to make 16 rolls in total. Serve with the dipping sauce.

NOTES: Kecap manis is also known as sweet soy sauce. It is a thick dark sauce used in Indonesian cooking as a seasoning and condiment. If it is not available, use soy sauce with a little soft brown sugar.

If square rice paper wrappers are not available, use round wrappers of the same diameter.

BELOW: Thai beef salad rice paper rolls

FRAGRANT CORN, COCONUT AND CHICKEN NOODLE SOUP

Preparation time: 20 minutes +
  10 minutes soaking
Total cooking time: 20 minutes
Serves 4

100 g (3^{1}/2 oz) dried rice vermicelli
1 cup (250 ml/8 fl oz) coconut cream
2 cups (500 ml/16 fl oz) coconut milk
1 cup (250 ml/8 fl oz) chicken stock
130 g (4^{1}/2 oz) creamed corn
500 g (1 lb) chicken thigh fillets, diced
  into 2 cm (^{3}/4 inch) squares
200 g (6^{1}/2 oz) baby corn, halved lengthways
5 cm (2 inch) piece of galangal, thinly sliced
6 makrut (kaffir) lime leaves, finely shredded
2 stems lemon grass, white part only, bruised
  and cut into 5 cm (2 inch) pieces

2 tablespoons fish sauce
2 tablespoons lime juice
1 tablespoon grated palm sugar
^{1}/2 cup (15 g/^{1}/2 oz) coriander (cilantro) leaves

1 Soak the vermicelli in boiling water for
6–7 minutes, or until soft. Drain.
2 Put the coconut cream, coconut milk, chicken
stock and creamed corn in a large saucepan
and bring to the boil, then reduce the heat
and simmer.
3 Add the chicken, baby corn, galangal, lime
leaves and lemon grass and simmer until the
chicken is tender.
4 Season with fish sauce, lime juice and palm
sugar. Stir through half the coriander leaves and
serve topped with the remaining leaves.

FISH AND NOODLE SOUP

Preparation time: 15 minutes
Total cooking time: 20 minutes
Serves 4

200 g (6^{1}/2 oz) dried rice vermicelli
1 tablespoon oil
2.5 cm (1 inch) piece of ginger, grated
3 small red chillies, finely chopped
4 spring onions (scallions), chopped
3^{1}/2 cups (875 ml/28 fl oz) coconut milk
2 tablespoons fish sauce
2 tablespoons tomato paste (purée)
500 g (1 lb) firm white fish fillets, cubed
2 ham steaks, diced
150 g (5 oz) snake beans, chopped
180 g (6 oz) bean sprouts, trimmed
1 cup (20 g/^{2}/3 oz) mint
^{1}/2 cup (80 g/2^{2}/3 oz) unsalted roasted peanuts

1 Soak the vermicelli in boiling water for
6–7 minutes, or until soft, then drain well.
Heat the oil in a large, heavy-based pan and
cook the ginger, chilli and spring onion for
3 minutes, or until golden.
2 Stir in the coconut milk, fish sauce and tomato
paste, cover and simmer for 10 minutes. Add
the fish, ham and snake beans and simmer for
10 minutes, or until the fish is tender.
3 Divide the vermicelli among four bowls and
top with bean sprouts and mint. Spoon the soup
into the bowls and sprinkle with peanuts.

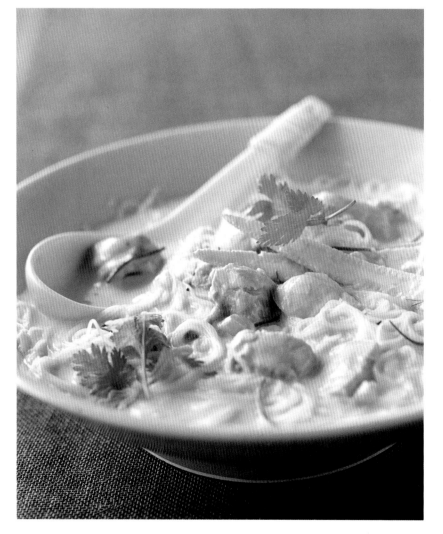

BELOW: Fragrant corn, coconut and chicken noodle soup

PENANG FISH LAKSA

Preparation time: 20 minutes +
 20 minutes soaking
Total cooking time: 40 minutes
Serves 4

1 whole snapper (750 g/1½ lb), scaled
 and cleaned
3 cups (750 ml/24 fl oz) chicken stock
6 Vietnamese mint stalks
4 dried red chillies
2 x 3 cm (¾ x 1¼ inch) piece of galangal,
 finely chopped
4 red Asian shallots, finely chopped
2 stems lemon grass, white part only,
 finely chopped
1 teaspoon ground turmeric
1 teaspoon shrimp paste
4 tablespoons tamarind purée
1 tablespoon sugar
500 g (1 lb) fresh round rice noodles
1 small Lebanese (short) cucumber, seeded
 and cut into strips
½ cup (10 g/¼ oz) Vietnamese mint
1 large green chilli, sliced

1 Trim the fins and tail off the fish with kitchen scissors. Make several deep cuts through the thickest part of the fish on both sides.

2 Pour the stock and 3 cups (750 ml/24 fl oz) water into a non-stick wok. Add the mint stalks and bring to the boil over high heat. Put the fish in the wok and simmer for 10 minutes, or until cooked. The fish should remain submerged during cooking; you might need to add some more boiling water. Lift the fish out of the wok and allow to cool.

3 Soak the chillies in 1 cup (250 ml/8 fl oz) boiling water for 20 minutes. Drain and chop. To make the laksa paste, put the chilli, galangal, shallots, lemon grass, turmeric and shrimp paste in a food processor or blender and blend to a smooth paste, adding a little water if needed.

4 Flake the flesh off the fish and remove all the bones, reserving both. Add the bones and tamarind to the stock in the wok and bring to the boil. Simmer for 10 minutes, then strain and return the liquid to a clean wok—make sure no bones slip through. Stir the laksa paste into the liquid and simmer over medium heat for 10 minutes. Stir in the sugar, add the fish flesh and simmer for 1–2 minutes, or until the fish is heated through.

5 Put the noodles in a heatproof bowl, cover with boiling water, then gently separate. Drain immediately and refresh under cold water. Divide the noodles among four bowls. Ladle on the fish pieces and broth, then sprinkle with cucumber, mint and chilli and serve.

ABOVE: Penang fish laksa

400 g (13 oz) chicken thigh fillets, cut
  into 2 cm (³/4 inch) pieces
3 cups (750 ml/24 fl oz) coconut milk
4 makrut (kaffir) lime leaves
2¹/2 tablespoons lime juice
2 tablespoons fish sauce
2 tablespoons grated palm sugar or
  soft brown sugar
250 g (8 oz) dried rice vermicelli
90 g (3 oz) bean sprouts, tailed
4 fried tofu puffs, julienned
3 tablespoons roughly chopped Vietnamese
  mint
²/3 cup (20 g/³/4 oz) coriander (cilantro) leaves
lime wedges, to serve

1 Roast the coriander and cumin seeds in a dry
saucepan or frying pan over medium heat for
1–2 minutes, or until fragrant, tossing the pan
constantly to prevent them burning. Grind finely
in a mortar and pestle or a spice grinder.
2 Put all the spices, onion, ginger, garlic, lemon
grass, candlenuts, chillies and shrimp paste in a
food processor or blender. Add about ¹/2 cup
(125 ml/4 fl oz) of the stock and blend to a paste.
3 Heat the oil in a wok or large saucepan
over low heat and gently cook the paste for
3–5 minutes, stirring constantly to prevent it
burning or sticking to the bottom. Add the
remaining stock and bring to the boil over high
heat. Reduce the heat to medium and simmer
for 15 minutes, or until reduced slightly. Add
the chicken and simmer for 4–5 minutes, or until
cooked through.
4 Add the coconut milk, lime leaves, lime
juice, fish sauce and palm sugar and simmer for
5 minutes over medium–low heat. Do not bring
to the boil or cover with a lid, as the coconut
milk will split.
5 Meanwhile, put the vermicelli in a heatproof
bowl, cover with boiling water and soak for
6–7 minutes, or until softened. Drain and
divide among large serving bowls with the
bean sprouts. Ladle the hot soup over the top
and garnish with some tofu strips, mint and
coriander leaves. Serve with a wedge of lime.
NOTES: Raw candlenuts are slightly toxic so
must be cooked before use.

  To roast the shrimp paste, wrap the paste
in foil and put under a hot grill (broiler) for
1 minute.

CHICKEN LAKSA

Preparation time: 30 minutes +
  10 minutes soaking
Total cooking time: 35 minutes
Serves 4–6

☆☆

1¹/2 tablespoons coriander seeds
1 tablespoon cumin seeds
1 teaspoon ground turmeric
1 onion, roughly chopped
1 tablespoon roughly chopped ginger
3 garlic cloves, peeled
3 stems lemon grass (white part only), sliced
6 candlenuts or macadamias (see Notes)
4–6 small red chillies
2–3 teaspoons shrimp paste, roasted
  (see Notes)
1 litre (32 fl oz) chicken stock
¹/4 cup (60 ml/2 fl oz) oil

ABOVE: Chicken laksa

BEEF PHO
(Vietnamese beef soup)

Preparation time: 15 minutes +
  40 minutes freezing
Total cooking time: 30 minutes
Serves 4

☆ ☆

400 g (13 oz) rump steak, trimmed

1/2 onion

1 1/2 tablespoons fish sauce

1 star anise

1 cinnamon stick

pinch of ground white pepper

1.5 litres (48 fl oz) beef stock

300 g (10 oz) fresh thin rice noodles

3 spring onions (scallions), thinly sliced

30 Vietnamese mint leaves

90 g (3 oz) bean sprouts, tailed

1 small white onion, cut in half and thinly sliced

1 small red chilli, thinly sliced on the diagonal

lemon wedges, to serve

1 Wrap the steak in plastic wrap and freeze for 40 minutes—this will make it easier to slice.
2 Meanwhile, put the onion, fish sauce, star anise, cinnamon stick, pepper, stock and 2 cups (500 ml/16 fl oz) water in a large saucepan. Bring to the boil, then reduce the heat, cover and simmer for 20 minutes. Discard the onion, star anise and cinnamon stick.
3 Cover the noodles with boiling water and gently separate. Drain and refresh under cold water. Thinly slice the meat across the grain.
4 Divide the noodles and spring onion among four deep bowls. Top with the beef, mint, bean sprouts, onion and chilli. Ladle the hot broth over the top and serve with the lemon wedges.

CRISP FRIED SHALLOTS

Peel red Asian shallots, then cut into very fine, even slices. Spread out to dry on a tray for a few hours. Fill a wok or deep-fat fryer one-third full of oil and heat to 180°C (350°F), or until a cube of bread dropped into the oil browns in 15 seconds. Deep-fry in batches until golden and crisp. Drain, then dry on crumpled paper towels.

VIETNAMESE MINT
Also called laksa leaf and Cambodian mint, this trailing herb with narrow, pointed, pungent-tasting leaves does not belong to the mint family, despite its name. Its flavour resembles coriander but is slightly sharper. The leaves are served as a garnish for laksa, beef pho and with spring rolls and dipping sauce. It can be used in salads to give a spicy flavour.

LEFT: Beef pho

CORIANDER

Also known as cilantro and Chinese parsley, all parts of this aromatic plant—seeds, leaves, stem and root—can be eaten. The leaves add an earthy, peppery flavour to curries and are used in salads and as a garnish, and the stems and roots are ground for curry pastes. Coriander is used extensively in Asian, South American, Middle Eastern and Mediterranean cuisines.

SPICY VIETNAMESE BEEF AND PORK NOODLE SOUP

Preparation time: 20 minutes +
   30 minutes freezing
Total cooking time: 40 minutes
Serves 4

300 g (10 oz) beef fillet steak

1/4 cup (60 ml/2 fl oz) vegetable oil

300 g (10 oz) pork leg fillet, cut into
   3 cm (1 1/4 inch) cubes

1 large onion, cut into thin wedges

2 litres (64 fl oz) good-quality beef stock

2 stems lemon grass

2 tablespoons fish sauce

1 teaspoon ground dried shrimp

1 teaspoon sugar

2 large red chillies, sliced

400 g (13 oz) fresh round rice noodles

2 cups (180 g/6 oz) bean sprouts, tailed

1/2 cup (10 g/1/4 oz) mint

1/2 cup (15 g/1/2 oz) coriander (cilantro) leaves

thinly sliced chilli, to serve (optional)

lemon wedges, to serve

1 Put the beef in the freezer for 20–30 minutes, or until partially frozen, then cut into paper-thin slices across the grain. Set aside.

2 Heat a wok until hot, add 1 tablespoon of the oil and swirl to coat the side of the wok. Stir-fry the pork in batches for 2–3 minutes, or until browned. Remove from the wok. Add another tablespoon of oil and stir-fry the onion for 2–3 minutes, or until softened. Pour in the stock and 2 cups (500 ml/16 fl oz) water. Bruise one of the lemon grass stems and add it to the wok. Return the pork to the wok and bring the liquid to the boil, then reduce the heat and simmer for 15 minutes, or until the pork is tender, periodically skimming off any scum that rises to the surface. Meanwhile, thinly slice the white part of the remaining lemon grass stem.

3 Remove the whole lemon grass stem from the broth and stir in the fish sauce, dried shrimp and sugar and keep at a simmer.

4 Heat the remaining oil in a small frying pan over medium heat and cook the sliced lemon grass and chilli for 2–3 minutes, or until fragrant. Stir into the broth. Just before serving, bring the broth to the boil over medium–high heat.

5 Put the rice noodles in a large heatproof bowl, cover with boiling water and gently separate the noodles. Drain immediately and rinse. Divide the noodles among four warm serving bowls. Top with the bean sprouts and cover with the boiling broth. Add the beef to the soup—the heat of the soup will cook it. Sprinkle with the mint and coriander, and chilli, if desired. Serve immediately with some wedges of lemon.

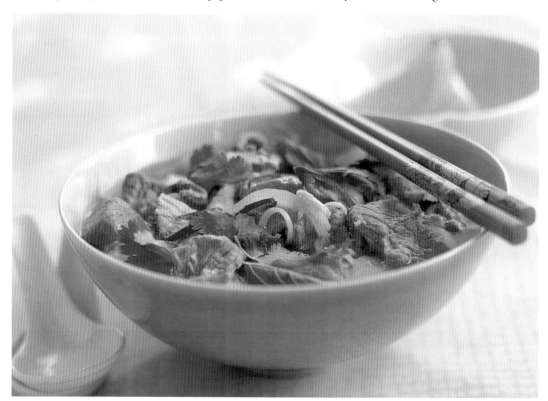

RIGHT: Spicy Vietnamese beef and pork noodle soup

RICE NOODLE SOUP WITH DUCK

Preparation time: 40 minutes
Total cooking time: 25 minutes
Serves 4–6

1 whole Chinese roast duck
4 coriander (cilantro) roots and stems,
  well rinsed
5 slices galangal
4 spring onions (scallions), sliced on the
  diagonal into 3 cm (1 1/4 inch) lengths
400 g (13 oz) Chinese broccoli, cut into
  5 cm (2 inch) lengths
2 garlic cloves, crushed
3 tablespoons fish sauce
1 tablespoon hoisin sauce
2 teaspoons grated palm sugar
1/2 teaspoon ground white pepper
500 g (1 lb) fresh rice noodles
crisp fried shallots, to garnish (optional)
coriander (cilantro) leaves, to garnish (optional)

1 To make the stock, cut off the duck's head with a sharp knife and discard. Remove the skin and fat from the duck, leaving the neck intact. Carefully remove the flesh from the bones and set aside. Cut any visible fat from the carcass along with the parson's nose, then discard. Break the carcass into large pieces, then put in a large stockpot with 2 litres (64 fl oz) water.
2 Bruise the coriander roots and stems with the back of a knife. Add to the pot with the galangal and bring to the boil. Skim off any foam that floats on the surface. Boil over medium heat for 15 minutes. Strain the stock through a fine sieve—discard the carcass and return the stock to a large clean saucepan.
3 Slice the duck flesh into strips. Add to the stock with the spring onion, Chinese broccoli, garlic, fish sauce, hoisin sauce, palm sugar and white pepper. Gently bring to the boil.
4 Cook the noodles in boiling water for 2–3 minutes, or until tender. Drain well. Divide the noodles and soup evenly among the serving bowls. If desired, garnish with the crisp fried shallots and coriander leaves. Serve immediately.

CHILLI PASTE

Remove the stalks from 200 g (6 1/2 oz) small red chillies. Put the chillies in a small saucepan with 1 cup (250 ml/8 fl oz) water and bring to the boil. Reduce the heat and simmer, partially covered, for 15 minutes. Remove from the heat and allow to cool slightly. Transfer the chillies and liquid to a food processor, then add 1 teaspoon each of salt and sugar, and 1 tablespoon each of vinegar and oil. Process until finely chopped and you have a paste. Store in a sealed container in the refrigerator for up to 2 weeks. Use in place of ready-made chilli paste in Asian dishes, or as a condiment.

ABOVE: Rice noodle soup with duck

PRAWN AND RICE NOODLE SALAD

Preparation time: 15 minutes +
   10 minutes soaking
Total cooking time: 15 minutes
Serves 4

☆ ☆

DRESSING

2 tablespoons lime juice

2 tablespoons dark soy sauce

1 tablespoon fish sauce

1 teaspoon grated lime zest

1 teaspoon caster (superfine) sugar

1 red chilli, seeded and finely chopped

2 teaspoons finely chopped ginger

SALAD

150 g (5 oz) dried rice vermicelli

100 g (3 1/2 oz) snow peas (mangetout),
   trimmed, cut in half widthways

1/4 cup (60 ml/2 fl oz) peanut oil

2/3 cup (100 g/3 1/2 oz) raw cashews, chopped

24 raw prawns (shrimp), peeled, deveined and
   tails intact

1/2 cup (10 g/1/4 oz) mint, chopped

1/2 cup (15 g/1/2 oz) coriander (cilantro)
   leaves, chopped

1 To make the dressing, combine the ingredients in a small bowl.

2 Soak the dried rice vermicelli in boiling water for 6–7 minutes. Drain and set aside.

3 Blanch the snow peas in boiling salted water for 10 seconds. Drain and refresh in cold water.

4 Heat the oil in a wok and swirl to coat. Add the cashews and stir-fry for 2 minutes, or until golden. Remove with a slotted spoon and drain on paper towels. Stir-fry the prawns over high heat for 2–3 minutes, or until just pink. Transfer to a bowl, pour on the dressing and toss. Chill.

5 Add the noodles, snow peas, mint, coriander and cashews, toss well and serve immediately.

BURMESE MIXED NOODLE AND RICE SALAD

Preparation time: 1 hour
Total cooking time: 40 minutes
Serves 6

☆

1 1/2 cups (300 g/10 oz) long-grain rice

120 g (4 oz) fine dried egg noodles

60 g (2 oz) dried mung bean vermicelli

120 g (4 oz) dried rice vermicelli

1 cup (90 g/3 oz) bean sprouts, tailed

2 potatoes, peeled and sliced

3 eggs

1 teaspoon oil

1/2 cup (125 ml/4 fl oz) peanut oil

4 large onions, quartered and thinly sliced

20 garlic cloves, thinly sliced

2 red chillies, seeded and sliced

3/4 cup (25 g/3/4 oz) dried shrimps, ground

1/2 cup (125 ml/4 fl oz) fish sauce

3/4 cup (185 ml/6 fl oz) tamarind concentrate

2 tablespoons chilli powder

BELOW: Prawn and rice noodle salad

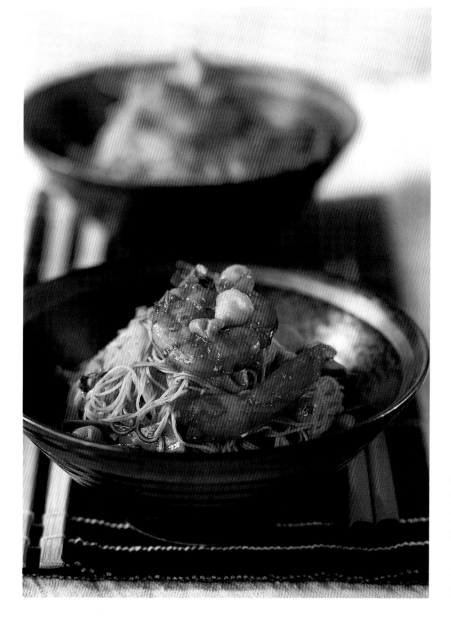

1 Fill two large saucepans with salted water and bring to the boil. Cook the rice in one for 12 minutes, or until tender. Drain, rinse and set aside. Add the egg noodles to the other pan and cook them for 2–3 minutes, or until tender. Transfer the egg noodles to a colander, rinse under cold water and set aside. Put the mung bean vermicelli and rice vermicelli in separate heatproof bowls, cover them with boiling water and soak until tender, then rinse under cold water and drain. Blanch the bean sprouts, rinse under cold water, then drain. Cook the potato in a large saucepan of boiling water for 10 minutes, or until tender, drain, then rinse under cold water and set aside.

2 Beat the eggs with 1/2 teaspoon salt and 1 tablespoon water. Heat the oil in a small frying pan, add the egg and cook over moderately low heat, gently drawing in the edges of the omelette to allow the uncooked egg to run to the outside. When cooked through, flip it over and lightly brown the other side. Remove from the pan and cool before cutting into thin strips.

3 Heat the peanut oil in a large frying pan and cook the onion, garlic and chilli separately over a moderately high heat until crispy, adding more oil if necessary.

4 Arrange the assorted noodles, rice, potato and bean sprouts on a large platter and place the omelette strips, garlic, onion, chilli, dried shrimp, fish sauce, tamarind and chilli powder in separate small dishes. The diners then serve themselves the salad ingredients and garnishes.

CHICKEN AND NOODLE SALAD WITH CASHEWS

Preparation time: 20 minutes +
  2 hours marinating
Total cooking time: 20 minutes
Serves 4

☆☆

2 garlic cloves, peeled

1/4 cup (60 ml/2 fl oz) fish sauce

1/4 cup (60 ml/2 fl oz) lime juice

2 teaspoons chilli paste

2 tablespoons soft brown sugar

2 cups (60 g/2 oz) firmly packed coriander
  (cilantro) leaves

1 cup (155 g/5 oz) unsalted roasted cashews,
  chopped

1/4 cup (60 ml/2 fl oz) oil

650 g (1 lb 5 oz) chicken thigh fillets

370 g (12 oz) rice noodle sticks

200 g (6 1/2 oz) tomatoes, diced

3 tablespoons coriander (cilantro) leaves, extra

1 To make the dressing, combine the garlic, fish sauce, lime juice, chilli paste, sugar, coriander and half the cashews in a food processor until smooth. With the motor running, slowly add the oil and mix well.

2 Put the chicken in a bowl with 1/2 cup (125 ml/4 fl oz) of the dressing. Cover and marinate in the refrigerator for at least 2 hours.

3 Cook the chicken in a non-stick frying pan for 5 minutes on each side, or until cooked through. Rest for 5 minutes, then cut into thin strips.

4 Cook the noodles in a saucepan of boiling water for 4 minutes, or until tender. Rinse and drain. Toss with the tomato and the remaining dressing.

5 Arrange the noodles on a platter. Top with the chicken, the remaining cashews and extra coriander leaves. Serve warm.

ABOVE: Chicken and noodle salad with cashews

CHINESE CELERY
Wild celery has been
used since ancient times,
though as a flavouring and
medicinal ingredient rather
than as a vegetable. The first
records of cultivated celery,
which is what we eat today,
date from the 1600s.
Chinese celery was
cultivated independently
and the result is a thinner,
juicier and more strongly
flavoured vegetable than
European celery.

*ABOVE: Crab and papaya
noodle salad*

CRAB AND PAPAYA NOODLE SALAD

Preparation time: 20 minutes +
    10 minutes soaking + 15 minutes refrigeration
Total cooking time: Nil
Serves 4

☆☆

80 g (2³/₄ oz) dried rice vermicelli
250 g (8 oz) green papaya
300 g (10 oz) fresh, cooked crab meat
2 tablespoons thinly sliced Chinese celery
    or celery
¹/₂ cup (10 g/¹/₄ oz) mint
4 tablespoons finely chopped Thai basil
    (see Note)
2 tablespoons crisp fried shallots
30 g (1 oz) roasted peanuts, crushed

DRESSING
2 tablespoons peanut oil
155 ml (5 fl oz) lime juice
1¹/₂ tablespoons fish sauce
2 tablespoons sugar
2 small red chillies, seeded
    and finely chopped

1 Put the vermicelli in a heatproof bowl, cover
with boiling water and soak for 6–7 minutes, or
until tender. Drain well, rinse in cold water and
drain again.
2 Meanwhile, peel the green papaya, cut in
half lengthways and scoop out the seeds with a
spoon. Cut the fruit into julienne strips and put
in a non-metallic bowl. Add the crab meat and
Chinese celery.
3 To make the dressing, whisk together the
peanut oil, lime juice, fish sauce, sugar and
chopped chillies in a small bowl.
4 Pour the dressing over the crab and papaya
mixture and toss well. Add the noodles, mint
and Thai basil and toss again, coating well in the
dressing. Cover with plastic wrap and refrigerate
for 15 minutes to allow the flavours to develop.
5 Sprinkle the salad with the crisp fried shallots
and crushed roasted peanuts just before serving.
NOTE: Thai basil is a member of the basil family
with smaller, darker leaves than normal basil and
a stronger aniseed flavour. If you can't find Thai
basil, replace it with the regular kind.

PORK NOODLE SALAD

Preparation time: 20 minutes + 10 minutes soaking
Total cooking time: 35 minutes
Serves 4–6

BROTH

1 cup (250 ml/8 fl oz) chicken stock

3 coriander (cilantro) roots

2 makrut (kaffir) lime leaves

3 x 3 cm (1¼ x 1¼ inch) piece of ginger, sliced

100 g (3½ oz) dried rice vermicelli

30 g (1 oz) fresh wood ear (see Note)

1 small red chilli, seeded and thinly sliced

2 red Asian shallots, thinly sliced

2 spring onions (scallions), thinly sliced

2 garlic cloves, crushed

250 g (8 oz) minced (ground) pork

¼ cup (60 ml/2 fl oz) lime juice

¼ cup (60 ml/2 fl oz) fish sauce

1½ tablespoons grated palm sugar

¼ teaspoon ground white pepper

½ cup (15 g/½ oz) coriander (cilantro) leaves, chopped, plus extra, to garnish

oakleaf or coral lettuce, to serve

lime wedges, to garnish

chilli strips, to garnish

1 To make the broth, combine the stock, coriander roots, lime leaves, ginger and 1 cup (250 ml/8 fl oz) water in a saucepan. Simmer for 25 minutes, or until the liquid has reduced to ¾ cup (185 ml/6 fl oz). Strain and return to the pan.

2 Soak the vermicelli in boiling water for 6–7 minutes. Drain, then cut into 3 cm (1¼ inch) lengths. Discard the woody stems from the wood ear, then thinly slice. Combine the vermicelli, wood ear, chilli, red Asian shallots, spring onion and garlic.

3 Return the stock to the heat and bring to the boil. Add the pork mince and stir, breaking up any lumps, for 1–2 minutes, or until the pork changes colour and is cooked. Drain, then add to the vermicelli mixture.

4 Combine the lime juice, fish sauce, palm sugar and white pepper, stirring until the sugar has dissolved. Add to the pork mixture with the coriander and mix well. Season with salt.

5 To assemble, tear or shred the lettuce, then arrange on a serving dish. Spoon on the pork and noodle mixture and garnish with the lime wedges, chilli and extra coriander.

NOTE: Wood ear (also called black fungus) is a cultivated wood fungus. It is mainly available dried; it needs to be reconstituted in boiling water for a few minutes until it expands to five times its dried size.

PORK NOODLE SALAD

Remove the woody stems from the fungus with a sharp knife.

LEFT: Pork noodle salad

PALM SUGAR
An unrefined sugar obtained from the sap of various palm trees. The sap is collected from the flower buds of mature (at least 15-year-old) palm trees— the job requires great agility as the flower buds are at the crown of the palm tree. The buds are beaten for a few days to start the sap flowing, then a container is attached and left to fill with sap. Shortly after collection, the sap is boiled down, evaporated and poured into moulds. Palm sugar is used not only in sweet dishes, but also to balance the flavours in savoury dishes. The best substitute if it is not available is equal parts of soft brown sugar and maple syrup.

ABOVE: Roast duck, lime, herb and noodle salad

ROAST DUCK, LIME, HERB AND NOODLE SALAD

Preparation time: 25 minutes +
  20 minutes soaking
Total cooking time: 10 minutes
Serves 4

☆☆

DRESSING
1/4 cup (60 ml/2 fl oz) fish sauce
2 tablespoons lime juice
1 tablespoon grated palm sugar
1 small red chilli, finely chopped

250 g (8 oz) dried flat rice stick noodles
  (5 mm/1/4 inch thick)
1 Chinese roast duck (see Note)
1 tablespoon julienned fresh ginger
90 g (3 oz) bean sprouts, tailed
1 small red onion, thinly sliced
3 tablespoons fresh coriander (cilantro) leaves
3 tablespoons fresh Thai basil or basil
1 lime, cut into wedges

1 To make the dressing, combine the fish sauce, lime juice, palm sugar and chilli in a small bowl.
2 Put the noodles in a large heatproof bowl, cover with warm water and soak for about 20 minutes, or until soft and pliable. Drain, then return to the bowl.
3 Preheat the oven to moderate 180°C (350°F/ Gas 4). Remove the flesh and skin from the duck in large pieces, then cut into thin strips, trying to keep some skin on every piece. Put the pieces of duck on a baking tray and heat in the oven for 10 minutes, or until the flesh is warmed through.
4 Add the ginger, bean sprouts, onion, coriander, basil and the dressing to the noodles and toss until well combined. Serve the salad on a platter, or on individual serving plates or bowls, and arrange the duck strips on top. Serve with lime wedges.
NOTE: Chinese roast duck can be bought ready to eat from Asian barbecue shops or restaurants. Often there are many hanging in the window to attract passers-by. Arguably the best part of these ducks is the crisp, dark glossy skin. If the skin on your duck has become limp, cook under the grill (broiler), skin-side up, under high heat for 1 minute, or until crisp.

BEEF AND NOODLE SALAD

Preparation time: 25 minutes +
  5 minutes soaking
Total cooking time: 10 minutes
Serves 4

500 g (1 lb) beef fillet, 5 cm (2 inches)
  in diameter
1¹/₂ tablespoons vegetable oil
1 teaspoon dried shrimp
1 teaspoon jasmine rice
1 stem lemon grass (white part only),
  finely chopped
1 small red chilli, seeded and finely chopped
2 coriander (cilantro) roots, finely chopped
2 makrut (kaffir) lime leaves, finely shredded
1–2 tablespoons lime juice
2 teaspoons finely chopped ginger
300 g (10 oz) dried rice vermicelli
1 Lebanese (short) cucumber, peeled, cut in half
  lengthways and cut into 1 cm (¹/₂ inch) pieces
1 vine-ripened tomato, cut into 1 cm (¹/₂ inch)
  wedges
1 red onion, cut into thin wedges
3 tablespoons torn Thai basil
3 tablespoons Vietnamese mint
1 tablespoon crisp fried shallots
2 tablespoons coriander (cilantro) leaves

Dressing
¹/₃ cup (80 ml/2³/₄ fl oz) lime juice
2 tablespoons grated palm sugar
1 tablespoon fish sauce
1 small red chilli, seeded and finely chopped
1 teaspoon sesame oil
¹/₂ teaspoon tamarind purée

1 Heat a chargrill plate or frying pan over high heat. Brush the beef with the vegetable oil and season generously with salt and black pepper. Sear on all sides for 3–4 minutes, ensuring the meat remains rare in the centre. Remove from the plate and allow to rest.

2 Dry-fry the dried shrimp and rice in a clean frying pan for 1–2 minutes, or until fragrant. Put in a spice grinder or mortar and pestle and grind to a fine powder. Mix the powder with the lemon grass, chilli, coriander roots, lime leaves, lime juice and ginger in a non-metallic bowl. Add the beef and turn to coat well on all sides. Cover with plastic wrap and marinate for at least 5 minutes, then cut into 1 cm (¹/₂ inch) thick slices across the grain.

3 To make the dressing, combine all the ingredients in a small bowl.

4 Put the vermicelli in a heatproof bowl, cover with boiling water and soak for 6–7 minutes, or until softened. Drain, rinse under cold water and drain again. Transfer the noodles to a large bowl, then add the beef, cucumber, tomato, onion, basil, mint and dressing and toss well. Serve garnished with the crisp fried shallots and coriander leaves.

BELOW: Beef and noodle salad

THAI FRIED NOODLES

Swirl the wok so that the egg spreads out to form a thin, eggy pancake.

PHAD THAI

(Thai fried noodles)

Preparation time: 40 minutes +
    20 minutes soaking
Total cooking time: 10 minutes
Serves 4–6

250 g (8 oz) flat dried rice stick noodles

1 tablespoon tamarind purée

1 small red chilli, chopped

2 garlic cloves, chopped

2 spring onions (scallions), sliced

1 1/2 tablespoons sugar

2 tablespoons fish sauce

2 tablespoons lime juice

2 tablespoons oil

2 eggs, beaten

150 g (5 oz) pork fillet, thinly sliced

8 large raw prawns (shrimp), peeled, deveined
    and tails intact

100 g (3 1/2 oz) fried tofu puffs, julienned

90 g (3 oz) bean sprouts, tailed

1/4 cup (40 g/1 1/4 oz) chopped roasted peanuts

3 tablespoons coriander (cilantro) leaves

1 lime, cut into wedges

ABOVE: Phad Thai

1 Put the noodles in a heatproof bowl, cover with warm water and soak for 15–20 minutes, or until soft and pliable. Drain well.

2 Combine the tamarind purée with 1 tablespoon water. Put the chilli, garlic and spring onion in a spice grinder or mortar and pestle and grind to a smooth paste. Transfer the mixture to a bowl and stir in the tamarind mixture along with the sugar, fish sauce and lime juice, stirring until combined.

3 Heat a wok until very hot, add 1 tablespoon of the oil and swirl to coat the side. Add the egg, swirl to coat and cook for 1–2 minutes, or until set. Remove, roll up and cut into thin slices.

4 Heat the remaining oil in the wok, stir in the chilli mixture, and stir-fry for 30 seconds. Add the pork and stir-fry for 2 minutes, or until tender. Add the prawns and stir-fry for a further minute, or until pink and curled.

5 Stir in the noodles, egg, tofu and the bean sprouts, and gently toss everything together until heated through.

6 Serve immediately topped with the peanuts, coriander and lime wedges.

PHAD SI-IEW
(Noodles with beef)

Preparation time: 20 minutes
Total cooking time: 20 minutes
Serves 4–6

500 g (1 lb) fresh rice noodle sheets

2 tablespoons peanut oil

2 eggs, lightly beaten

500 g (1 lb) rump steak, thinly sliced
   across the grain

1/4 cup (60 ml/2 fl oz) kecap manis

1 1/2 tablespoons soy sauce

1 1/2 tablespoons fish sauce

300 g (10 oz) Chinese broccoli (gai larn),
   cut into 5 cm (2 inch) lengths

1/4 teaspoon ground white pepper

lemon wedges, to serve

1 Cut the noodle sheets lengthways into 2 cm (3/4 inch) strips. Cover with boiling water, then gently separate the strips.

2 Heat a wok over medium heat, add 1 tablespoon of the oil and swirl to coat the side. Add the egg, swirl to coat and cook for 1–2 minutes, or until set. Remove, roll up and cut into shreds.

3 Reheat the wok over high heat, add the remaining oil and swirl to coat. Stir-fry the beef in batches for 3 minutes, or until brown. Remove the beef to a side plate.

4 Reduce the heat to medium, add the noodles and stir-fry for 2 minutes. Combine the kecap manis, soy sauce and fish sauce. Add to the wok with the broccoli and white pepper, then stir-fry for a further 2 minutes. Return the egg and beef to the wok and stir-fry for another 3 minutes, or until the broccoli has wilted and the noodles are soft but not falling apart. Serve with the lemon wedges on the side.

NOTE: Rice noodles should not be refrigerated, as they are very difficult to separate when cold.

KECAP MANIS
Kecap (pronounced 'ketchap') is the Indonesian word for their version of soy sauce, which is darker and thicker than the Chinese and Japanese kinds. It is made from soya beans, palm sugar and some spices. Thick, sweet and dark, it is used as a condiment, a dipping sauce, an ingredient and as a marinade. There are many varieties and these range from sweet to the salty *kecap asin*. Buy from supermarkets or Asian food stores. Once opened, store in the refrigerator.

LEFT: Phad si-iew

BEEF KEUH TEOW

Preparation time: 15 minutes
Total cooking time: 15 minutes
Serves 4

600 g (1 1/4 lb) fresh flat rice noodles
  (about 2 cm/3/4 inch wide)
1/4 cup (60 ml/2 fl oz) peanut oil
150 g (5 oz) bacon, thinly sliced
300 g (10 oz) beef round, blade or sirloin steak,
  thinly sliced across the grain
3 garlic cloves, crushed
4 small red chillies, seeded and thinly sliced
12 spring onions (scallions), thinly sliced
250 g (8 oz) bean sprouts, tailed

1/4 cup (55 g/2 oz) sugar
1/3 cup (80 ml/2 3/4 fl oz) soy sauce
1/3 cup (80 ml/2 3/4 fl oz) oyster sauce
3 eggs, lightly beaten
4 spring onions (scallions) (green part only),
  thinly sliced, extra

1 Briefly soak the noodles in boiling water, then gently separate the noodles and drain.
2 Heat a wok over high heat, add 1 tablespoon of the oil and swirl to coat. Stir-fry the bacon until crispy. Remove from the wok. Heat another tablespoon of the oil, then stir-fry the beef for 2 minutes. Remove from the wok.
3 Heat the remaining oil in the wok, add the garlic, chilli and spring onion and stir-fry over high heat for 5 seconds. Add the bean sprouts and stir-fry for another 10 seconds, then add the sugar, soy sauce, oyster sauce and noodles and stir-fry for 1–2 minutes, or until the noodles brown slightly. Return the bacon and beef to the wok and toss well until heated through.
4 Push the noodle mixture to one side of the wok, then pour in the egg. Turn the noodle mixture on top of the egg and let it cook, without stirring, for 5 seconds. Invert the noodles and egg in one turn onto a serving dish so a little of the egg is on top of the noodles. Garnish with the extra spring onion and serve.

CHILLI JAM

Soak 3 tablespoons dried shrimp in hot water for 5 minutes, drain, then dry and chop. Heat 2 cups (500 ml/16 fl oz) oil in a small saucepan over medium heat, add 2 cups (220 g/7 oz) sliced red Asian shallots, 1 cup (110 g/3 1/2 oz) thinly sliced garlic and cook for 10 minutes, stirring constantly, until golden. Add the shrimp and 5 seeded and finely chopped long, red chillies and cook for 5 minutes, stirring constantly. Drain, reserving the oil. Transfer to a food processor and blend gradually, adding 1/4 cup (60 ml/2 fl oz) of the reserved cooking oil to form a paste. Transfer to a saucepan over medium heat and, when it begins to simmer, add 1/2 cup (90 g/3 oz) grated light palm sugar, 3 tablespoons tamarind purée and 2 tablespoons fish sauce. Cook for 5 minutes, stirring frequently, until it thickens. Cool before serving. Store in a clean jar in the fridge for up to 6 months. Makes about 3 cups.

BELOW: Beef keuh teow

CHILLI JAM
Chilli jam (sometimes called chilli paste) is made with tomato, onion, chilli, oil, tamarind, garlic, sugar, salt, spices and vinegar. It is available in Asian food stores, or you can make your own (page 200). Among its many uses, chilli jam can be a condiment for rice or noodle dishes, or it can be added to stir-fries or curries.

CHICKEN, CHILLI JAM AND NOODLE STIR-FRY

Preparation time: 15 minutes +
    20 minutes soaking
Total cooking time: 10 minutes
Serves 4

250 g (8 oz) flat rice stick noodles
    (1 cm/^{1}/$_2$ inch wide)
400 g (13 oz) chicken breast fillet
1 onion
1 red capsicum (pepper)
1 tablespoon peanut oil
2 tablespoons chilli jam
2 teaspoons fish sauce
2 tablespoons light soy sauce
90 g (3 oz) bean sprouts, tailed
100 g (3^1/$_2$ oz) unsalted cashew nuts
1 cup (30 g/1 oz) loosely packed basil,
    plus extra, to garnish

1 Put the noodles in a large heatproof bowl, cover with warm water and soak for about 20 minutes, or until soft. Drain well.
2 Meanwhile, cut the chicken breast fillets into 5 mm (^{1}/4 inch) slices against the grain. Slice the onion into thin wedges. Thinly slice the capsicum.
3 Heat a wok over high heat, add the peanut oil and swirl to coat the side. Cook the onion for 1–2 minutes, or until lightly golden. Add the chicken slices and cook for a further 3–5 minutes, or until browned and almost cooked through. Stir in the chilli jam, then add the capsicum and cook for another minute.
4 Add the fish sauce, soy sauce, bean sprouts, cashew nuts, basil and the noodles to the wok and toss until warmed through and well combined. Garnish with the extra basil and serve immediately.

ABOVE: Chicken, chilli jam and noodle stir-fry

RED ASIAN SHALLOTS
Shallots are very closely related to the onion, but have a milder, more delicate flavour. They also differ from the onion family in that instead of having a single bulb, shallots grow in clusters and are joined with a common root end. There are several varieties, most with long brown bulbs. The Asian variety has papery pinkish–red skin. They are often made into pickles in Southeast Asia.

PORK AND PRAWN VERMICELLI

Preparation time: 25 minutes +
 10 minutes soaking
Total cooking time: 10 minutes
Serves 4

100 g (3¹/₂ oz) dried rice vermicelli

2 tablespoons peanut oil

200 g (6¹/₂ oz) lean minced (ground) pork

100 g (3¹/₂ oz) red Asian shallots, finely chopped

2 garlic cloves, finely chopped

2 small red chillies, finely chopped

100 g (3¹/₂ oz) Chinese celery or celery,
 finely chopped

12 raw prawns (shrimp), peeled and deveined

1 makrut (kaffir) lime leaf, shredded

1¹/₂ tablespoons fish sauce

1 tablespoon sugar

2¹/₂ tablespoons lime juice

2 tablespoons mint

3 tablespoons Thai basil

4 tablespoons coriander (cilantro) leaves

1 Put the vermicelli in a large heatproof bowl, cover with boiling water and soak for 6–7 minutes, or until tender. Drain well and set aside.
2 Heat a wok until very hot, add 1 tablespoon of the oil and swirl to coat. Add the pork and stir-fry for 1–2 minutes, or until slightly brown, stirring to break up any lumps. Drain and transfer to a plate lined with paper towel.
3 Heat the remaining oil in the wok over high heat and stir-fry the shallots, garlic, chilli and celery for 1 minute. Add the prawns, lime leaf, fish sauce, sugar and lime juice and continue to stir-fry for 1 minute, or until the prawns start to turn pink.
4 Add the vermicelli and pork to the wok and stir-fry for 1–2 minutes, or until well combined and heated through. Divide among the serving dishes, then toss in the mint, basil and coriander. Serve immediately.
NOTE: It is important to toss the herbs through the stir-fry after the mixture has been transferred to the serving bowls—if the herbs are tossed through in the wok, the heat of the wok will cause them to wilt very quickly.

*ABOVE: Pork and
prawn vermicelli*

RICE STICK NOODLES WITH KECAP BEEF

Preparation time: 15 minutes +
  10 minutes soaking
Total cooking time: 10 minutes
Serves 4

250 g (8 oz) narrow, dried rice stick noodles

1/4 cup (60 ml/2 fl oz) peanut oil

300 g (10 oz) rump steak, sliced

2 garlic cloves, finely chopped

1 stem lemon grass, white part only,
  finely chopped

3 spring onions (scallions), sliced

200 g (6 1/2 oz) sugar snap peas

1 bunch broccolini, roughly chopped

1/4 cup (60 ml/2 fl oz) kecap manis

2 tablespoons soy sauce

1 tablespoon fish sauce

2 tablespoons snipped garlic chives (see Note)

1 Pour boiling water over the noodles and allow them to stand for 10 minutes or until tender and pliable. Drain.

2 Heat half the oil in a wok, add the meat, garlic and lemon grass in batches and stir-fry over high heat until the meat is browned. Add the spring onions, snap peas and broccolini and stir-fry for a few minutes, or until bright green and tender, but still slightly crisp. Remove from the wok and keep warm.

3 Add the remaining oil to the wok and then the noodles. Stir-fry for 1 minute. Stir in the kecap manis, soy sauce and fish sauce to coat the noodles.

4 Return the meat and the vegetables to the wok, along with any juices, and toss together until heated through. Stir in the chives and serve.

NOTE: Garlic chives (also known as Chinese chives) have a stronger flavour than regular chives, and they look wider and flatter. If you can't find them, use regular chives instead.

LEFT: Rice-stick noodles with kecap beef

GINGER
Ginger is the name of this tropical plant and its rhizomes, which are eaten fresh and are also dried, preserved and ground into a powder. Thought to be native to Southeast Asia, ginger is now unknown in the wild, but is grown commercially all over the world in tropical climates and can be bought fresh year-round. Young, fresh ginger often has pink tips. The skin can be removed easily by rubbing with your fingers. Older ginger will need to be peeled. The older the ginger the stronger the flavour and the more fibrous the flesh. Store ginger in the vegetable crisper for several weeks, and break off just what you need to use.

GINGER AND CHILLI VEGETABLES WITH NOODLES

Preparation time: 15 minutes
Total cooking time: 10 minutes
Serves 4

☆

1/4 cup (60 ml/2 fl oz) sweet chilli sauce
2 tablespoons fish sauce
2 tablespoons dark soy sauce
1 tablespoon lime juice
500 g (1 lb) fresh rice noodle sheets, at room temperature
2 tablespoons peanut oil
1 teaspoon sesame oil
3 tablespoons grated ginger
1 onion, thinly sliced
1 red capsicum (pepper), sliced
100 g (3 1/2 oz) fresh shiitake mushrooms, sliced
200 g (6 1/2 oz) baby corn
500 g (1 lb) Chinese broccoli (gai larn), sliced
200 g (6 1/2 oz) snow peas (mangetout)
16 Thai basil leaves

1 To make the stir-fry sauce, mix together the sweet chilli sauce, fish sauce, soy sauce and lime juice in a small bowl.
2 Cut the noodle sheets into 3 cm (1 1/4 inch) wide strips, then cut each strip into three. Gently separate the noodles (you may need to run a little cold water over them to do this).
3 Heat the peanut and sesame oils in a wok, add the ginger and onion and stir-fry for a few minutes, or until the onion is soft. Add the vegetables and stir-fry until brightly coloured and just tender. Add the noodles and stir-fry until soft. Stir in the stir-fry sauce. Remove from the heat and toss in the basil leaves.

RIGHT: Ginger and chilli vegetables with noodles

MEE GROB
(Crispy noodles)

Preparation time: 30 minutes +
  20 minutes soaking
Total cooking time: 15 minutes
Serves 4–6

4 dried Chinese mushrooms
oil, for deep-frying
100 g (3¹/₂ oz) dried rice vermicelli
100 g (3¹/₂ oz) fried tofu puffs, julienned
4 garlic cloves, crushed
1 onion, chopped
1 chicken breast fillet (about 200 g/6¹/₂ oz),
  thinly sliced
8 green beans, sliced on the diagonal
6 spring onions (scallions), thinly sliced
  on the diagonal
8 raw prawns (shrimp), peeled and deveined,
  tails intact
30 g (1 oz) bean sprouts, tailed
coriander (cilantro) leaves, to garnish

SAUCE
1 tablespoon light soy sauce
¹/₄ cup (60 ml/2 fl oz) white vinegar
5 tablespoons sugar
¹/₄ cup (60 ml/2 fl oz) fish sauce
1 tablespoon sweet chilli sauce

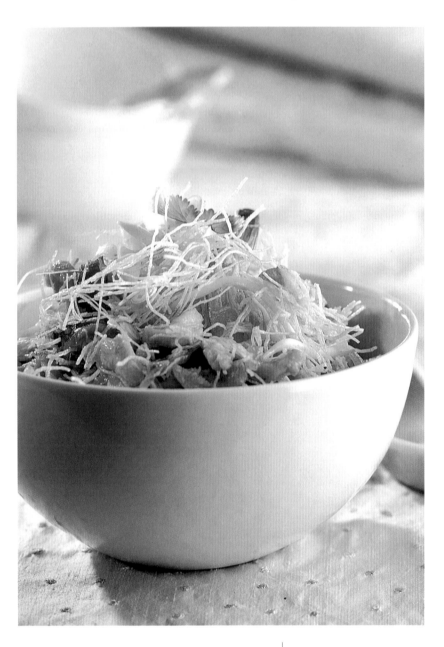

1 Put the mushrooms in a heatproof bowl, cover with boiling water and soak for 20 minutes. Drain, discard the woody stems and thinly slice the caps.
2 Fill a wok or deep-fat fryer one-third full of oil and heat to 180°C (350°F), or until a cube of bread dropped into the oil browns in 15 seconds. Cook the vermicelli in batches for 5 seconds, or until puffed and crispy. Drain on paper towels.
3 Add the tofu to the wok in batches and deep-fry for 1 minute, or until crisp. Drain on paper towels. Cool the oil slightly and carefully remove all but 2 tablespoons of the oil.
4 Reheat the wok over high heat until very hot. Add the garlic and onion, and stir-fry for 1 minute. Add the chicken slices, mushrooms, green beans and half the spring onion and stir-fry for 2 minutes, or until the chicken has almost cooked through. Add the prawns and stir-fry for a further 2 minutes, or until the prawns just turn pink.
5 To make the sauce, combine the soy sauce, white vinegar, sugar, fish sauce and sweet chilli sauce. Add to the wok and stir-fry for 2 minutes, or until the meat and prawns are tender and the sauce is syrupy. Remove the wok from the heat and stir in the vermicelli, tofu and bean sprouts. Garnish with the coriander and the remaining spring onion.

ABOVE: Mee grob

DRIED SHRIMP
These tiny shelled, salted and sun-dried shrimp are available whole or ground into a powder. They impart a salty flavour to Asian food. They have an intense flavour, some more so than others, but can be soaked in water before use to reduce their potency. If kept refrigerated, they should last for several months.

SINGAPORE NOODLES

Preparation time: 15 minutes + 1 hour soaking
Total cooking time: 15 minutes
Serves

2 tablespoons dried shrimp

300 g (10 oz) dried rice vermicelli

100 g (3 1/2 oz) Chinese barbecued pork (char siu)

100 g (3 1/2 oz) bean sprouts, tailed

1/3 cup (80 ml/2 3/4 fl oz) oil

2 eggs, beaten

1 onion, thinly sliced

1 teaspoon salt

1 tablespoon Chinese curry powder

2 tablespoons light soy sauce

2 spring onions (scallions), shredded

2 red chillies, shredded

1 Soak the dried shrimp in boiling water for 1 hour, then drain. Soak the noodles in hot water for 6–7 minutes, then drain. Thinly slice the pork. Wash the bean sprouts and then drain them thoroughly.

2 Heat a wok over high heat, add 1 tablespoon of the oil and heat until very hot. Pour in the egg and swirl to coat the wok, then cook for 1–2 minutes, or until set. Remove from the wok and cut into small pieces.

3 Preheat the wok over high heat, add the remaining oil and heat until very hot. Stir-fry the onion and bean sprouts with the pork and shrimp for 1 minute, then add the noodles, salt, curry powder and soy sauce, blend well and stir for 1 minute. Add the omelette, spring onion and chilli and toss to combine.

ABOVE: Singapore noodles

VIETNAMESE CREPES WITH PORK, PRAWNS AND NOODLES

Preparation time: 45 minutes + 4 hours resting
Total cooking time: 35 minutes
Serves 6

1 1/2 cups (260 g/8 oz) rice flour

1 teaspoon baking powder

1 1/2 teaspoons sugar

1/2 teaspoon ground turmeric

1 cup (250 ml/8 fl oz) coconut milk

3 teaspoons peanut oil

lime wedges, to serve

DIPPING SAUCE

2 tablespoons lime juice

1 tablespoon fish sauce

1 tablespoon caster (superfine) sugar

1 small red chilli, finely chopped

SALAD

1 carrot, coarsely grated

120 g (4 oz) iceberg lettuce, shredded

1 Lebanese (short) cucumber, julienned

100 g (3 1/2 oz) bean sprouts, tailed

1 cup (20 g/3/4 oz) mint

1 cup (30 g/1 oz) coriander (cilantro) leaves

FILLING

75 g (2 1/2 oz) dried rice vermicelli, broken

1 tablespoon peanut oil

1 large onion, thinly sliced

6 garlic cloves, crushed

200 g (6 1/2 oz) lean pork fillet, minced (ground)

250 g (8 oz) raw prawns (shrimp), peeled, deveined and chopped

1 small red capsicum (pepper), thinly sliced

75 g (2 1/2 oz) button mushrooms, thinly sliced

1 tablespoon light soy sauce

1/4 teaspoon ground white pepper

4 spring onions (scallions), thinly sliced

1 To make the crepe batter, blend the rice flour, baking powder, sugar, turmeric, coconut milk, 1/2 teaspoon salt and 1 cup (250 ml/8 fl oz) water in a blender to a smooth batter. Cover and leave in a warm place for 2–4 hours.

2 Mix together all the dipping sauce ingredients in a small bowl.

3 Toss all the salad ingredients together in a large bowl.

4 To make the filling, soak the vermicelli in boiling water for 6–7 minutes, or until soft. Drain. Heat a wok over high heat, add the oil and swirl to coat. Add the onion and cook for 2 minutes, then the garlic, cooking for a further 30 seconds. Add the pork and cook for 2 minutes, or until browned. Stir in the prawns, capsicum and mushrooms and cook until the prawns change colour. Stir in the noodles, soy sauce, white pepper and spring onion.

5 To make the crepes, whisk the batter until smooth. Heat 1/2 teaspoon of the oil in a 30 cm (12 inch) non-stick frying pan. Pour 1/3 cup (80 ml/2 3/4 fl oz) of the batter into the centre of the pan, and swirl to spread to the edges. Cook over medium heat for 1–2 minutes, or until golden and crispy. Turn and repeat on the other side. Repeat with the remaining oil and batter to make six crepes in total.

6 To assemble, place a portion of the filling on half a crepe, folding the other side on top. Repeat with the remaining crepes and filling. Serve with the sauce, salad and lime.

BELOW: Vietnamese crepes with pork, prawns and noodles

VIETNAMESE DUCK RICE PAPER ROLLS

Preparation time: 20 minutes
Total cooking time: Nil
Serves 4 as a light meal

16 x 22 cm (9 inch) round rice paper wrappers
1 whole Chinese roast duck, meat removed
   from the bones and chopped
1 telegraph cucumber
150 g (5 oz) bean sprouts, tailed

SAUCE
1 tablespoon hoisin sauce
2 teaspoons chilli sauce
1 tablespoon plum sauce

1 Half-fill a large bowl with warm water and a second bowl with cold water. Dip each wrapper into the warm water for 10 seconds and then into the cold water. Drain on paper towels and stack on a serving plate with a piece of baking paper between each wrapper.
2 Remove any remaining bones from the duck and shred the meat. Place in a serving dish. Cut the cucumber in half lengthways and scrape out the seeds. Cut the cucumber flesh into 1 x 6 cm (½ x 2½ inch) strips. Put in a serving dish. Put the bean sprouts in a separate serving dish. Combine the sauce ingredients in a small dish.
3 Invite your guests to assemble their rolls at the table. To assemble, spread a little sauce onto the rice paper wrapper, then arrange the filling ingredients on the top half of the wrapper. Fold over the bottom edge then roll up, tucking in the sides.

GROW YOUR OWN BEAN SPROUTS

Bean sprouts are the edible, crisp young shoots of mung beans or soya beans. They are often used in Asian cooking. To grow your own mung bean sprouts, wash the beans thoroughly, then put them in a large jar and fill it with tepid water. Cover the top with muslin or cheesecloth, secure it with a rubber band, then drain the water out through the cloth. Leave the jar on its side in a dark, warm place (light causes the sprouts to turn green). Repeat this rinsing process morning and evening. Sprouting will begin after 2–3 days and they will be ready to eat after 4–6 days. You can follow the same process to grow soya bean sprouts but they take longer to germinate than mung beans.

RIGHT: Vietnamese duck rice paper rolls

THAI STICKY RICE WITH MANGOES

Preparation time: 10 minutes +
  overnight soaking + 20 minutes resting
Total cooking time: 1 hour 5 minutes
Serves 4

☆ ☆

2 cups (400 g/13 oz) long-grain glutinous rice

1 tablespoon white sesame seeds, to serve

1 cup (250 ml/8 fl oz) coconut milk

1/2 cup (90 g/3 oz) grated palm sugar or
  soft brown sugar

2–3 mangoes, peeled, seeded and sliced

1/4 cup (60 ml/2 fl oz) coconut cream

mint sprigs, to garnish

1 Put the rice in a sieve and wash under cold running water until the water runs clear. Put the rice in a glass or ceramic bowl, cover with water and soak overnight, or for at least 12 hours. Drain the rice.

2 Line a metal or bamboo steamer with a piece of muslin cloth. Put the rice on top of the muslin and cover the steamer with a tight-fitting lid. Put the steamer over a pot or wok of boiling water and steam over moderately low heat for 50 minutes, or until the rice is cooked. Replenish the pot with boiling water as necessary. Transfer the rice to a large bowl and fluff it up with a fork.

3 Toast the sesame seeds in a dry pan over medium heat for 3–4 minutes, shaking the pan gently, until the seeds are golden brown. Remove from the pan immediately to prevent them burning.

4 Pour the coconut milk into a small saucepan, add the sugar and 1/4 teaspoon salt. Slowly bring the mixture to the boil, stirring constantly, until the sugar is dissolved. Reduce the heat and simmer for 5 minutes, or until the mixture is slightly thickened. Stir the mixture often while it is simmering, to prevent it sticking to the bottom of the pan.

5 Slowly pour the coconut milk over the top of the rice. Use a fork to lift and fluff up the rice. Do not stir the liquid through, otherwise the rice will become too gluggy. Let the rice mixture rest for 20 minutes before carefully spooning it into the centre of four warmed serving bowls. Arrange the mango slices on the rice mounds. Spoon a little coconut cream over the rice, sprinkle over the sesame seeds and garnish with the mint.

ABOVE: Thai sticky rice with mangoes

BANANA

The banana is fruit native to the tropics, and there are a huge number of varieties of banana available that are rarely seen outside of Asia. The banana plant is not a tree, but a giant perennial herb that looks like a palm tree.

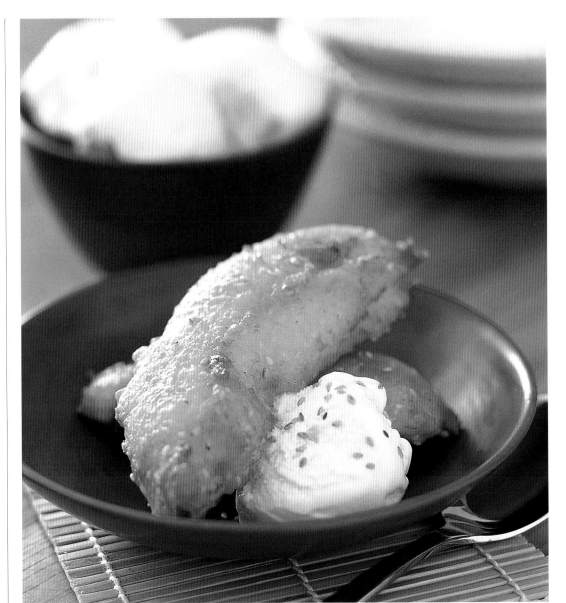

BANANA FRITTERS IN COCONUT BATTER

Preparation time: 15 minutes +
   1 hour standing
Total cooking time: 20 minutes
Serves 6

☆ ☆

100 g (3¹/2 oz) glutinous rice flour
100 g (3¹/2 oz) freshly grated coconut or
   ²/3 cup (60 g/2 oz) desiccated coconut
50 g (1³/4 oz) sugar
1 tablespoon sesame seeds
¹/4 cup (60 ml/2 fl oz) coconut milk
6 sugar bananas
oil, for deep-frying

ABOVE: Banana fritters in coconut batter

1 Combine the flour, coconut, sugar, sesame seeds, coconut milk and ¹/4 cup (60 ml/2 fl oz) water in a large bowl. Whisk to a smooth batter—add more water if the batter is too thick. Set aside to rest for 1 hour.
2 Peel the bananas and cut in half lengthways (cut each portion in half again crossways if the bananas are large).
3 Fill a wok or deep-fat fryer one-third full of oil and heat to 180°C (350°F), or until a cube of bread dropped into the oil browns in 15 seconds. Dip each piece of banana into the batter, then drop gently into the hot oil. Cook in batches for 4–6 minutes, or until golden brown all over. Remove with a slotted spoon and drain on crumpled paper towels. Serve hot with vanilla ice cream and a sprinkling of extra toasted sesame seeds, if desired.

STICKY BLACK RICE PUDDING

Preparation time: 10 minutes +
 overnight soaking + 15 minutes standing
Total cooking time: 30 minutes
Serves 6–8

2 cups (400 g/13 oz) black rice
3 fresh pandan leaves (see Notes)
2 cups (500 ml/16 fl oz) coconut milk
80 g (2³/₄ oz) palm sugar, grated
¹/₄ cup (55 g/2 oz) caster (superfine) sugar
coconut cream, to serve
mango or papaya cubes, to serve

1 Put the rice in a large glass or ceramic bowl and cover with water. Leave to soak for at least 8 hours, or preferably overnight. Drain, then put in a saucepan with 1 litre (32 fl oz) water and slowly bring to the boil. Cook at a low boil, stirring frequently, for 20 minutes, or until tender. Drain.

2 Pull your fingers through the pandan leaves to shred them and then tie them in a knot. Pour the coconut milk into a large saucepan and heat until almost boiling. Add the palm sugar, caster sugar and pandan leaves and stir until the sugars have dissolved.

3 Add the cooked rice to the pan of coconut milk and cook, stirring, for 8 minutes without boiling. Turn off the heat, cover and leave for 15 minutes to absorb the flavours. Remove the pandan leaves.

4 Spoon into bowls and serve warm with coconut cream and fresh mango.

NOTES: The long flat leaves of the pandanus are crushed and used as a flavouring in many Thai sweets. They are sold fresh, frozen, dried or as a flavouring essence or paste.

Don't refrigerate the black rice pudding or it will dry out and harden.

VARIATION: Any fresh tropical fruit, such as banana, pineapple or lychee is also delicious served with this dish.

STICKY BLACK RICE PUDDING

In Asia this sweet, sticky rice pudding based on black rice (closer to purple than black) is usually eaten for breakfast or as a sweet snack. However, in Asian restaurants outside Asia, this dish usually appears on the dessert menu.

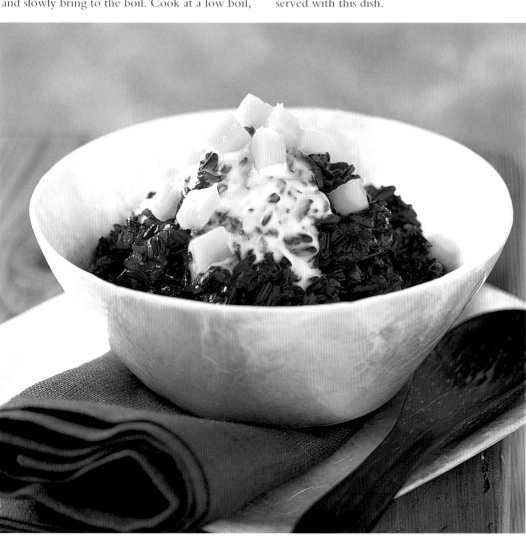

LEFT: Sticky black rice pudding

CHINA

The cuisine of China is incredibly diverse, but it does have one unifying feature—rice. There is barely a meal that is not accompanied by rice. In fact, such is the importance of this staple grain in China that it is regarded as the focal point of most meals. Everything else, from stir-fries to braises, is secondary. In most cases, rice makes its appearance as a simple perfectly steamed dish, but it is also enjoyed as fried rice, rice noodle dishes and even at breakfast time, as the comforting rice soup, congee.

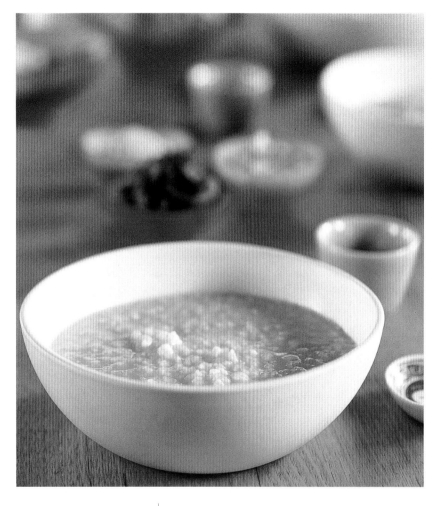

1 Put the rice in a clay pot, casserole dish or saucepan and stir in the stock or water. Bring to the boil, then reduce the heat and simmer very gently, stirring occasionally, for 1^3/4–2 hours, or until it has a porridge-like texture and the rice is breaking up.

2 Add a sprinkling of soy sauce, sesame oil and white pepper to season the congee. The congee can be served plain, or choose a selection from the toppings listed and serve in bowls alongside the congee for guests to help themselves.

NOTE: You'll need access to an Asian or Chinese grocery store to acquire preserved turnip, one-thousand-year-old eggs and fried dough sticks; if you don't have one nearby, choose some of the more easily available toppings instead.

PORK CONGEE

Preparation time: 15 minutes
Total cooking time: 1 hour 45 minutes
Serves 4–6

1^1/2 cups (300 g/10 oz) long-grain rice, rinsed and drained
^{1}/2 star anise
2 spring onions (scallions), white part only
4 x 4 cm (1^1/2 x 1^1/2 inch) piece of ginger, cut into slices
3.5 litres (112 fl oz) chicken stock
1 tablespoon peanut oil
2 garlic cloves, crushed
1 teaspoon grated ginger, extra
400 g (13 oz) minced (ground) pork
ground white pepper
^{1}/4 cup (60 ml/2 fl oz) light soy sauce
roasted sesame oil, to drizzle

1 Put the rice in a large saucepan with the star anise, spring onions, sliced ginger and stock. Bring to the boil, then reduce the heat and simmer for 1^1/2 hours, stirring occasionally.

2 Heat the oil in a frying pan over high heat. Cook the garlic and grated ginger for 30 seconds. Add the pork and cook for 5 minutes, or until browned, breaking up any lumps with the back of a wooden spoon.

3 Discard the star anise, spring onions and ginger from the soup, add the pork mixture and simmer for 10 minutes. Season with white pepper and stir in the soy sauce. Serve with a drizzle of sesame oil.

PLAIN CONGEE WITH ACCOMPANIMENTS

Preparation time: 15 minutes
Total cooking time: 2 hours
Serves 4

☆☆

1 cup (220 g/7 oz) short-grain rice, rinsed and drained
2.5 litres (80 fl oz) chicken stock or water
light soy sauce, to taste
roasted sesame oil, to taste

TOPPINGS
3 spring onions (scallions), chopped
4 tablespoons chopped coriander (cilantro)
30 g (1 oz) sliced pickled ginger
4 tablespoons finely chopped preserved turnip
4 tablespoons roasted peanuts
2 one-thousand-year-old eggs, cut into slivers
2 tablespoons sesame seeds, toasted
2 fried dough sticks, diagonally sliced

ABOVE: Plain congee with accompaniments

RAINBOW CONGEE

Preparation time: 15 minutes +
  30 minutes soaking
Total cooking time: 2 hours 15 minutes
Serves 6

200 g (6½ oz) short-grain rice
2 dried Chinese mushrooms
85 g (3 oz) snow peas (mangetout), trimmed
2 Chinese sausages (lap cheong)
2 tablespoons oil
¼ red onion, finely diced
1 carrot, cut into 1 cm (½ inch) dice
2 litres (64 fl oz) chicken stock or water
3 teaspoons light soy sauce

1 Put the rice in a bowl and, using your fingers as a rake, rinse under cold running water to remove any dust. Drain the rice in a colander.
2 Soak the dried mushrooms in boiling water for 30 minutes, then drain and squeeze out any excess water. Remove and discard the stems and chop the caps into 5 mm (¼ inch) dice. Cut the snow peas into 1 cm (½ inch) pieces.
3 Place the sausages on a plate in a steamer. Cover and steam over simmering water in a wok for 10 minutes, then cut them into 1 cm (½ inch) pieces.
4 Heat a wok over medium heat, add the oil and heat until hot. Stir-fry the sausage until it is brown and the fat has melted out of it. Remove with a wire sieve or slotted spoon and drain. Pour the oil from the wok, leaving 1 tablespoon.
5 Reheat the reserved oil over high heat until very hot. Stir-fry the red onion until soft and transparent. Add the mushrooms and carrot and stir-fry for 1 minute, or until fragrant.
6 Put the mushroom mixture in a clay pot, casserole dish or saucepan and stir in the soy sauce, rice, 2 litres (64 fl oz) stock or water and ¼ teaspoon salt. Bring to the boil, then reduce the heat and simmer very gently, stirring occasionally, for 1¾–2 hours, or until it has a porridge-like texture and the rice is breaking up. If it is too thick, add the remaining stock and return to the boil. Toss in the snow peas and sausage, cover and stand for 5 minutes before serving.

CONGEE
A popular breakfast meal or filling snack, congee is also prepared for convalescents because it is so soothing to eat. Plain congee is served with lots of different condiments; the idea being that each diner can choose their own favourite combination to sprinkle over the top. A fried dough stick is one of the most common accompaniments—dough sticks are available in Chinese markets and are sold as long thin sticks. Congee can also be made into a more substantial meal by adding meat or fish.

LEFT: Rainbow congee

215

EGG FRIED RICE

Preparation time: 15 minutes
Total cooking time: 15 minutes
Serves 4

☆

4 eggs
1 spring onion (scallion), chopped
50 g (1³/₄ oz) fresh or frozen peas (optional)
¹/₄ cup (60 ml/2 fl oz) oil
3 cups (550 g/1 lb 1³/₄ oz) cold cooked white
   long-grain rice (see Note)

BELOW: Egg fried rice

1 Beat the eggs with a pinch of salt and
1 teaspoon of the spring onion. Cook the

peas in a saucepan of simmering water for
3–4 minutes for fresh or 1 minute for frozen.
2 Heat a wok over high heat, add the oil and
heat until very hot. Reduce the heat, add the
egg and lightly scramble. Add the rice before
the egg is set too hard, increase the heat and
stir to separate the rice grains and break the egg
into small bits. Add the peas and the remaining
spring onion and season with salt. Stir constantly
for 1 minute.
NOTE: You'll need 1 cup (200 g/6¹/₂ oz)
uncooked rice to obtain 3 cups cooked.

FRIED RICE WITH CHINESE BARBECUED PORK

Preparation time: 15 minutes
Total cooking time: 10 minutes
Serves 4

☆

6 spring onions (scallions)
150 g (5 oz) snow peas (mangetout)
200 g (6¹/₂ oz) Chinese barbecued pork
   (char siu)
3 teaspoons roasted sesame oil
2 eggs, lightly beaten
2 garlic cloves, finely chopped
3 cups (550 g/1 lb 1³/₄ oz) cold cooked white
   long-grain rice (see Note)
2 tablespoons soy sauce

1 Cut the spring onions and snow peas
diagonally into very thin shreds. Cut the pork
into thin slices.
2 Heat a wok until hot, add 1 teaspoon of
the oil and swirl to coat the base of the wok.
Add the egg and swirl over the base until it
has just set. Turn the egg over and cook for
30 seconds, or until lightly browned, then
remove from the wok. Allow the egg to cool
slightly, then roll up and cut into 1 cm (¹/₂ inch)
thick slices.
3 While the wok is still very hot, add the
remaining oil, then the garlic, spring onion and
snow peas and stir-fry for 1–2 minutes, or until
slightly soft. Add the pork, rice, soy sauce and
strips of omelette and toss until heated through
and thoroughly combined—the soy sauce should
turn the rice brown. Remove from the heat and
serve immediately.
NOTE: You'll need 1 cup (200 g/6¹/₂ oz)
uncooked rice to obtain 3 cups cooked.

YANGZHOU FRIED RICE WITH PRAWNS

Preparation time: 20 minutes
Total cooking time: 10 minutes
Serves 6

125 g (4 oz) cooked prawns (shrimp)

150 g (5 oz) fresh or frozen peas

1 tablespoon oil

3 spring onions (scallions), finely chopped

1 tablespoon finely chopped ginger

2 eggs, lightly beaten

3 cups (550 g/1 lb 1³/₄ oz) cold cooked white
  long-grain rice (see Note)

1¹/₂ tablespoons chicken stock

1 tablespoon Chinese rice wine

2 teaspoons light soy sauce

¹/₂ teaspoon roasted sesame oil

1 Peel the prawns and cut then in half through the back, removing the dark intestinal vein.

2 Cook the peas in a saucepan of simmering water for 3–4 minutes for fresh or 1 minute if you're using frozen.

3 Heat a wok over high heat, add the oil and heat until hot. Stir-fry the spring onion and ginger for 1 minute. Reduce the heat, add the egg and lightly scramble. Add the prawns and peas and toss lightly to heat through, then add the rice before the egg is set too hard. Increase the heat and stir to separate the rice grains and break the egg into small bits.

4 Add the stock, rice wine, soy sauce, sesame oil, ¹/₂ teaspoon salt and ¹/₄ teaspoon freshly ground black pepper, and toss lightly.

NOTE: You'll need 1 cup (200 g/6¹/₂ oz) uncooked rice to obtain 3 cups cooked.

CHINESE FRIED RICE
In China, plain cooked rice is served with everyday meals, while fried rice is only eaten as a snack on its own or at banquets, when it is served at the end of the meal. Fried rice is an excellent way to use up leftover cooked rice and any odds and ends.

*ABOVE: Yangzhou fried rice
with prawns*

RICE IN CHINA

Chinese meals are always centred around a staple, known as *fan* in Mandarin. In most cases the *fan* is rice; however, in the northern and western areas of China where the climate is harsh, wheat or millet products, which are easier to grow, may replace rice as the *fan*. Rice, always white and polished, is served in small bowls accompanied by platters of secondary dishes, or *cai*, of meat, seafood or vegetables, pickles and condiments.

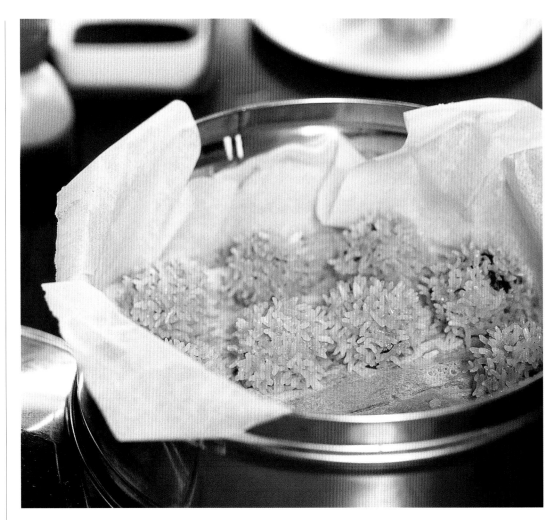

PEARL BALLS

Preparation time: 25 minutes +
 1 hour standing + 30 minutes soaking
Total cooking time: 30 minutes
Serves 6

☆ ☆

330 g (11 oz) glutinous or sweet rice
8 dried Chinese mushrooms
150 g (5 oz) peeled water chestnuts
450 g (14 oz) minced (ground) pork
1 small carrot, grated
2 spring onions (scallions), finely chopped
1 1/2 tablespoons finely chopped ginger
2 tablespoons light soy sauce
1 tablespoon Chinese rice wine
1 1/2 teaspoons roasted sesame oil
2 1/2 tablespoons cornflour (cornstarch)
soy sauce, to serve

1 Put the rice in a bowl and, using your fingers as a rake, rinse under cold running water to remove any dust. Drain the rice in a colander, then place it in a bowl with enough cold water to cover. Set aside for 1 hour. Drain the rice and transfer it to a baking tray in an even layer.

2 Soak the dried mushrooms in boiling water for 30 minutes, then drain and squeeze. Remove and discard the stems and chop the caps.

3 Blanch the water chestnuts in a saucepan of boiling water for 1 minute, then refresh in cold water. Drain, pat dry and finely chop them.

4 Place the pork in a bowl, add the mushrooms, water chestnuts, carrot, spring onion, ginger, soy sauce, rice wine, sesame oil and cornflour. Stir the mixture vigorously to combine.

5 Roll the mixture into 2 cm (3/4 inch) balls, then roll each meatball in the glutinous rice so that it is completely coated. Lightly press the rice to make it stick to the meatball. Place the pearl balls well apart in three steamers lined with greaseproof paper punched with holes, or some damp cheesecloth or muslin. Cover and steam over simmering water in a wok, swapping the steamers halfway through, for 25 minutes. If the rice is still firm, continue to cook for a little longer until it softens. Serve with the soy sauce.

ABOVE: Pearl balls

STEAMED CHICKEN AND SAUSAGE RICE

Preparation time: 30 minutes + 30 minutes soaking
Total cooking time: 50 minutes
Serves 4

4 dried Chinese mushrooms
250 g (8 oz) skinless chicken thigh fillet
1 teaspoon Chinese rice wine
2 teaspoons cornflour (cornstarch)
3 Chinese sausages (lap cheong)
200 g (6¹/2 oz) long-grain rice
1 spring onion (scallion), chopped

SAUCE
2 tablespoons light soy sauce
1 tablespoon Chinese rice wine
¹/2 teaspoon caster (superfine) sugar
¹/2 garlic clove, chopped (optional)
¹/2 teaspoon chopped ginger
¹/2 teaspoon roasted sesame oil

1 Soak the dried mushrooms in boiling water for 30 minutes, then drain and squeeze out any excess water. Remove and discard the stems and shred the caps.
2 Cut the chicken into bite-sized pieces and combine with the rice wine, cornflour and a pinch of salt.
3 Put the sausages on a plate in a steamer. Cover and steam over simmering water in a wok for 10 minutes, then thinly slice on the diagonal.
4 Put the rice in a bowl and, using your fingers as a rake, rinse under cold running water to remove any dust. Drain in a colander. Place in a large clay pot or casserole dish or four individual clay pots and add enough water so that there is 2 cm (³/4 inch) of water above the surface of the rice. Bring the water slowly to the boil, stir, then place the chicken pieces and mushrooms on top of the rice, with the sausage slices on top of them. Cook, covered, over very low heat for about 15 minutes, or until the rice is cooked.
5 To make the sauce, combine the soy sauce, rice wine, sugar, garlic, ginger and sesame oil in a small saucepan and heat until nearly boiling. Pour the sauce over the chicken and sausage and garnish with the spring onion.

BELOW: Steamed chicken and sausage rice

STEAMED GLUTINOUS RICE IN LOTUS LEAVES

Preparation time: 30 minutes +
    overnight soaking + 1 hour soaking
Total cooking time: 1 hour 20 minutes
Makes 8

☆☆

3 cups (600 g/1 1/4 lb) glutinous rice
4 large lotus leaves (see Note)

FILLING
2 tablespoons dried shrimp
4 dried Chinese mushrooms
2 tablespoons oil

BELOW: Steamed glutinous
rice in lotus leaves

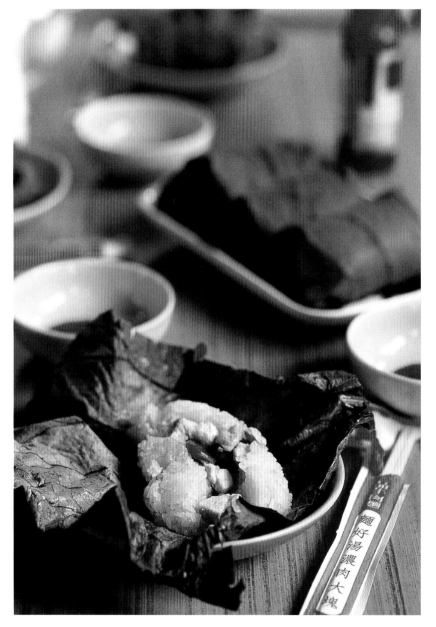

360 g (12 oz) skinless chicken breast fillet,
    cut into 1 cm (1/2 inch) cubes
1 garlic clove, crushed
2 Chinese sausages (lap cheong), thinly sliced
2 spring onions (scallions), thinly sliced
1 tablespoon oyster sauce
3 teaspoons light soy sauce
3 teaspoons sugar
1 teaspoon roasted sesame oil
1 tablespoon cornflour (cornstarch)
chilli sauce, to serve

1 Put the rice in a bowl, cover with cold water and leave to soak overnight. Drain in a colander, then put the rice in a steamer lined with greaseproof paper punched with holes. Steam, covered, over simmering water in a wok for 30–40 minutes, or until the rice is cooked. Cool slightly before using.
2 Soak the lotus leaves in boiling water for 1 hour, or until softened. Shake dry and cut the leaves in half to give eight equal pieces.
3 Meanwhile, to make the filling, soak the dried shrimp in boiling water for 1 hour, then drain. Soak the dried mushrooms in boiling water for 30 minutes, then drain and squeeze out any excess water. Remove and discard the stems and finely chop the caps.
4 Heat a wok over high heat, add half the oil and heat until very hot. Stir-fry the chicken for 2–3 minutes, or until browned. Add the shrimp, mushrooms, garlic, sausage and spring onion. Stir-fry for another 1–2 minutes, or until fragrant. Add the oyster sauce, soy sauce, sugar and sesame oil and toss well. Combine the cornflour with 220 ml (7 fl oz) water, add to the sauce and simmer until thickened.
5 With wet hands, divide the rice into 16 balls. Place the lotus leaves on a work surface, put a ball of rice in the centre of each leaf and flatten the ball slightly, making a slight indentation in the middle. Spoon one-eighth of the filling onto each rice ball, top with another slightly flattened rice ball and smooth into one ball. Wrap up firmly by folding the leaves over to form an envelope.
6 Place the parcels in three steamers. Cover and steam over simmering water in a wok, swapping the steamers halfway through, for 30 minutes. To serve, open up each leaf and eat straight from the leaf while hot with some chilli sauce.
NOTE: Lotus leaves are the dried leaves of the lotus. They are sold in packets in Chinese markets.

STEAMED BEEF WITH RICE FLOUR

Preparation time: 20 minutes +
    30 minutes marinating
Total cooking time: 25 minutes
Serves 4

450 g (14 oz) rump or sirloin steak, trimmed
2 tablespoons soy sauce
1 tablespoon chilli bean paste (toban jiang)
1 tablespoon Chinese rice wine
1 tablespoon finely chopped ginger
1/4 teaspoon freshly ground white pepper
1 tablespoon oil
125 g (4 oz) glutinous rice flour
1/2 teaspoon ground cinnamon
1 teaspoon roasted sesame oil
1 spring onion (scallion), shredded

1 Cut the beef into 2.5 mm (1/8 inch) slices and then cut the slices into bite-sized pieces. Combine with the soy sauce, chilli bean paste, rice wine, ginger, pepper and oil in a non-metallic bowl. Marinate in the fridge for 30 minutes.

2 Dry-fry the rice flour in a wok until it is brown and smells roasted. Add the cinnamon. Drain the beef and toss in the rice flour to coat.
3 Place the beef slices in a steamer lined with greaseproof paper punched with holes. Cover and steam over simmering water in a wok for 20 minutes. Sprinkle with the sesame oil and garnish with the spring onion.

CRISPY RICE

Put 2/3 cup (135 g/4 1/2 oz) white long-grain rice in a bowl and, using your fingers as a rake, rinse under cold running water to remove any dust. Drain the rice in a colander. Put the rice and 220 ml (7 fl oz) water in a heavy-based saucepan and bring to the boil. Reduce the heat to low and simmer, covered, for 15–18 minutes. Continue to cook, uncovered, until the rice has formed a cake that comes loose from the pan. Leave to cool. Tip the cake out and dry completely. Fill a wok one-quarter full of oil. Heat the oil to 180°C (350°F), or until a cube of bread dropped in the oil turns golden brown in 15 seconds. Cook the rice cake until it is brown and crisp. Serves 4.

CHINESE RICE WINE
Also known as Shaoxing rice wine. Made from rice, millet, yeast and Shaoxing's local spring water, the wine is aged for at least 3 years, then bottled either in glass or decorative earthenware bottles. The best and most expensive grades are aged for up to 100 years and are served as a drink. Chinese rice wine has a rich, sweetish taste and a clear or amber colour. Dry sherry is an acceptable substitute in cooking.

ABOVE: Steamed beef with rice flour

1 tablespoon oyster sauce

1 tablespoon Chinese rice wine

1 carrot, grated

8 water chestnuts, finely chopped

4 spring onions (scallions), thinly sliced

200 g (6½ oz) Chinese cabbage (wom bok),
  finely shredded

1 tablespoon sweet chilli sauce

2 teaspoons cornflour (cornstarch)

20 large spring roll wrappers

oil, for deep-frying

1 Soak the dried mushrooms in boiling water for 30 minutes, then drain and squeeze. Remove and discard the stems and chop the caps. Put the vermicelli in a heatproof bowl, cover with boiling water and soak for 6–7 minutes, or until soft and transparent. Drain and cut into 5 cm (2 inch) lengths.

2 Heat the oil in a wok over high heat and swirl to coat. Add the garlic and ginger, and cook for 1 minute. Add the pork mince and cook for another 3 minutes, stirring to break up any lumps. Add the prawns and cook for 1 minute, or until they just turn pink. Stir in the soy sauce, oyster sauce, rice wine, carrot, water chestnuts, spring onion, Chinese cabbage and sweet chilli sauce and cook for 2 minutes, or until warmed through. Season to taste with salt and pepper. Stir in the mushrooms and vermicelli.

3 Combine the cornflour and 2 tablespoons water in a small bowl until smooth.

4 Lay the spring roll wrappers under a damp tea towel. Working with one at a time, place a wrapper on the work surface with one corner facing you. Place 2 tablespoons of the filling along the centre of each spring roll wrapper. Brush the edges with the cornflour paste and roll up firmly, tucking in the ends as you go, and sealing with the cornflour paste. Continue, covering the completed rolls with a damp tea towel to prevent them drying out.

5 Fill a wok one-third full of oil and heat to 180°C (350°F), or until a cube of bread dropped in the oil browns in 15 seconds. Cook the spring rolls in batches of 2–3 rolls, turning gently to brown evenly, for 2 minutes, or until golden. Drain on crumpled paper towels. Serve with light soy sauce or your favourite dipping sauce. NOTE: If the rolls are too big, serve cut in half on the diagonal.

SPRING ROLLS

Preparation time: 30 minutes +
  30 minutes soaking
Total cooking time: 25 minutes
Makes 20

☆☆

4 dried Chinese mushrooms

80 g (2¾ oz) dried rice vermicelli

1 tablespoon peanut oil

2 garlic cloves, chopped

2 teaspoons grated ginger

250 g (8 oz) minced (ground) pork

250 g (8 oz) raw prawns (shrimp),
  peeled and finely chopped

1 tablespoon light soy sauce

ABOVE: Spring rolls

CHINESE STEAMED CHICKEN AND RICE PARCELS

Preparation time: 20 minutes +
  2 hours soaking + 10 minutes standing
Total cooking time: 30 minutes
Serves 4

☆ ☆ ☆

2 lotus leaves
6 dried Chinese mushrooms
1¼ cups (275 g/9 oz) short-grain rice
1 tablespoon peanut oil
250 g (8 oz) chicken thigh fillets, cut into
  1.5 cm (⅝ inch) cubes
2 garlic cloves, chopped
3 teaspoons grated ginger
50 g (1¾ oz) water chestnuts, chopped
¼ cup (60 ml/2 fl oz) light soy sauce
1 tablespoon Chinese rice wine
1 teaspoon cornflour (cornstarch)

1 Soak the lotus leaves in warm water for 2 hours, then cut in half. Soak the dried mushrooms in boiling water for 30 minutes, then drain and squeeze, reserving the soaking liquid. Remove and discard the stems and chop the caps.

2 Rinse the rice, then put it in a saucepan with 1½ cups (375 ml/12 fl oz) water. Bring to the boil, reduce the heat, cover and cook over low heat for 10 minutes. Stand, covered, for a further 10 minutes.

3 Heat a wok over high heat, add the oil and swirl to coat. Add the chicken and cook for 3 minutes, or until browned. Add the garlic, ginger, water chestnuts and mushrooms and cook for a further 30 seconds. Add the rice wine, 2 tablespoons of the soy sauce and ¼ cup (60 ml/2 fl oz) of the mushroom soaking liquid. Mix the cornflour with 1 tablespoon water, add to the wok and cook until the mixture thickens. Add the rice and the remaining soy sauce.

4 Lay each piece of lotus leaf, brown-side down, on a work surface. Place one-quarter of the rice mixture in the middle of each piece of lotus leaf, making a mound about 6 x 8 cm (2½ x 3 inches). Fold in the short sides, then roll lengthways to create a parcel. Repeat with the remaining mixture. Put the parcels, seam-side down, in a large steamer that has been lined with greaseproof paper punched with holes. Cover and steam over simmering water in a wok for 20 minutes, replenishing the water if necessary. Serve, and unwrap the parcels to eat.

CHINESE MUSHROOMS
Also known as shiitake. Often the dried ones are called Chinese mushrooms and the fresh ones are called shiitake, which is the Japanese name for them. Chinese cuisine usually features dried ones, which have a strong flavour and aroma and need to be soaked for 30 minutes in boiling water to reconstitute them before they are used.

LEFT: Chinese steamed chicken and rice parcels

CLAY POTS

Also known as sand pots, these earthenware, lidded pots are used for braised dishes, soups and rice dishes that need to be cooked slowly on the stove. The pots come in different shapes: the squatter ones are for braising and the taller ones for soups and rice. The pots are fragile and should be heated slowly, preferably with a liquid inside. Clay pots should be soaked in cold water for 24 hours before the first use and allowed to dry thoroughly.

ABOVE: Pork and rice clay pot

PORK AND RICE CLAY POT

Preparation time: 15 minutes +
　30 minutes soaking
Total cooking time: 1 hour 45 minutes
Serves 4

☆☆

15 g (1/2 oz) dried Chinese mushrooms
1 1/2 cups (300 g/10 oz) white long-grain rice
1/4 cup (60 ml/2 fl oz) vegetable oil
500 g (1 lb) lean fillet pork, cut into
　2 cm (3/4 inch) pieces
1 1/2 tablespoons hoisin sauce
2 teaspoons shredded ginger
3 garlic cloves, crushed
1 cinnamon stick
2 star anise
2 tablespoons dark soy sauce
1 tablespoon light soy sauce
2 tablespoons Chinese rice wine
2 cups (500 ml/16 fl oz) chicken stock
140 g (4 1/2 oz) tin straw mushrooms,
　drained and rinsed
125 g (4 oz) tin sliced bamboo shoots, drained
shredded spring onions (scallions), to garnish
　(optional)

1 Preheat the oven to warm 170°C (325°F/ Gas 3). Soak the dried mushrooms in boiling water for 30 minutes, then drain and squeeze. Remove and discard the stems. Meanwhile, soak the rice in cold water for 30 minutes, then rinse under cold running water until the water runs clear. Drain thoroughly.

2 Heat a wok over a high heat, add a tablespoon of oil and swirl to coat. Cook the pork until lightly browned, then stir in 2 teaspoons of the hoisin sauce, remove from the wok and set aside. Heat the rest of the oil in the wok, add the ginger, garlic, cinnamon stick and star anise and stir-fry for 30 seconds.

3 Add the rice to the wok and stir-fry over medium heat for 1 minute. Return the pork to the wok, add the soy sauces, rice wine and remaining hoisin sauce and stir well to combine. Remove from the heat and transfer to a clay pot or casserole dish. Pour the stock over the rice, arrange the Chinese mushrooms, straw mushrooms and bamboo shoot slices on top, then cover with the lid.

4 Bake for 1 1/4 hours, or until the meat is tender and the rice is cooked and almost has the texture of sticky rice. Remove the cinnamon stick and star anise. Garnish with the shredded spring onions, if desired. Serve with stir-fried Asian greens.

BARBECUED ASIAN PORK RIBS WITH SPRING ONION RICE

Preparation time: 15 minutes +
  overnight marinating
Total cooking time: 40 minutes
Serves 4

1 kg (2 lb) American-style pork ribs,
  cut into sections of 4–5 ribs
1/4 cup (60 ml/2 fl oz) hoisin sauce
1/4 cup (60 ml/2 fl oz) soy sauce
1 tablespoon Chinese rice wine
2 garlic cloves, chopped
2 tablespoons oil
3 spring onions (scallions), finely chopped
1 tablespoon grated ginger
1 1/4 cups (250 g/8 oz) long-grain rice
600 g (1 1/4 lb) baby bok choy (pak choi),
  leaves separated

1 Put the ribs in a non-metallic bowl. Combine the hoisin sauce, soy sauce, rice wine, garlic, 1 tablespoon of the oil, 2 tablespoons of the spring onion and half the ginger. Pour onto the ribs and mix to coat. Marinate for at least 10 minutes, or overnight in the refrigerator, if time permits.

2 Bring a large saucepan of water to the boil. Add the rice and cook for 12 minutes, stirring occasionally. Drain well.

3 Heat the remaining oil in a small saucepan over medium–low heat. When the oil is warm but not smoking, remove the pan from the heat and add the remaining spring onion and ginger. Season with 1/4 teaspoon salt, stirring quickly to combine. Stir this mixture through the rice.

4 Preheat a chargrill pan or barbecue plate and brush with oil. Remove the ribs from the marinade with tongs and reserve the marinade. Cook the ribs, in batches, if necessary, for 8–10 minutes on each side, or until cooked through, occasionally basting with the marinade.

5 About 5 minutes before the ribs are cooked, pour the reserved marinade into a small saucepan. If there is not much liquid, add 1/3 cup (80 ml/ 2 3/4 fl oz) water. Boil for 2 minutes, then add the bok choy, stirring to coat. Cook, covered, for 1–2 minutes, or until just wilted. Serve the ribs with the rice and bok choy, and drizzle with the marinade.

BOK CHOY
Also known as pak choi and little Chinese white cabbage, this is a mild, open-leaved cabbage with a fat white or pale green stem and dark green leaves. A smaller version is called Shanghai or baby bok choy. Separate the leaves and wash well before use.

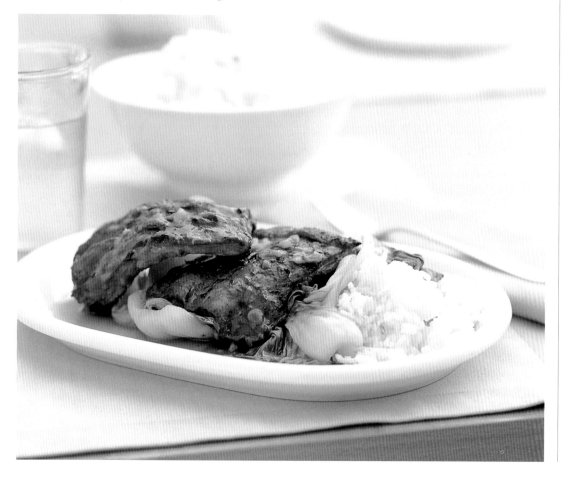

LEFT: Barbecued Asian pork ribs with spring onion rice

225

CHICKEN, SEAFOOD AND MEAT DISHES

BEEF WITH SPRING ONIONS

Thinly slice 500 g (1 lb) beef, then cut into bite-sized pieces. Put in a bowl with 2 finely chopped garlic cloves, 2 tablespoons light soy sauce, 1 tablespoon Chinese rice wine, 1 tablespoon cornflour (cornstarch) and 2 teaspoons sugar. Marinate for 1 hour. Drain. Combine ¼ cup (60 ml/ 2 fl oz) light soy sauce, 2 teaspoons sugar and ½ teaspoon roasted sesame oil. Heat a wok over high heat, add ¼ cup (60 ml/ 2 fl oz) oil and heat until very hot. Cook the beef in two batches for 1½ minutes,

or until brown. Remove and drain. Pour the oil from the wok, leaving 1 tablespoon. Reheat the wok over high heat and stir-fry 5 chopped spring onions (scallions) for 1 minute. Add the beef and the sauce. Toss well. Serves 6.

LAMB AND LEEKS

Thinly slice 300 g (10 oz) lamb fillet and combine with 1 tablespoon light soy sauce, 2 teaspoons Chinese rice wine, 2 teaspoons cornflour (cornstarch), ½ teaspoon sugar, ½ teaspoon roasted

sesame oil and ¼ teaspoon Sichuan peppercorns. Marinate in the fridge for 2 hours. Soak 3 tablespoons dried black fungus in cold water for 20 minutes, then drain and squeeze. Heat a wok over high heat, add 1⅔ cups (410 ml/13 fl oz) oil and heat until very hot. Stir-fry the lamb for 1 minute, or until brown. Remove from the wok and drain. Pour the oil out of the wok, leaving 2 tablespoons. Reheat the wok over high heat and stir-fry 4 small pieces of ginger, 200 g (6½ oz) young leeks that have been cut into short lengths (white part only) and the fungus for 1 minute, then stir in 2 tablespoons yellow bean sauce. Return the lamb to the wok and cook for 1 minute. Serves 4.

SQUID FLOWERS
Open up 400 g (13 oz) squid tubes, scrub clean, then score the inside with a fine crisscross pattern—do not cut all the way through. Cut the squid into 3 x 5 cm (1¼ x 2 inch) pieces. Blanch in boiling water for 30 seconds. Remove and refresh in cold water, then drain and dry well. Heat a wok over high heat, add ¼ cup (60 ml/2 fl oz) oil and heat until very hot. Stir-fry 2 tablespoons salted, fermented, rinsed and mashed black beans, 1 chopped small onion, 1 chopped small green capsicum (pepper), 4 small slices of ginger, 1 sliced spring onion (scallion) and 1 chopped red chilli for 1 minute. Add the squid and 1 tablespoon

Chinese rice wine, mix well and stir for 1 minute. Serves 4.

SHREDDED CHICKEN
Shred 250 g (8 oz) chicken. Combine the chicken with a pinch of salt, ¼ egg white and 2 teaspoons cornflour (cornstarch). Shred 3 celery stalks. Heat a wok over high heat. Add 410 ml (13 fl oz) oil to the wok and heat until hot, then turn off the heat. Blanch the chicken in the oil for 1 minute. Stir to separate the shreds, then remove and drain. Pour the oil from the wok, leaving 2 tablespoons. Reheat the wok over high heat and stir-fry 1 tablespoon shredded ginger, 2 shredded spring onions (scallions), 1 shredded red chilli and the celery for 1 minute. Add 1 teaspoon salt and ½ teaspoon sugar, blend well, then add the chicken with 2 tablespoons chicken stock, 1 tablespoon soy sauce and

1 tablespoon Chinese rice wine. Stir-fry for 1 minute. Serves 4.

RED-COOKED CHICKEN
Put 2 cinnamon sticks, 1 star anise, 2 pieces of dried orange peel, ½ teaspoon fennel seeds, 280 ml (9 fl oz) dark soy sauce, 90 g (3 oz) sugar and ½ cup (125 ml/ 4 fl oz) Chinese rice wine in a casserole dish with 1.5 litres (48 fl oz) water. Bring to the boil, then simmer for 30 minutes. Put a cleaned whole chicken breast-side down in the cooking liquid and cook for 1½ hours, turning twice. Turn off the heat and leave in the liquid for 30 minutes, then remove. Cut into bite-sized pieces. Spoon over a little liquid and serve hot or cold. Serves 6.

FROM LEFT: Beef with spring onions, Lamb and leeks, Squid flowers, Shredded chicken, Red-cooked chicken

FRIED NOODLES

Preparation time: 20 minutes
Total cooking time: 15 minutes
Serves 4

500 g (1 lb) thick fresh rice noodles

2 tablespoons oil

2 Chinese sausages (lap cheong), thinly
   sliced on the diagonal

2 garlic cloves, finely chopped

1 onion, finely chopped

3 red chillies, seeded and chopped

250 g (8 oz) Chinese barbecued pork
   (char siu), finely chopped

400 g (13 oz) raw prawns (shrimp),
   peeled and deveined

1/2 bunch garlic chives, cut into short lengths

2 tablespoons kecap manis

3 eggs, lightly beaten

1 tablespoon rice vinegar

100 g (3 1/2 oz) bean sprouts, tailed

BELOW: Fried noodles

1 Cover the noodles with boiling water, then gently separate.
2 Heat the oil in a large wok. Stir-fry the sausage slices for a few minutes, or until golden and very crisp. Using a slotted spoon, remove from the wok and drain on paper towels.
3 Reheat the oil in the wok, add the garlic, onion, chilli and pork and stir-fry for 2 minutes. Add the prawns and toss constantly until they change colour. Add the noodles, chives and kecap manis and toss. Cook for 1 minute or until the noodles begin to soften. Pour the combined eggs and vinegar over the top of the mixture and toss for 1 minute. Be careful not to let the egg-coated noodles burn on the base of the pan. Add the bean sprouts and toss.
4 Arrange the noodles on a large serving platter, scatter the drained pork sausages over the top and toss gently. Garnish with a few extra chives and serve immediately.

CRISPY VERMICELLI CAKES WITH SESAME VEGETABLES

Preparation time: 20 minutes +
   10 minutes soaking
Total cooking time: 15 minutes
Makes about 12

400 g (13 oz) dried rice vermicelli

peanut oil, for shallow-frying

2 teaspoons roasted sesame oil

1 tablespoon peanut oil, extra

2 carrots, cut into julienne strips

1 red capsicum (pepper), cut into julienne strips

2 zucchini (courgettes), cut into julienne strips

4 spring onions (scallions), cut into
   julienne strips

1/2–1 tablespoon oyster sauce

1 Soak the vermicelli in boiling water for 6–7 minutes, then drain thoroughly.
2 Heat the peanut oil in a large heavy-based frying pan over medium heat. Shape tablespoons of the noodles into flat discs and shallow-fry in batches for 3 minutes, or until crisp and golden. Drain on crumpled paper towels.
3 Heat the sesame oil and extra peanut oil in a wok and stir-fry the vegetables for 3 minutes, or until softened slightly. Stir in the oyster sauce and cook for 2 minutes. Serve the crispy vermicelli cakes topped with the vegetables.

SAN CHOY BAU WITH NOODLES

Preparation time: 20 minutes
Total cooking time: 15 minutes
Serves 6

vegetable oil, for deep-frying
100 g (3¹/₂ oz) dried rice vermicelli
¹/₄ cup (60 ml/2 fl oz) chicken stock
2 tablespoons Chinese rice wine
2 tablespoons soy sauce
2 tablespoons hoisin sauce
1 tablespoon brown bean sauce
¹/₂ teaspoon sugar
¹/₄ cup (60 ml/2 fl oz) peanut oil
1 garlic clove, crushed
1 tablespoon finely chopped ginger
3 spring onions (scallions), thinly sliced and
    green ends reserved for garnish
150 g (5 oz) minced (ground) pork
500 g (1 lb) raw prawns (shrimp), peeled,
    deveined and roughly chopped
12 iceburg lettuce leaves, trimmed into
    neat cups

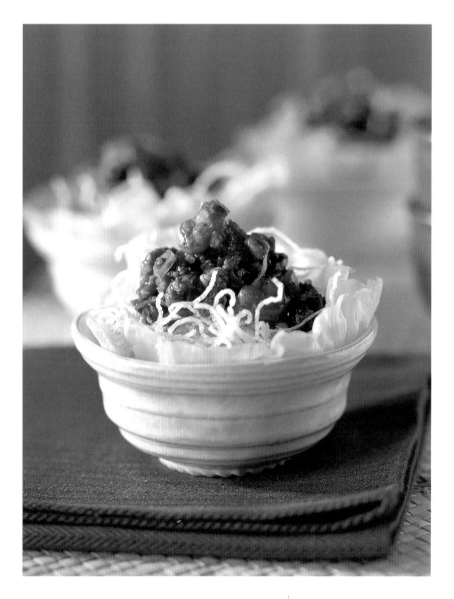

1 Fill a deep heavy-based saucepan or deep-fat fryer one-third full of oil and heat to 170°C (325°F), or until a cube of bread dropped into the oil browns in 20 seconds. Add the dried rice vermicelli to the oil in batches and deep-fry until puffed up but not browned—this will only take a few seconds, so watch it carefully. Remove with a slotted spoon and drain well on crumpled paper towels.
2 To make the stir-fry sauce, put the chicken stock, Chinese rice wine, soy sauce, hoisin sauce, brown bean sauce, sugar and ¹/₂ teaspoon salt in a small bowl and stir together until well combined.
3 Heat the peanut oil in a wok over high heat and swirl to coat the side of the wok. Add the garlic, ginger and spring onion and stir-fry for 1 minute, being careful not to burn the garlic.
4 Add the pork to the wok, breaking up the lumps with the back of a wooden spoon, then cook for a further 4 minutes. Add the prawns and stir-fry for 2 minutes, or until they begin to change colour.
5 Add the stir-fry sauce and stir until combined. Cook over high heat for 2 minutes, or until the mixture thickens slightly.

6 Divide the noodles among the lettuce cups, spoon the pork and prawn mixture over the noodles and garnish with the reserved spring onion. Serve at once.
NOTES: Make sure the pork mince is not too lean or the mixture will be dry.

When deep-frying the vermicelli, take care not to allow the oil to become too hot as the noodles will expand and brown very quickly. It helps to make sure you have everything you need by your side before you start deep-frying— a slotted spoon for removing the noodles and a tray lined with crumpled paper towels. Remember to deep-fry the noodles in small batches as they will dramatically increase in volume when cooked.

ABOVE: San choy bau with noodles

MANDARINS

Mandarin (also called tangerine) is the general name given to a group of citrus, orange-like fruits with loose skins. The name mandarin was originally a nickname, deriving from the English word for Chinese court official. These fruits have long been admired in China, as much for their fragrance as their taste. Though rarely used in cooking, the skin of certain varieties is dried and used as a flavouring or ground for use as a spice.

MANDARIN AND DUCK RICE PAPER ROLLS

Preparation time: 40 minutes
Total cooking time: Nil
Makes 24

1 whole Chinese roast duck
24 small rice paper wrappers
3 mandarins, peeled and segmented
1 cup (20 g/³/4 oz) mint
60 g (2 oz) chives, cut into 3 cm
  (1¹/4 inch) lengths
2 tablespoons hoisin sauce
2 tablespoons fresh mandarin juice

1 Remove the flesh and skin from the duck and shred into 1 x 3 cm (¹/2 x 1¹/4 inch) pieces, trying to keep some skin on each piece of flesh.
2 Working with one wrapper at a time, briefly soak each wrapper in cold water until softened, then place on a dry tea towel. Arrange 2–3 pieces of duck at the end of the wrapper closest to you. Top with 2 segments of mandarin, 3 mint leaves and several lengths of chives. Fold the end closest to you over the filling, fold in the sides and firmly roll up the rice paper.
3 Combine the hoisin sauce and mandarin juice in a bowl and serve as a dipping sauce with the rice paper rolls. Serve immediately.

PRAWNS IN RICE PAPER

Preparation time: 30 minutes +
  10 minutes soaking
Total cooking time: Nil
Makes 8

DIPPING SAUCE
1 teaspoon sugar
2 tablespoons fish sauce
1 tablespoon white vinegar
1 small red chilli, finely chopped
1 tablespoon chopped coriander
  (cilantro) leaves and stems

50 g (1³/4 oz) dried rice vermicelli
8 rice paper wrappers
16 cooked prawns (shrimp), peeled
  and deveined
16 Thai basil leaves
1 cup (30 g/1 oz) coriander (cilantro) leaves
1 carrot, cut into short thin strips
1 tablespoon grated lime zest
2 tablespoons sweet chilli sauce,
  plus extra, to serve

1 To make the dipping sauce, dissolve the sugar in ¹/4 cup (60 ml/2 fl oz) water, then stir in the

ABOVE: Mandarin and duck rice paper rolls

fish sauce, vinegar, chilli and coriander.

2 Soak the vermicelli in boiling water for 6–7 minutes, or until softened. Drain well.

3 Working one at a time, briefly soak a rice paper wrapper in lukewarm water until it softens, then lay it on a work surface. Put 2 prawns side by side in the centre of the wrapper and top with 2 basil leaves, 1 tablespoon coriander, a few carrot strips, a little lime zest and a small amount of vermicelli. Spoon a little chilli sauce over the top. Press the filling down to flatten it a little. Fold in the two sides, then roll up the parcel. Lay seam-side down on a serving plate and sprinkle with a little water, then cover with plastic wrap or a damp tea towel while you prepare the rest of the wrappers. Serve immediately with the dipping sauce and a little extra sweet chilli sauce.

PRAWN RICE NOODLE ROLLS

Preparation time: 20 minutes
Total cooking time: 15 minutes
Serves 4

☆

1 tablespoon peanut oil

2 garlic cloves, crushed

200 g (6¹/₂ oz) fresh shiitake mushrooms, thinly sliced

5 spring onions (scallions), chopped

¹/₃ cup (60 g/2 oz) drained and chopped water chestnuts

150 g (5 oz) fresh baby corn, roughly chopped

650 g (1 lb 5 oz) raw medium prawns (shrimp), peeled, deveined and roughly chopped

500 g (1 lb) fresh rice noodle rolls

oil, for brushing

SAUCE

¹/₄ cup (60 ml/2 fl oz) light soy sauce

2 teaspoons roasted sesame oil

1 teaspoon grated ginger

1 teaspoon sugar

2 tablespoons Chinese rice wine

1 Heat a wok over high heat, add the oil and swirl. Add the garlic and mushrooms and stir-fry for 1 minute, or until soft. Cook the spring onion, water chestnuts, corn and prawns for 2 minutes, or until the corn is just tender and the prawns are starting to turn pink, then remove from the heat.

2 Carefully unroll the rice noodle roll and cut it in half. You need two 16 x 23 cm (6¹/₂ x 9 inch) rectangles. Place ¹/₄ cup (3 tablespoons) of the prawn mixture along one short end of each rectangle, leaving a 3 cm (1¹/₄ inch) border. Fold both sides of the noodle roll towards the centre, then roll up like a spring roll. Cover with a damp tea towel and repeat with the remaining noodle rolls and prawn mixture.

3 Place the rolls seam-side down in a steamer lined with greaseproof paper punched with holes and lightly brushed with oil. Cover and steam over simmering water in a wok for 4–5 minutes, or until the prawns are cooked.

4 Meanwhile, to make the sauce, put the soy sauce, sesame oil, ginger, sugar and rice wine in a small saucepan and stir over medium heat until it is heated through. Place the rice noodle rolls on a platter and drizzle with the sauce just before serving.

BELOW: Prawn rice noodle rolls

VEGETABLE DISHES

CHINESE BROCCOLI IN OYSTER SAUCE

Wash 1 kg (2 lb) Chinese broccoli (gai lan). Discard any tough stems and diagonally cut into 2 cm (³/4 inch) pieces through the stem and the leaf. Blanch for 2 minutes, or until just tender, then refresh in cold water and dry. Heat a wok over high heat, add 1¹/2 tablespoons oil and heat until very hot. Stir-fry 2 finely chopped spring onions (scallions), 1¹/2 tablespoons grated ginger and 3 finely chopped garlic cloves for 10 seconds. Add the broccoli and cook until it is heated through. Add a combined mixture of ¹/2 cup (125 ml/ 4 fl oz) chicken stock, ¹/4 cup (60 ml/ 2 fl oz) oyster sauce, 1¹/2 tablespoons light soy sauce, 1 tablespoon Chinese rice wine, 2 teaspoons cornflour (cornstarch), 1 teaspoon sugar and 1 teaspoon roasted sesame oil. Cook until it has thickened, tossing to coat the broccoli. Serves 6.

TOFU IN YELLOW BEAN SAUCE

Cut 400 g (13 oz) firm, drained tofu into bite-sized pieces. Heat a wok over medium heat, add 2 tablespoons oil and heat until hot. Cook the tofu until golden. Add 1 crushed garlic clove, 1¹/2 tablespoons yellow bean sauce, 2 teaspoons oyster sauce and 2 teaspoons sugar and toss well. Combine 2 teaspoons cornflour (cornstarch) with 170 ml (5¹/2 fl oz) water, add to the sauce with 1 sliced spring onion (scallion) and simmer until the sauce has thickened and the spring onion has softened slightly. Serves 4.

SICHUAN-STYLE EGGPLANT

Peel 500 g (1 lb) Chinese or thin eggplants (aubergines) and trim off the ends. Cut in half lengthways and cut each half into strips 2 cm (³/4 inch) thick. Cut the strips into 5 cm (2 inch) lengths. Put the eggplant in a bowl with ¹/2 teaspoon salt and toss lightly, then leave for 1 hour. Pour off any liquid. Put the eggplant on a heatproof plate and sit in a steamer. Cover and steam over simmering water in a wok for 15 minutes, or until tender. Combine ¼ cup (60 ml/2 fl oz) light soy sauce, 1 tablespoon Chinese rice wine, 1 tablespoon roasted sesame oil, 2 teaspoons clear rice vinegar, 1 teaspoon sugar, 1 finely chopped spring onion (scallion), 2 finely chopped garlic cloves and 1 teaspoon chilli bean paste (toban jiang), then pour the sauce over the eggplant, tossing lightly to coat. Serves 6.

HOT AND SOUR CABBAGE

Separate the leaves from 1 small Chinese cabbage (wom bok) and trim off the stems. Cut the leaves across their length into 1 cm (½ inch) wide strips, separating the stems from the leaves. Combine ⅓ cup (80 ml/2¾ fl oz) Chinese black vinegar, ¼ cup (60 ml/2 fl oz) light soy sauce, 2 tablespoons sugar and ½ teaspoon salt. Heat a wok over high heat, add 1 tablespoon oil and heat until

very hot. Stir-fry 1 chopped red chilli and 2½ tablespoons finely chopped ginger for 15 seconds. Add 1½ diced red capsicums (peppers) and stir-fry for 30 seconds, then add 1½ tablespoons Chinese rice wine and stir-fry for 30 seconds. Add the cabbage stems, toss lightly and cook for 1 minute. Add the leaves and toss lightly, then pour in the soy sauce mixture, tossing lightly to coat. Cook for 30 seconds, then add 1 teaspoon roasted sesame oil. Serves 6.

STIR-FRIED WATER SPINACH

Wash and dry 1 kg (2 lb) water spinach. Remove any tough lower stalks and only use the young stems and leaves. Heat a wok over high heat, add 1½ tablespoons oil and heat until very hot. Stir-fry the water spinach for 1 minute, or until it begins to wilt. Drain in a colander. Add another tablespoon of oil to the wok

with 2 teaspoons shrimp paste, 3 crushed garlic cloves and 1–2 seeded and chopped red chillies, and toss over medium heat for 1 minute. Add the water spinach, 2 teaspoons oyster sauce and 2 teaspoons sugar and toss for 1 minute. Serves 4.

FROM LEFT: Chinese broccoli in oyster sauce, Tofu in yellow bean sauce, Sichuan-style eggplant, Hot and sour cabbage, Stir-fried water spinach

LION'S HEAD MEATBALLS

This dish is so named because the large meatballs are said to look like lion's heads surrounded by a mane of bok choy (pak choi). Originally the meatballs tended to be made from pork and pork fat and were coarser in texture than the ones featured here.

LION'S HEAD MEATBALLS

Preparation time: 20 minutes +
  30 minutes soaking
Total cooking time: 45 minutes
Serves 4

☆ ☆

6 dried Chinese mushrooms
100 g (3 1/2 oz) dried rice noodles
600 g (1 1/4 lb) minced (ground) pork
1 egg white
4 garlic cloves, finely chopped
2 tablespoons finely grated ginger
1 tablespoon cornflour (cornstarch)
1 1/2 tablespoons Chinese rice wine
6 spring onions (scallions), thinly sliced
2 tablespoons peanut oil
2 litres (64 fl oz) home-made chicken stock or
  1.5 litres (48 fl oz) purchased stock diluted
  with 2 cups (500 ml/16 fl oz) water
1/4 cup (60 ml/2 fl oz) light soy sauce
1 teaspoon sugar
400 g (13 oz) bok choy (pak choi), cut in half
  lengthways and leaves separated

1 Soak the dried mushrooms in 1 cup (250 ml/ 8 fl oz) boiling water for 30 minutes, then drain and squeeze, reserving the soaking liquid. Remove and discard the stems and chop the caps. Meanwhile, put the noodles in a heatproof bowl, cover with boiling water and soak for 4–5 minutes, or until soft. Drain and rinse.
2 Put the pork, egg white, garlic, ginger, cornflour, rice wine, two-thirds of the spring onion, and a pinch of salt in a food processor. Using the pulse button, process until smooth and well combined. Divide the mixture into eight portions and shape into large balls using wet hands.
3 Heat a wok over high heat, add the peanut oil and swirl to coat. Cook the meatballs in batches for 2 minutes on each side, or until golden but not cooked through. Drain.
4 Clean and dry the wok, then pour the stock into the wok and bring to the boil. Add the meatballs, soy sauce, sugar and mushrooms with the soaking liquid, then cover and cook over low heat for 20–25 minutes, or until the meatballs are cooked through.
5 Add the bok choy and noodles, cover and cook for 5 minutes, or until the noodles are heated through. Sprinkle with the remaining spring onion, then serve.

ABOVE: Lion's head meatballs

MONGOLIAN HOTPOT

Preparation time: 15 minutes + 10 minutes soaking
Total cooking time: 5 minutes
Serves 6

1/3 cup (80 ml/2 3/4 fl oz) light soy sauce

2 tablespoons Chinese sesame paste

3 tablespoons Chinese rice wine

1 teaspoon chilli and garlic paste

250 g (8 oz) dried rice vermicelli

600 g (1 1/4 lb) lamb backstraps or loin fillet,
    thinly sliced across the grain

4 spring onions (scallions), sliced

1.5 litres (48 fl oz) chicken stock

6 thin slices of ginger

300 g (10 oz) silken firm tofu, cut into
    1.5 cm (5/8 inch) cubes

300 g (10 oz) Chinese broccoli (gai lan),
    cut into 4 cm (1 1/2 inch) lengths

2 cups (75 g/2 1/2 oz) shredded Chinese
    cabbage (wom bok)

1 To make the sauce, combine the soy sauce, sesame paste, 1 tablespoon of the rice wine and the chilli and garlic paste in a small bowl.

2 Put the vermicelli in a large heatproof bowl, cover with boiling water and soak for 6–7 minutes. Drain well and divide among six serving bowls. Top with the lamb slices and spring onion.

3 Put the stock, ginger and remaining rice wine in a 2.5 litre (80 fl oz) flameproof hotpot or large saucepan. Cover and bring to the boil over high heat. Add the tofu, Chinese broccoli and Chinese cabbage and simmer, uncovered, for 1 minute, or until the broccoli has wilted. Divide the tofu, broccoli and cabbage among the serving bowls, then ladle on the hot stock—it should be hot enough to cook the lamb. Drizzle a little of the sauce on top and serve the rest on the side.

NOTE: This recipe traditionally uses a Chinese steamboat—this is an aluminium pot with a steam spout in the middle, placed on a propane burner in the middle of the dining table. You could also use a fondue pot.

TOFU
Also known as bean curd, or *doufu* by the Chinese. Tofu products are made from yellow soya beans that have been soaked, ground, combined with water and then cooked for a short time until they solidify. It is sold in blocks, either soft, firm or pressed, depending on the water content. Keep the blocks in water in the fridge, changing the water frequently, for up to 2 to 3 days.

LEFT: Mongolian hotpot

RICE NOODLE
PANCAKES WITH
ROAST DUCK

Carefully ease the skin
and flesh away from the
duck carcass.

Fry the pancakes on
both sides until crispy
and golden.

RICE NOODLE PANCAKES WITH ROAST DUCK

Preparation time: 20 minutes +
 5 minutes soaking
Total cooking time: 30 minutes
Serves 4–6

☆☆

1 Chinese roast duck (1.4 kg/2 lb 13 oz)
400 g (13 oz) fresh flat rice noodles
 (about 5 mm/^{1}/4 inch wide)
2 small red chillies, seeded and
 finely chopped
3 spring onions (scallions), thinly sliced
1 teaspoon peanut oil
1 cup (250 ml/8 fl oz) vegetable oil
^{1}/4 cup (60 ml/2 fl oz) hoisin sauce
1 Lebanese (short) cucumber, seeded
 and julienned
2 spring onions (scallions), extra, julienned
 into 5 cm (2 inch) lengths
coriander (cilantro) leaves, to garnish

1 Preheat the oven to moderate 180°C (350°F/
Gas 4). Remove the legs and wings from the
duck by twisting the joints away from the body
and cutting through the bones. Carefully ease
the skin and flesh away from the carcass in one
piece, trimming away any excess fat. Place the
flesh on a baking tray.
2 Cut the noodles into 10 cm (4 inch) long
pieces. Place in a large heatproof bowl, cover
with boiling water and soak briefly, gently
separating with your fingers. Drain, rinse with
cold water and drain again. Drain the noodles
on paper towels.
3 Combine the noodles, chilli, spring onion
and peanut oil in a large bowl. Heat the
vegetable oil in a large heavy-based frying pan
over high heat. Pour ^{1}/4 cup (3 tablespoons)
of the noodle mixture per pancake into the
pan and cook for 2–3 minutes on each side,
or until crispy and golden brown. Drain on
paper towels. Repeat with the remaining
mixture to make 12 noodle pancakes in total.
4 Meanwhile, roast the duck for 10 minutes,
or until the skin is crispy, then cut into 1 cm
(^{1}/2 inch) thick strips. Spread a little hoisin sauce
onto each pancake, add some cucumber and
spring onion and top with the slices of duck.
Garnish with the coriander leaves.

*ABOVE: Rice noodle
pancakes with roast duck*

ASIAN ROASTED DUCK WITH RICE NOODLES

Preparation time: 25 minutes
Total cooking time: 15 minutes
Serves 4

 ☆ ☆

1 whole Chinese roast duck
500 g (1 lb) fresh flat rice noodles
   (1 cm/¹/₂ inch wide)
3¹/₂ tablespoons peanut oil
3 small (180 g/6 oz) slender eggplants
   (aubergines), cut into 1 cm (¹/₂ inch)
   thick slices
2 x 2 cm (³/₄ x ³/₄ inch) piece of ginger,
   julienned
2 small red chillies, finely chopped
4 spring onions (scallions), thinly sliced
   on the diagonal
3 tablespoons torn basil
¹/₄ cup (60 ml/2 fl oz) Chinese barbecue sauce

1 Remove the crispy skin and the meat from the duck, discarding the carcass and fat. Finely slice the meat and skin and place in a bowl—there should be at least 350 g (11 oz) of meat.
2 Place the noodles in a heatproof bowl, cover with boiling water and soak briefly. Gently separate the noodles with your hands. Rinse under cold water and drain well.
3 Heat a wok over high heat, add 2¹/₂ tablespoons of the peanut oil and swirl to coat the side of the wok. When hot, add the eggplant and stir-fry for 3–4 minutes, or until softened. Transfer to a bowl.
4 Heat the remaining oil in the wok over high heat. Cook the ginger, chilli and spring onion for 30 seconds, stirring constantly. Return the eggplant to the wok. Add the duck, basil and barbecue sauce, and gently toss together for 1–2 minutes, or until heated through. Add the noodles and stir-fry for 1–2 minutes, or until well combined and heated through, taking care not to break up the noodles. Serve immediately.

SLENDER EGGPLANT
The slender eggplant (aubergine) is much narrower than the European eggplant. It has a similar taste, but a much more tender skin. Look for firm, heavy eggplants that have shiny, smooth skins with no brown patches.

LEFT: Asian roasted duck with rice noodles

FRESH NOODLES
WITH BEEF AND
GARLIC CHIVES

Slice the fresh noodle
roll into thick slices, which
will unroll and separate
into noodles.

FRESH NOODLES WITH BEEF AND GARLIC CHIVES

Preparation time: 20 minutes +
   overnight marinating
Total cooking time: 10 minutes
Serves 6

☆☆

250 g (8 oz) rump or sirloin steak, trimmed

2 large garlic cloves, crushed

3 teaspoons cornflour (cornstarch)

1/4 teaspoon roasted sesame oil

1/4 cup (60 ml/2 fl oz) oyster sauce

2 teaspoons sugar

1 tablespoon dark soy sauce

1 kg (2 lb) fresh rice noodle rolls

1/4 cup (60 ml/2 fl oz) vegetable oil

1 red capsicum (pepper), thinly sliced

150 g (5 oz) Chinese garlic chives,
   cut into 5 cm (2 inch) lengths

chilli sauce, to serve

1 Cut the beef across the grain into thin bite-sized strips—you may find this easier if you freeze the steak for 15–20 minutes beforehand. Combine with the garlic, cornflour, sesame oil, 1 tablespoon of the oyster sauce, 1 teaspoon of the sugar and 2 teaspoons of the soy sauce. Marinate in the fridge for at least 30 minutes, or overnight, if time permits.

2 Cut the noodle rolls into 2 cm (3/4 inch) slices, then separate them slightly with your hands.

3 Heat a wok over high heat, add the vegetable oil and swirl to coat the side of the wok and heat until very hot. Stir-fry the capsicum for 1–2 minutes, or until it begins to soften. Add the beef and toss constantly for several minutes, or until it changes colour. Add the garlic chives and noodles and toss for 1–2 minutes, or until they soften. Add the remaining oyster sauce, sugar and soy sauce and toss well until combined. Serve with some chilli sauce on the side.

ABOVE: Fresh noodles with beef and garlic chives

RAINBOW NOODLES

Preparation time: 25 minutes +
  10 minutes soaking
Total cooking time: 10 minutes
Serves 4

225 g (7 oz) prawns (shrimp)

1 tablespoon Chinese rice wine

1 teaspoon roasted sesame oil

2¹/₂ tablespoons finely chopped ginger

300 g (10 oz) dried rice vermicelli

2 leeks, white part only

¹/₃ cup (80 ml/2³/₄ fl oz) peanut oil

1¹/₂ tablespoons Chinese curry powder
  (see Note)

200 g (6¹/₂ oz) bean sprouts, tailed

¹/₄ cup (60 ml/2 fl oz) chicken stock or water

2 tablespoons light soy sauce

¹/₂ teaspoon sugar

1 Peel the prawns, leaving the tails intact. Using a sharp knife, score lengthways along the back and remove the vein. Place in a bowl, add the rice wine, sesame oil and 2 teaspoons of the ginger and toss to coat.

2 Soak the noodles in boiling water for 6–7 minutes, then drain. Cut the leeks into roughly 5 cm (2 inch) lengths and shred finely. Wash well and dry thoroughly.

3 Heat a wok over high heat, add 1 tablespoon of the peanut oil and heat until very hot. Stir-fry the prawns in batches for 1¹/₂ minutes, or until they turn opaque. Remove with a wire sieve or slotted spoon and drain. Pour off the oil and wipe out the wok.

4 Reheat the wok over high heat, add the remaining oil and heat until very hot. Stir-fry the curry powder for a few seconds, or until fragrant. Add the leek and remaining ginger and stir-fry for 1¹/₂ minutes. Add the bean sprouts and cook for 20 seconds, then add the prawns, stock or water, soy sauce, sugar and 1 teaspoon salt and ¹/₂ teaspoon freshly ground black pepper, and stir to combine.

5 Add the noodles and toss until they are cooked through and have absorbed all the sauce. Transfer to a serving dish and serve.

NOTE: Chinese curry powder is much milder than its Indian counterpart and has a similar flavour to five-spice powder, with the addition of turmeric and coriander. You could use a mild Indian curry powder instead.

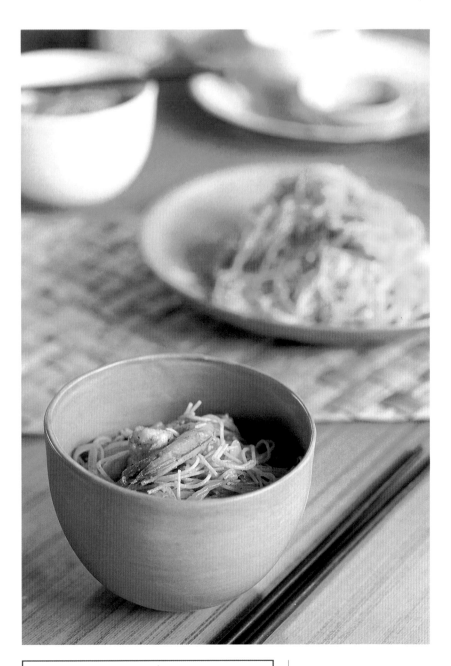

CHILLI SAUCE

Remove the stems from 1 kg (2 lb) red chillies, then put the chillies in a saucepan with ¹/₃ cup (80 ml/2³/₄ fl oz) water. Cover with a lid and bring to the boil. Cook until the chillies are tender, then stir in 3 teaspoons salt, ¹/₃ cup (75 g/2¹/₂ oz) sugar and 170 ml (5¹/₂ fl oz) clear rice vinegar. Cool slightly, then transfer to a blender or food processor and blend to a paste. Alternatively, push through a strainer. Store in a jar in the fridge for up to 1 month or freeze in small portions. Use as an ingredient or dipping sauce for Chinese dishes. Makes 1²/₃ cups (410 ml/13 fl oz).

ABOVE: Rainbow noodles

CROSSING-THE-BRIDGE
NOODLES

Pull off the head and peel
the shell from the body.

CROSSING-THE-BRIDGE NOODLES

Preparation time: 25 minutes +
  40 minutes soaking
Total cooking time: 10 minutes
Serves 4

100 g (3¹/₂ oz) prawns (shrimp)

100 g (3¹/₂ oz) skinless chicken breast fillet

100 g (3¹/₂ oz) squid tubes

100 g (3¹/₂ oz) Chinese ham, thinly sliced

8 dried Chinese mushrooms

125 g (4 oz) bean sprouts, tailed

350 g (11 oz) fresh rice noodles or
  250 g (8 oz) rice stick noodles

chilli sauce, to serve

light soy sauce, to serve

1 litre (32 fl oz) chicken stock

4 spring onions (scallions), finely chopped

*ABOVE: Crossing-the-bridge
noodles*

1 Peel the prawns, remove the heads, then cut
them in half through the back, removing the
vein. Slice the prawns and the chicken breast
thinly on the diagonal.

2 Open up the squid tubes by cutting down one
side, scrub off any soft jelly-like substance and
slice thinly on the diagonal. Arrange the prawns,
chicken, squid and ham on a plate, cover and
refrigerate until needed.

3 Soak the dried mushrooms in boiling water
for 30 minutes, then drain and squeeze out any
excess water. Remove and discard the stems.
Add the mushrooms to the plate. Wash the bean
sprouts and drain thoroughly. Add to the plate.

4 Separate the rice noodles into four bundles.
If you are using dried rice noodles, soak in hot
water for 10 minutes, then drain.

5 Give each guest a small saucer of chilli sauce
and a saucer of soy sauce. Place the ingredients
and dipping sauces on the table. Heat four soup
bowls either in a low oven or by running them
under very hot water for a few minutes. Put
the chicken stock in a clay pot, casserole dish
or saucepan with the spring onion and bring to
the boil. When the stock has reached a rolling
boil, fill the soup bowls.

6 Give each guest a hot bowl filled with stock
and let them cook the meat, vegetables and
noodles in the stock.

CINNAMON BEEF NOODLES

Preparation time: 15 minutes
Total cooking time: 1 hour 40 minutes
Serves 6

1 teaspoon oil
10 spring onions (scallions), cut into
    4 cm (1 1/2 inch) lengths, lightly crushed
10 garlic cloves, thinly sliced
6 slices of ginger
1 1/2 teaspoons chilli bean paste (toban jiang)
2 cassia or cinnamon sticks (see Note)
2 star anise
1/2 cup (125 ml/4 fl oz) light soy sauce
1 kg (2 lb) chuck steak, trimmed and
    cut into 4 cm (1 1/2 inch) cubes
250 g (8 oz) rice stick noodles
250 g (8 oz) baby spinach
3 tablespoons finely chopped spring onion
    (scallions)

1 Heat a wok over medium heat, add the oil and heat until hot. Stir-fry the spring onion, garlic, ginger, chilli bean paste, cassia and star anise for 10 seconds, or until fragrant. Transfer to a clay pot, casserole dish or saucepan. Add the soy sauce and 2.25 litres (72 fl oz) water. Bring to the boil, add the beef, then return to the boil. Reduce the heat and simmer, covered, for 1 1/2 hours, or until the beef is very tender. Skim the surface occasionally to remove any impurities and fat. Remove and discard the ginger and cassia.

2 Meanwhile, soak the noodles in hot water for 10 minutes, then drain and divide among six soup bowls.

3 Add the spinach to the beef and bring to the boil. Spoon the beef mixture over the noodles and sprinkle with the spring onion.

NOTE: In China cassia bark is more often used than cinnamon to make this recipe. The bark of the cassia tree is similar to cinnamon, but the flavour is more woody.

STAR ANISE
An aromatic ingredient in Chinese cooking, this is a star-shaped dried seed pod from a native Chinese tree containing a flat seed in each of its eight points. It has a similar flavour and aroma to fennel seed and aniseed. It is used whole in braised dishes or ground into one of the ingredients of five-spice powder.

LEFT: Cinnamon beef noodles

NOODLES WITH
SEAFOOD AND DRIED
SCALLOPS

Shred the steamed scallops into pieces. They have a strong flavour and are best eaten in small pieces.

NOODLES WITH SEAFOOD AND DRIED SCALLOPS

Preparation time: 25 minutes +
  10 minutes soaking
Total cooking time: 40 minutes
Serves 4

☆ ☆

4 dried scallops (see Note)

12 prawns (shrimp)

200 g (6 1/2 oz) squid tubes

400 g (13 oz) thin rice stick noodles

1 tablespoon oil

2 tablespoons shredded ginger

2 spring onions (scallions), thinly sliced

150 g (5 oz) Chinese cabbage (wom bok), finely shredded

1 cup (250 ml/8 fl oz) chicken stock

2 tablespoons light soy sauce

2 tablespoons Chinese rice wine

1 teaspoon roasted sesame oil

1 Put the dried scallops in a heatproof bowl with 1 tablespoon water and put them in a steamer. Cover and steam over simmering water in a wok for 30 minutes, or until they are completely tender. Remove the scallops and shred the meat.
2 Peel the prawns and cut them in half through the back, removing the vein.
3 Open up the squid tubes by cutting down one side, scrub off any soft jelly-like substance, then score the inside of the flesh with a fine crisscross pattern, making sure you do not cut all the way through. Cut the squid into 3 x 5 cm (1 1/4 x 2 inch) pieces.
4 Soak the noodles in hot water for 10 minutes, then drain.
5 Heat a wok over high heat, add the oil and heat until very hot. Stir-fry the ginger and spring onion for 1 minute, then add the prawns and squid and stir-fry until just opaque. Add the scallops and Chinese cabbage and toss together. Pour in the stock, soy sauce and rice wine and boil for 1 minute. Add the noodles and sesame oil, toss together and serve.
NOTE: Dried scallops, known as conpoy, are highly prized. Available at Chinese markets.

ABOVE: Noodles with seafood and dried scallops

NOODLE PANCAKES WITH PEKING DUCK

Preparation time: 20 minutes
Total cooking time: 15 minutes
Serves 4 as a starter

½ Chinese roast duck

500 g (1 lb) fresh rice noodle sheets

1 teaspoon roasted sesame oil

¼ cup (40 g/1¼ oz) sesame seeds, toasted

2 tablespoons vegetable oil

50 g (1¾ oz) snow pea (mangetout) sprouts, to garnish

SAUCE
¼ cup (60 ml/2 fl oz) hoisin sauce
1 tablespoon plum sauce

1 Remove the flesh and skin from the duck, trying to keep some of the skin on each piece.
2 Cut the noodle rolls into 5 cm (2 inch) slices, then halve them. Rinse them under cold water and separate them slightly with your hands. Drain and pat dry, then transfer to a bowl and mix in the sesame oil, sesame seeds and 1 tablespoon of the vegetable oil.
3 Lightly grease eight egg rings and place four of them in a large non-stick frying pan with a little of the oil. Press the noodle mixture firmly into the rings and cook the pancakes over medium heat until crisp and golden. Remove the egg rings and turn the pancakes over. Repeat with the remaining noodle mixture until you have eight noodle pancakes. Keep the pancakes warm.
4 To make the sauce, put the hoisin and plum sauces in a saucepan with 1 tablespoon water and bring to the boil.
5 To serve, place two noodle pancakes on top of one another on each plate, top with snow pea sprouts and barbecued duck and drizzle with the sauce.

ROASTED SESAME OIL
Chinese sesame oil is made from roasted white sesame seeds and is a rich amber liquid, unlike the pale unroasted Middle Eastern sesame oil. Buy small bottles as it loses its aroma quickly. It does not fry well on its own because it burns quickly. Roasted sesame oil can be mixed with other oils for stir-frying or sprinkled on food as a seasoning—only a small amount is needed because it has a strong flavour.

LEFT: Noodle pancakes with Peking duck

CHINESE BARBECUED PORK
A Cantonese speciality, these pork pieces have been marinated in a mixture of soy sauce and five-spice powder, then coated in maltose or honey and roasted until they have a red, lacquered appearance. Available at Chinese barbecue shops. Also called char siu.

ABOVE: Steamed rice noodle rolls

STEAMED RICE NOODLE ROLLS

Preparation time: 15 minutes
Total cooking time: 10 minutes
Makes 4

PORK FILLING
350 g (11 oz) Chinese barbecued pork (char siu), chopped
3 spring onions (scallions), finely chopped
2 tablespoons chopped coriander (cilantro)

OR PRAWN FILLING
250 g (8 oz) small prawns (shrimp)
1 tablespoon oil
3 spring onions (scallions), finely chopped
2 tablespoons chopped coriander (cilantro)

OR VEGETABLE FILLING
300 g (10 oz) Chinese broccoli (gai lan)
1 teaspoon light soy sauce
1 teaspoon roasted sesame oil
2 spring onions (scallions), chopped
4 fresh rice noodle rolls, at room temperature
oyster sauce, to serve

1 To make the pork filling, combine the pork with the spring onion and coriander.
2 To make the prawn filling, peel and devein the prawns. Heat a wok over high heat, add the oil and heat until very hot. Stir-fry the prawns for 1 minute, or until they are pink and cooked through. Season with a little salt and ground white pepper. Add the spring onion and coriander and mix well.
3 To make the vegetable filling, wash the Chinese broccoli well. Discard any tough-looking stems and chop the rest of the stems. Put on a plate in a steamer, cover and steam over simmering water in a wok for 3 minutes, or until the stems and leaves are just tender. Combine the Chinese broccoli with the soy sauce, sesame oil and spring onion.
4 Carefully unroll the rice noodle rolls (don't worry if they crack or tear a little at the sides). Trim each one into a neat rectangle about 15 x 18 cm (6 x 7 inches) (you may be able to get two out of one roll if they are very large). Divide the filling among the rolls, then re-roll the noodles. Put the rolls on a plate in a large steamer, cover and steam over simmering water in a wok for 5 minutes. Serve the rolls cut into pieces and drizzled with some oyster sauce.
NOTE: These are a dim sum favourite.

RICE NOODLE ROLLS FILLED WITH PRAWNS

Preparation time: 20 minutes
Total cooking time: 20 minutes
Makes 8

500 g (1 lb) fresh rice noodle rolls,
    at room temperature
1 teaspoon roasted sesame oil
1 tablespoon peanut oil
1 tablespoon grated ginger
3 spring onions (scallions), thinly sliced
200 g (6$^{1}/_{2}$ oz) water chestnuts, chopped
500 g (1 lb) raw prawns (shrimp), peeled,
    deveined and chopped
1 tablespoon fish sauce
1 tablespoon soft brown sugar
1 tablespoon snipped garlic chives
2 tablespoons vegetable oil

$^{1}/_{3}$ cup (80 ml/2$^{3}/_{4}$ fl oz) light soy sauce
1 teaspoon roasted sesame oil, extra
$^{1}/_{2}$ teaspoon white sugar
extra garlic chives, to garnish

1 Open out the rice noodle sheets and cut eight 15 cm (6 inch) squares. Heat the sesame and peanut oils in a wok, add the ginger and spring onions and cook over medium heat for 2 minutes. Add the water chestnuts and prawns and cook, stirring, for 5 minutes, or until the prawns turn pink. Stir in the fish sauce, sugar and chives. Remove from the wok and allow to cool slightly.
2 Spoon the mixture down the centre of each rice noodle sheet and roll over to enclose the filling.
3 Heat the vegetable oil in a clean, non-stick frying pan. Cook the noodle rolls in batches over medium heat until golden on both sides. Serve drizzled with the combined soy sauce, sugar, extra sesame oil and garnish with the extra garlic chives.

WATER CHESTNUTS
These are the rhizomes of a plant that grows in paddy fields in China. The nut has a dark-brown shell and a crisp white interior. The raw nuts need to be peeled with a knife and blanched, then stored in water. Canned ones need to be drained and rinsed. Freshly peeled water chestnuts are occasionally available from Chinese markets.

LEFT: Rice noodle rolls filled with prawns

SICHUAN PEPPERCORNS
Not a true pepper, but the berries of a shrub called the prickly ash. Sichuan pepper, unlike ordinary pepper, has a pungent flavour and the aftertaste, rather than being simply hot, is numbing. The peppercorns should be crushed and dry-roasted to bring out their full flavour.

LAMB HOTPOT WITH RICE NOODLES

Preparation time: 20 minutes +
  2 hours marinating
Total cooking time: 2 hours
Serves 4

☆ ☆

2 garlic cloves, crushed
2 teaspoons grated ginger
1 teaspoon five-spice powder
1/4 teaspoon ground white pepper
2 tablespoons Chinese rice wine
1 teaspoon sugar
1 kg (2 lb) boneless lamb shoulder, trimmed
  and cut into 3 cm (1 1/4 inch) pieces
30 g (1 oz) dried Chinese mushrooms
1 tablespoon peanut oil
1 large onion, cut into wedges
2 cm (3/4 inch) piece of ginger, julienned
1 teaspoon Sichuan peppercorns, crushed
2 tablespoons sweet bean paste
1 teaspoon black peppercorns, ground
  and toasted
2 cups (500 ml/16 fl oz) chicken stock
1/4 cup (60 ml/2 fl oz) oyster sauce
2 star anise
1/4 cup (60 ml/2 fl oz) Chinese rice wine, extra

80 g (2 3/4 oz) tin sliced bamboo shoots, drained
100 g (3 1/2 oz) tin water chestnuts, drained
  and sliced
400 g (13 oz) fresh rice noodles, cut into
  2 cm (3/4 inch) wide strips
1 spring onion (scallion), sliced on the diagonal

1 Combine the garlic, grated ginger, five-spice powder, white pepper, rice wine, sugar and 1 teaspoon salt in a large bowl. Add the lamb and toss to coat. Cover and marinate for 2 hours.
2 Meanwhile, soak the dried mushrooms in boiling water for 30 minutes, then drain and squeeze out any excess water. Remove and discard the stems and chop the caps.
3 Heat a wok over high heat, add the oil and swirl to coat. Stir-fry the onion, julienned ginger and Sichuan peppercorns for 2 minutes. Add the lamb in batches and cook for 2–3 minutes, or until starting to brown. Return all the lamb to the wok. Stir in the bean paste and ground peppercorns and cook for 3 minutes. Transfer to a 2 litre (64 fl oz) flameproof clay pot or casserole dish. Stir in the stock, oyster sauce, star anise and extra rice wine and simmer, covered, over low heat for 1 1/2 hours, or until the lamb is tender. Stir in the bamboo shoots and water chestnuts and cook for 20 minutes. Add the mushrooms.
4 Cover the noodles with boiling water and gently separate. Drain and rinse, then add to the hotpot, stirring for 1–2 minutes, or until heated through. Sprinkle with spring onion.

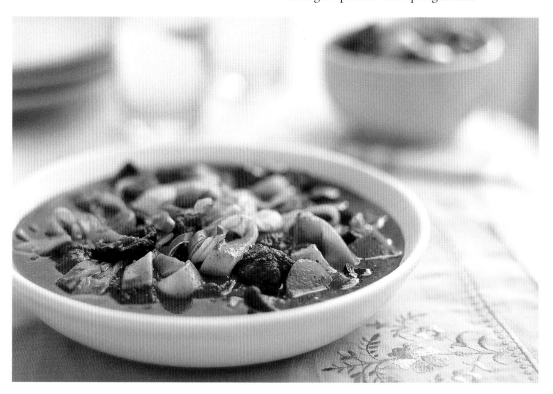

*RIGHT: Lamb hotpot
with rice noodles*

EIGHT-TREASURE RICE

Preparation time: 20 minutes +
  30 minutes soaking
Total cooking time: 3 hours
Serves 8

☆ ☆ ☆

12 whole blanched lotus seeds (see Notes)

12 jujubes (dried Chinese dates) (see Notes)

20 fresh or tinned gingko nuts, shelled
  (see Notes)

225 g (7 oz) glutinous rice

2 tablespoons sugar

2 teaspoons oil

30 g (1 oz) slab sugar (see Notes)

8 glacé cherries

6 dried longans, pitted (see Notes)

4 almonds or walnuts

225 g (7 oz) red bean paste (see Notes)

1 Soak the lotus seeds and jujubes in bowls
of cold water for 30 minutes, then drain.
Remove the seeds from the jujubes. If using
fresh gingko nuts, blanch in a saucepan of
boiling water for 5 minutes, then refresh in
cold water and dry thoroughly.
2 Put the glutinous rice and 300 ml (9$^{1}/_{2}$ fl oz)
water in a heavy-based saucepan and bring to
the boil. Reduce the heat to low and simmer
for 10–15 minutes. Stir in the sugar and oil.
3 Dissolve the slab sugar in 220 ml (7 fl oz) water
and bring to the boil. Add the lotus seeds, jujubes
and gingko nuts and simmer for 1 hour, or until
the lotus seeds are soft. Drain, reserving the liquid.
4 Grease a 1 litre (32 fl oz) heatproof bowl and
decorate the base with the lotus seeds, jujubes,
gingko nuts, cherries, longans and almonds.
Smooth two-thirds of the rice over this to form
a shell on the surface of the bowl. Fill with the
bean paste, cover with the remaining rice and
smooth the surface.
5 Cover the rice with a piece of greased foil
and put the bowl in a steamer. Cover and steam
over simmering water in a wok for 1–1$^{1}/_{2}$ hours,
replenishing with boiling water during cooking.
6 Turn the pudding out onto a plate and pour
the reserved sugar liquid over the top. Serve hot.
NOTES: Eight-treasure rice is a Chinese rice
pudding. It is a favourite at banquets and
Chinese New Year. The eight treasures vary,
but can also include other preserved fruits. You
will need access to a Chinese grocer to obtain
most of the ingredients.

Lotus seeds are the seeds from the lotus.
  Jujubes (Chinese dates) are an olive-sized
dried fruit with a red, wrinkled skin. They are
thought to be lucky because of their red colour.
  Gingko nuts are the nuts of the maidenhair
tree. The hard shells are cracked open and the
inner nuts soaked to loosen their skins. Shelled
nuts can be bought in cans and are easier to use
than unshelled ones.
  Slab sugar is dark brown sugar with a caramel
flavour sold in a slab. Soft brown sugar can be
used instead.
  Longans are from the same family as lychees.
Available fresh, canned or dried.
  Red bean paste is made from crushed adzuki
beans and sugar.

BELOW: Eight-treasure rice

ABOVE: New Year sweet dumplings

(the dough will be very hot) to form a soft, slightly sticky dough. Dust your hands with extra rice flour, roll the dough into a cylinder, then divide it into cherry-size pieces. Cover the dough with a tea towel and, using one piece at a time, form each piece of dough into a flat round, then gather it into a cup shape. The dough should be fairly thin.

3 Fill each cup shape with 1 teaspoon of paste and fold the top over, smoothing the dough so you have a round ball with no visible joins.

4 Bring 1 litre (32 fl oz) water to the boil, add the rock sugar and stir until dissolved. Return to the boil, add the dumplings in batches and simmer for 5 minutes, or until they rise to the surface. Serve warm with a little of the syrup.

NOTE: Yellow rock sugar comes as uneven lumps of sugar, which may need to be further crushed before use if very big. It is a pure sugar that produces a clear syrup and makes sauces shiny and clear. You can use sugar cubes instead.

DEEP-FRIED ICE CREAM IN COCONUT

Preparation time: 20 minutes +
  several days freezing
Total cooking time: 1 minute
Serves 6

☆ ☆ ☆

2 litres (64 fl oz) vanilla ice cream
1 egg
$1/2$ cup (60 g/2 oz) plain (all-purpose) flour
$1/2$ cup (90 g/3 oz) rice flour
$1 1/2$ cups (150 g/5 oz) fine dry breadcrumbs
2 tablespoons desiccated coconut
oil, for deep-frying

1 Make six large scoops of ice cream. Return to the freezer.

2 Make a thick batter of the egg, flours and $3/4$ cup (185 ml/6 fl oz) water. Coat the ice cream balls with the batter, then roll in the breadcrumbs and coconut to coat thickly. Return to the freezer to freeze for several days.

3 Heat the oil to 190°C (375°F) or until a cube of bread dropped in the oil browns in 10 seconds. Slide in one ice cream ball at a time and cook for a few seconds until the surface is golden. Remove from the oil and serve at once with fresh fruit.

NOTE: It is crucial that the ice cream is solidly frozen and that the oil is sufficiently hot.

NEW YEAR SWEET DUMPLINGS

Preparation time: 40 minutes
Total cooking time: 15 minutes
Makes 24

☆ ☆ ☆

60 g (2 oz) black sesame paste, red bean paste
  or smooth peanut butter
$1/3$ cup (80 g/$2^3/4$ oz) caster (superfine) sugar
250 g (8 oz) glutinous rice flour
30 g (1 oz) rock sugar (see Note)

1 Combine the sesame paste with the caster sugar in a small bowl.

2 Sift the rice flour into a bowl and stir in 220 ml (7 fl oz) boiling water. Knead carefully

CHINESE ALMOND PUDDING

Preparation time: 5 minutes +
  3 hours chilling
Total cooking time: 1 hour 15 minutes
Serves 6

1 cup (100 g/3½ oz) ground almonds
½ cup (90 g/3 oz) glutinous rice flour
2½ cups (625 ml/20 fl oz) milk
½ cup (115 g/4 oz) caster (superfine) sugar

1 Combine the ground almonds and rice flour in a heavy-based saucepan and mix in about ⅓ cup (80 ml/2¾ fl oz) cold water to form a thick, smooth paste. Add a little more water if necessary. Then stir in the milk until smooth.
2 Place the pan over low heat and cook, stirring almost constantly so that it does not catch, for about 1¼ hours, or until thick and smooth. Gradually add the sugar, stirring until dissolved.
3 Pour the mixture into six small Chinese rice bowls. You can either serve the pudding warm, or allow to cool slightly, then refrigerate for 3 hours, or until firm. When chilled, it is nice served with fresh mango.
VARIATION: Stir in 50 g (1¾ oz) pitted and chopped jujubes (Chinese dates).

CHINESE ALMOND
PUDDING

Slowly pour in the milk and stir constantly until the mixture is smooth.

Slowly add the sugar and keep stirring until it has dissolved.

LEFT: Chinese almond pudding

JAPAN

The history of food in Japan is inseparable from that of rice. A sophisticated cuisine has developed around creating dishes to serve with and complement rice. Seafood, seaweed and vegetables are the other mainstays of the Japanese diet. The emphasis is on the pure flavours of the ingredients, so in general recipes are simple, but they depend on really fresh ingredients to bring them to life. Sushi is probably the most famous of any Japanese food—and today sushi bars are popping up in cities across the globe. This chapter offers a wide range of achievable sushi recipes to make at home, as well as many other delicious Japanese meals.

HOW TO MAKE THE PERFECT SUSHI
The secret to making great sushi at home is the rice—get that right and you're halfway there.

Sushi, one of Japan's most well-known food exports, is essentially a combination of ingredients (often seafood) with vinegared rice, traditionally served with pickled ginger and wasabi.

Sushi originated as a method of preserving fish—it was discovered that by salting fish and wrapping it in boiled rice, the fish would ferment and be preserved. Originally the rice itself decomposed and was discarded. It was only later, in the fifteenth century, that a new fermentation method shortened the process to a couple of weeks, which meant that the rice could be eaten as well, and a popular snack food was born. In its final transformation, at the end of the eighteenth century, sushi was united with sashimi, resulting in sushi as we now know it.

FLAVOURS
Sushi fillings usually comprise seafood, vegetables (mostly cooked), omelette, tofu or pickles. The rolls are wrapped in thin sheets of lightly toasted nori (seaweed), which has a nutty flavour.

The accompaniments are just as important as the sushi itself—sharp, biting wasabi, sweet pickled ginger and salty soy sauce.

THE FRESHER THE BETTER
Most seafood is suitable for use in sushi, except for oysters. The only requirement is that the seafood must be exquisitely fresh—tell your fishmonger that you want it for sushi.

WHICH RICE?
The rice in sushi is not just plain rice. It has been cooked, then specially dressed for use. To make good sushi, you must first prepare good sushi rice. Use white short-grain japonica rice in the Japanese style. Japanese rice grains look translucent in their raw state and have a light powder on them. Japan itself does not produce enough rice to export, but other countries including the United States of America and Korea grow rice in the Japanese style.

TEXTURE
Japanese rice absorbs less water than other varieties of rice, so when properly cooked, the rice should be slightly sticky but with firm, not soft, grains.

TOOLS
Sushi can be successfully made with only a few simple kitchen tools, though there is specialist equipment available.

To cook the rice, you can either use an electric rice cooker or a large, heavy-based saucepan with a lid.

Once the rice is cooked, it must be cooled. The Japanese use a special flat, shallow wooden bowl, called a *hangiri*, but a large shallow bowl or platter will also serve—the aim is to spread the rice out so it will cool. Many recipes specify to fan the rice cool—a newspaper or magazine makes a good fan. While fanning, the dressing should be added to the rice.

There are special rice paddles, usually wooden, that have tapered ends designed to separate the grains without crushing them. A spatula does the same job.

You'll need a very sharp knife to cut the fish—cut it across the grain into thin slices about 5 cm (2 inches) long and 2 cm (³/4 inch) wide.

And lastly, you'll need a bamboo sushi mat for rolling the sushi; these are very cheap and are available at Asian food stores. If you can't access a sushi mat, try using baking paper or plastic wrap; though it will be hard to achieve a really neat roll.

BASIC TECHNIQUE

The first step is to make the sushi rice. Wash Japanese short-grain rice under cold running water until the water runs clear, then leave in the strainer to drain for an hour.

Put the rice in a saucepan or rice cooker with water and a piece of kombu (seaweed), if desired, and bring to the boil. If using a rice cooker, follow the manufacturer's instructions.

If using a saucepan, bring the rice to the boil and cook for 5–10 minutes, or until tunnels form on the surface of the rice, then reduce the heat to low, cover and cook the rice for 12–15 minutes, or until the rice is cooked and all the water has been absorbed. The absorbency of the rice will vary from brand to brand and according to how old it is.

Remove from the heat, take the lid off the pan, cover the rice with a clean tea

towel and leave it to stand for 15 minutes.

The dressing always includes rice vinegar, but may also include mirin, sugar and salt. Stir the ingredients together until the sugar has dissolved.

Spread the rice over the base of a *hangiri* or non-metallic dish or bowl, pour the dressing over the top and use a rice paddle or spatula to mix the dressing through the rice, separating the grains—the aim is to make the rice grains stick together slightly. Fan the rice until it cools to room temperature. Cover with a damp, clean tea towel until ready to use.

You can leave the sushi rice covered with the tea towel for up to 6 hours until you're ready to make your sushi. Don't refrigerate the rice or it will become hard and crusty.

MAKI ZUSHI

Maki zushi is probably the most well-known sushi roll—the one that you will usually find in a Japanese lunchbox. It can be filled with a variety of ingredients such as strips of sashimi tuna or salmon, cucumber, pickled daikon, dried mushrooms, kampyo (dried gourd), pickled ginger, omelette or sesame seeds.

To prevent rice sticking to your hands when assembling sushi, dip your fingers in a bowl of warm water with a few drops of rice vinegar added.

Place a sheet of nori on a sushi mat with the shiny side facing down. Spread cooled sushi rice about 1 cm (¹/2 inch)

STEPS TO MAKING THE PERFECT SUSHI
STEP ONE: Wash the rice under cold running water, then leave it to drain in a sieve for anywhere between 30 minutes to 1 hour.
STEP TWO: Cook the rice until steam holes appear in the surface.
STEP THREE: Spread out the rice either in a shallow bowl and stir the dressing through.
STEP FOUR: Spread cooled sushi rice about 1 cm (¹/2 inch) thick over the nori, leaving a 1 cm (¹/2 inch) border on each side.
STEP FIVE: Spread a small amount of wasabi along the groove in the rice. Place a selection of strips of your filling ingredients on top of the wasabi.
STEP SIX: Dip a sharp knife in vinegared water, trim the ends, then cut the roll in half and then each half into three.

thick over the nori, leaving a 1 cm (¹/2 inch) border on each side.

Make a shallow groove down the centre of the rice towards one short end. Spread a small amount of wasabi along the groove. Put a selection of strips of your filling ingredients on top of the wasabi.

Lift up the edge of the bamboo mat and roll the sushi, starting from the edge nearest to you. When you've finished rolling, press the mat to make either a round or square roll. Push in any rice that may be escaping from the ends.

Wet a sharp knife in vinegared water, trim the ends and cut the roll in half and then each half into three. Repeat with the remaining nori, rice and fillings.

SUSHI

Preparation time: 45 minutes +
  1 hour draining + cooling
Total cooking time: 10 minutes
Makes about 30

☆ ☆ ☆

1 cup (220 g/7 oz) Japanese short-grain rice
2 tablespoons rice vinegar
1 tablespoon caster (superfine) sugar
125 g (4 oz) sashimi grade salmon, tuna
  or trout
1 small Lebanese (short) cucumber, peeled
1/2 small avocado (optional)
4 sheets of roasted nori
wasabi paste, to taste, plus extra, to serve
3 tablespoons pickled ginger
Shoyu (Japanese soy sauce), for dipping

BELOW: Sushi

1 Wash the rice under cold running water until the water runs clear, then drain thoroughly. Leave the rice in the strainer to drain for an hour. Put the rice in a saucepan with 2 cups (500 ml/16 fl oz) water and bring to the boil. Reduce the heat and simmer for about 5 minutes, or until all the water has been absorbed. Reduce the heat to very low, cover and cook for another 4–5 minutes. Remove the pan from the heat and leave, covered, for about 10 minutes.

2 To make the sushi dressing, combine the rice vinegar, caster sugar and 1 teaspoon salt in a small bowl.

3 Spread the rice over the base of a non-metallic dish or bowl, pour the sushi dressing over the top and use a rice paddle or spatula to mix the dressing through the rice, separating the grains as you do so. Fan the rice until it cools to room temperature.

4 Using a very sharp knife, cut the fish into thin strips. Cut the cucumber and avocado into julienne strips about 5 cm (2 inches) in length.

5 Place a sheet of nori on a sushi mat with the shiny side facing down. Position the nori with the longest sides at the top and bottom. Pat a quarter of the rice over about half of the nori sheet along one long side, leaving a 2 cm (3/4 inch) border around the sides. Spread a very small amount of wasabi down the centre of the rice. Arrange a quarter of the pieces of fish, cucumber, avocado (if using) and ginger along the top of the wasabi stripe.

6 Lift up the edge of the mat and roll the sushi, starting from the edge nearest you. Press the nori edges together to seal the roll and form into a round roll. Push in any rice that is escaping from the ends. Using a sharp flat-bladed or electric knife, cut the roll into 2.5 cm (1 inch) rounds. Repeat with the remaining ingredients.

7 Serve the sushi on small individual plates with small bowls of soy sauce and extra wasabi—your guests can mix them together to their taste for a dipping sauce.

NOTE: Sushi can be made up to 4 hours in advance and kept on a plate, covered with plastic wrap. If you are planning to make the sushi ahead of time, keep the large rolls intact and slice them into rounds just before serving. Don't refrigerate sushi or the rice will become hard.

MIRIN
A sweet spirit-based rice liquid used predominantly in Japanese cooking in basting sauces and marinades. Its high sugar content adds a sheen to the food. Mirin, when mixed with soy sauce, forms the basis of yakitori and teriyaki marinades. The real thing, *hon mirin*, contains 14 per cent alcohol, and is far superior to the low-alcohol imitation mirin.

INARI SUSHI

Preparation time: 10 minutes +
    1 hour draining + cooling
Total cooking time: 15 minutes
Makes 6

☆ ☆

1 cup (220 g/7 oz) Japanese short-grain rice
2 tablespoons white sesame seeds
2 tablespoons rice vinegar
1 tablespoon caster (superfine) sugar
1 teaspoon mirin
6 inari pouches (see Notes)

1 Wash the rice under cold running water until the water runs clear, then drain thoroughly. Leave the rice in the strainer to drain for an hour. Put the rice in a saucepan with 2 cups (500 ml/16 fl oz) water and bring to the boil. Reduce the heat and simmer for about 5 minutes, or until all the water has been absorbed. Reduce the heat to very low, cover and cook for another 4–5 minutes. Remove the pan from the heat and leave, covered, for about 10 minutes.

2 Toast the sesame seeds in a dry frying pan over medium heat for 3–4 minutes, shaking the pan gently, until the seeds are golden brown—watch them carefully so they don't brown too quickly. Remove the seeds from the pan at once to prevent them burning.
3 To make the sushi dressing, combine the rice vinegar, sugar, mirin and 1 teaspoon salt in a small bowl.
4 Spread the rice over the base of a non-metallic dish or bowl, pour the sushi dressing over the top and use a rice paddle or spatula to mix the dressing through the rice, separating the grains as you do so. Fan the rice until it cools to room temperature.
5 Gently separate the inari pockets and open them up. Form the rice into balls and place a ball of rice inside each pocket. Sprinkle the rice with the toasted sesame seeds and press the inari closed with your fingers. Serve on a plate, cut-side down.
NOTES: Inari pouches (*aburage*) are slightly sweet pockets made from bean curd. They are available from Japanese food shops.

You can serve the inari sushi as they are or tie each parcel with a blanched chive.

ABOVE: Inari sushi

WASABI
Though often compared to horseradish, wasabi is, in fact, an unrelated herb. In Japan, it grows wild near freshwater streams, but it is also cultivated widely. It is the green root of the plant that is eaten with sushi and sashimi, sometimes on its own and sometimes mixed with soy sauce. Most of the so-called wasabi—in powder or paste form—available commercially is dyed horseradish. Real wasabi is expensive, and if seeking it, ask for *hon* (real) wasabi.

ABOVE: Nigiri zushi

NIGIRI ZUSHI

Preparation time: 20 minutes +
    1 hour draining + 15 minutes standing
Total cooking time: 25 minutes
Makes 16–20

☆☆

2¹/2 cups (550 g/1 lb 1³/4 oz) Japanese
    short-grain rice
5 cm (2 inch) piece of kombu (see Note)
100 ml (3¹/2 fl oz) rice vinegar
1 tablespoon mirin
¹/4 cup (60 g/2 oz) caster (superfine) sugar
250 g (8 oz) sashimi grade tuna or salmon
lemon juice
wasabi paste, to taste
nori, cut into strips (optional)

1 Wash the rice under cold running water until the water runs clear, then leave it in the strainer to drain for an hour. Put the rice and kombu in a saucepan with 3 cups (750 ml/24 fl oz) water and bring to the boil. Cook for 5–10 minutes, or until tunnels form on the surface of the rice, then lift out the piece of kombu. Reduce the heat to low, cover with a lid and cook the rice for 12–15 minutes, or until the rice is cooked and all the water has been absorbed. Remove from the heat, remove the lid from the pan, cover the rice with a clean tea towel and leave for 15 minutes.
2 To make the sushi dressing, combine the rice vinegar, mirin, caster sugar and 1 teaspoon salt in a small bowl and keep stirring until the sugar is dissolved.
3 Spread the rice over the base of a non-metallic dish or bowl, pour the dressing over the top and use a rice paddle or spatula to mix the dressing

through the rice, separating the grains—the aim is to make the grains stick together slightly. Fan the rice until it cools to room temperature.

4 Trim the tuna or salmon into a neat rectangle, removing any blood or connective tissue. Using a sharp knife, cut paper-thin slices of fish from the trimmed fillet, cleaning your knife in a bowl of water and lemon juice after cutting each slice.

5 Form a tablespoon of your sushi rice into an oval about the same length and width as your rectangles of fish. Place a piece of fish on the open palm of your left hand, then spread a small dab of wasabi over the centre of the fish. Place the rice on the fish and gently cup your palm to make a curve. Using the middle and index fingers of your right hand, press the rice onto the fish, firmly pushing. Turn over and repeat the shaping process, finishing with the fish on top of the rice. Nigiri zushi can be served with a strip of nori tied around the centre.

NOTE: Kombu is a large, flat and olive green seaweed also known as kelp and tangle kelp. Sold in dried sheets, it is often coated with a white salty mould—this imparts flavour and should not be washed off—wipe over with a damp cloth and cut into pieces. Kombu is often used to flavour Japanese dashi (stock), or cooked as a vegetable with fish.

HAND-SHAPED TUNA SUSHI

Preparation time: 20 minutes +
  1 hour draining + 15 minutes standing
Total cooking time: 20 minutes
Makes about 30

☆☆

1 cup (220 g/7 oz) Japanese short-grain rice

2 tablespoons rice vinegar

1 tablespoon caster (superfine) sugar

300 g (10 oz) sashimi grade tuna

wasabi paste, to taste, plus extra, to serve

Shoyu (Japanese soy sauce), to serve

1 Wash the rice under cold running water until the water runs clear, then leave in the strainer to drain for an hour. Put the rice and 2 cups (500 ml/16 fl oz) water in a saucepan. Bring the rice to the boil and cook for 5 minutes, or until tunnels form on the surface of the rice, then reduce the heat to low, cover and cook for 10–15 minutes, or until the rice is cooked and all the water has been absorbed. Remove from the heat, remove the lid from the pan, cover the rice with a clean tea towel and leave for 15 minutes.

2 To make the sushi dressing, combine the vinegar, sugar and 1 teaspoon salt in a small bowl and stir until the sugar is dissolved.

3 Spread the rice over the base of a non-metallic dish or bowl, pour the sushi dressing over the top and use a rice paddle or spatula to mix the dressing through the rice, separating the grains—the aim is to make the rice grains stick together slightly. Fan the rice until it cools to room temperature.

4 Cut the tuna into thin strips about 5 cm (2 inches) long, then put a dab of wasabi on each.

5 Using your hands, roll a tablespoon of rice into a ball. Place the rice ball onto a strip of fish, with the wasabi side against the fish and then gently mould the tuna around the rice. Flatten the ball slightly to elongate, then lay the balls on a tray, seam-side down. Repeat with the rest of the ingredients. Serve with the Shoyu and wasabi.

BELOW: Hand-shaped tuna sushi

RICE SOUP WITH PRAWN AND EGG

Preparation time: 15 minutes
Total cooking time: 15 minutes
Serves 4

3 teaspoons dashi granules
1/4 cup (60 ml/2 fl oz) Shoyu (Japanese
   soy sauce)
2 tablespoons sake
1 tablespoon mirin
4 cups (740 g/1 1/2 lb) cold cooked Japanese
   short-grain rice, rinsed well
12 raw prawns (shrimp), peeled and deveined
3 eggs, beaten
2 teaspoons ginger juice (see Notes)
2 spring onions (scallions), finely chopped
mitsuba or shiso, to garnish (optional)
   (see Notes)

1 Dissolve the dashi granules in 1.5 litres (48 fl oz) hot water, then combine with the Shoyu, sake, mirin and 1/2 teaspoon salt in a large saucepan and bring to the boil over high heat. Reduce the heat to low, then add the rice and simmer for 4 minutes, or until heated through. Add the prawns and cook for a further 3 minutes, or until the prawns are pink and starting to curl.

2 Remove the pan from the heat and drizzle the eggs over the top, place the lid on the pan and allow to sit for 1 minute before stirring the eggs through the soup along with the ginger juice and the spring onions. Season to taste, garnish with mitsuba or shiso if using and serve immediately as the eggs should not be allowed to set completely.

NOTES: Ginger juice is available in some health food stores.

Mitsuba is a Japanese herb that resembles flat-leaf (Italian) parsley. It is used as a garnish.

Shiso (also called perilla) is a member of the mint family.

JAPANESE MEALS

Being a mountainous country of volcanic islands not suited to agriculture, Japanese food centres around fresh seafood and seaweed, vegetables and rice. After the Meiji Restoration of 1868, Japan increasingly began to adopt Western practices. Meat began to appear in the largely vegetable-based diet. Today, meat is still popular, though expensive. Other Western practices have also been adopted. For breakfast, many Japanese (particularly in the urban areas) now eat bread or rolls instead of the traditional bowl of rice porridge (*okayu*). However, most Japanese still eat rice for lunch and dinner.

RIGHT: Rice soup with prawn and egg

OMELETTE RICE

Preparation time: 15 minutes
Total cooking time: 25 minutes
Serves 4

☆ ☆

20 g (^{3}/$_4$ oz) butter

1 onion, finely chopped

2 garlic cloves, crushed

2 teaspoons very finely chopped ginger

250 g (8 oz) chicken thigh fillets, cut into dice

^{1}/$_2$ cup (125 g/4 oz) tomato sauce

^{1}/$_3$ cup (50 g/1^3/$_4$ oz) cooked peas

3 cups (255 g/7 oz) cooked Japanese
    short-grain rice, rinsed well

Japanese mayonnaise, to serve (see Notes)

tomato sauce, to serve (optional)

OMELETTES

8 eggs

1 tablespoon Shoyu (Japanese soy sauce)

1 tablespoon mirin

1 Melt the butter in a large frying pan, add the onion and cook over medium heat for about 8–10 minutes, or until golden. Add the garlic, ginger and chicken and cook, stirring, for 1 minute, or until the chicken starts to change colour, then add the tomato sauce and peas and mix well. Add the rice and mix again until the rice is evenly pink from the tomato sauce. Continue cooking, stirring occasionally, for about 5 minutes until the chicken is cooked and the rice is completely heated through. Season to taste, then cover and set aside while you make the omelettes.

2 Put all the omelette ingredients in a bowl and lightly beat. Spray a non-stick frying pan with a little cooking oil spray. Heat over medium heat, then pour one-quarter of the egg mixture in. Using chopsticks or a soft spatula, gently drag the outside edges of the egg into the centre until it just starts to set, then leave to cook for 1 minute. Spoon one-quarter (about 1 cup) of the rice mixture along the centre line of the egg, then very carefully fold two sides towards the centre, over the rice so you have a rectangular omelette. Put a serving plate over the top and very carefully invert the omelette onto the plate so the seam is underneath. Repeat with the remaining mixture to make four omelettes.

3 If desired, squeeze a little mayonnaise and tomato sauce over the top—you'll get the best result if you use a squeeze bottle. Serve immediately, accompanied by a green salad.

NOTES: Japanese mayonnaise typically comes in easy-to-use squeeze bottles. If you can't find it, use whole-egg mayonnaise instead.

Try experimenting with other filling ingredients such as mushrooms, ham, corn or cheese.

Another simpler version of Omelette rice is to make the omelettes, then serve them over the rice or to break them up and mix through the rice mixture.

ABOVE: Omelette rice

CHICKEN TERIYAKI

Preparation time: 20 minutes +
  10 minutes standing
Total cooking time: 10 minutes
Serves 4

1/3 cup (80 ml/2³/4 fl oz) mirin
1/3 cup (80 ml/2³/4 fl oz) Shoyu (Japanese
  soy sauce)
1/3 cup (60 g/2 oz) soft brown sugar
1 tablespoon finely chopped ginger
2 small garlic cloves, crushed
500 g (1 lb) chicken breast fillets, cut into
  3 cm (1¹/4 inch) cubes
1/4 cup (60 ml/2 fl oz) peanut oil, plus extra,
  for brushing
10 spring onions (scallions), cut into
  3 cm (1¹/4 inch) lengths

1 Combine the mirin, Shoyu, sugar, ginger and garlic in a large shallow non-metallic dish and stir to dissolve the sugar. Add the chicken and toss well. Marinate for 10 minutes.
2 Drain the chicken, reserving the marinade. Add the peanut oil to the marinade. Thread the chicken onto 12 metal skewers, alternating with the spring onions. Brush with the marinade.
3 Cook the chicken under an oiled hot grill (broiler) for 2 minutes. Turn over and brush with more marinade. Cook for 5 minutes, or until the chicken is cooked through.
4 Put any remaining marinade in a small saucepan over medium heat and bring to the boil. Serve the chicken with rice, and the marinade on the side.

STEAMED SAKE CHICKEN

Preparation time: 25 minutes +
  30 minutes marinating
Total cooking time: 20 minutes
Serves 4

500 g (1 lb) chicken breast fillets with skin on
1/3 cup (80 ml/2³/4 fl oz) sake
2 tablespoons lemon juice
4 cm (1¹/2 inch) piece of ginger, thinly sliced
2 tablespoons Shoyu (Japanese soy sauce)
1 tablespoon mirin
1 teaspoon sesame oil
1 spring onion (scallion), sliced on the diagonal,
  plus extra, to garnish
1/2 small red capsicum (pepper), skin removed,
  flesh cut into very fine 3 cm (1¹/4 inch) strips

1 Use a fork to prick the skin on the chicken in several places. Place the chicken, skin-side up, in a shallow dish, then pour on the combined sake, lemon juice, ginger and 1 teaspoon salt. Cover and marinate in the refrigerator for 30 minutes.
2 Combine the Shoyu, mirin, sesame oil and spring onion in a small bowl.
3 Line a steamer with baking paper. Arrange the chicken, skin-side up, in the steamer. Fill a saucepan with 2 cups (500 ml/16 fl oz) water and sit the steamer over the top. Cover and cook over simmering water for 20 minutes, or until cooked. Cut the chicken into bite-sized pieces, arrange on a platter and drizzle with the Shoyu mixture. Arrange the capsicum strips in a bundle on the side of the platter, then scatter spring onion over the chicken. Serve with rice.

BELOW: Chicken teriyaki

SUSHI CREPES

Preparation time: I hour + I hour draining
Total cooking time: 30 minutes
Makes about 40

4 eggs

SUSHI

I cup (220 g/7 oz) Japanese short-grain rice

2 tablespoons rice vinegar

I tablespoon sugar

I tablespoon mirin

a little wasabi paste

125 g (4 oz) sashimi grade tuna, cut into
   thin strips

I small cucumber, peeled and cut into
   julienne strips

1/2 avocado, cut into julienne strips

3 tablespoons pickled ginger, cut into thin strips

Shoyu (Japanese soy sauce), for dipping

1 To make the crepes, gently whisk the eggs with 2 tablespoons cold water and a pinch of salt in a bowl until combined. Heat and lightly oil a small crepe pan or heavy-based frying pan, and pour enough of the egg mixture into the pan to lightly cover the base. Cook over low heat for 1 minute, being careful not to allow the crepe to brown. Turn the crepe over and cook for 1 minute. Transfer to a plate and repeat with the remaining mixture.

2 To make the sushi, wash the rice under cold running water until the water runs clear, then drain. Leave the rice in the strainer to drain thoroughly for 1 hour. Put the rice in a saucepan with 2 cups (500 ml/16 fl oz) water, bring to the boil, then reduce the heat and simmer for 5 minutes, or until small tunnels begin to appear in the rice. If using gas, cover and turn the heat to very low, and continue cooking for 7 minutes, or until all the liquid is absorbed. If using an electric stove-top, remove the pan from the heat, cover and leave the rice to steam for 10–12 minutes.

3 To make the sushi dressing, combine the rice vinegar, sugar, mirin and 1 teaspoon salt in a jug and stir until the sugar dissolves.

4 Spread the rice over the base of a non-metallic dish or bowl, pour the sushi dressing over the top and use a rice paddle or spatula to mix the dressing through the rice. Fan the rice until it cools to room temperature.

5 Place one egg crepe on a sushi mat. Spread 4 tablespoons of the sushi rice over a third of the crepe, using a spatula or the back of a spoon.

6 Spread a tiny amount of wasabi along the centre of the rice. Place some tuna, cucumber, avocado and ginger over the wasabi.

7 Using the sushi mat to help you, fold the crepe over to enclose the filling and roll up firmly in the mat. Trim the ends with a sharp knife and cut the crepe roll into 2 cm (3/4 inch) rounds with a sharp knife. Serve with Shoyu for dipping.

NOTE: The crepes can be made ahead and stored in an airtight container in the refrigerator. Do not slice until serving or they may dry out.

ABOVE: Sushi crepes

MAKI ZUSHI

Preparation time: 25 minutes +
    1 hour draining + cooling
Total cooking time: 20 minutes
Makes 48

☆ ☆ ☆

1 cup (220 g/7 oz) Japanese short-grain rice
2 tablespoons rice vinegar
1 tablespoon caster (superfine) sugar
250 g (8 oz) sashimi grade tuna
1 small Lebanese (short) cucumber
1/2 avocado
8 sheets of roasted nori
3 teaspoons wasabi paste

1 Wash the rice under cold running water until the water runs clear, then drain thoroughly.

Leave the rice in the strainer to drain for an hour. Put the rice in a saucepan with 2 cups (500 ml/16 fl oz) water and bring to the boil. Reduce the heat and simmer for about 5 minutes, or until all the water has been absorbed. Reduce the heat to very low, cover and cook for another 4–5 minutes. Remove the pan from the heat and leave, covered, for about 10 minutes.

2 To make the sushi dressing, combine the rice vinegar, caster sugar and 1 teaspoon salt in a small bowl.

3 Spread the rice over the base of a non-metallic dish or bowl, pour the sushi dressing over the top and use a rice paddle or spatula to mix the dressing through the rice, separating the grains as you do so. Fan the rice until it cools to room temperature.

4 Cut the tuna, cucumber and avocado into thin strips. Place a sheet of nori on a sushi mat, shiny-side down, with a short end towards you. Spread the rice about 1 cm (1/2 inch) thick over the nori, leaving a 1 cm (1/2 inch) border. Make a shallow groove down the centre of the rice towards the short end closest to you. Spread a small amount of wasabi along the groove. Place a selection of strips of your filling ingredients on top of the wasabi. Lift up the edge of the bamboo mat and roll the sushi, starting from the edge nearest to you. When you have finished rolling, press the mat to make either a round or square roll. Push in any rice that is escaping from the ends. Wet a sharp knife, trim the ends and cut the roll in half and then each half into three. Repeat with the remaining ingredients.

BELOW: Maki zushi

INSIDE-OUT ROLLS

Use 8 sheets of roasted nori and 6 cups (1.2 kg/2 lb 6 1/2 oz) cooked sushi rice. Place a sheet of nori on a bamboo mat and spread 1 cm (1/2 inch) rice over the top, leaving a 1 cm (1/2 inch) border. Cover with a sheet of plastic wrap, slightly larger than the nori. In one quick motion, turn the nori and rice over, then place it back on the mat, so the plastic is under the rice and the nori on top. Spread a little wasabi on the nori, along the short end, 4 cm (1 1/2 inches) from the edge. Lay strips of cucumber, avocado and fresh crab on top of the wasabi, then roll from this end, using the plastic as a guide. Rewrap in plastic, then roll up in the mat. Remove the plastic and roll in flying fish roe. Cut in half, trim the ends, and cut each half into three. Serve with Shoyu (Japanese soy sauce). Makes 48.

LAYERED SUSHI

Preparation time: 25 minutes + 1 hour draining + cooling + 1 hour refrigeration
Total cooking time: 35 minutes
Makes 36

☆☆☆

2¹/₂ cups (550 g/1 lb 1³/₄ oz) Japanese
  short-grain rice
1 piece of kombu (optional)
100 ml (3¹/₂ fl oz) rice vinegar
1 tablespoon mirin
¹/₄ cup (60 g/2 oz) caster (superfine) sugar
¹/₃ cup (90 g/3 oz) Japanese mayonnaise
  (see Note)
2 teaspoons wasabi paste
4 sheets of roasted nori
300 g (10 oz) smoked salmon
¹/₄ cup (40 g/1¹/₄ oz) pickled ginger slices
black sesame seeds, to garnish

1 Wash the rice under cold running water until the water runs clear, then leave in the strainer to drain for an hour. Put the rice and kombu in a saucepan with 3 cups (750 ml/24 fl oz) water if desired, and bring to the boil. Cook for 5–10 minutes, or until tunnels form on the surface of the rice, then remove the kombu. Reduce the heat to low, cover and cook the rice for 12–15 minutes, or until the rice is cooked and all the water has been absorbed. Remove from the heat, remove the lid from the pan, cover the rice with a clean tea towel and leave for 15 minutes.

2 To make the sushi dressing, combine the vinegar, mirin, sugar and 1 teaspoon salt in a small bowl and stir until the sugar is dissolved.

3 Spread the rice over the base of a non-metallic dish or bowl, pour the sushi dressing over the top and use a rice paddle or spatula to mix the dressing through the rice, separating the grains—the aim is to make the rice grains stick together slightly. Fan the rice until it cools to room temperature.

4 Combine the mayonnaise and wasabi in a small bowl. Lay a sheet of nori, shiny-side up, on top of a piece of baking paper on a dry tray. Entirely cover the nori with a cup of loosely packed rice. Spread with a little wasabi mayonnaise, then top with a layer of smoked salmon and some slices of pickled ginger. Place another sheet of nori on top and flatten lightly with a rolling pin. Repeat the layering twice, to form three layers, finishing with a sheet of nori, and again flattening with the rolling pin. Reserve the remaining wasabi mayonnaise.

5 Cover and refrigerate for at least an hour, then, using a very sharp knife dipped in water, trim any filling protruding from the edges and slice into 2 cm (³/₄ inch) squares. Garnish with wasabi mayonnaise, pickled ginger and black sesame seeds.

NOTE: Japanese mayonnaise typically comes in easy-to-use squeeze bottles. If you can't find it, use whole-egg mayonnaise instead.

ABOVE: Layered sushi

CALIFORNIA ROLLS

Preparation time: 25 minutes +
  1 hour draining + cooling
Total cooking time: 25 minutes
Makes 12

☆ ☆ ☆

NORI
Nori is a type of seaweed, called laver in Great Britain, but known by its Japanese name, nori, in most other parts of the world. The Japanese consume many billions of sheets of nori annually—as a wrapper for sushi, eaten on its own and dipped into soy sauce or made into nori rolls. You can buy plain nori sheets and toast them yourself over a gas flame to bring out the nutty flavour, or buy nori sheets that have already been toasted.

1 cup (220 g/7 oz) Japanese short-grain rice
1 tablespoon rice vinegar
2 generous pinches of caster (superfine) sugar
1 large egg
1 teaspoon sake
1 teaspoon oil
2 sheets of roasted nori, 20 x 18 cm (8 x 7 inches)
2 crabsticks, 40 g (1 1/4 oz) each, cut into strips
25 g (3/4 oz) pickled daikon, cut into julienne strips
25 g (3/4 oz) carrot, cut into julienne strips
25 g (3/4 oz) cucumber, cut into julienne strips
Shoyu (Japanese soy sauce), to serve
wasabi paste, to serve
pickled ginger, to serve

1 Wash the rice under cold running water until the water runs clear, then drain thoroughly. Drain for an hour. Put the rice into a saucepan and cover with 220 ml (7 fl oz) cold water.

Cover the pan and bring the water to the boil. Reduce the heat and simmer for 10 minutes. When the rice is cooked, remove the pan from the heat and leave, covered, for 10 minutes.
2 To make the sushi dressing, mix together the vinegar, a pinch of the sugar and a pinch of salt.
3 Spread the rice over the base of a non-metallic dish or bowl, pour the sushi dressing over the top and use a rice paddle or spatula to mix the dressing through the rice, separating the grains as you do so. Fan the rice until it cools to room temperature. Cover the pan with a damp tea towel and set aside—do not refrigerate.
4 To make the omelette, gently combine the egg, sake, a pinch of sugar and a pinch of salt. Heat the oil in a small frying pan. Add the egg mixture and cook until firm around the edges but still slightly soft in the middle. Roll the omelette, then tip it out of the pan. Cool, then slice into strips.
5 Put a nori sheet on a sushi mat, shiny-side down. Add half of the rice, leaving a 2 cm (3/4 inch) gap at the edge furthest away from you. Lay half of the fillings on the rice in the following order: omelette, crabstick, daikon, carrot, cucumber. Starting with the end nearest to you, tightly roll the mat and the nori. Repeat this process with the remaining ingredients.
6 Using a sharp knife, cut each roll into six slices. After cutting each slice, rinse the knife under cold running water to prevent sticking. Serve with Shoyu, wasabi and pickled ginger.

RIGHT: California rolls

VEGETARIAN CALIFORNIA ROLLS

Preparation time: 35 minutes +
    1 hour draining + 15 minutes standing
Total cooking time: 15 minutes
Makes 30

☆ ☆ ☆

500 g (1 lb) Japanese short-grain rice

1/4 cup (60 ml/2 fl oz) rice vinegar

1 tablespoon caster (superfine) sugar

5 sheets of roasted nori

1 large Lebanese (short) cucumber, cut
    lengthways into long batons

1 avocado, thinly sliced

1 tablespoon black sesame seeds, toasted

30 g (1 oz) pickled ginger slices

1/2 cup (125 g/4 oz) Japanese or
    whole-egg mayonnaise

3 teaspoons wasabi paste

2 teaspoons Shoyu (Japanese soy sauce)

1 Wash the rice under cold running water until
the water runs clear, then drain thoroughly.

Drain for an hour. Put the rice and 3 cups
(750 ml/24 fl oz) water in a saucepan. Bring to
the boil over low heat and cook for 5 minutes,
or until tunnels form in the rice. Remove from
the heat, cover and leave for 15 minutes.
2 To make the sushi dressing, put the vinegar,
sugar and 1 teaspoon salt in a small saucepan and
stir over low heat until the sugar and salt dissolve.
3 Spread the rice over the base of a non-metallic
dish or bowl, pour the sushi dressing over the
top and use a rice paddle or spatula to mix the
dressing through the rice, separating the grains
as you do so. Fan the rice until it cools to
room temperature.
4 To assemble, lay a nori sheet, shiny-side
down, on a sushi mat and spread out one-fifth
of the rice, leaving a 2 cm (3/4 inch) border at
one end. Arrange one fifth of the cucumber,
avocado, sesame seeds and ginger lengthways
over the rice, 3 cm (1 1/4 inches) from the
border. Spread on some of the combined
mayonnaise, wasabi and Shoyu and roll to
cover the filling. Continue rolling tightly to join
the edge, then hold in place for a few seconds.
Trim the ends and cut into 2 cm (1/2 inch) slices,
wetting your knife in vinegared water between
each slice. Repeat. Serve with any remaining
wasabi mayonnaise.

SESAME SEEDS
The demand for sesame
seeds in Japan far exceeds
the country's ability to grow
sesame (the herb that
produces the seeds). The
plant produces small, pear-
shaped white, brown or
black seeds. All three
varieties taste the same;
the choice of which seed to
use seems to be a matter
of aesthetics, habit or both.
The seeds are usually
toasted before use to bring
out their flavour.

*ABOVE: Vegetarian
California rolls*

CHICKEN DONBURI

Preparation time: 20 minutes + cooling
Total cooking time: 30 minutes
Serves 4

☆ ☆

2 cups (440 g/14 oz) Japanese short-grain rice
2 tablespoons oil
200 g (7 oz) chicken breast fillet, cut into
   thin strips
2 onions, thinly sliced
4 tablespoons Shoyu (Japanese soy sauce)
2 tablespoons mirin
1 teaspoon dashi granules
5 eggs, lightly beaten
2 sheets of nori
2 spring onions (scallions), sliced

1 Wash the rice in a colander under cold running water until the water runs clear. Put the rice in a medium, heavy-based saucepan, add 2½ cups (625 ml/20 fl oz) water and bring to the boil over high heat. Cover the pan with a tight-fitting lid, reduce the heat to the lowest setting to prevent the rice burning at the bottom of the pan and cook for 15 minutes. Turn the heat to very high for 15–20 seconds and remove the pan from the heat. Set the pan aside for 12 minutes, without lifting the lid (so the steam does not escape).

2 Heat the oil in a frying pan over high heat, then stir-fry the chicken until it is golden and tender, and set aside. Reheat the pan, add the onion and cook, stirring occasionally, for 3 minutes, or until it begins to soften. Add the Shoyu, mirin, dashi granules and 2 tablespoons water. Stir to dissolve the dashi and bring the stock to the boil. Cook for 3 minutes, or until the onion is tender.

3 Return the chicken to the pan and pour in the eggs, stirring gently. Cover and simmer over very low heat for 2–3 minutes, or until the eggs are just set. Remove the pan from the heat.

4 Toast the nori by holding it over low heat and moving it back and forth for about 15 seconds, then crumble it into a dish.

5 Transfer the rice to an earthenware dish, carefully spoon over the prepared chicken and egg mixture, and sprinkle with the nori. Garnish with the spring onion.

NOTE: This meal is also known as Oyakodon.

BELOW: Chicken donburi

TOFU MISO SOUP

Cut 250 g (8 oz) tofu into cubes. Slice 1 spring onion (scallion) diagonally into 1 cm (½ inch) lengths. Set the tofu and onion aside. Using a wooden spoon, combine 1 litre (32 fl oz) water and ½ cup (80 g/ 2¾ oz) dashi granules in a small saucepan, then bring the mixture to the boil. Combine 100 g (3½ oz) miso paste and 1 tablespoon mirin in a small bowl, then add to the boiling liquid in the pan. Stir the miso over medium heat, taking care not to let the mixture boil once the miso has dissolved, or it will lose flavour. Add the tofu cubes to the hot stock and heat, without boiling, over medium heat for 5 minutes. Serve in individual bowls, garnished with the spring onion. This is a quick soup to accompany a rice meal. Serves 4.

DONBURI
Donburi are one-dish meals in which a dish of cooked rice is topped with well-flavoured meat, eggs, tofu or a combination of all of them. The name comes from the bowl that the dish is traditionally served in.

VEGETABLE DONBURI

Preparation time: 20 minutes +
  15 minutes soaking
Total cooking time: 35 minutes
Serves 4

2 cups (440 g/14 oz) Japanese short-grain rice

10 g (1/4 oz) dried whole shiitake mushrooms

2 tablespoons oil

1 onion, sliced

2 slender eggplants (aubergines), sliced
  on the diagonal

100 g (3 1/2 oz) green beans, cut into 4 cm
  (1 1/2 inch) lengths

5 spring onions (scallions), cut into 2 cm
  (3/4 inch) lengths

100 ml (3 1/2 fl oz) Shoyu (Japanese soy sauce)

100 ml (3 1/2 fl oz) mirin

1/4 cup (60 g/2 oz) sugar

4 eggs, lightly beaten

1 Wash the rice and place in a saucepan with 2 1/2 cups (625 ml/20 fl oz) water. Bring to the boil, reduce the heat and simmer, covered, for 15 minutes. Leave, covered, for 10 minutes.
2 Soak the mushrooms in 1 2/3 cups (410 ml/ 13 fl oz) boiling water for 15 minutes. Drain and reserve the soaking liquid. Remove the stems and cut the caps in half.
3 Heat the oil in a deep frying pan. Cook the onion over medium heat for 4 minutes, or until softened but not browned. Add the eggplant and cook for 3–4 minutes, or until softened. Add the beans, mushrooms and spring onion and cook for 2–3 minutes, or until almost cooked. Combine the Shoyu, mushroom soaking liquid, mirin and sugar, and stir through the vegetables. Simmer for 4 minutes.
4 Pour the egg over the vegetables, cover and simmer for 1 minute, or until partly cooked. Serve the rice in bowls, spoon on the vegetable mixture and pour on the cooking sauce.

ABOVE: Vegetable donburi

1 Wash the rice under cold running water until the water runs clear, then drain thoroughly. Drain for an hour. Put the rice into a saucepan and cover with 220 ml (7 fl oz) cold water. Cover the pan and bring the water to the boil, then reduce the heat and simmer for 10 minutes. When the rice is cooked, remove it from the heat and let it stand, covered, for 10 minutes.

2 To make the sushi dressing, mix together 1 tablespoon of the vinegar, the sugar and 1/4 teaspoon salt.

3 Spread the rice over the base of a non-metallic dish or bowl, pour the sushi dressing over the top and use a rice paddle or spatula to mix the dressing through the rice, separating the grains as you do so. Fan the rice until it cools to room temperature. Cover with a damp tea towel and set it aside, but do not refrigerate.

4 Meanwhile, using a sharp knife, cut the fish into 16 paper-thin pieces, measuring 2 x 5 cm (3/4 x 2 inches). Cut each sheet of nori in half. Thinly slice the avocado and sprinkle with a little lemon juice. Mix the remaining vinegar with 1/4 cup (60 ml/2 fl oz) water in a small bowl. Use the vinegar water to stop the rice sticking to your fingers as you form the sushi. Taking 1 tablespoon of rice at a time, carefully mould the rice into oval shapes—you should end up with 12 ovals.

5 Holding a piece of nori seaweed in the palm of your hand, smear a little wasabi over it, put an oval of rice on top, then fill it with a piece of fish, avocado, daikon and cucumber. Wrap the nori around the ingredients in a cone shape, using a couple of grains of cooked rice to secure the rolls. Alternatively, put the ingredients on the table for guests to help themselves. Serve with Shoyu, extra wasabi and pickled ginger.

SUSHI HAND-ROLLS

Preparation time: 25 minutes +
  1 hour draining + cooling
Total cooking time: 15 minutes
Serves 6

☆☆

1 cup (220 g/7 oz) Japanese short-grain rice

2 tablespoons rice vinegar

generous pinch of caster (superfine) sugar

175 g (6 oz) sashimi grade fish, such as
  tuna or salmon

6 sheets of roasted nori, 20 x 18 cm (8 x 7 inches)

1 small avocado

1 tablespoon lemon juice

wasabi paste

60 g (2 oz) pickled daikon

85 g (3 oz) cucumber, cut into thin strips

Shoyu (Japanese soy sauce), to serve

pickled ginger, to serve

ABOVE: Sushi hand-rolls

PICKLED GINGER

Peel 500 g (1 lb) young ginger, then slice crossways into very thin slices. Put the ginger in a bowl with 1 teaspoon sea salt, toss together well and let stand for 10 minutes. Rinse under boiling water, then drain thoroughly. Pour 2 cups (500 ml/ 16 fl oz) rice vinegar, 3/4 cup (185 g/6 oz) caster (superfine) sugar and 1 1/2 tablespoons sea salt into a small saucepan and cook over medium heat until the sugar has dissolved. Put the ginger in a sterilized 1 litre (32 fl oz) jar, then pour on the vinegar mixture. Cover tightly, then leave overnight before using. Keeps for 2 months. NOTE: The ginger won't be as pink as the commercial variety.

NORI CONES

Preparation time: 45 minutes + 1 hour draining
  15 minutes standing + 5 minutes soaking
Total cooking time: 15 minutes
Makes 40

☆ ☆

2 cups (440 g/14 oz) Japanese short-grain rice

2 tablespoons rice vinegar

2 tablespoons caster (superfine) sugar

10 g (¹/₄ oz) sliced dried shiitake mushrooms

250 g (4 oz) choy sum (Chinese flowering
  cabbage), shredded and blanched

1 tablespoon pickled ginger, shredded

1 tablespoon sesame seeds, toasted

1 tablespoon kecap manis

¹/₂ teaspoon wasabi paste

2 teaspoons mirin

1 tablespoon Shoyu (Japanese soy sauce)

10 sheets of roasted nori

ready-made sushi dipping sauce,
  to serve

1 Wash the rice under cold running water until the water runs clear, then drain. Drain for an hour. Put in a saucepan with 2 cups (500 ml/ 16 fl oz) water. Bring to the boil, then reduce the heat and simmer for 10 minutes. Remove from the heat, cover and stand for 15 minutes.
2 To make the sushi dressing, put the vinegar, sugar, ¹/₂ teaspoon salt and 2 tablespoons water in a saucepan and stir over low heat until the sugar and salt have dissolved.
3 Spread the rice over the base of a non-metallic dish or bowl, pour the sushi dressing over the top and use a rice paddle or spatula to mix the dressing through the rice, separating the grains as you do so. Fan the rice until it cools.
4 Soak the mushrooms in boiling water for 5 minutes. Drain, squeeze dry and roughly chop.
5 Put the rice in a bowl and stir in the choy sum, mushrooms, ginger, sesame seeds and the combined kecap manis, wasabi, mirin and Shoyu.
6 Lay the nori sheets shiny-side down and cut each one into four squares. Brush the joining edge with water and put 1 tablespoon of the mixture in the centre of the square. Roll up on the diagonal to form a cone and top up with 2 teaspoons of filling. Repeat. Serve with the dipping sauce.

SHIITAKE

Shiitake is the Japanese name for a type of fungus grown on tree trunks. It is customary to call the fresh mushrooms shiitake and the dried ones dried Chinese mushrooms, perhaps because in Japan the fresh ones are used more than the dried, and the reverse is true in China. Shiitake mushrooms have dark-brown caps. Cut a cross in the top of the cap of large mushrooms to allow them to cook through the thickest part.

LEFT: Nori cones

RICE BALLS

Preparation time: 20 minutes +
  1 hour draining + 20 minutes standing
Total cooking time: 25 minutes
Serves 4

1 1/4 cups (275 g/9 oz) Japanese short-grain rice
55 g (2 oz) smoked salmon, chopped
2 tablespoons finely chopped pickled ginger
2 spring onions (scallions), finely chopped
2 teaspoons black sesame seeds, toasted

1 Wash the rice under cold running water until the water runs clear, then drain. Drain for an hour. Put the rice in a saucepan with 1 1/3 cups (350 ml/11 fl oz) water and bring to the boil. Reduce the heat to very low, cover and cook for 15 minutes. Remove the pan from the heat and stand, covered, for about 20 minutes.
2 Combine the salmon, ginger and spring onion in a small bowl. Using wet hands, form a small handful of rice into a ball, push 2 teaspoons of the smoked salmon mixture into the centre of the rice and remould the ball around it. Repeat with the remaining rice and salmon, keeping your hands wet to prevent the rice from becoming sticky. Sprinkle with the sesame seeds.

CHIRASHI SUSHI

Preparation time: 25 minutes +
  10 minutes standing
Total cooking time: 30 minutes
Serves 4

2 cups (440 g/14 oz) Japanese short-grain rice
4 dried shiitake mushrooms
1/3 cup (80 ml/2 3/4 fl oz) rice vinegar
1/3 cup (80 g/2 3/4 oz) caster (superfine) sugar
1 tablespoon soy sauce
2 large eggs
1 tablespoon sake
1–2 teaspoons oil
1 avocado
1 tablespoon lemon juice
1 small carrot, cut into thin strips and blanched
300 g (10 1/2 oz) salmon fillet, skinned and cut
  into small chunks
2 spring onions (scallions), finely shredded
2 tablespoons crushed roasted white sesame
  seeds or 50 g (1 3/4 oz) fish roe
sliced pickled ginger, wasabi paste and
  Shoyu (Japanese soy sauce), to serve

1 Wash the rice under cold running water until the water runs clear, then drain. Drain for 1 hour. Put the rice in a saucepan, and cover with 2 cups (500 ml/16 fl oz) cold water. Bring to the boil, reduce the heat and simmer for 10 minutes. When the rice is cooked, remove the pan from the heat and leave, covered, for 10 minutes.
2 Meanwhile, put the mushrooms in a saucepan with 300 ml (10 1/2 fl oz) boiling water.
3 To make the sushi dressing, combine the vinegar, 2 tablespoons of the sugar and 2 teaspoons salt.
4 Spread the rice over the base of a non-metallic dish or bowl, pour the dressing over the top and use a rice paddle or spatula to mix the dressing through the rice, separating the grains. Fan the rice until it cools to room temperature. Cover with a damp tea towel and leave to one side.

BELOW: Rice balls

5 Add the remaining sugar and the soy sauce to the mushrooms, bring the liquid to the boil, then simmer, covered, for 15 minutes. Drain.
6 Beat the eggs with the sake and a pinch of salt. Heat the oil in a small frying pan, add half of the egg mixture and cook until just set. Roll the omelette to one side of the pan. Pour in the remaining egg and lift the cooked omelette so the raw egg runs underneath it. When the second omelette is cooked, roll the two together to make one roll, and allow to cool. Cut into thin slices.
7 Thinly slice the mushroom caps, discarding the stems. Toss the avocado in the lemon juice. Arrange the mushrooms, omelette, carrot, avocado, salmon and spring onions on the rice. Scatter the sesame seeds over the top. Serve with pickled ginger, wasabi and soy sauce on the side.
NOTE: The name translates as 'scattered' sushi.

RICE WITH FIVE THINGS

Preparation time: 25 minutes +
    1 hour 20 minutes resting
Total cooking time: 25 minutes
Serves 6

2 cups (440 g/14 oz) Japanese short-grain rice
5 dried shiitake mushrooms
20 g (³/₄ oz) deep-fried tofu
100 g (3¹/₂ oz) Konnyaku (see Notes)
1 small carrot
70 g (2¹/₄ oz) bamboo shoot
4 chicken thigh fillets (about 500 g/1 lb)
1 teaspoon dashi granules dissolved in
    2 cups (500 ml/16 fl oz hot water
2 tablespoons mirin
¹/₃ cup (80 ml/2³/₄ fl oz) Shoyu (Japanese
    soy sauce)
3 tablespoons chopped mitsuba (optional)
    (see Note)

1 Wash the rice under cold running water until the water runs clear, then soak for 1 hour. Drain.
2 Soak the mushrooms in 1¹/₂ cups (375 ml/ 12 fl oz) hot water for 30 minutes, then drain, reserving the liquid. Discard the stems and thinly slice the caps. Put the tofu in a heatproof bowl and cover with boiling water for a few minutes then drain and squeeze gently between paper towel to remove excess oil.
3 Cut the konnyaku, carrot, bamboo shoot and tofu into 3 cm (1¹/₄ inch) long, 5 mm (¹/₄ inch)

wide strips and place in a bowl with the mushrooms. Cut the chicken into bite-sized pieces and add to the bowl. Combine the dashi, mushroom liquid, mirin, Shoyu and 1 teaspoon salt, then pour over the chicken and vegetables and allow to sit for about 20 minutes.
4 Drain the rice and spread over the base of a large saucepan. Pour the chicken and vegetable mixture over but do not stir. Place over high heat and bring to the boil then cover, reduce the heat to low and cook for 15 minutes. Turn off the heat but leave the pan on the stove and rest for another 10 minutes before stirring to combine all the ingredients well. Stir through the mitsuba if desired, then serve.
NOTES: This dish was traditionally only made with rice and 5 vegetables; however, now it often contains other ingredients for extra flavour.

Konnyaku is a chewy, brownish grey, speckled, gelatinous paste and is made from the starchy root of the Konjac or Devil's tongue plant. It is usually formed into blocks or thin strings (commonly known as shirataki noodles).

Mitsuba is a herb resembling flat-leaf (Italian) parsley; its flavour is a cross between parsley and cucumber with a slightly peppery bite. Both konnyaku and mitsuba are available at Japanese specialist stores or Asian supermarkets.

ABOVE: Rice with five things

273

PICKLED GINGER
The soft, delicate slices of pickled ginger are a common accompaniment to Japanese food. The ginger acts as a palate cleanser, with its sharp, slightly sweet taste. To make your own, see page 270.

PORK SCHNITZEL CURRY

Preparation time: 25 minutes
Total cooking time: 30 minutes
Serves 4

☆

1 tablespoon oil
1 onion, cut into thin wedges
2 large carrots, cut into 2 cm (³/₄ inch) cubes
1 large potato, cut into 2 cm (³/₄ inch) cubes
60 g (2 oz) Japanese curry paste block, broken into small pieces (see Note)
plain (all-purpose) flour, for coating
4 x 120 g (4 oz) pork schnitzels, pounded to 5 mm (¹/₄ inch) thickness
2 eggs, lightly beaten
150 g (5 oz) Japanese breadcrumbs (panko)
oil, for deep-frying
pickled ginger, pickled daikon and umeboshi (baby pickled plums), to serve

1 Heat the oil in a saucepan, add the onion, carrot and potato, and cook over medium heat for 10 minutes, or until starting to brown. Add 2 cups (500 ml/16 fl oz) water and the curry paste, and stir until the curry paste dissolves and the sauce becomes smooth. Reduce the heat and simmer for 10 minutes, or until the vegetables are cooked through. Season.

2 Season the flour well with salt and pepper. Dip each schnitzel into the flour, shake off any excess, then dip into the beaten egg, allowing any excess to drip off. Coat with the Japanese breadcrumbs by pressing each side of the schnitzel firmly into the crumbs on a plate.

3 Fill a deep-fat fryer or heavy-based saucepan one-third full of oil and heat to 180°C (350°F), or until a cube of bread dropped into the oil browns in 15 seconds. Cook the schnitzels, one at a time, turning once or twice, for 5 minutes, or until golden brown all over and cooked through. Drain on crumpled paper towels.

4 Slice each schnitzel into 5–6 pieces and arrange, keeping the original shape, over cooked rice. Ladle the curry sauce over the schnitzels. Serve with the pickles on the side.

NOTE: Japanese curry comes in a solid block or in powder form and is available in Asian supermarkets. You can buy Japanese curry of varying heat, from mild to very hot, whichever is most suitable to your taste.

ABOVE: Pork schnitzel curry

SWEET RED BEAN SOUP WITH MOCHI

Preparation time: 5 minutes
Total cooking time: 3 hours 10 minutes
Serves 4

1 cup (220 g/7 oz) azuki beans
2/3 cup (145 g/5 oz) caster (superfine) sugar
pinch of salt
4 squares of mochi (see Note)

1 Rinse the beans, then place in a large saucepan of water and bring to the boil. Drain, then return the beans to the pan with 1 litre (32 fl oz) fresh water. Bring to the boil again, cover, reduce the heat to low and cook for 2 hours, or until the beans are tender and almost all the water has been absorbed. Check the beans occasionally as you may need to add a little more water.

2 Add the sugar and 1.5 litres (48 fl oz) water and stir to combine. Increase the heat to high and cook for about 40 minutes, or until the beans are soft but not mushy. You should have a thin but chunky 'soup'; if you prefer, you can make the soup thicker by mashing some of the beans with a fork or make it thinner by adding a little extra water. Remove the pan from the heat, cover and set aside.

3 Preheat the grill (broiler) to high. Line a baking tray with foil and place the mochi on top. Cook, turning frequently, for 10 minutes, or until mottled golden and puffed up to about twice their size. Place a rice cake in the base of four small, deep serving bowls and ladle the soup over the top. Traditionally the chewy mochi is eaten with chopsticks, then the soup is drunk directly from the bowl.

NOTES: Mochi cakes, often sold as *kirimochi* are glutinous rice cakes. They are available at Japanese speciality stores and Asian supermarkets. Mochi cakes are traditional celebratory fare at New Year.

Another way of cooking the mochi is to simmer it in water for a few minutes until tender.

AZUKI BEANS
Also known as adzuki beans. These small red beans are the second most widely used legume in Japanese cookery after the soya bean. The main use is to pound the sweet beans, add some sugar syrup and make a sweet bean paste popular in desserts.

LEFT: Sweet red bean soup with mochi

FUSION

Rice is so popular and versatile that even countries without a history of rice cultivation have embraced the grain and adapted it to their local cuisine. This can result in a wonderful fusion of traditional rice recipes made with non-traditional ingredients. For example, the classic Italian rice dish, risotto, is transformed into something completely different by adding Asian flavours; the native American wild rice is used to make a colourful salad with Chinese roast duck; and the retro classic prawn cocktail has rice noodles added for some extra crunch.

WILD RICE SALAD WITH CHINESE ROAST DUCK

Preparation time: 15 minutes
Total cooking time: 50 minutes
Serves 4–6

1 cup (200 g/6¹/2 oz) wild rice
1 cup (200 g/6¹/2 oz) basmati or jasmine rice
16 thin asparagus spears, sliced
8 spring onions (scallions), thinly sliced
100 g (3¹/2 oz) pecans, roughly chopped
100 g (3¹/2 oz) dried cranberries
zest and juice 1 orange
1 whole Chinese roast duck

Dressing
¹/2 cup (125 ml/4 fl oz) soy sauce
2 tablespoons sugar
1¹/2 tablespoons balsamic vinegar
1¹/2 tablespoons peanut oil
2 teaspoons sesame oil
2 teaspoons grated ginger
2 small red chillies, finely chopped

1 Put the wild rice in a saucepan of cold, salted water, bring to the boil and cook for 30 minutes. Add the basmati or jasmine rice and continue to cook for a further 10 minutes, or until both rices are just cooked. Drain and refresh under cold water, then drain again and transfer to a large bowl.

2 Blanch the asparagus in a saucepan of boiling water, then drain and refresh under cold water. Add to the bowl with the rice.

3 Add the spring onions, pecans, dried cranberries and orange zest to the rice and mix together well.

4 Combine all the dressing ingredients and the orange juice in a screw-top jar and shake well.

5 Heat the oven to moderately hot 200°C (400°F/Gas 6). Remove the skin from the duck and break it into rough pieces. Shred the duck meat and add it to the salad. Place the skin on a baking tray and bake for 5 minutes, or until crispy. Drain on paper towel, then slice.

6 If necessary, shake the dressing again before pouring it over the salad. Toss everything together. Serve the salad in individual bowls, topped with pieces of crispy duck skin.

CITRUS ZEST
The zest of lemons, limes and oranges is often added to food for flavour or for decorating cakes and desserts. The easiest way to remove the zest is to use a purpose-designed citrus zester. The angle of the blade is shallow enough to ensure that only the flavoursome zest is removed, not the bitter pith below it.

RIGHT: Wild rice salad with Chinese roast duck

BAKED FISH WITH NOODLE FILLING

Preparation time: 20 minutes +
   10 minutes soaking
Total cooking time: 50 minutes
Serves 10–12

2 kg (4 lb) ocean trout or 1 whole salmon,
   boned and butterflied (see Note)
100 g (3½ oz) rice stick noodles
1 tablespoon peanut oil
6 red Asian shallots, chopped
2 red chillies, chopped
2 tablespoons grated ginger
200 g (6½ oz) water chestnuts, chopped
200 g (6½ oz) bamboo shoots, chopped
6 spring onions (scallions), sliced
2 tablespoons chopped coriander
   (cilantro) root
3 tablespoons chopped coriander
   (cilantro) leaves
2 tablespoons fish sauce
2 tablespoons grated palm sugar

Lime butter sauce
4 makrut (kaffir) lime leaves, finely shredded
2 tablespoons lime juice
125 g (4 oz) butter

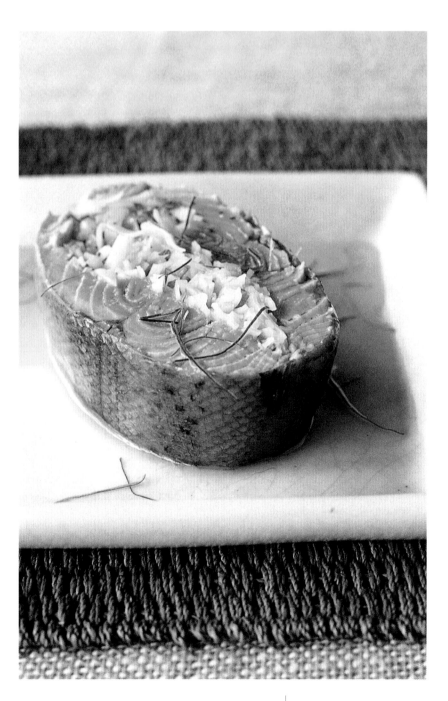

1 Preheat the oven to 180°C (350°F/Gas 4).
Pat the fish dry and use tweezers to remove
any remaining small bones.
2 Soak the noodles in boiling water for
10 minutes. Drain well, pat dry and cut into
short lengths.
3 Heat the oil in a frying pan and cook the
shallots, chillies and ginger over medium heat
for about 5 minutes, or until the shallots are
golden. Transfer to a bowl. Add the noodles,
water chestnuts, bamboo shoots, spring onions,
coriander root and leaves, fish sauce and palm
sugar to the bowl and mix well.
4 Open the salmon or trout fillet out flat and
spread the noodle filling over the centre. Fold
the fish over to enclose the filling and secure
with string every 5 cm (2 inches) along the fish.
Place onto a baking tray lined with foil and bake
for 30–40 minutes, or until tender.
5 To make the sauce, place the lime leaves,
lime juice and butter in a saucepan and cook

over medium heat until the butter turns nutty
brown. Cut the salmon into slices, discarding
the string, then serve topped with the sauce.
NOTE: A fish that has been butterflied has been
carefully slit through the middle, along the
bones, but not all the way through. The effect
is of having a hinge on one side of the fish.
Another term for this is 'pocket boning'. Ask
your fishmonger to do this for you.

*ABOVE: Baked fish with
noodle filling*

1 Break the vermicelli into smaller pieces. Fill a deep-fat fryer or large saucepan one-third full of oil and heat to 180°C (350°F), or until a cube of bread dropped into the oil browns in 15 seconds. Add the noodles to the oil in batches and cook for 10 seconds or until puffed, white and crisp. Drain on crumpled paper towels and sprinkle with sea salt.

2 Peel and devein the prawns. Arrange the lettuce and crispy noodles in six shallow bowls and top with the cucumber, avocado and prawns.

3 Put the mayonnaise, tomato sauce, Tabasco sauce and 1 tablespoon water in a small bowl and whisk to combine. Drizzle the sauce over the prawns. Serve with lime wedges, if desired.

DUCK AND RICE SALAD WITH SWEET GINGER DRESSING

Preparation time: 30 minutes
Total cooking time: 1 hour
Serves 4–6

☆ ☆

DRESSING

1/3 cup (80 ml/2 3/4 fl oz) oil

1 teaspoon walnut oil

1 teaspoon orange zest, plus extra, to garnish

1 tablespoon orange juice

1 tablespoon finely chopped preserved ginger

1 teaspoon sambal oelek

1 teaspoon white wine vinegar

1/2 cup (90 g/3 oz) wild rice

2 teaspoons oil

1/2 cup (50 g/1 3/4 oz) pecans

1/2 teaspoon ground cumin

1/2 teaspoon garam masala

1/4 teaspoon cayenne pepper

75 g (2 1/2 oz) long-grain white rice

1 celery stick, thinly sliced

20 yellow pear tomatoes or red cherry tomatoes, cut in half lengthways

20 g (3/4 oz) small English spinach leaves

4 spring onions (scallions), thinly sliced

450 g (14 oz) Chinese roast duck, with skin, cut into pieces (see Note)

CRUNCHY PRAWN COCKTAILS

Preparation time: 20 minutes
Total cooking time: 5 minutes
Serves 6

☆ ☆

50 g (1 3/4 oz) dried rice vermicelli

oil, for deep-frying

sea salt

750 g (1 1/2 lb) cooked, medium-sized prawns (shrimp)

1 small iceberg lettuce, leaves separated

1 Lebanese (short) cucumber, sliced

1 avocado, sliced

1/2 cup (125 g/4 oz) whole-egg mayonnaise

1 tablespoon tomato sauce

a few drops of Tabasco sauce

lime wedges, to serve (optional)

ABOVE: Crunchy prawn cocktails

1 To make the dressing, mix the ingredients together thoroughly. Season.

2 Rinse the wild rice under cold water and add to 300 ml (9½ fl oz) of simmering water. Cook, covered, for 45 minutes, or until the grains puff open. Drain off any excess water.

3 Meanwhile, heat the oil in a large frying pan. Add the pecans and cook, stirring, until golden. Remove from the pan and allow to cool. Coarsely chop the nuts. Add the cumin, garam masala, cayenne pepper and a pinch of salt to the pan and cook for 1 minute, or until aromatic. Add the pecans and toss to coat.

4 Add the white rice to a saucepan of boiling water and simmer until tender. Drain and mix with the wild rice and pecans in a large, shallow bowl. Add the celery, tomato, spinach and spring onion. Add half of the dressing and toss well. Arrange the pieces of duck on top with the skin uppermost. Drizzle with the remaining dressing and garnish with the orange zest.

NOTE: Chinese roast duck can be purchased from any Chinatown, or from your local Chinese restaurant.

CHICKPEAS WITH RICE

Preparation time: 15 minutes
Total cooking time: 25 minutes
Serves 4

☆

2 tablespoons olive oil

1 onion, finely chopped

1 garlic clove, crushed

1 red chilli, finely chopped

1 litre (32 fl oz) chicken stock

4 ripe tomatoes, peeled, seeded and diced
   (see Note)

1 cinnamon stick

1 bay leaf

1 cup (220 g/7 oz) short- or medium-grain rice

400 g (13 oz) tin chickpeas, drained

2 tablespoons chopped parsley

2 tablespoons chopped mint

olive oil, for drizzling

fetta cheese, crumbled

1 Heat the oil in a large saucepan and add the onion, garlic and chilli. Cook, stirring frequently, until all the ingredients are soft and the onion is translucent. Add the stock,

tomatoes, cinnamon, bay leaf and rice and bring to the boil.

2 Reduce the heat to low and simmer for 15 minutes, or until the rice is almost tender.

3 Stir in the chickpeas and cook for another 2–3 minutes, then stir in the parsley and mint and season well. Serve in soup bowls drizzled with olive oil and topped with crumbled fetta cheese.

NOTE: The easiest way to peel tomatoes is to score a cross in their bases, then to put them in a bowl, cover with boiling water and leave for 30 seconds. Drain, then plunge into cold water. You should be able to easily peel the skin away from the cross.

BELOW: Chickpeas with rice

BROWN RICE SALAD WITH BEEF

Preparation time: 15 minutes
Total cooking time: 50 minutes
Serves 4

1 cup (220 g/7 oz) short-grain brown rice

2 tablespoons oil

1 garlic clove, thinly sliced

4 spring onions (scallions), thinly sliced

2 tablespoons pickled ginger, thinly sliced

1/2 daikon, grated

1 tablespoon mirin

2 teaspoons sesame oil

2 tablespoons sesame seeds, toasted

2 fillet steaks

2 tablespoons teriyaki sauce

BELOW: Brown rice salad with beef

1 Cook the rice in a saucepan of boiling water for about 40 minutes, or until tender but firm. Drain, then leave to cool in a large bowl.
2 Heat 1 tablespoon of the oil in a frying pan and cook the garlic and spring onion until fragrant, then add to the rice along with the ginger and daikon. Sprinkle on the mirin, sesame oil and sesame seeds. Toss together.
3 Brush the steak fillets with teriyaki sauce and fry in the remaining oil for 3 minutes on each side. Rest for 1 minute, slice thinly and add to the top of the rice salad.

WILD RICE PANCAKES WITH TOFU AND MUSHROOMS

Preparation time: 25 minutes +
    1 hour standing
Total cooking time: 1 hour
Serves 6–12

6 eggs, lightly beaten

3 cups (750 ml/24 fl oz) milk

185 g (6 oz) butter, melted

1 1/2 cups (185 g/6 oz) plain (all-purpose) flour

1/2 teaspoon baking powder

2 tablespoons kecap manis

2 tablespoons chopped coriander
    (cilantro) leaves

1/4 cup (60 ml/2 fl oz) vegetable oil

2 tablespoons grated ginger

1 red chilli, finely chopped

2 spring onions (scallions), finely chopped

1/2 cup (95 g/3 1/4 oz) wild rice, cooked

1 teaspoon sesame oil

125 g (4 oz) firm tofu, cut into cubes

315 g (10 oz) mixed fresh mushrooms

2 teaspoons white miso paste (see Note)

2 tablespoons soy sauce

1 tablespoon lime juice

2 garlic cloves, crushed

1 Put the eggs, milk and 125 g (4 oz) of the butter in a large bowl and whisk to combine.
2 Sift the flour and baking powder into a bowl. Gradually whisk the flour into the egg mixture. Add the kecap manis and coriander and whisk until smooth. Cover and refrigerate for 1 hour.
3 Meanwhile, heat 2 tablespoons of the vegetable oil in a wok. Add the ginger, chilli

and spring onion and stir-fry over high heat for 3 minutes. Remove from the heat and place in a bowl with the the wild rice; cover and set aside.

4 Add the rice mixture to the batter and mix well. Heat the remaining butter in a non-stick frying pan, spoon ¼ cup (3 tablespoons) of the batter into the pan, tilt the pan so the batter covers the base, then cook for 2 minutes, or until it begins to bubble. Turn over and cook the other side until golden. Repeat with the remaining batter.

5 Heat the sesame oil and remaining vegetable oil in a wok. Stir-fry the tofu over high heat for 5 minutes, or until golden. Add the mushrooms, miso, soy sauce and lime juice and cook for 4 minutes, or until the mixture is heated through. Add the garlic and stir for 1 minute. Serve two filled pancakes per person as a first course, or four each as a main.

NOTE: White miso paste is a mild-flavoured paste made from fermented soya beans. Available in large supermarkets or Asian food stores.

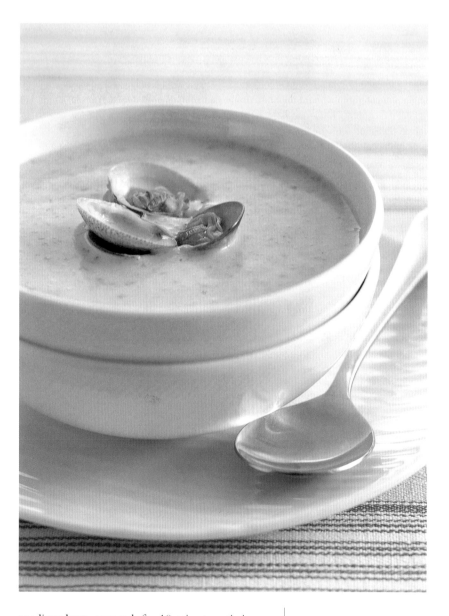

CREAMY CLAM SOUP

Preparation time: 20 minutes + cooling
Total cooking time: 1 hour 10 minutes
Serves 4

1.8 kg (4 lb 8 oz) clams, in shells, cleaned

1 litre (32 fl oz) good-quality fish stock

60 g (2 oz) butter

1 onion, chopped

1 celery stalk, chopped

1 large carrot, chopped

2 large leeks, sliced into rings

1 bay leaf

85 g (3 oz) long-grain white rice

¾ cup (185 ml/6 fl oz) cream

3 tablespoons finely chopped parsley

1 Tip the clams into a large saucepan with 1 cup (250 ml/8 fl oz) water. Put it over high heat, bring the liquid to the boil, then reduce the heat to medium and add a tight-fitting lid. Cook for 7–10 minutes—the shells will open when the clams are cooked. Drain and set aside the clams, discarding any that have not opened. Reserve the cooking liquid. Add enough fish stock to the liquid to make 1 litre (32 fl oz).

2 Rinse the saucepan, then return to the heat with the butter. Once the butter has melted, add the onion, celery, carrot and leek. Cook over medium heat, covered, for 10 minutes, stirring occasionally. Add the stock and bay leaf, bring to the boil, reduce the heat and simmer for a further 10 minutes. Add the rice, bring the mixture back to the boil, cover and cook on medium heat for 15–20 minutes, or until the rice and vegetables are tender.

3 Meanwhile, remove all but eight of the cooked clams from the shells. When ready, remove the soup from the heat and stir in the shelled clams. Remove the bay leaf and allow to cool for 10 minutes.

4 Purée the soup in batches in a blender (a food processor can be used but it will not achieve the same smooth consistency). Rinse the saucepan. Pass the soup through a sieve back into the saucepan.

5 Stir in the cream and season. Gently reheat the soup. When it is hot, add some parsley, then serve, adding two clams in the shell to each bowl.

ABOVE: Creamy clam soup

HARVESTING WILD RICE
Hundreds of years ago, in the big lakeland district between Canada and the United States of America, it would have been a familiar sight to find two American-Indian women harvesting wild rice in a canoe. Traditional harvesting still goes on today, but less so since the discovery of effective mechanical harvesting methods.

ABOVE: Wild rice, thyme and mixed mushroom pilaff

WILD RICE, THYME AND MIXED MUSHROOM PILAFF

Preparation time: 20 minutes +
  5 minutes standing
Total cooking time: 45 minutes
Serves 4

☆☆

^{2}/3 cup (100 g/3^1/2 oz) wild rice

1^1/2 cups (375 ml/12 fl oz) vegetable stock

60 g (2 oz) butter

1 large onion, finely chopped

2 garlic cloves, crushed

1^1/3 cups (265 g/8 oz) long-grain rice

300 g (10 oz) mixed mushrooms, sliced
  (e.g. button, field, Swiss brown)

1^1/2 tablespoons chopped thyme

1 fresh bay leaf

2 tablespoons chopped flat-leaf (Italian) parsley

toasted pine nuts, to serve

1 Rinse the wild rice and cook in a saucepan of plenty of boiling water for 25 minutes—it will only be partially cooked after this time. Drain.
2 When the rice is nearly done, pour the stock into a large saucepan with 1^1/2 cups (375 ml/ 12 fl oz) water and bring to the boil. Reduce the heat to a simmer.
3 Meanwhile, melt the butter in a large heavy-based frying pan, add the onion and garlic and cook until the onion is softened but not browned. Add the white rice and stir until the rice grains are coated with butter, then stir in the mushrooms.
4 Add the wild rice, stock, thyme and bay leaf. Bring to the boil while stirring, then reduce the heat, cover tightly with a lid and simmer for 15 minutes, or until the rice is tender and the stock has been absorbed.
5 Leave to stand for 5 minutes. Remove the bay leaf. Season, add the parsley and fluff up the rice with a fork. Sprinkle with pine nuts and serve.

PORK WITH RICE NOODLE CAKE AND CUCUMBER SALAD

Preparation time: 40 minutes + 5 minutes soaking
Total cooking time: 25 minutes
Serves 4

500 g (1 lb) thin fresh rice noodles,
   at room temperature
2 Lebanese (short) cucumbers, halved
   lengthways and thinly sliced
2 tablespoons chopped coriander
   (cilantro) leaves
1 tablespoon lime juice
1 tablespoon fish sauce
2 teaspoons caster (superfine) sugar
1/4 cup (60 ml/2 fl oz) oil
1 red capsicum (pepper), thinly sliced
3 garlic cloves, finely chopped
1 tablespoon white vinegar
1/4 cup (60 ml/2 fl oz) black bean sauce
1/3 cup (80 ml/2 3/4 fl oz) chicken stock
1 tablespoon soft brown sugar
300 g (10 oz) Chinese barbecued pork
   (char siu), sliced

1 Pour boiling water over the noodles and leave for 5 minutes, or until softened. Drain, then separate by pulling apart slightly.
2 To make the cucumber salad, toss the cucumber, coriander, lime juice, fish sauce and sugar together in a large bowl.
3 Heat 1 tablespoon of the oil in a large non-stick frying pan. Place four deep 10 cm (4 inch) rings in the frying pan. Fill as firmly as possible with the noodles and press down with the back of a spoon. Cook over medium heat for 10 minutes, or until crisp, pressing the noodles down occasionally. Turn over and repeat on the other side, adding another tablespoon of the oil if necessary. Cover and keep warm.
4 Meanwhile, heat 1 tablespoon of the remaining oil in a wok, add the capsicum and stir-fry over high heat for 2 minutes, or until the capsicum has softened slightly. Add the garlic to the wok and toss for 1 minute, or until softened, then add the vinegar, black bean sauce, stock and sugar. Stir until the sugar has dissolved, then simmer for 2 minutes, or until the sauce thickens slightly. Add the Chinese barbecued pork and stir to coat with the sauce.
5 To serve, place a noodle cake on each plate and top with some of the pork mixture. Arrange the cucumber salad around the noodle cake and then serve.

LEFT: Pork with rice noodle cake and cucumber salad

SCALLOPS ON ASIAN RISOTTO CAKES

Preparation time: 35 minutes +
  3 hours 10 minutes refrigeration
Total cooking time: 40 minutes
Serves 4 as a starter

☆☆

2 cups (500 ml/16 fl oz) vegetable stock
2 tablespoons mirin
1 stem lemon grass (white part only), bruised
2 makrut (kaffir) lime leaves
3 coriander (cilantro) roots
2 tablespoons fish sauce
20 g (³/4 oz) butter
2–3 tablespoons peanut oil
3 red Asian shallots, thinly sliced
4 spring onions (scallions), chopped
3 garlic cloves, chopped

2 tablespoons finely chopped ginger
1¹/4 teaspoons white pepper
²/3 cup (140 g/4¹/2 oz) arborio rice
2 tablespoons toasted unsalted
  chopped peanuts
1 cup (50 g/1³/4 oz) chopped coriander
  (cilantro) leaves
2 garlic cloves, chopped, extra
1 teaspoon finely chopped ginger, extra
¹/4 cup (60 ml/2 fl oz) lime juice
1–2 teaspoons grated palm sugar
vegetable oil, for pan-frying
plain (all-purpose) flour, to dust
1 tablespoon vegetable oil, extra
16 large white scallops without roe,
  beard removed
lime wedges, to serve

BELOW: Scallops on Asian risotto cakes

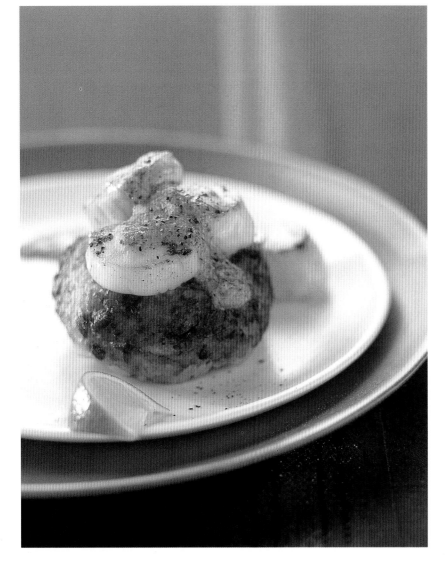

1 Heat the stock, mirin, lemon grass, lime leaves, coriander roots, half the fish sauce and 1 cup (250 ml/8 fl oz) water in a saucepan, bring to the boil, then reduce the heat and keep at a simmer.
2 Heat the butter and 1 tablespoon of the peanut oil in a large saucepan over medium heat until bubbling. Add the shallots, spring onion, garlic, ginger and 1 teaspoon of the white pepper and cook for 2–3 minutes, or until fragrant and the onion is soft. Add the rice and stir until coated.
3 Add ¹/2 cup (125 ml/4 fl oz) of the stock (avoid the lemon grass and coriander roots). Stir constantly over medium heat until nearly all the liquid is absorbed. Continue adding the stock ¹/2 cup (125 ml/4 fl oz) at a time, stirring constantly, for 20–25 minutes, or until all the stock is absorbed and the rice is tender and creamy. Remove from the heat, cool, then cover and refrigerate for 3 hours, or until cold.
4 To make the pesto, combine the peanuts, coriander, extra garlic and ginger and the remaining pepper in a blender or food processor and process until finely chopped. With the motor running, slowly add the lime juice, sugar and remaining fish sauce and peanut oil and process until smooth—you might not need all the oil.
5 Divide the risotto into four balls, then mould into patties. Cover and refrigerate for 10 minutes. Heat the oil in a large frying pan over medium heat. Dust the patties with flour and cook in batches for 2 minutes each side, or until crisp. Drain on paper towels. Cover and keep warm.
6 Heat the extra oil in a clean frying pan over high heat. Cook the scallops in batches for 1 minute each side. Serve a cake with four scallops, some pesto and lime wedges.

PARMESAN CHEESE
A hard cow's milk cheese used either grated and added to dishes or shaved to use as a garnish. Always buy Parmesan in a chunk and grate it as you need it, rather than use the ready-grated variety. *Parmigiano Reggiano*, from Parma in northern Italy, is the most superior Parmesan. It has markings on the rind that indicate the place and date of manufacture as well as the words *Parmigiano Reggiano*.

CHICKEN AND MUSHROOM RISOTTO

Preparation time: 15 minutes
Total cooking time: 45 minutes
Serves 4

1.25 litres (40 fl oz) vegetable or chicken stock

2 tablespoons olive oil

300 g (10 oz) chicken breast fillets, cut into
  1.5 cm ($^5/_8$ inch) wide strips

250 g (8 oz) small button mushrooms, halved

pinch of nutmeg

2 garlic cloves, crushed

20 g ($^3/_4$ oz) butter

1 small onion, finely chopped

1$^2/_3$ cups (360 g/12 oz) arborio rice

$^2/_3$ cup (170 ml/5$^1/_2$ fl oz) dry white wine

$^1/_4$ cup (60 g/2 oz) sour cream

$^1/_2$ cup (50 g/1$^3/_4$ oz) grated Parmesan cheese

3 tablespoons chopped parsley

1 Bring the stock to the boil over high heat, then reduce the heat and keep at a simmer. Heat the oil in a large saucepan. Cook the chicken pieces over high heat for 3–4 minutes, or until golden brown. Add the mushrooms and cook for 1–2 minutes more, or until starting to brown. Stir in the nutmeg and garlic, and season with salt and freshly ground black pepper. Cook for 30 seconds, then remove from the pan.

2 Melt the butter in the same pan and cook the onion over low heat for 5–6 minutes. Add the rice, stir to coat, then stir in the wine. Once the wine is absorbed, reduce the heat and add $^1/_2$ cup (125 ml/4 fl oz) of the stock, stirring constantly over medium heat until all the liquid is absorbed. Continue adding more liquid, $^1/_2$ cup (125 ml/4 fl oz) at a time, until all the stock has been used and the rice is creamy. This will take about 20–25 minutes. Stir in the mushrooms and the chicken with the last of the chicken stock.

3 Remove the pan from the heat and stir in the sour cream, Parmesan and parsley. Season with salt and freshly ground black pepper, then serve, with a little extra Parmesan, if desired.

ABOVE: Chicken and mushroom risotto

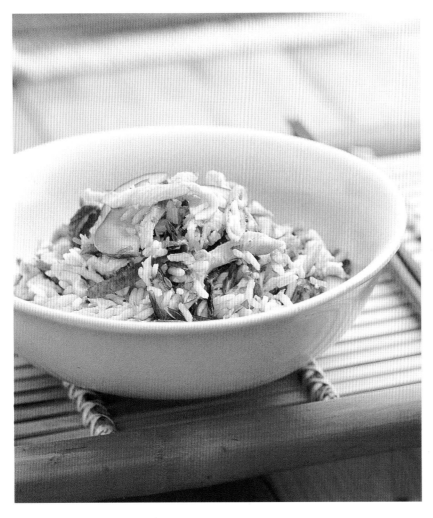

1 Bring a large saucepan of water to the boil and add the wild rice and 1 teaspoon salt. Cook for 30 minutes, then add the jasmine rice and cook for a further 10 minutes, or until tender. Drain the rice, refresh under cold water and drain again.
2 Shred the chicken (both the skin and flesh) into bite-sized pieces, place in a large bowl and add the mint and coriander. Cut the cucumber through the centre (do not peel) and slice thinly on the diagonal. Slice the spring onions on the diagonal. Add the cucumber, spring onion, rice and peanuts to the bowl.
3 Mix together the mirin, rice wine, soy sauce, lime juice and sweet chilli sauce in a small jug, pour over the salad and toss to combine. Pile the salad onto serving platters and serve with a little extra chilli sauce.
NOTE: It is important to use an Asian barbecued chicken, available from Asian barbecue shops, as the flavours of five spice and soy used to cook it will add to the flavour of the salad.

THREE RICE SALAD

Preparation time: 50 minutes +
  2 hours marinating
Total cooking time: 50 minutes
Serves 6–8

☆

3/4 cup (150 g/5 oz) long-grain rice
3/4 cup (165 g/5 1/2 oz) brown rice
100 g (3 1/2 oz) wild rice
1 red capsicum (pepper)
1 green capsicum (pepper)
1/3 cup (80 ml/2 3/4 fl oz) olive oil
1 garlic clove, crushed
2 cups (310 g/10 oz) frozen baby peas
2–3 teaspoons lemon juice, to taste
pinch of mustard powder
4 tomatoes, peeled, seeded and chopped
4 spring onions (scallions), finely chopped
4 tablespoons finely chopped parsley
1/3 cup (60 g/2 oz) small black olives

1 Cook the rices separately, according to the packet instructions. Rinse, drain, cool and set aside.
2 Halve, seed, then quarter the capsicums. Place, skin-side up, under a hot grill (broiler) and cook for 10 minutes, or until the skin blisters and blackens. Place in a plastic or paper bag for 5 minutes (this will make removing the skin

WILD RICE AND ROAST CHICKEN SALAD

Preparation time: 15 minutes
Total cooking time: 40 minutes
Serves 8

☆ ☆

1 cup (190 g/6 1/2 oz) wild rice
1 cup (200 g/6 1/2 oz) jasmine rice
1 Chinese barbecued chicken (see Note)
3 tablespoons chopped mint
3 tablespoons chopped coriander (cilantro)
1 large Lebanese (short) cucumber
6 spring onions (scallions)
1/2 cup (80 g/2 3/4 oz) roasted peanuts, roughly chopped
1/3 cup (80 ml/2 3/4 fl oz) mirin
2 tablespoons Chinese rice wine
1 tablespoon soy sauce
1 tablespoon lime juice
2 tablespoons sweet chilli sauce, plus extra, to serve

ABOVE: Wild rice and roast chicken salad

easier). Peel away the skin and discard, then slice the capsicum into thin strips. Combine the oil and garlic in a bowl; add the capsicum strips and leave to marinate for at least 2 hours.

3 Place the peas in a large saucepan of boiling salted water and cook for 2 minutes, then cool under cold water and drain. Place the capsicum in a strainer and leave to drain over a bowl to collect the oil. Whisk the oil, lemon juice and mustard together. Add salt and pepper, to taste.

4 Mix together the rice, capsicum, peas, tomato and spring onion. Stir through the dressing and parsley. Spoon onto a platter and scatter with olives.

ASIAN MUSHROOM RISOTTO

Preparation time: 20 minutes +
　30 minutes soaking
Total cooking time: 45 minutes
Serves 4

10 g (³/4 oz) dried Chinese mushrooms

2 cups (500 ml/16 fl oz) vegetable stock

2 tablespoons soy sauce

¹/3 cup (80 ml/2³/4 fl oz) mirin

150 g (5 oz) Swiss brown mushrooms

150 g (5 oz) oyster mushrooms

100 g (3¹/2 oz) fresh shiitake mushrooms

150 g (5 oz) shimeji mushrooms

40 g (1¹/4 oz) butter

1 tablespoon olive oil

1 onion, finely chopped

3 garlic cloves, crushed

1 tablespoon finely chopped ginger

2 cups (440 g/14 oz) arborio rice

100 g (3¹/2 oz) enoki mushrooms, trimmed

2 tablespoons snipped chives

shaved Parmesan, to garnish (optional)

1 Put the Chinese mushrooms in a bowl, cover with 2¹/2 cups (625 ml/20 fl oz) boiling water and soak for 30 minutes, then drain, reserving the liquid. Remove and discard the stems and thinly slice the caps.

2 Heat the vegetable stock, soy sauce, mirin, reserved mushroom liquid and 1 cup (250 ml/ 8 fl oz) water in a large saucepan, bring to the boil, then reduce the heat and keep at a low simmer, skimming off any scum that forms on the surface.

3 Trim and slice the Swiss brown, oyster and shiitake mushrooms, discarding any woody ends. Trim the shimeji and pull apart into small clumps. Melt 1 tablespoon of the butter in a large saucepan over medium heat, add all the mushrooms except the Chinese and enoki and cook, stirring, for 3 minutes, or until wilted, then remove from the pan.

4 Heat the oil and remaining butter in the same saucepan over medium heat, add the chopped onion and cook, stirring, for 4–5 minutes, or until the onion is soft and just starting to brown. Add the garlic and ginger and stir well until fragrant. Add the rice and stir for 1 minute, or until it is well coated in the oil mixture.

5 Gradually add ¹/2 cup (125 ml/4 fl oz) of the hot stock to the rice. Stir constantly over medium heat until nearly all the liquid has been absorbed. Continue adding more stock, ¹/2 cup (125 ml/4 fl oz) at a time, stirring constantly for 20–25 minutes, or until all of the stock has been absorbed and the rice is tender.

6 Add all the mushrooms and stir well. Season to taste with salt and pepper. Garnish with the chives and shaved Parmesan and serve.

BELOW: Asian mushroom risotto

DRIED RICE VERMICELLI
One of Asia's most popular
and versatile noodles, rice
vermicelli are made from
rice flour paste. They are
often formed into rounds
before being dried, so they
form a sort of nest. When
deep-fried, the vermicelli
will expand to nearly four
times its original size; the
fried noodles are often
used for garnish.

TERIYAKI BEEF WITH GREENS AND CRISPY NOODLES

Preparation time: 20 minutes +
  2 hours marinating
Total cooking time: 15 minutes
Serves 4

☆☆

450 g (14 oz) sirloin steak, cut into thin strips
100 ml (3½ fl oz) teriyaki marinade
oil, for deep-frying
100 g (3½ oz) dried rice vermicelli
2 tablespoons peanut oil
1 onion, sliced
3 garlic cloves, crushed
1 red chilli, seeded and finely chopped
200 g (6½ oz) carrots, julienned
600 g (1¼ lb) choy sum, cut into
  3 cm (1¼ inch) lengths
1 tablespoon lime juice

1 Combine the beef and teriyaki marinade in a non-metallic bowl and marinate for 2 hours.
2 Fill a deep-fat fryer or wok one-third full of oil and heat to 190°C (375°F), or until a cube of bread dropped into the oil browns in 10 seconds. Separate the noodles into small bundles and deep-fry until they sizzle and puff up. Drain well on paper towels. Drain the oil, and carefully pour into a heatproof bowl to cool before discarding.
3 Heat 1 tablespoon of the peanut oil in the wok. When the oil is nearly smoking, lift the beef out of the marinade (reserving the marinade) and cook in batches over high heat for 1–2 minutes. Remove to a plate. Heat the remaining oil, then stir-fry the onion for 4 minutes before adding the garlic and chilli and cooking for 30 seconds. Add the carrot and choy sum and stir-fry for 3–4 minutes, or until tender.
4 Return the beef to the wok with the lime juice and reserved marinade and cook over high heat for 3 minutes. Add the noodles, toss well briefly, then serve immediately.

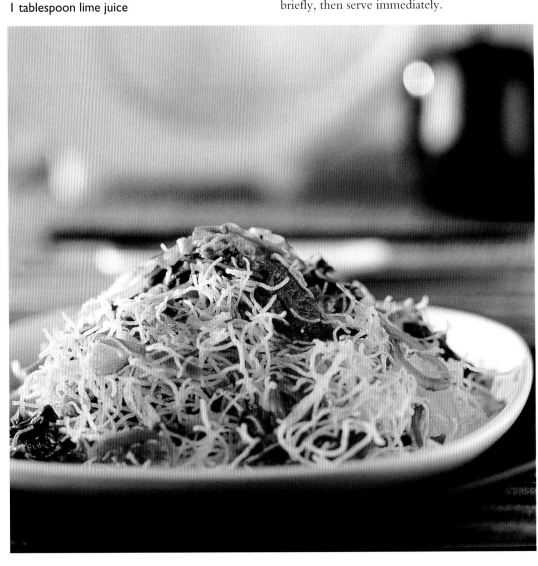

RIGHT: Teriyaki beef with greens and crispy noodles

BAKED RISOTTOS
Though risottos are traditionally prepared on the stove-top, they can also be made in the oven in a casserole dish. The result may not be quite as creamy as a stove-top risotto, but the method is much kinder on your wrists.

BAKED CHICKEN AND LEEK RISOTTO

Preparation time: 10 minutes
Total cooking time: 40 minutes
Serves 4–6

60 g (2 oz) butter

1 leek, thinly sliced

2 chicken breast fillets, cut into
2 cm (3/4 inch) cubes

2 cups (440 g/14 oz) arborio rice

1/4 cup (60 ml/2 fl oz) white wine

1.25 litres (40 fl oz) chicken stock

1/3 cup (35 g/1 1/4 oz) freshly grated
Parmesan cheese, plus extra, to garnish

2 tablespoons thyme, plus extra,
to garnish

1 Preheat the oven to slow 150°C (300°F/Gas 2) and place a 5 litre (160 fl oz) ovenproof dish with a lid in the oven to warm. Heat the butter in a saucepan over medium heat, add the leek and cook for 2 minutes, or until softened but not browned.

2 Add the chicken and cook, stirring, for 2–3 minutes, or until it colours. Add the rice and stir so that it is well coated with butter. Cook for 1 minute.

3 Add the wine and stock and bring to the boil. Pour the mixture into the warm ovenproof dish and cover. Place in the oven and cook for 30 minutes, stirring halfway through. Remove from the oven and stir through the Parmesan and thyme leaves. Season with salt and freshly ground black pepper. Sprinkle with extra thyme and Parmesan and serve.

ABOVE: Baked chicken and leek risotto

291

GLOSSARY

AL DENTE Meaning 'to the tooth'. Pasta and risotto rice are cooked until they are al dente—the outside is tender but the centre still has a little resistance or 'bite'.

ARROZ Spanish and Portuguese for rice.

ASAFOETIDA This yellowish powder is made from the dried latex of a type of fennel. Its pungent smell has earned it the name 'devil's dung'. It is said to be one of the secret ingredients of Worcestershire sauce. Asafoetida is used as a meat tenderizer and is also added to pulses to make them more digestible. It comes in small airtight containers and is available from Indian food shops.

BORLOTTI BEANS Slightly kidney shaped, this large bean is a beautifully marked pale, pinkish brown with burgundy specks.

CAPERS The pickled flowers of the caper bush. Available preserved in brine, vinegar or salt and should be rinsed well and squeezed dry before use.

CHINESE BARBECUED PORK Also known as char siu. A pork fillet that has been marinated in a mixture of soy sauce, five-spice powder and sugar, then barbecued over charcoal.

CHINESE MUSHROOMS The Chinese usually cook with dried mushrooms, which have a strong flavour and aroma, and need to be soaked to reconstitute them before they are used. The flavourful soaking liquid can be added to dishes. Dried mushrooms are widely available.

CHINESE RICE WINE Made from rice, millet, yeast and Shaoxing's local water, this is aged for at least three years, then bottled either in glass or decorative earthenware bottles. Several varieties are available. As a drink, rice wine is served warm in small cups. In cooking, dry sherry is the best substitute.

CHORIZO A highly seasoned ground pork sausage flavoured with garlic, chilli powder and other spices. It is widely used in both Mexican and Spanish cooking. Mexican chorizo is made with fresh pork, while the Spanish version uses smoked pork.

CLAMS Also sold as vongole, these bivalves are slightly chewy and salty, and have a hard, ridged shell, measuring about 4 cm (1½ inches). They are often confused with pipi, which have a smooth shell, and a sweeter meat.

COCONUT CREAM AND MILK Both extracted from the flesh of fresh coconuts. The cream is pressed out first and is thicker than the milk.

CRISP FRIED SHALLOTS Thin slices of red Asian shallots that are deep-fried. Commonly used as a garnish in Southeast Asia. Store in the refrigerator.

DAL OR DHAL is used to describe not only an ingredient but also a dish made from it. In India, dal relates to any type of dried split pea, bean or lentil. All dal should be rinsed before use, and cooking times vary.

DASHI GRANULES Made from dried kelp and dried fish, dashi is available as granules or as a powder. Dissolve in hot water to make the Japanese stock, dashi.

DRIED SHRIMP Small sun-dried prawns (shrimp) that are available whole or shredded, but they are usually ground before use. Some require soaking and rinsing before use.

FETTA CHEESE A soft, white cheese ripened in brine. Originally made from the milk of sheep or goats, but often now made with the more economical cow's milk. It has a sharp and salty taste.

FLAT-LEAF PARSLEY Also known as Italian or continental parsley. Used as an ingredient rather than a garnish.

GHEE A highly clarified butter made from cow or water buffalo milk. Ghee can be heated to a high temperature without burning.

GINGER The rhizome of a tropical plant which is sometimes referred to as a 'root'. Fresh young ginger has a smooth, pinkish beige skin. As it ages, the skin toughens and the flesh becomes more fibrous. Choose pieces you can snap easily.

HARISSA A fiery red paste from North Africa, made of chilli which is soaked, then pounded with coriander, caraway, garlic and salt, and moistened with oil.

IKAN BILIS The fry of anchovies, similar to whitebait, which are salted and sundried. Ikan bilis is used in Southeast Asian dishes and is available in Asian food stores.

JULIENNE To cut a vegetable or citrus rind into short, thin 'julienne' strips.

KECAP MANIS A thick, dark, sweet, aromatic soy sauce used in Indonesian cooking. Traditionally it is flavoured with garlic, star anise and galangal, and sweetened with palm syrup.

LEMON GRASS A lemon-scented tropical grass with leaves and a central rib. It is popular in Southeast Asia, mostly because lemons do not grow so easily in the tropics. Only the lower stalk is used in cooking. You can substitute one stalk of lemon grass for three thin strips of lemon zest. Do not use dried lemon grass because it has little flavour.

MAKRUT (KAFFIR) LIME LEAVES The highly fragrant, dark green leaves of a citrus tree, which are available fresh, frozen or dried from greengrocers.

MIRIN Sometimes incorrectly described as 'rice wine', this spirit-based sweetener from Japan is used for cooking, especially in marinades and glazes, and simmered dishes. It is sold in Asian food shops.

MOZZARELLA A smooth, fresh white cheese with a mild, slightly sweet flavour. It melts well.

NORI A seaweed which is pressed into sheets and dried. It is mostly used as a wrapper in sushi or is shredded and added to Japanese soups as a garnish.

ONE-THOUSAND-YEAR-OLD EGGS Also known as century eggs, these are eggs that have been preserved by coating them in wood ash, slaked lime and rice husks. They are left to mature for 40 days. When ready to eat, the coating is scraped off and the shell peeled. These eggs are eaten as an hors d'oeuvre or with congee.

PANCETTA Cured belly of pork, somewhat like streaky bacon. Available in flat pieces or rolled up.

PANDANUS LEAF Also known as pandan leaf, this flavour enhancer is used in both savoury and sweet dishes of Sri Lanka, Malaysia, Indonesia and Thailand. It has a delicate, almost sweet taste. A strip may be added to rice on cooking or to simmering curries. It is also used to wrap ingredients, such as chicken and rice.

PASSATA Meaning 'puréed', this most commonly refers to a smooth uncooked tomato pulp bought in tins or jars.

PICKLED DAIKON A yellow-coloured, firm and crunchy pickle made from daikon—a large white radish. It is usually pickled in dry rice bran after being hung to dry. It is available as whole pieces or presliced in supermarkets or Asian food stores.

PICKLED GINGER Whole, sliced or shredded peeled ginger root preserved in brine, rice wine or rice vinegar. It usually takes on a light pink colouring through chemical reaction. Thinly sliced pickled ginger is frequently used as a garnish in Japanese dishes.

PORCINI MUSHROOMS Used in Italian and French cooking, these have a brown cap and a thick white stem. Also known as cep mushrooms, they come fresh or dried. Soak dried ones in warm water, then rinse. The strained soaking water can be used.

PRESERVED LEMONS Lemons that have been preserved in a salt–lemon juice mixture (sometimes with spices such as cinnamon, cloves and coriander) for about 30 days. They are an indispensable ingredient in Moroccan cooking. Rinse and remove the white pith before using.

PROSCIUTTO An Italian ham that has been cured by salting then drying in the air. It doesn't require cooking.

ROCKET This salad green, also known as arugula is native to the Mediterranean. The peppery flavour increases with age.

SAFFRON The dried dark orange stigmas of a type of crocus flower, which are used to add aroma and flavour to food. Only a few threads are needed for each recipe as they are very pungent (and expensive).

SAKE is a Japanese alcoholic drink which is often called rice wine—a misnomer since it is brewed. It is often served warm in restaurants, but is also used as an ingredient to tenderize, tone down saltiness and to remove unwanted flavours and scents. Sake is stronger than mirin, so it should be used sparingly.

SALT COD Brought to Europe from Newfoundland as long ago as the fifteenth century, salt cod's popularity in France is a legacy of the religious requirement to eat fish on Fridays. Salt cod has been gutted, salted and dried, and is different from stockfish, which is dried but not salted. A centre-cut fillet tends to be meatier than the thinner tail end, and some varieties are drier than others so soaking time varies. Salt cod is also sold as morue or bacalao.

SASHIMI Thinly sliced raw fish, typically served with grated horseradish or ginger and soy sauce. The preparation of the fish is a skill perfected with long practice.

TAMARIND A large, brown, bean-like pod with a fruity, tart flavour. It is available as a dried shelled fruit, a block of compressed pulp, a purée or a concentrate. It adds a sweet–sour flavour.

TOMATO PASSATA This is a bottled tomato sauce commonly used in Italian cooking. The sauce is made with fresh, ripe tomatoes which are peeled, seeded and slowly cooked down with basil, onion and garlic. The thickened sauce is then passed through a sieve before being bottled.

TURMERIC Dried turmeric, sold whole or ground, is a deep yellow colour, and has a slightly bitter flavour and pungent aroma. Turmeric is added to dishes for both colour and flavour.

VANILLA EXTRACT Made by using alcohol to extract the vanilla flavour from vanilla beans. Vanilla extract is strong and should be used sparingly. Avoid using artificial vanilla essence made with synthetic vanillin.

VINE LEAVES Young leaves from the grape vine, blanched then preserved in brine. Available in packets, jars and cans.

WASABI PASTE A pungent Japanese flavouring resembling horseradish in taste. It comes from the herb Wasabia japonica and is turned into a green powder (which is reconstituted with water) or wasabi paste, both available from Asian food stores.

WATER CHESTNUTS Small, rounded crisp vegetables, usually sold canned.

ZEST The outer layer of citrus fruit, which is coloured and contains the essential oils.

INDEX

Page numbers in *italics* refer to photographs. Page numbers in **bold** type refer to margin notes.

ACKNOWLEDGEMENTS

FOOD PREPARATION: Alison Adams, Shaun Arantz, Rekha Arnott, Ross Dobson, Jo Glynn, Sonia Grieg, Valli Little, Olivia Lowndes, Briget Palmer, Kim Passenger, Justine Poole, Julie Ray, Dimitra Stais, Angela Tregonning.

PHOTOGRAPHY: Alan Benson, Cris Cordeiro, Craig Cranko, Ben Dearnley, Joe Filshie, Scott Hawkins, Ian Hofstetter, Chris L. Jones, Jason Lowe, Ashley Mackevicius, André Martin, Rob Reichenfeld, Brett Stevens.

STYLISTS: Kristen Anderson, Marie-Hélène Clauzon, Cherise Koch, Jane Collins, Carolyn Fienberg, Sarah de Nardi, Jane Hann, Mary Harris, Katy Holder, Michelle Noerianto, Sarah O'Brien, Sally Parker.

RECIPE DEVELOPMENT: Sophie Braimbridge, Belinda Frost, Jo Glynn, Deh-Ta Hsiung, Jane Lawson, Carol Selva Rajah, Sarah Randell, Nina Simonds, Jody Vassallo, Priya Wickramasinghe and the Murdoch Books Test Kitchen.

The publisher wishes to thank the following, all in NSW, for their assistance in the photography for this book: AEG Kitchen Appliances; Breville Holdings Pty Ltd; Chief Australia; Kitchen Aid; The Bay Tree; ici et la; Malcolm Greenwood; MUD Australia; No Chintz.